# FORCES IN AMERICAN CRITICISM

# FORCES

# IN AMERICAN CRITICISM

## A STUDY IN THE

## HISTORY OF AMERICAN LITERARY THOUGHT

*Bernard Smith*

*New York*

COOPER SQUARE PUBLISHERS, INC.

1971

130879

Originally Published and Copyright © 1939 by
Harcourt, Brace and Company, Inc.
Copyright © Renewed 1967 by Bernard Smith
Published 1971 by Cooper Square Publishers, Inc.
59 Fourth Avenue, New York, N. Y. 10003
International Standard Book No. 0-8154-0384-4
Library of Congress Catalog Card No. 71-156805

Printed in the United States of America

# PREFACE — 1971

THIS work was first published in 1939. The edition sold out fairly quickly, considering its rather special subject. Needless to say, its sale was chiefly to university and public libraries and to professional students of American literary history.

For some twenty-five years after it went out of print there was no evidence of any interest in reviving it. Then, suddenly, within just two years, five publishers specializing in reprinting scholarly works asked for the right to reissue it. I could only conclude that the inquiries were inspired by a new interest in the social and literary attitudes of the pre-World War II period. Certainly this work reflected one aspect of that period: a serious effort to apply the Marxist analytical method to the study of historical and literary materials.

For several years I rejected all invitations to reissue the work, simply because it no longer adequately reflected my thinking. Indeed, I feared that it presented a rather misleading view of American literary criticism because of its almost total emphasis on the ideological and sociological elements in the critical writings of our often naive and awkward but sometimes remarkably sophisticated literary history.

Of course, even when it was first published I made an effort —as the original preface clearly reveals—to discriminate between the narrow area of my study and the objective totality of literary criticism. But I do not think my discrimination was good enough. I had devised an isolate, as the scientists call it. That isolate was the ideological current in criticism, largely divorced from considerations of taste, aesthetic principles, and poetic insight.

In theory it can work; in reality it doesn't quite. Literary criticism, when it is valid, useful to either the creator or the

*vii*

audience—when it is more, that is to say, than personal aggrandizement or scholastic morphology—is a rich and complex fabric
of feeling and thought. No strand can be removed from it safely
(including, of course, the ideological bias). For no strand can
be studied and evaluated by itself without to some degree distorting the whole.

I have come to feel, however, that I should not withhold the
work from today's students of American literature. If they are
*that* interested in what happened in the 1930's—what was written
then, what was felt and thought—they are entitled to have at
their disposal the products of that period. Accordingly, I have
agreed to permit the reissuance of this work without a single
alteration of the original text.

I do not mean to imply that I question everything in it. Not
at all. Many of the observations and judgments herein still seem
to me to be provocative and useful. Moreover, it *organizes* the
history of American literary criticism, as no other work did before it. A few very kind reviewers suggested, at the time of first
publication, that the volume was a worthy supplement to Parrington's "Main Currents in American Thought." I was flattered then;
I remain flattered. I hope its new generation of readers will find
it equally illuminating—at least in so far as it expresses the over-
simplified Marxist approach to intellectual problems in that particular time.

It was a time when the United States had suffered through a
decade of severe economic depression and its attendant social
and cultural dislocations; and a time when the world had begun
to explode into devastating wars between reactionary and socialist forces, with the liberal democracies seemingly torn between the two, when not actually biased in favor of the former.
Perhaps the current interest in the 1930's derives from an uneasy suspicion on the part of the young that we may have entered a comparable time.

London
January 1971

# PREFACE

SOME years ago I became interested in finding out to what degree one could relate the history of American literature to the history of American life. It occurred to me that the real link in that relationship is the attitude toward literature that men have had under varying circumstances—the ideas they have had regarding its value and purpose and the way its excellence or lack of it may be determined. In other words, literary criticism seemed to me more clearly related to social history than are poetry and fiction.

It proved to be a missing link. There were, of course, a few essays on our critical history, and since then a few more have been published. But there is still no systematic study of the subject, and nothing at all that treats of it from the point of view in which I am interested, although the need for it has long been felt.

This volume is an attempt to survey the field. It is neither a formal nor a complete history of American critical writing. I am keenly aware that there are lines of inquiry I have not pursued, that there are critics I have not mentioned, that there are others I have dealt with inadequately, and that I have not touched on many aspects of those I have dealt with at length. All that I have tried to do is to indicate the main currents and to sketch the principal figures. The definitive work in the field remains to be done. It must be done in several volumes—when there are more special studies and monographs than are now available—by someone who has more leisure than I have had during the past eight years.

It is a work worth doing. The history of our literary thought is a significant thread in the history of our culture. We cannot understand the former without an understanding of the latter, but the former throws light upon the latter. Once we have established the connections that have existed between these two histories, we may find it possible to establish the connections between literature and society.

The reader will, no doubt, wonder what my own ideas about criticism and culture are. It should be said here, then, that I believe in the use of scientific methods in so far as they are applicable to literary history; that I am antagonistic to mysticism; and that I am biased in favor of the broadest possible democracy. What other ideas and sentiments I possess are explicit in the text that follows.

Something should also be said about the meaning of certain words. "Bourgeois" has often been an epithet. I do not use it as such. I use it as it is used in the social sciences—as a nominative term for a class that developed a describable culture. On the other hand, such words as "spiritual," "noble," and "sophisticated" are used for their suggestiveness; they are not fixed categories. I hope their meanings are clear in their contexts.

Organizing the book presented the usual problems. How much knowledge of the subject on the part of one's readers can be assumed in a work of literary history that is not aimed specifically at an academic audience but which will probably be read by teachers and referred to by students? I have done my best to effect a useful compromise between detailed analysis and generalized discussion.

Finally, a few words about documentation: the footnotes are few where the material cited is familiar or easily obtained; they are therefore most numerous in the earlier sections of the book.

Many friends have encouraged and advised me. But my debt to my wife, Frances Newmark, is especially great: she made it possible for me to complete this work.

B. S.

# CONTENTS

# FORCES IN AMERICAN CRITICISM

CHAPTER I

# PROVINCIAL CRITICISM

THE founding of New England begins the history of literary criticism in America. In the credo of Puritanism there were certain definite ideas about the moral and social value of art, and especially of poetry and drama. By any definition, that constitutes a philosophy of literature.

"Puritanism" is a label that has often been applied to the dogma that art should be judged in terms of morality. It is obviously a false use of the term, for moralistic criticism is centuries older than Cotton Mather or Cromwell. It was the essence of Greek criticism. The fact is that many American Puritans were opposed, at least in theory, to every kind of imaginative writing, rather than being advocates of one kind, and they were therefore really not literary moralists at all. The scholarly and cultivated men of the community had no such antagonism to belles-lettres; on the contrary, on this point they were bitterly antagonistic to the group that wanted to suppress esthetic pursuits. The conflict was genuine and was directly inspired by social differences. The educated among the settlers were much closer in spirit to the aristocratic merchants and intellectuals whom Milton represented in England than to the struggling, maligned, barely literate craftsmen and farmers who formed the rank and file of the Massachusetts Bay Colony. Both classes were rebelling against feudal privilege and both decried the vices that arose from it, but it was only the commoners who considered the enjoyment of art a vice.

Unfortunately, in the early days, the fanatics in the latter class were able to force the community to adopt their attitude toward literature. Intent upon creating a state of holiness in a sinful

3

world, they were emotionally exhausted by their incessant moral self-criticism and intellectually by their absorption in theological debates. At best they considered secular learning a luxury which was certainly dispensable in a frontier community. The most zealous, in condemning all worldly joys and sensual pleasures, effectively condemned the poetic spirit itself. They believed that the library of a righteous man is composed of the Bible, the works of Calvin, and the sermons of the approved divines. Hence they could logically favor only the writing of histories and records and religious treatises.

Poetry with an orthodox connotation—verse, that is, which might be used as a testimonial to Calvinism—was nevertheless tolerated, even encouraged, and such verse was actually produced in quantity. The dogmas of the church were occasionally supplemented by piety in general, but the result was always the same: a sermon in meter. Thus it became an assumption of the group that poetry's single reason for being was that it could describe the Holy Word picturesquely and memorably. The seed of didacticism was thereby planted in American literature. A few strangely moving poems have survived from that barren period, and we have discovered here and there, in the annals of colonizers and explorers, fine passages on the glories of the virgin country; but most of this superior writing came from the aristocracy of the commonwealth, the few who had enjoyed some contact with English culture, and it proves simply that the iron grip of a theocracy could not altogether kill the soul of man. It was outside the representative body of writing in Puritan America, and it was born *in spite of* the hostile esthetic climate.

The arts of the theatre, partly on account of their pagan origins and their relation to Catholic ritual, and partly because in Europe they were traditionally patronized by the court and the "mob," were loathed and publicly denounced.

A people cursed with an official critique so inimical to art would have been sterile, so far as creative endeavor is concerned, even if their energies had not been consumed by hardships in the wilderness. But if the theology was responsible for the Puritan's fear of beauty, it was the environment that determined the duration of this blight. Puritanism was the creed of a despised class—the emerging bourgeoisie warring for honor and position against a caste system. It was a doctrinal compensation for their social inferiority. R. H. Tawney called it "the schoolmaster of the English middle classes. It heightened their virtues, sanctified, without eradicating, their convenient vices, and gave them an inexpugnable assurance that, behind virtues and vices alike, stood the majestic and inexorable laws of an omnipotent Providence. . . ." Transported to an unbroken land, it became an instrument of discipline: it held the settlers together and heartened them by providing a conviction of infallibility and visions of a glorious destiny. The theocracy collapsed when the land was conquered and wealth began to flow into the towns, for prosperity removed the need for the harsh discipline of Calvinism. Early in the eighteenth century the merchants and their representatives rose to power. They created a secular community and a leisure class. Then, naturally, came the beginnings of literature and criticism.

2

Those who now owned the property and wealth of the colonies, and who were therefore the cultured and articulate, formed a bustling and willful class, and yet one whose social horizon was circumscribed by the orderly processes of trade. Theirs was a mercantile aristocracy, founded upon the simplest type of commerce. Their possession of the means of production, or rather of distribution, was the result of royal grant, inheritance, and priority, and the conduct of their business consisted primarily in the exchange of goods and the slow accumulation of real things—ships, buildings, land, and so on. Allied with them were the governors who had supplanted the "theocratic oligarchy," the bankers, the professionals (such as lawyers, doctors, and professors, who filled a very respectable niche

in the structure of this static society), and, finally, the ministers, who had reconciled themselves to their political subordination and had made their peace with the new lords.

These were the upper classes. They lived in the cities—Boston, New York, Philadelphia, Baltimore, and Charleston—the
ports where ships from England arrived with manufactures, articles of luxury, books, journals, and news of European capitals,
and returned with the products of inland agriculture, trapping,
and forestry, and the fruits of West Indian trade. Except perhaps for a small group of resident servants of the King before
the Revolution, they were the social equals of the English
bourgeoisie. This was especially true of our richer, urban class
in whose hands lay the great, growing capitalism of commerce,
and they developed an identical psychology with the British.
More than that, the Americans considered themselves English-
men and looked upon the cultural heritage of Britain as their
own. Not even the war and independence could kill this sense
of kinship with the fatherland; they still tried to associate their
own life with that of London and still looked to the British for
their intellectual sustenance. Not even the Revolutionary shibboleths of equality could destroy their contempt for the crude
mechanics and the rough yeomanry of the States. Years of political isolation, the opening up of a new life here in America
when the riches of the West were discovered, the decay of
mercantilism when the industrial revolution promised opportunities beyond the wildest dreams of the trader, the infiltration of
native sons, children of the lower classes, into the government,
the universities, and business—all this had to happen before the
transatlantic mind disintegrated and a distinctive national tradition could begin to transform the dominant culture and assert
itself in the arts. Still, when it did come, it came from below
rather than from above, and among the gentry the old ways
lingered on for a long time.

Nevertheless, we find that the earliest magazines desired a
separate literature, and indeed it is almost impossible to name a

periodical which did not repeatedly celebrate the appearance of American poets and scholars and which did not attempt to encourage their activity and win for them a measure of public esteem. In 1774 Isaiah Thomas's *Royal American Magazine*, announcing that Britain's literary fame had begun to decline, boasted that "it is reserved for this new world to produce those noble works of genius to which past ages can afford nothing parallel." In 1788 the *Columbian Magazine* published an article entitled "An Account of two Americans of extraordinary genius in Poetry and Music" which severely reprimanded the Abbé Raynal for stating that we had not yet produced a distinguished artist or man of genius. "When we consider," it said, "the strong enthusiasm which he has himself felt in favor of America . . . we must suppose, for his justification, either that he has been misinformed by the enemies of our glory, or (what is still more probable) that our friends have neglected to make him acquainted with the names and abilities of the several eminent men which America has produced." Then followed a long account of the achievements of a Mr. Robert Bolling, "one of the greatest poetical geniuses that ever existed," author of two volumes of Horatian verse, and so proficient in Latin, French, and Italian that he was "able to write elegant poetry in every one of those languages." As for music, the *Columbian* pointed to William Billings and referred to him as the rival of Handel. Similarly, Noah Webster's *American Magazine*, founded in 1787, and the *Massachusetts Magazine*, founded in 1789, turned their magnifying lenses on the microscopic talents of home poetasters and perceived genius. This sort of self-deception was practiced for a generation, continuing into fairly sensible journals like the *Monthly Anthology*, founded in 1803, and conservative ones like the *Portico*, founded in 1816.

Such patriotism did not indicate a national spirit, the impulse toward an indigenous and original culture. It was rather a provincial spirit, the impulse which moves the country to emulate the metropolis, to prove that it is less gauche and raw than the former thinks it is and that it, too, has intelligence, good taste, and ambition. It was a "desire to demonstrate American abilities," remarked Professor Mott.[1] Exactly: a desire to demonstrate ability to the parent country, just as a child desires to show off before his father. It is not necessarily an attribute of a colony; it is a characteristic of any province which senses its inferiority to an older, more civilized center. Consider how Los Angeles persistently strives to be as sophisticated as San Francisco, and how for a while Chicago belligerently challenged the reputation of New York as the sanctuary of American writers. (And perhaps this impulse was the initial motive in American criticism—the reason why the first magazines went to the trouble of establishing review sections at all.) There was rarely, during this early period, evidence of true nationalism. The quest was for poets who would live here but carry on the traditions of England. At the very moment that Isaiah Thomas hailed the future of the "new world" he eulogized the Addisonian essay— "those publications which appeared under the titles of Spectators, Guardians, Tattlers, etc."—and assumed that the writers of this continent would aspire at most to step into the shoes of Mr. Steele and Mr. Addison and march forward in them. No, they were not likely to think often of an art that would be altogether American, those gentlemen who made up the literate segment of the population and who were the guides and paymasters of its culture.

The sun of the mercantile aristocracy reached its zenith toward the end of the eighteenth century, hung high until about 1820, and thereafter set rapidly. Its society was well regulated, unchanging, and relatively simple. It attained a considerable elegance, elaborate though derivative, and a keen, supple intelligence in statecraft. Its ideas were offshoots of English rationalism, the social philosophy of the middle classes; its religion was Protestant; and its local politics were Federalist. The other main

[1] Frank Luther Mott: *A History of American Magazines: 1741-1850* (New York, 1930), p. 22.

stream of philosophical thought in America, borrowed from France, was physiocratic, but since it was strong chiefly among plantation-owners—the Virginian and Carolinian friends of Jefferson—it need not concern us. The agrarian Jeffersonians were mighty in law and political economy, but they had little influence upon the current literary journals, all of which were published in the cities. North or South, the city mind was a constant. Charleston, for instance, as Professor Parrington pointed out, "was more sympathetic with capitalism than with agrarianism." Later on, many years after the French Revolution, the French ideal of liberty and democracy swept through American literature, but that was a movement that is properly named after Andrew Jackson. It appealed to the undistinguished citizenry of the frontier and of industry, not to gentlemen planters. By then the merchant classes had lost control of the state, and the nation's culture was no longer exclusively theirs.

In their heyday, however, their taste was successfully and completely expressed. The nature of this taste is easily deduced from their Anglicism and their sovereignty in a static, stubborn, complacent society. It was, of course, classical. The earliest indications of an interest in literary opinion may be found in the colonial newspapers, most of which were actually literary weeklies, with a minimum of news and a maximum of trivial essays blandly patterned after the papers of Addison and Steele; and what these origins consisted of were scattered remarks on the coffee-house wits, on Defoe, Swift, and Pope, as well as excerpts from the original *Spectator*.[1] From then on until the *North American Review* began to yield to the influence of Coleridge and Wordsworth (around 1825), the prevailing models were Augustan and Johnsonian, with occasional leanings toward the sentimental transition poets, Blair, Gray, Thomson, and Akenside. The one important exception at this time was

[1] Elizabeth C. Cook: *Literary Influences in Colonial Newspapers: 1704-1750* (New York, 1912), Introduction.

Charles Brockden Brown, whose patron saint was William Godwin.

Imitations of Addison were accompanied by adulations of him. Dryden and Pope were worshiped, and articles on their supernatural merits loaded the chief periodicals year after year. All were poorly written, merely "informed," and dull, and all had almost exactly the same things to say. To one who sneered at Johnson—for example, Joseph Brown Ladd, who, in that respect, anticipated the romantic writers by many years [1]—there were a hundred who admired him. In addition, pieces were published frequently on Homer, Tasso, Virgil, Horace, Pindar, and other classic poets, some on Milton and many on Shakespeare, and all from the point of view of English classicism. On the other hand, no one wrote on behalf of Wordsworth and Goethe, although a generation later they were exalted as demigods. Coleridge was rarely appreciated.[2] Southey had only a few friends, and even Gray was not without enemies.[3] Byron alone, of the romantic poets, was championed, but the usual procedure was to apologize for his behavior and to regret the "immoralities" in both his life and poetry before applauding the poetry itself. The one romantic who could always inspire applause in every camp was Sir Walter Scott—but that is easily understood. The writers of the *North American Review*, soon after its founding in 1815, said a few kind words about Leigh Hunt and Southey. They were aware of Wordsworth, but ignored Shelley and Keats long after the publication of their first work. "In 1817, a year before the appearance of *Endymion*, Willard Phillips could still assert, with a dogmatic certainty worthy of Bysshe, that the heroic couplet is the greatest of all English meters." [4] And as late as 1830 a *North American* critic

[1] *The Literary Remains of Joseph Brown Ladd, M.D.*, edited by Elizabeth Haskins (New York, 1832), pp. 181 ff.

[2] *The Portico*, among others, never let pass an opportunity to attack him.

[3] *The Monthly Anthology*, for instance, published scornful as well as fulsome criticisms of Gray—in the same issue! Vol. V, July 1808, pp. 357, 367-9.

[4] G. E. De Mille: *Literary Criticism in America* (New York, 1931), p. 23.

stated that "Pope carried the sustained harmony and sweetness of English versification to a degree unexcelled before. It is difficult to detect much that is delicate and harmonious in the earlier English poets. The rhymes of Chaucer form no exception to this remark."

What seems most obnoxious about classicism in the young United States was its handmaiden—the cult of authority. Not only were the ancient classics and the recent English classicists adored for their own sake, revered with an almost religious fanaticism, but they were also upheld as irreproachable and imperishable models of literary eloquence, which no sane person should want, let alone try, to amend or modify, and writers were commanded to go only to them for advice on style, philosophy, and the propriety of emotions. If reviewers had been forced to refrain from testing a work by what they thought were the dicta of Aristotle, Dryden, and Johnson, and from comparing it with the works of the approved Greek and Latin poets, most of them would apparently have had nothing to say about it and no way of deciding whether it were good or bad. Nothing could have been more injurious to the budding arts of the country than such insistence upon authority and tradition.

It put a premium on fear and cautiousness, legitimated imitation, and discouraged those qualities—imagination, adventurousness, and a sense of freedom—which were necessary to the rise of an original art. How much the critics of the magazines and colleges really affected the poets of this time we do not know, but it is altogether probable that they were not unheard. Critics, in their roles as editors, reviewers, and teachers, have always been the tutors not merely of the public taste but to some extent of the artists' desires as well, and here they were almost in unanimous agreement as to the nature of the poetic ideal. Who were the rebels, the misanthropes and prophets? A literary equivalent of Tom Paine did not exist. And suppose there had been one—he would have had no audience to lend dignity to his experiments. Writers and readers were members of the same social class, and this class owned the magazines and controlled the narrow education that was then available at Harvard, Yale, and Princeton.

It is laughable: an aristocracy without a court, antiquarians without a past, bowing to authority on the morrow of a social "revolution." There is no cause for wonder that the contemporary literature was intellectually timid and morally stagnant (but not unpretentious). It is literally painful to read today the works of Timothy Dwight, John Trumbull, Joseph Dennie, Robert Treat Paine, Mrs. Mercy Warren, Lemuel Hopkins, William Crafts, John Neal, William Tudor, and the host of nameless amateurs who contributed stale and wretched verse and sickly copies of Johnson and Addison to the magazines. The "liberals" or Jeffersonian democrats, such as Brown and Philip Freneau, stood for ideas to which we are presumably more sympathetic than to those of the tories, and in fact it is pleasant to come across a little humanity in that belletristic desert of smugness and arrogance. But, alas, they were not much less imitative and conventional than the tories; it needed only a tiny pinch of unorthodoxy to be distinguished from that company. Brown was no Godwin, and Freneau, aside from being a poor poet, never dared to follow the flights even of the earlier English romantics. Their American environment was not calculated to inspire great boldness. Not until after the War of 1812, when hints of the coming of romance appeared and multiplied, was there any effective resistance to the dogmatic eighteenth-century spirit. The younger writers then found that spirit baleful and stifling. They were looking for newer, livelier, more passionate models. So prominent a citizen and writer as Richard Henry Dana, one of the first of New England's aristocrats to exhibit a sympathy for romanticism, was then moved to protest against stand-pat pedantry and to call for liberalism and impartiality—to urge critics to judge a work on its own merits, and not on whether it were patterned after or followed or failed to follow the accepted guides.[1]

To complete our analysis of the character of American criticism in this period of beginnings (1780-1820), it must be admitted that it possessed other and still more objectionable traits. Professor Mott was rather mild when he said that during these years "criticism in the United States was not on a very high plane. It was full of prejudice, ulterior motives and pretence. Political partisanships and personal animosities vitiated much of it." [2] Yet to the modern reader the unconscious vanity of those forgotten critics, their assumption of infallibility and the pompousness of their writing, may be merely amusing. He may even find their attempts at systematic criticism—their practice of a cramped and strangled logic in technical studies, aping badly the conservative English reviews—no more than annoying, although he will wonder how any poet could have found aid or counsel in their strictures. Knowing how slight was the nation's interest in art in an age of pioneering, he will pass over their parochialism and their superficiality. Knowing, too, that the best minds were absorbed in problems of state, he will doubtless forgive their dullness and their lack of inquisitiveness. It is, rather, the dishonesty of their judgments that he will really find odious.

Perhaps, however, it would be juster to speak of untrustworthiness instead of dishonesty. When a critic wrote a distorted and perverse report of the work of a romantic poet, that may not have reflected his intention; his utter inability to comprehend an ideology opposed to his own may have led him unwillingly to falsify. When a critic puffed the dreadful work of an American, it may be fairer to suspect the warping effect of patriotism than of a neighborly sentiment. When a critic attacked the art of his political enemies and praised that of his

[1] R. H. Dana: "Men and Books," in *The Idle Man*, No. IV (New York, 1822).
[2] Mott, op. cit., p. 182.

allies, irrespective of the intrinsic worth of either, that may not have been an instance of premeditated misstatement so much as of that blindness to merit in the hated object which so often accompanies ardent devotion to a subject. Untrustworthiness is not a euphemism for dishonesty, for if the acts in question were not deliberate, they were produced by a complex of emotions which were not entirely conscious. Still, the modern reader finds them odious—to the same degree that he finds any corruption of the truth odious. But he does not find them causes for indignation. It is, indeed, somewhat refreshing to encounter critics who were naïve about their participation in social struggles and frankly employed their craft in the interests of class, party, and state.

3

Charles Brockden Brown and Joseph Dennie were the literary boundaries of their age. Between them they exhausted the intellectual possibilities of the class from which they came in the society in which they lived. And since it is but a short step from social philosophy to philosophy of art, they marked off accurately the range of esthetic taste and theory.

Brown and Dennie were America's first professional men of letters. Historians remember the former chiefly for his grotesque novels and the latter for his collection of "moral" essays, *The Lay Preacher,* and his magazine, *The Port Folio,* but they have another claim to bibliographic immortality—one too little known. They were the first in this country to make criticism a vocation. Neither of them ever wrote a review or article worthy of inclusion in a pedant's anthology, and yet each has a certain retrospective importance. In a generative decade, one which awakened public interest to periodical literature and demonstrated the existence of a belletristic need which had heretofore hardly been felt, both edited magazines that were explicitly critical and literary, each representing a somewhat different—in some respects, an opposite—tendency. In 1799 Brown founded his *Monthly Magazine, and American Review,* with a relatively large review section. In 1801 Dennie brought out his *Port Folio*, in the beginning without reviews, but later emphatically with a critical cast.

Brown's position in American literature may be indicated simply by noting that he aspired to be here what William Godwin was in England. It is a commonplace that he became an exponent of the Gothic novel by imitating—ineptly, of course—Godwin's *Caleb Williams*, but he acquired from that erratic British disciple of the French Revolution a literary mood as well as a manner, for he absorbed greedily his romantic humanitarianism in addition to his theory of fiction. A romanticist in temperament, Brown's opinions were easily influenced by the romantic and rationalist works he read—the works of the French reformers and the more sentimental Germans, of William Cowper, Rousseau, Holcroft, and Mary Wollstonecraft, and, above all, the *Political Justice* of Godwin. As a result he became one of the very few liberal critics of his time. It is "significant that the poetry which measured up to his idea of greatness was that of Thomson, Akenside, and Cowper. Southey's early poems, romantic and revolutionary in spirit, he hailed as works of genuine value." [1]

The simplest and clearest statement of what his social philosophy meant to his contemporaries was that written by his friend and biographer, William Dunlap, who said in his "life" of Brown that the latter "imputed to wrong causes the defects which are but too apparent in existing systems. He saw the wrong and injustice and evil which exist, and instead of attributing them to the ignorance and selfishness of individuals, he assigned as the cause the errors or inefficiency of those codes which are intended to enlighten or to restrain." Obviously, Brown was a liberal Daniel in a den of conservative lions—but, as we shall see, they managed eventually to lie down together.

He edited two periodicals, in addition to his *Monthly Maga-*

[1] David L. Clark, in *Studies in English*, No. 7, University of Texas Bulletin No. 2743 (November 15, 1927), pp. 166-7.

*zine,* in the years from 1799 to 1807: the *American Review, and Literary Journal* and the *Literary Magazine, and American Register.* Although each died abruptly, leaving few regrets and fewer memories, his motives and tastes were evident in all of them. He was pious, romantic, and patriotic. He became a forerunner in the movement to emancipate American letters from English domination; he recognized thematic possibilities in such material as the borderland and the Indian. He did not succeed, however, in freeing his own writing from English influences.

His *Monthly Magazine* was founded with the aid and encouragement of the New York Friendly Club, one of the many fraternal organizations of literary gentlemen which existed then in the larger cities. Their membership consisted of respectable citizens of some wealth and social prestige but with little talent. They sought to foster a "national" literature, and perhaps in this respect they did some good. The more ambitious members of the Friendly Club contributed reviews to Brown's journal, and hence liberal and tory opinions appeared side by side. Since they were all unsigned, except for an occasional initial, it is difficult to know exactly where Brown ended and the Club began, but one is surely justified in assuming that the pieces plainly colored by a rather sober romanticism were either his or those of a rare contributor who sympathized with his views. (The same difficulty, by the way, is met in examining other and later periodicals, for anonymity was the general custom.)

In the first issue of the *Monthly Magazine* there appeared an article "On the State of American Literature" which had something new and startling to say to the provincial Anglophiles. The author asserted bluntly that "the literary character of America is extremely superficial." His explanations were several, among them being the "defective plans of tuition in colleges" and the inadequacy of the rewards offered to writers of serious works. But the first and primary cause, in the author's opinion, was "the love of gain, which, in a very remarkable degree, pervades the United States. . . . When a young man of active and enterprising talents comes forward, instead of studying to distinguish himself in the paths of literature and science, he reads and improves himself no more than will qualify him to pursue the main chance." Here was the genesis of that universal yet peculiarly American conflict between the practical business man and the literary idealist; and nothing could give us a deeper insight into Brown's character. Written suavely and with the correct admixture of high-mindedness and cosmopolitanism, that article might have been a contribution to Harold E. Stearns's 1922 symposium, *Civilization in the United States*.

An idealism so genteel as Brown's, however, could not maintain itself against the pressure of that environment. The limitations of his liberalism became more and more evident as time went on. He compromised: a professed romantic, he nevertheless printed antagonistic reviews of Percy's *Reliques* and Warton's *History of English Poetry*. Despite his own admiration for the young Southey, he published a bitterly reactionary attack upon him by some tory who complained grimly: "Southey affects to follow no predecessor, and to acknowledge the supremacy of no tribunal. He looks with jealous and contemptuous eyes on the old aristocracy of the literary world, and denies the jurisdiction of its kings and elders. . . . He honors his great predecessors neither in word nor deed; and not only withholds from them that tribute of applause to which they are legally entitled, but sedulously avoids all imitation of their manner, and refuses, on all occasions, to be swayed by their example." [1]

He played safe with the clergy: the sermons of the most prominent ministers were scrupulously reviewed. He took care not to prick the moral prejudices of his community: Persian poetry displeased him on the ground that he could find nothing in it except celebrations of alcoholic and sexual joys. In fact, his capitulation went still further: he announced an editorial

[1] *The Literary Magazine*, Vol. V, No. 30 (March 1806), pp. 200-1.

policy for his last magazine which was hardly sympathetic to the spirit of William Godwin. "In an age like this," he said, "when the foundations of religion and morality have been so boldly attacked, it seems necessary . . . to be particularly explicit as to the path which the editor means to pursue. He, therefore, avows himself to be, without equivocation or reserve, the ardent friend and the willing champion of the Christian religion. Christian piety he reveres as the highest excellence of human beings. . . . Everything that savours of indelicacy or licentiousness will be rigorously proscribed. His poetical pieces may be dull, but they shall, at least, be free from voluptuousness or sensuality, and his prose, whether seconded or not by genius and knowledge, shall scrupulously aim at the promotion of public and private virtue."

His position in the end was plainly not that of a truly liberated mind. Perhaps his companions in the Friendly Club dissipated his youthful unconventionality; perhaps the fate of the French Revolution was a factor. At any rate, the point is worth stressing. Because of the views expressed in his novels, historians with diverse biases have used Brown's name as a synonym for whatever radicalism there was in the forenoon of American literature. Dunlap's disapproval was echoed a generation later by William Hickling Prescott, while, on the other hand, Professor Parrington was enthusiastic about his "political romanticism" and Dr. Charles A. Beard has written warmly of "the spirit of left wing politics" revealed in his work. Whether or not this may be justified by his fiction, it does not pertain to his critical writing, most of which was done after the last of his novels had appeared. One may recognize his detachment from the widespread and powerful literary toryism of his day and one may credit him with inaugurating a liberal-romantic spirit in American criticism without exaggerating either his independence or his courage. It is enough to say that he was probably as adventurous a dissenter as he could comfortably be under the circumstances.

The circumstances were more favorable for Joseph Dennie. He spoke for an applauding constituency, and he was therefore a complete and consistent personality. To speak of him as a conservative or to designate his philosophy as classical is almost to subtract from the fervor that animated both the man and his work. He was virulent even for an age when most literary gentlemen were zealous in their defense of tradition and the status quo. His nom de plume, "Oliver Oldschool, Esq.," symbolized perfectly his political, social, literary, and religious beliefs. He was an admirer of English literature, politics, and culture. He hated France, Thomas Jefferson, and Tom Paine. He knew no viler epithet than "Jacobin." His essays in praise of the classics and in dispraise of romanticism verged on the hysterical. He was the author of the statement that "the *common people*, in any country, in every age, are nearly the same. Their praise is often to be dreaded, and their censure is generally proof of the merit of the object."

For these opinions he was rather well rewarded. In 1799 "he received the appointment of private and confidential Secretary to the Department of State." [1] Because his *Port Folio* was published in Philadelphia, home of a large and articulate upper-class population that was both aristocratic and Anglocentric, his magazine lived longer and more prosperously than any of its predecessors or contemporaries. The rewards, however, were incidental. He was sincere, and Clapp's sketch proves that he was always an impassioned belletrist, even while engaged in the practice of law and while serving as lay reader for an Episcopal church in New Hampshire. He was unique, for if there were few then who cherished a deep affection for literature, there were still fewer who were willing to sacrifice in its favor the possibility of a successful career in either jurisprudence or theology.

His literary creed may be adequately described in his own words. "Nothing is a source of purer pleasure to the Editor of

[1] W. W. Clapp: *Joseph Dennie* (Cambridge, 1880), p. 32.

The Port Folio," he wrote, "than to have it often in his power to reposit, in that Miscellany, every liberal encomium, and every vigorous defense of that portion of literature, which is correctly denominated *classical*." [1] The current "neglect of elegant letters" he attributed in boldface type to an administration "utterly destitute of classical taste." Elsewhere he sneered: "the chief ruler of our republick is a person by the name of Jefferson, formerly, we believe, an *obscure provincial advocate* in Virginia and afterwards a voyager to France, where he contracted a fondness for false philosophy, and French idioms." It is therefore understandable why he was able to read a dreary poem "with some pleasure" simply because the author seemed to be a "friend to the cause of religion and morality."

But if in matters of religion and morality he was at one with Brockden Brown, he was personally less the prig. He was robust enough to enjoy masculine prose, and he was not shocked by the poems on love and wine that Brown found a little too indelicate for his taste. Brown's magazines were much concerned with the novels of Richardson, whereas Dennie wrote frequently of his admiration for Fielding and Sterne. "Henry Fielding is one of my favourite authors," he said, "and his Tom Jones I generally have read at least twice a year since my boyhood. I admire this original writer not only for his wit, humor, and perfect knowledge of the human heart, but for his clear and manly style." It was characteristic of Dennie that he concluded this appreciation of Fielding with the remark that "above all, he is to be venerated for his love of *Classical Literature*, and to be studied for his successful imitations of some of the finest reliques of antiquity." It may be observed in passing that we have long since become familiar with the "niceness" of certain types of liberals as compared with the hearty vitality of certain types of tories.

[1] An example of the consequences of his mania: he published serially a ponderous, incredibly dull essay on "Classical Learning" which first appeared toward the end of 1807 and continued through eighteen separate issues during the half-year from January to July 1808.

Dennie adored above all living writers Thomas Moore, which is not surprising in view of the latter's cultivation of elegant formal verse and his ultra-conservative politics. He called Moore "one of the politest scholars of Great Britain, who has emulated the Grecian graces of Anacreon, and who has warbled the songs of Festivity and Love, in a mode so faithful to feeling, and so responsive to taste, that Waller himself is not more enchanting." Nor is it surprising that Dennie, the snob, infatuated with upper-class English society, should defend and uphold Moore when after visiting the United States he caused a scandal by speaking aloud his hatred for democracy and the "rudeness" of American life. In short, there was not a trace of liberalism in Dennie. True, he could sometimes see poetical virtues even in his political enemies: Coleridge, he said, "however erroneous in his political creed, is a man of genius and a poet"; Freneau, the faithful and obedient disciple of Jefferson, he praised for style and imagination. But here he was simply being true to his admittedly genuine love for literature. Our final estimate of what he was and what he stood for must be based upon his animosity toward a state which professed to be more interested in furthering the welfare of the commonalty than in patronizing the arts and letters created for the diversion of the wealthy.

CHAPTER II

# THE RISE OF CRITICAL TRADITIONS

ONE may almost describe numerically the changes that took place in the life of the American people during the two or three decades after the Treaty of Ghent. We speak of an industrial revolution: from 1790 to 1811 the Patent Office reported an average of seventy-seven inventions annually, but in the year 1830 alone there were five hundred and forty-four patents recorded. We speak of a westward migration: the sale of public lands was negligible at the beginning of the century, but in 1834 about four million acres were sold, and the totals for 1835 and 1836 were fifteen million and twenty million respectively. We speak of economic hope and speculative enterprise: during the five years before the panic of 1837, the valuation of New York City real property jumped from $250,000,000 to $403,000,000, while "building lots in such a place as Bangor, Maine, rose from $300 to $1,000." We speak of a boom in commerce: from 1800 to 1830 the value of our total imports decreased approximately thirty million dollars, but from 1830 to 1860 it *gained* two hundred and ninety million, while the value of our exports, which had increased only about one million dollars in the first period, increased about two hundred and sixty million in the second.

These were the decades which opened with a craze for canal and highway building and ended with a forecast of the railroad mania. They witnessed the development of the factory system in textile and machine production. Immigration on the grand scale began then. Cities grew: in 1800 about four per cent of our population was urban, in 1820 slightly less than five per cent, in 1830 more than six and one-half per cent, in 1840 ap-

22

proximately eight and one-half per cent. The country had started on its march to riches and power.

Intellectual and moral changes accompanied the sociological and economic. The maturation of a simple static society into a complex dynamic one—from commerce to industry, from aggrandizement to exploitation—could not help disturbing traditional manners and ideals. It was in this period, for instance, in New England that the milder Calvinistic gospel that had replaced Puritanism itself declined—in favor of a religion that was even more tolerant and liberal (the Unitarian). We have already noted the fact that the development of the interior of the United States and the growth of economic independence brought forth a vigorous nationalism. Still more significant, however—at least to our immediate concern—was the effect upon the general mood and temper of the age. Its reflections in the arts and letters we call romanticism. "The loveliest romantic dreams," wrote Parrington, "spring from a parentage that is humbly prosaic. There is no more fruitful source of romantic hope than a fluid economics that overflows all narrow preemptions and sweeps away the restrictions that hamper free endeavor. . . . The cautious ways of earlier generations were become as much out of date as last year's almanac. . . . It was our first great period of exploitation, and from it emerged, as naturally as the cock from the mother egg, the spirit of romance, gross and tawdry in vulgar minds, dainty and refined in the more cultivated." [1]

The rise of romance in literary criticism may be traced in the early history of the *North American Review*. Immediately upon its founding, in 1815, this autocrat among magazines was recognized to be the spokesman of conservative New England. Its editor, William Tudor, and its first contributors were perfect representatives of the administrative and professional aristocracy. In their hands the conventions of their class were

[1] V. L. Parrington: *Main Currents in American Thought* (New York, 1927), Vol. II, p. 190.

secure. They never suffered its dogmas to be tampered with grossly or to feel too strongly the impress of foreign philosophies. Such men as Jared Sparks, John Adams, Alexander Everett, Willard Phillips, Edward Channing, and John G. Palfrey were politically reliable. By and large they were imbued with the spirit of England at the end of the eighteenth century, and they could all be depended upon to remember that one of the reasons for establishing the magazine was "to neutralize the effects of the French Revolution on American political thought." [1]

At the outset of its career, as we observed above, the *North American* was unfriendly to romanticism. Its slighting of Keats, Shelley, and Coleridge were but negative symptoms of a calculated toryism. Alexander Everett expressed the general attitude quite frankly in an essay on Byron in 1825. After an extended and cordial appraisal of Byron's poetic gifts, Everett stated (with regret) that "almost the whole mass of Lord Byron's writings is, in one way or another, tainted with immorality. . . . Others, which are wholly free from this stain, are infected with faults more dangerous, perhaps, because less obvious to the unsuspecting or uninformed reader; such as the exhibition, under a favorable point of view, of unnatural and vicious characters, and the introduction of false principles in morals and religion. . . . Lord Byron appears to have thrown off very early, (if he ever felt it,) the wholesome restraint, which is generally imposed upon young minds by the authority of received opinions; and never to have attained any firm or distinct conception of the sublime truths, which these received opinions rest upon and represent." [2]

By the "authority of received opinions" Everett meant little more than the authority of government and church. Examine the magazine as a whole and you will find that its literary and

[1] W. B. Cairns, in *The Cambridge History of American Literature* (New York, 1918), Vol. II, p. 164.
[2] *The North American Review*, Vol. XX, No. 36 (January 1825), p. 40.

social prejudices corresponded. There was a consistent strain of snobbishness in it; it exuded a cold disdain for the rebellious classes who were everywhere upsetting political apple-carts, and especially for the intellectuals who were preaching unquiet doctrines. It sought to act as a bulwark against the encroaching tide of philosophical unorthodoxies; it stood for the conventions and proprieties, for "good taste" and the traditional morality. It was, in short, the organ of the class that dominated New England's culture. And that was its role not only in this particular period; always during the sixty years of its eminence it maintained its position as the weathervane of the ruling thought. Hence when eventually it changed its bias and became sympathetic to the romantics, it was because the New England mind was undergoing a similar metamorphosis. Never, of course, did this highly reputable journal turn to the more extreme or subversive of the romantic movements, but it could hardly resist the influence of the times. Who was now not tainted?

Signs of the change came soon enough—in the work, not of stray visionaries or obscure radicals, but of the most respectable contributors of whom the magazine could boast. In 1832 W. H. Prescott, writing on "English Literature of the Nineteenth Century," dared to say of the Augustan age: "Taste became paramount to every other consideration. The rules, although professing to be founded on nature, were consulted instead of her. . . . A character of timidity, sobriety, an artificial and somewhat monotonous elegance, was thus gradually substituted for the bold, irregular, but spontaneous movements of the age of Shakespeare." Pope, he intimated, was not one of his major admirations, and he was even less an admirer of Johnson. "He was strangely insensible," wrote Prescott, "to the beauties of sentiment, as well as those of external nature. . . . He was equally destitute of imagination and taste, as is shown by his habitually cumbrous and pedantic style, and by the perversity of his criticisms on some of the higher specimens of English poetry. His stiff reverence for authority and his Tory prejudices, equally intolerant and illiberal, made him high gravel blind, to borrow Launcelot Gobbo's phrase, not merely on political or religious topics, but on the most abstract questions of literature." But to Wordsworth, despite his dislike for the Englishman's concept of the ideal man and his theory of poetic diction, Prescott, who was anything but a radical, was significantly responsive: "He had nothing in him foreign to humanity. His contemplative habits led him to scrutinize his species with a philosophic eye, and by levelling in his mind the artificial distinctions of society, extending his sympathies to the humblest of his fellow creatures. A holy calm is shed over his writings, whose general purpose seems to be to reconcile man with himself and his destiny, by furnishing him with a key to the mysteries of his present condition. Wordsworth's soul is instinct with such a pure love of nature, loyalty of purpose, that had he not entangled himself in an unlucky theory, he might have shared the popularity of Cowper, whom he must be admitted to surpass in the general elevation, as well as the benevolence of his sentiments." [1]

Romanticism was on the way! A few years later even the arrogantly sensible pages of the *North American* revealed an incomplete immunity to the contagion of transcendentalism, which had apparently just infected the better part of New England's intelligentsia. The following appeared in a review of Coleridge's *The Friend:* "To Wordsworth and Coleridge, the latter the greatest philosopher and highest poetical genius, the other the most philosophic poet of modern times, the age is indebted in obligations, which it is difficult adequately to measure or acknowledge. If to exert an almost magic power over minds of the noblest structure, and brightest promise; if to turn the hearts of the young with keen and animated gaze to the unveiled countenance of truth; if to waken and call forth their best energies of intellect; if to form them to habits of thought and meditation; if to rescue them from the baneful influence of

[1] *The North American Review*, Vol. XXXV, No. 96 (July 1832), pp. 166-74.

that materialism, which has lain with a weight like death upon universal science . . . if to detect and reprove the usurpations of the understandings, and give freedom to faith as above the understanding; if to lead them to the contemplation of law in nature, and to the insight of principles in their own being, and to a reverential acknowledgement of the universal presence of the dread ground of all being;—if all this can constitute a claim to admiration and love, surely these venerable men may demand it." [1]

These brief excerpts from the work of representative critics are indicative enough, perhaps, of the trend, but when we recall, in addition, that now Longfellow and E. P. Whipple, and soon young Lowell, were contributors to the magazine, it is obvious that, in its own narrow sphere, it had completed a major cycle in the history of modern literature. It had not become an adventurer in new ideas; it was no whit less scholarly than before, no less genteel, no less conscious of its obligation to preserve the "best" in New England's culture; but it was certainly more buoyant and liberal than it had been at its founding. Instead of looking back to the glories of the past, it looked forward to the possibilities of the future—which, indeed, was true equally of State Street bankers and Harvard lecturers. It was not these men, but the transcendentalists, who pushed the premises of romanticism to their logical ends in the arts and philosophy, yet they too were shaking off the restraints of the classical ideology and groping for a freer emotional expression.

The *North American*, as a matter of fact, merely confirmed what was happening everywhere in the United States. In the South and West the same phenomena were apparent. In the East many had turned to romanticism a decade or more earlier. The path that Charles Brockden Brown had started to pursue had been eagerly pursued by others. The *United States Literary Gazette*, for instance, in 1824 praised the *Reliques* of Percy, denounced the Pope-Johnson school, and hailed with joy the

[1] Ibid., Vol. XL, No. 117 (April 1835), p. 350.

*Poetical Works* of Wordsworth. By the beginning of the third decade of the century ecstatic references to the beauties of nature, the simple life, the humble people, the truths of the spirit, and so on were commonplace.

## 2

It was in this period that a national literature was born. There had been previous attempts to utilize American themes, but no one until now had been able to detach himself from English influences sufficiently to create a work of unquestionable individuality and with characteristics peculiar to the American environment. Brockden Brown—a familiar example—could set his tales in Philadelphia, yet they would remain, in style and spirit, the minor offshoots of English romanticism. It was quite just of his countrymen to call him "the American Godwin," for his novels were plainly derivative. So, too, did Irving fail to embody in his stories anything essentially American. His use of local history and neighborhood legends could never disguise his affinity with the London wits of half a century before. With Cooper, however, we enter the new phase. True, he also was catalogued by means of a comparison with a British predecessor—he was called "the American Scott"—but there was much more in him than that label implied. There were certain psychological traits, certain sentimentalities and boldnesses, that were really native. A little later came Hawthorne and Melville, and about them there could be no doubt as to origins.

In this period nationalism developed in critical as well as imaginative writing. The developments were more or less parallel; if anything the tendency manifested itself in criticism first, it being easier to have the ambition or desire than the accomplishment, and easier to perceive the possibilities than to exploit them.

The ground was cleared psychologically by the death of the generation whose cultural ties were principally with England. The men who had sown the seeds of American letters, most of them tories, others of them Southern gentlemen with Anglican Church affiliations, all of them closer in spirit to the English bourgeoisie than to the natives of the colonies, had died off by now, and the new generation was home-bred and without personal mature memories of transatlantic relations. The blossoming of a society based upon an internal economy furthered the process. The rise of an indigenous personality and way of life— the pioneer and the frontier—completed it.

Esthetically the ground was cleared by an attempt to appraise honestly the deficiencies of American literature. It had been customary—it was a quality of the provincial mind—to applaud the slightest efforts of American writers. On the other hand, there had also existed an excessive humility, a tendency to self-abasement. Some writers went out of their way to make clear their reliance upon English culture and their despair over the low state of American letters. This was a form of provincialism too, and Professor Norman Foerster has pointed out that "the two forms could coexist in the same person." We may return to our simile of the child and his father. At one moment he will boast of his prowess and independence, at another he will cling to the older man's hand and seek his protection. Even when he is trying to prove his abilities, he is actually striving to duplicate some act of his father's which seems to him admirable, for he is not yet mature enough to be individual. That is provincialism.

In the 1820's and '30's, however, when men's eyes were turned upon themselves, there was a little less interest in winning the approval of the English; and now that the nation began to grow, began to take stock of its exploits and heroisms, its vastness and wealth, there was a little less need to sustain the ego by falsifying the achievements in the arts. Of course, it took a long time, almost a century, before that interest and that need disappeared entirely, but their decline dated from these years. Correspondingly, when the nation began to realize its worth—

and its potentialities—it became reluctant to accept complacently its previous cultural subservience to England.

Thus the gradual appearance of a judicious attitude toward American poetry, of a determination to estimate its actual value in terms of reasonably civilized standards and to publish the truth in the face of English sneers, may well be regarded as the preparatory stage for nationalism in our critical writing. We cannot consider Joseph Dennie's impassioned denunciations of our literature in 1805 as instances of courage and honesty. His motives were suspect; his statements sprang from political partisanship, for they were part of his campaign against Jefferson. Moreover, what he sought was not an *American* literature, but American proficiency in following and imitating eighteenth-century models. For this reason we cannot consider any of the early lamentations over the condition of our belles-lettres as examples of true independence. Such lamentations were, indeed, common: the *North American Review* published two in the first year of its existence. All of them were reactionary, for they had in mind the absence of what, if it had arisen and flourished, would have been at best a lukewarm revival of a mode that was already dead in its British source. Interesting and symptomatic was Stephen Simpson's "View of the Present State of Polite Learning," which ran through eight issues of *The Portico* in 1816. Simpson, noted for his ecstatic Americanism, here argued ponderously that the arts, letters, and sciences of Western civilization were decaying because of the spread of democracy and radicalism, which, he maintained, were incompatible with intellectual advancement. What a heart-breaking cry for a renaissance of classicism—which is to say, of social and literary *conservatism!* What gloom at the beginning of one of the most brilliant centuries in European history! It certainly has nothing to do with the mood out of which came an American national spirit.

Nor was the Anglo-American literary war which Professor

Mott described [1]—the bickering and quarreling between American writers and English reviewers that marked the first quarter of the nineteenth century and reached its peak in 1819-20—a valid manifestation of nationalism. The resentment aroused among American writers by the contempt of British critics was, like many of the provincial flutterings, a sign of progress in that it signified the drift toward introspection, but it did not contain within itself any real feeling about the American character or any real desire for a wholly new and original literature. The latter (it is worth repeating) are the distinguishing traits of nationalism, and they were not strongly or widely expressed until the following quarter-century, the Jacksonian era. Then, too, came the development of regionalism, which is part of nationalism and is, in fact, its logical goal.

It is obvious that nationalism was connected with the romantic movement—not only in point of time, but of spirit—and that they had certain common roots. It is to be expected, therefore, that the kind of judiciousness that indicated stirrings of self-respect should be found chiefly among the forerunners of romanticism. We have already seen how Brockden Brown published a bold yet not humiliating article on the weaknesses of American literature. In 1818, at the age of twenty-four, William Cullen Bryant contributed his famous essay on "Early American Verse" to the *North American Review*. It was the justest survey of the field published up to that time. It was neither self-castigating nor self-adulatory, and it completed its message with the hope that the natural beauties of *this* country would be used as subjects by our poets. Soon afterwards the urge toward individuality was quite general. Bryant himself, in 1825, in an essay in the *North American* entitled "American Society as a Field for Fiction," outlined a basis for nationalism. He not only described the United States as a good source of material and advised writers to refrain from foreign themes, but intimated as well that American society, with all its strange diversity, its

[1] Mott, op. cit., pp. 390-1.

regional and sectarian idiosyncrasies elsewhere unknown, would form "a national character" which should find literary expression. Moreover, he wrote, "it is a native writer only that must and can do this. It is he that must show how infinite diversities of human character are yet further varied by causes that exist in our own country, exhibit our peculiar modes of thinking and action and mark the effect of these upon individual fortunes and happiness."

In 1824 Edward Everett, in his address to the Phi Beta Kappa Society at Harvard, had uttered still prouder, still more optimistic sentiments. The rather hollow oratorical tone in which he spoke did not imply insincerity when he said that it was "impossible to foresee what garments our native muses will weave to themselves . . . to mark out, beforehand, the probable direction in which the intellect of this country will move, under the influence of institutions as new and peculiar as those of Greece, and so organized as to secure the best blessings of popular government, without the evils of anarchy. But if, as no one will deny, our political system brings more minds into action, on equal terms, and extends the advantages of education, more equally, throughout the community; if it provides a prompter and wider circulation of thought; if, by raising the character of the masses, it swells to tens of thousands and millions those 'sons of emulation, who crowd the narrow strait where honor travels,' it would seem not too much to anticipate new varieties and peculiar power in the literature, which is but the voice and utterance of all this mental action."

A less pompous prediction, and one more intrinsically literary, was that quoted by Professor Mott from an issue of the *Knickerbocker* in 1833: "The formation of a literature of our own— *a National American Literature*—is the dearest idol of our heart. . . . We do not despair of witnessing the time when, in this country, the noble language which we speak shall in structure indeed be English, but in tone, in character, in power, purely and decidedly American." Obviously, we have reached the stage at which nationalism was the familiar currency of the critic. In 1837 Emerson delivered his famous oration on "The American Scholar," which linked the concept of a national literature to romantic and democratic sentiments. And in 1847 Rufus W. Griswold, in his introduction to *The Prose Writers of America*, set down in a few simple words, without excessive eloquence or overemphasis, the major principle of the movement: "Whatever we do well must be done in a national spirit. The tone of a great work is given or received by the people among whom it is produced, and so is national, as an effect or as a cause. . . . The spirit which animates the best literature of any country must be peculiar to it." Elsewhere in the essay Griswold attained an intensity of national feeling that verged on jingoism. In him the nationalistic movement, in criticism, reached a peak. Beyond him there could be only irrationality.[1]

Curiously, the tide of nationalism seemed to subside after the Civil War. The emotion itself still existed, but it was not nearly so often or so vehemently flaunted. Perhaps it was because all that could be said on the subject for the time being had already been said. Perhaps it was because there was no longer any need for it—Melville, Thoreau, and Whitman had published their masterpieces. Certainly there were now other issues of greater moment to deal with. At any rate, the movement declined, and not until after the Spanish-American War did it enjoy a revival. But then it took wholly different forms, animated by different motives and directed at different goals.[2]

[1] It is perhaps useful to note here that nationalism was not confined to New England and the Middle Atlantic states. Witness Alexander B. Meek's Phi Beta Kappa oration, "Americanism in Literature," at the University of Georgia in 1844, later reviewed and echoed by William Gilmore Simms, another nationalist.

[2] A good survey of literary nationalism may be found in a dissertation, "A National Literature, 1837-1855," published in *American Literature*, Vol. VIII, No. 2 (May 1936).

3

If we except only the quest for literary independence, the chief characteristic of early American criticism was its preoccupation with problems of morality. It was evidently impossible, or unwise, to criticize a novel or poem without commenting on its moral tendency. It goes without saying that the standards of judgment were orthodox.

This orthodoxy was, of course, that of the bourgeoisie. It is now hardly necessary to explain the term "bourgeois morality." The works of R. H. Tawney, Max Weber, and other writers have adequately defined and illustrated the origins, causes, and nature of that code of social conduct which arose with the middle classes and attained the status of a universal convention in the nineteenth century. It will be sufficient to recall that it entailed such rules as industriousness, sobriety, chastity, monogamy, conjugal fidelity, and abstention from gambling; that it condemned improvidence and professed to scorn all those forms of play—physical, mental, or emotional—which are indulged in solely for the pleasure inherent in their pursuit; and that all these precepts and abjurations were imposed with a practical material end in view. As an ethical system it was no doubt beneficial to an emerging class of which the economic base was commerce; it was a system which, if conscientiously followed, would tend to strengthen the group, increase its wealth and give it a sense of social superiority. "If virtue is advantageous," Tawney has remarked, "vice is ruinous"—in business. Where riches are derived from selling at a profit, time is money, opportunity knocks but once, and you must keep your eye on the main chance! Where credit is the foundation of an economy, your reputation for "steadiness" is your principal asset. We remember that William Cobbett's chief objections to "good eating and drinking" were their unremunerative consumption of time *and* money.

This narrow moral code has commonly been referred to as

"Puritanism." It is a dangerous and probably misleading label. In *The Religious Background of American Culture* Dr. Thomas Cuming Hall insisted that Lollardry, rather than Puritanism, was the pre-eminent force in conditioning the American mind. That may not be true, yet it is certain that the morality we are studying was not a distinctive feature of the Puritan philosophy. It was part of that philosophy, but not the part that made it *Puritanism*, for the same morality was advocated by other Protestant groups—by petty-bourgeois Protestantism in general. We now realize, moreover, that it could not have been the Puritan—if we use the term with any degree of precision—who introduced that code into American criticism. His theocratic state had disintegrated and his theological ideals had almost been forgotten at the time when critical writing first began to appear here. It is true, as we previously observed, that he created a favorable atmosphere for the rise of moralistic criticism by associating poetry with religious instruction; but that is not the same thing as judging a poem by the fidelity of its sentiments to a moral, as distinguished from a doctrinal, code. In short, it seems wise to avoid the label entirely; its use is unnecessary and would erroneously restrict the origin of the point of view under consideration.

In the first period of criticism the test of morality was applied baldly and directly, in a manner at once sententious and diffident; and it was applied on every relevant occasion. Richardson's declaration that he wrote his *Pamela* "to promote the cause of religion and virtue" could well have been the exemplary attitude. Thus one reviewer praised Mrs. Mercy Warren's *Poems* because "the fervency of conjugal affection, the fondness of maternal love," and "a most sacred regard for the interests of religion" were "amiably conspicuous" in them.[1] Another reported, with gratitude, that in Peter Markoe's comic opera, *The Reconciliation*, "the sentiments are in general fine" and "the moral inculcated throughout the whole is, a confi-

[1] *The Massachusetts Magazine*, November 1790, p. 692.

dence in the ways of Providence, and an adherence to probity and rectitude." [1] Another announced that in Philenia's *Ouabi* "the sentiments are such as ought to govern man in his best estate." [2] On the other hand, it was noted with pain that in *The Hapless Orphan* "at one time atrocity is kindly veiled without the least animadversion on crime." [3] Phrases like "moral feelings," "noble objects," and "the pure and the good" were omnipresent, and even as late as 1826, in the *United States Literary Gazette*, a critic felt himself obliged (unnecessarily, one would have thought) to say: "Never be our literature increased by works of profligacy. Never be the principle admitted among us, that beauty may be pursued in a literary work without regard to moral influence. Indeed beauty has no real existence, independent of morality. . . ." It is clear that while the last sentence was written as if it were a statement of fact or a law of nature, there is a strain of anxiety and hope in the sentences before it that is anything but expressive of confidence.

Is there not, in fact, something in all of the foregoing quotations that suggests a feeling of insecurity? Bumptiousness and uncertainty are not seldom allied! Where in those simple moral commandments were there any of the accretions of familiarity? Where was there a sense of tradition behind the code? They had neither the sophistication of analysis nor the sophistication of allusiveness; the writers never attempted to prove their case nor dared to assume that their readers could take it for granted. Their declarations of principle were emphatic and constantly recurring—too emphatic and too frequently repeated if it is true that they entertained no doubts and were assured of the community's approval. Are we to suspect that the writers felt subconsciously that really they were *not* secure? In literary criticism the sanctions of the bourgeois morality were not yet established; there were no precedents; there were no authorities to

[1] *The Universal Asylum, and Columbian Magazine,* July 1790, p. 46.
[2] *The Massachusetts Magazine,* December 1790, p. 759.
[3] Ibid., July 1793, p. 432.

appeal to. On the one hand there was perhaps a realization that the philosophies of literature which had created the indisputable masterpieces of the balladists, the Elizabethans, and the Cavaliers were in direct conflict with the philosophy now prevalent; on the other hand there was perhaps a memory of the contempt for belles-lettres—nay, the vituperative condemnation of them as either frivolous and fruitless or positively corrupting—of some of the fanatical Puritan fathers. In these circumstances there would be nothing surprising if beneath their dogmatism the moralists were on the defensive.

But it is evident that they knew the solution to their dilemma. The critics of the time were almost without exception the ardent exponents of a principle which comprised the entire esthetic philosophy of their class and religion. This was the principle of moral utility. It may be defined in a few words: art must have a moral purpose or socially useful content—a purpose consonant with the ethic of the class and a use beneficial to its stability and growth. In its earlier, cruder, more primitive applications it was a raw demand that, for example, a poem have "a moral"; in its later polished form it was a refusal to admit that, for example, "immoral" characters are fit subjects for art, or—if the novelist did persist in depicting "free love"—that sexual relations outside the normal pattern of Victorian family life could result in anything but misfortune and tragedy. Moral utility, in one form or another, was the supreme esthetic principle of our nineteenth century; its influence and consequences are still with us. It was, certainly, a natural expression of the period, for it was nothing but an application to esthetics of the utilitarian philosophy of Bentham and Adam Smith, which is the whole social philosophy of the bourgeoisie; but it was also, specifically, a handy tool for the perplexed and fumbling critic. First of all, obviously, it provided a justification for literature. Secondly, it provided a consistent stand in regard to the art of the past: the critic could now pick out whatever was acceptable and point to the rest as evidence of the evil and backwardness of older societies—of courts, Catholicism, and kingdoms—while congratulating his readers upon living in the most advanced and civilized of all nations and all ages, and the nearest to nature and God.

Thus what seems to us the awkwardness and bluster of the early literary moralists lay not in the lack of a tool but in their ineptness in employing it. To say that they were over-militant is to say simply that they were not subtle—which is a trait of the parvenu. As an instance of this we may cherish Mrs. Mercy Warren's letter to her son on the *Letters* of Lord Chesterfield. The "amiable and accomplished" Mrs. Warren wrote that she was "charmed with the correct style, the elegant diction, the harmony of language, the thousand beauties of expression, that run parallel with the knowledge of the world and the arts of life, through this complete system of refinement." Yet she said: "I never see this fascinating collection of letters taken up by the youthful reader, but I tremble, lest the honied poison that lurks beneath the fairest flowers of fancy and rhetorick, should leave a deeper tincture on the mind, than even his documents for external decency and the semblance of morality. I have no quarrel with the *Graces*—I love the *Douceurs* of civility, the placid manners l'amiable. . . . But I love better that frankness and sincerity that bespeak a soul above dissimulation; that genuine, resolute, manly fortitude, that equally despises and resists the temptation to vice, in the purlieus of the brothel, or the anti-chamber of the princess." In conclusion, Mrs. Warren found that "The utile is so studiously blended with the vile, that in some of his letters, one would mistake Lord Chesterfield for a saint, was not his cloven hoof discovered by his precipitance to procure an arrangement for his noviciate." [1] Mrs. Warren's pathetic yearning to be worldly, her false elegance, her priggishness, her remarkable intermingling of coyness with righteousness, may impress or amuse us as elements in a pen-portrait of the *nouveau riche* of that period; but they are not nearly

[1] *The Massachusetts Magazine*, January 1790, pp. 36-8.

so striking as her deliberate opposition of the useful (the "utile"!) to the vile. It expresses, in the barest and briefest possible form, the point of view that made the bulk of American criticism the poor thing it is.

Grace is the ornament of custom, and custom is that effortless familiarity which is the fruit of time. Two generations after Mrs. Warren's correspondence with her young son, there were men in high station—in the universities, in the pulpits, in the editorial chairs of the fashionable and popular magazines—who were writing and speaking about poetry and the novel in phrases which, although they would never have occurred to her, would not have shocked her. They were graceful phrases, polished, unself-conscious, perfumed with scholarship, but in essence identical with hers. They sprang from the principle of moral utility as surely as hers did, and the audience to which they were directed was an embodiment of its spirit.

Gone were the bluster, the pretentiousness, the uneasy insistence upon the rectitude of a morality too often explained, and in their place were poise, refinement, and the aspect of tolerance. That is to say, at bottom nothing had changed. For nothing had happened to that segment of American society from which these writers came or in which they lived—nothing except the passing of time. I refer, of course, to the superior classes of the East who were not threatened by industrialism or who had adjusted themselves to its coming. Their wealth, power, and position were now almost hereditary. They lived in an atmosphere of security and stability. They had enjoyed from childhood the blessings of comfort, of a certain leisure, of travel and education. Hence while they still adhered to and swore by the code which had identified and elevated them, they were used to it and sure of it. Just as their social status had become traditional, so had their culture. Thus, too, had the principle of moral utility mellowed into a tradition. Not within the memory of living men had its tenets been the subject of serious doubt; therefore they could command obeisance by virtue of universality and antiquity. The art-thought of the group had evolved with the group itself from an intellectually raw, untested, unvenerated position to one of a supremacy so familiar that it seemed necessary and eternal.

Now, any code so established is less a faith to be guarded or a law to be enforced as a means of ensuring the survival of a community, than a pattern to which one conforms because of habit and a fear of that stigma which the community attaches to moral irresponsibility. In this stage of its history some of the purposes of the code are forgotten, its implications ignored, its significance misunderstood. It is simply a way of life which (because the ruling caste upholds it) one does not ordinarily think of violating. The well-bred person, the gentleman, the good man behaves admirably—in accordance with the rules— just because that is the way to behave.

Moral utility in literary criticism had reached precisely that stage in the period under discussion (1830-50). It was no longer a principle. It was a habit. It was a tradition. How and why it had arisen were questions that occurred to no one. The function of the critic to make the artist toe the moral mark of the time was no more debated than the morality itself. Consequently the critic tended to express his function as a mere *attitude*. It was not necessary to go into detail, to explain the axioms and precepts of the philosophy. No one had to be told what "immorality" was or why it should be shunned. No one had to be told why certain of the "facts of life" could not be treated by the novelist. An allusion sufficed. Audience, artist, and critic understood each other perfectly. The conduct of a gentleman, you understand, is "instinctive." When that can be said of it —when it has been so completely absorbed into the subconscious mind of society—the concept of moral utility is known in criticism as *gentility*.

In the plainest, least evasive of words, then, gentility is conservatism. It is the moral and social orthodoxy of the bourgeois who has, so to speak, been "refined." It is a way of thinking, if not of living, that conserves the code by which the sovereignty of the class is ultimately secured. Gentility is placid; it cannot long exist where there is no order. Nor does it bloom in a cosmopolitan soil; it favors an insular or provincial people. Although the characteristic of a whole class, it was best exhibited, and in its purest form, by that segment of the class which did not need to dirty its hands with unscrupulous finance or the suppression of labor uprisings, or even with the kind of creative work that was frankly conditioned by the market-place. It is inconceivable that this segment could have lived without the rest of its class, for it lived with it almost parasitically; yet it possessed some slight detachment, for which it was properly grateful. For it was to that pleasant, cherished aloofness that the intellectual emissaries of the class, the gowned and cloistered scholars, owed their grace and charm, and to that aloofness that its social idols, the coupon-clipping grandsons of pirates, owed their "good manners." They were attractive garments, and they hid, for quite a while, the other and meaner implications of orthodoxy.

Any adequate definition of gentility is also a perfect description of the contents of the *North American Review*. To thumb the pages of its issues from about 1825 to 1875 is to soak oneself in criticism that was generally sound, judicious, and "correct" and which never disobeyed the canons of good taste by including anything crude or violent. Therefore it also executed the amazing feat of passing through the most ebullient years in our literary history without ever illuminating obscure realities or ever bursting into that magnificent intolerance that accompanies a passion for unpalatable truth.

This was no mere accident, but neither was it the consequence of a deliberate policy. The magazine was founded by a coherent group of articulate gentlemen who wrote as they thought, and naturally it became the inheritance of their own kind. Its bias at birth was prophetic of its career, for the seeping in from time to time of new moods and sentiments barely touched its nuclear tradition. Hence it needed no watchful control: the existence of the society it spoke for guaranteed the perpetuation of its spirit. Who were its editors and writers? *Professor* Channing, *Judge* Phillips, *Professor* Kirkland, *Professor* Bowen, *Chief Justice* Shaw, *Judge* Story, the *Reverend* Mr. Peabody, *President* Quincy, *Admiral* Davis, *Colonel* Whiting, *Professor* Willard, *Governor* Cass, *Captain* McKenzie, *Professor* Parsons, *Professor* Everett. . . .[1] Almost every writer who personified gentility in criticism in its first stage was a contributor to the *North American Review*.

On one of its least satisfactory levels, Henry Wadsworth Longfellow was its supreme example. There is no longer any need to deflate the extraordinary reputation that his name once enjoyed among school-teachers. That task has been accomplished pretty thoroughly during the past twenty or twenty-five years. Even in his own lifetime he was sometimes regarded with a "peculiar" kindliness (by Poe, for instance, and Margaret Fuller), and yet it is worth remembering that as recently as 1913 John Macy's essay in *The Spirit of American Literature* shocked many reputedly intelligent persons.

The most charitable estimate of him possible today is Parrington's: "A gentle, lovable soul, widely read and in maturer years possessing a ripe literary scholarship, he was a skillful purveyor of gentle, lovable ideals. Although he drew his materials from Spain and Sweden and Italy, from primitive New England and aboriginal America, it was Germany that largely provided the staple of his romance . . . not Königsberg with its transcendental metaphysics, nor Weimar with its pagan culture, nor Tübingen with its higher criticism. Such things, transcendental and critical, he was not concerned about; it was the

---

[1] A fairly complete list can be found in *The North American Review*, Vol. C, No. 206 (January 1865), pp. 315-30.

minor romantics, Freiligrath rather than Heine, the gentle melancholy and pervasive *Sehnsucht* of the German folk-nature, that drew him irresistibly and quickened his sympathetic pen. There was little intellect in Longfellow, little creative originality. . . ." [1]

The sweetness and sentimentality of his verse was present also in his criticism. Hawthorne's *Twice-Told Tales* moved him to this very audible sigh: "Everything about it has the freshness of morning and of May. These flowers and green leaves of poetry have not the dust of the highway upon them. They have been gathered fresh from the secret places of a peaceful and gentle heart. There flow deep waters, silent, calm, and cool; and the green trees look into them and 'God's blue heaven.' . . . The true poet is a friendly man. He takes to his arms even cold and inanimate things, and rejoices in his heart, as did St. Francis of old, when he kissed the bride of snow. To his eye all things are beautiful and holy; all are objects of feeling and of song, from the great hierarchy of the silent, saint-like stars, that rule over night, down to the little flowers which are 'stars in the firmament of the earth.' " [2]

Such writing is manifestly not criticism at all. Impressionists are not critics, and eclectics are often impressionists only. At their best they make excellent anthologists and charming lecturers, and that, of course, is just what Longfellow was. His writing was never analytical, but expository and superficial. His scholarship was decorative, not instrumental, and his mind was not so much inquisitive as receptive. He was thus superbly qualified for the role of elementary tutor to an uncultured people.

Withdrawn as he unquestionably was from vital issues, it would nevertheless be a serious mistake to minimize his real significance in American literary thought, as Parrington did

[1] Parrington, op. cit., Vol. II, p. 439.
[2] Henry Wadsworth Longfellow: *Prose Works* (Boston, 1886), Vol. I, p. 362.

when he said in passing: "He was the poet of an uncritical and unsophisticated generation, as yet untroubled by science and industrialism, and his mind was detached from politics and his conscience rarely disturbed by social questions." [1] All this may be true, and yet—his philosophy of art had social implications.

It was supported by sanctions derived from a world much less remote than Dante's. He had the ear of an enormous audience, and it would be absurd to suppose that his taste did not influence theirs. Would it have done so if it had not in some way touched the problems that arose out of their tangible life? Let us scrutinize his fundamental creed. In his "Defence of Poetry" he wrote that poetry "may be made, and should be made, an instrument for improving the condition of society, and advancing the great purpose of human happiness. Man must have his hours of meditation as well as of action. The unities of time are not so well preserved in the great drama, but that moments will occur, when the stage must be left vacant, and even the busiest actors pass behind the scenes. There will be eddies in the stream of life, though the main current sweeps steadily onward, till 'it pours in full cataract over the grave.' There are times, when both mind and body are worn down by the severity of daily toil; when the grasshopper is a burden; and thirsty with the heat of labor, the spirit longs for the waters of Shiloah, that go softly. At such seasons, both mind and body should unbend themselves; they should be set free from the yoke of their customary service, and thoughts take some other direction, than that of the beaten, dusty thoroughfare of business." This is followed by a flaccid passage on the stirrings of "divinity" experienced by the imaginative man, which immediately leads to this plea: "Let the cares and business of the world sometimes sleep, for the sleep is the awakening of the soul." He concludes: "To fill up these interludes of life with a song, that shall soothe our worldly passions and inspire us

[1] Parrington, op. cit., Vol. II, pp. 439-40.

with a love of heaven and virtue, seems to be the peculiar province of poetry. . . ." [1]

What do we find in this ardent "Defence"? Above all, there is a yearning for a pleasanter and more peaceful world than existed. Yet Longfellow did not repudiate or condemn the crass business community which so obviously wearied and offended him. He assumed that it *had* to function as it did and to continue doing so. What place, then, could poetry find in it? His answer, in effect, was that it could serve as a drug or sedative to alleviate the significantly painful disturbances that he well realized must result, to mind and spirit, from the ordinary conduct of commerce. In other words, it could help calm the troubled waters of everyday life.

To suggest such a role to the artist and to teach people to ask him to fulfill it is an attempt—it matters not that it was unconscious—to violate the highest and truest purposes of art. It transforms art from an experience, an essential element of conscious living, a conduit of wisdom and sensitivity, into an escape. It encourages sentimentality, weakness, and evasiveness in art, instead of making art a distilled intensification of reality. The emotion from which it springs is juvenile, and its expression in an adult cannot help being saccharine—and Longfellow's achievement, and that of his fellows, was to sprinkle upon it the holy water of academic approval. By so doing they gave it a respectable career. It is still with us, in the form of a somewhat inarticulate commonplace of literary criticism. Has not every one of us heard someone say of a play that he did not enjoy it because "he's got enough troubles of his own without seeing them on the stage"?

So it is of no consequence in our study of Longfellow's gentility as a social influence that his conscience was "rarely disturbed by social questions." A critic of literature need not write a sociological treatise in order to reveal his outlook on

[1] *The North American Review,* Vol. XXXIV, No. 74 (January 1832), pp. 63-4.

society. It is, moreover, hardly necessary to add that a critic need not make a statement regarding a specific issue in order to reveal the extent of his adjustment to the society in which he makes his home. On this point one may simply recall Van Wyck Brooks's remark that Longfellow "had an unerring eye for the 'practical application' that lurks in every shred of romance." That indicates a high degree of adjustment, in spite of the fact that he was a cloistered soul.

The point of view that Longfellow illustrates permeated the writing of most of the critics who formed what was then considered New England's aristocracy of mind—such men, for example, as George Ticknor, Edward Everett, W. H. Prescott, and George Stillman Hillard. That strange and potent union of romanticism and respectability was the vital principle in all of their work, and although it was recorded in various ways, depending upon the personality of the writer, their approach to belles-lettres invariably started with it as a premise and encompassed only what could somehow be made to seem consistent with it.

These were not mean and bigoted men, nor men without accomplishments. On the contrary, they were as broad and cultured and worldly as the best of their contemporaries. Their limitations as critics were those of their environment, not personal ones. Hence when Prescott extolled Scott above Burns, or when he said of the Spanish romances that they "could not fail to debauch both the taste and the morals of the youthful reader," or when he derived from *Don Quixote* this merchant's maxim: "Perhaps, after all, if we are to hunt for a moral as the key of the fiction, we may . . . pronounce it to be the necessity of proportioning our undertakings to our capacities"—he was not being obtuse or narrow. The man whose histories of Spain, Peru, and Mexico helped establish in this country an academic tradition of disinterested scholarship, painstaking research, and cautious generalization was no fool. He was only, in the passage quoted, expressing the "official," the conventional esthetic philosophy of his town, so to speak. He was not superior to it.

Precisely the same things may be said of the others whose names are mentioned above. Everett—professor of Greek at Harvard, editor of the *North American Review*, member of Congress, Governor of Massachusetts, Secretary of State, president of Harvard, etc., etc.—was one of the first of American scholars to study in a German university. He brought to Cambridge the fruits of his learning. Together with Ticknor and Follen, he introduced the young men of New England to the European mind, to the spirit of an ancient civilization unadulterated by Anglo-Saxon influences. Because they were ripe for it, his teaching proved to be literally a revolutionary inspiration to them.[1] There was nothing, however, revolutionary about Everett himself. He emerged from his Teutonic and Greco-Roman learning as the complete American orator—capable of delivering the ordinary sentiments of a solid citizen and good patriot in smoothly polished, hollow sentences. That applies to his literary as well as his political and secular speeches. Ticknor—professor of French and Spanish at Harvard and author of a history of Spanish literature that is still consulted—was best characterized by one of his spiritual heirs, Barrett Wendell. Professor Wendell justly described his work as "scholarly" and "authoritative," but not interesting. It is "heavily respectable reading," he said. It is indeed respectable, and in more senses than Wendell meant.

There is another aspect of gentility that became apparent at this time—a kind of "social consciousness" that is quite unlike anything that that term ordinarily signifies today. An excellent example of it is Hillard's essay, *The Relation of the Poet to His Age*, in which he argued that poets are not Olympian, but, on the contrary, related to their age and indebted to it, and that

[1] Ralph Waldo Emerson: "Historic Notes of Life and Letters in New England," in *Lectures and Biographical Sketches*. Also Richard Henry Dana, Jr.: *An Address upon the Life and Services of Edward Everett* (Cambridge, 1865).

they therefore had a social function and should feel it obligatory to deal with "real life." This sounds astonishingly radical from a man who was genteel to the marrow of his bones—a man who could write of Landor, although admiring him, that "his vehemence of expression is not always restrained by decorum," and of Spanish literature that it is full of "vicious propensities." It all depends on what is meant by reality and by social function. Concerning the latter we note the following: "The office of poetry is to idealize human life; to connect the objects of thought with those associations which embellish, dignify and exalt, and to keep out of sight, those which debase and deform; to extract from the common world, which lies at our feet, the elements of the romantic, the impassioned and the imaginative." [1] From this we may conclude that when the genteel critic urged upon the poet an awareness of the world around him, he had in mind not what we think of as realism, but rather a deliberate and purposeful idealization of the material realm—an embellishment of fact. Hillard's plea was not unrelated to Longfellow's "Defence of Poetry"; it was only a more conscious statement of its potential social uses. This was a fundamental part of the "romantic-respectable" esthetic creed. Even Dr. Channing, who was not at all inclined to shy away from public problems, knew no other. Poetry, he said, "far from injuring society, is one of the great instruments of its refinement and exaltation. It lifts the mind above ordinary life, gives it a respite from depressing cares. . . ." [2]

The prevalence of "defenses of poetry" indicates a necessity to justify it, as a non-productive secular activity, against the old Calvinistic tradition plus the new philistinism of an expanding commercial society. The nature of these "defenses" indicates that the writers were contaminated by the very spirit against which they seemed to be struggling, for their strategy did not entail a head-on collision, or any forthright attempt to

[1] Op. cit. (Boston, 1843), p. 506.
[2] *The Works of William E. Channing, D.D.* (Boston, 1875), p. 498.

destroy the corrupting forces, but sought rather to clear the field for the enemy by removing literature from the "practical world" to a wholly different sphere of conduct and thought, where it could not distract anyone from the business of accumulating money. They may not have realized it, but their work tended to make poetry serve the ends of the philistines.

It must not be assumed, however, that this school of romantic gentility produced nothing of value. In William Cullen Bryant, for example, it brought forth some serious and quite sensitive critical writing. If Longfellow represented the period on a mediocre level, Bryant represented it on a high one. In some ways he was the ablest, certainly the best balanced of the men among whom he is naturally grouped. He was as scholarly as most and as alive to poetic values, yet more than most he was interested in current affairs and willing, especially in his journalistic career, to participate in movements for immediate social benefits. He was neither excessively sentimental nor pedantic. Some have accused him of austerity; Lowell and Hawthorne found him "cold." Yet although he was not a passionate nature, he could be moved. "He is never carried out of sight of common sense by his imagination," remarked one of his contemporaries in the *North American Review*. But neither was he so prosaic that his imaginative powers were atrophied. In short, he was a sensible man. He was too sensible to be swayed by the claims of the provincial patriots or the negations of the Anglophobes—and too "sensible" not to be in accord with the critical conventions.

Bryant was twenty-four years old when he proved his worth as a critic. The occasion was the appearance of the essay on "Early American Verse," probably the most judicious estimate of the subject published up to that time. "National gratitude, national pride," he wrote, "ask of us that we should foster the infant literature of our country. . . . [But] it is not necessary for these purposes—it is even detrimental—to bestow on mediocrity the praise due to excellence, and still more so is the attempt to persuade ourselves and others into an admiration of the faults of favorite writers. We make but a contemptible figure in the eyes of the world, and set ourselves up as objects of pity to our posterity, when we affect to rank the poets of our own country with those mighty masters of song who have flourished in Greece, Italy, and Britain." With this brief statement he made it clear that he could not be fooled by poetasters and that his interest in poetry was a serious esthetic one, not one of national egotism. From that point he could go on to define his conception of poetry and its relation to life.

Basically his ideas did not differ from his contemporaries', but they were better expressed—more reasonably, more sensitively. In a lecture "On the Nature of Poetry" in 1825 he put forth the usual argument for moral utility. He added, however, the proviso that it be emotionally rather than cerebrally stated. He was aware, he said, that poetry "does not concern itself with abstract reasonings, nor with any course of investigation that fatigues the mind. Nor is it merely didactic; but this does not prevent it from teaching truths which the mind instinctively acknowledges. . . . The truths of which I have spoken, when possessing any peculiar force or beauty, are properly within the province of the art of which I am treating, and, when recommended by harmony of numbers, become poetry of the highest kind." It should, of course, be borne in mind that "the truths" of which he spoke were the "moral truths" as interpreted by the genteel people of Boston and New York.

A second lecture, "On the Value and Uses of Poetry," is even more explicit in regard to its usefulness as an inspiration (perhaps a goad?) to virtue. Here, among other things, he recommends poetry in so far as it "withdraws us from the despotism of many of those circumstances which mislead the moral judgment. It is dangerous to be absorbed continuously in our own immediate concerns." Let us tarry awhile in the poetic sphere, he suggests, so that we may be "sent back to the world with our moral perceptions cleared and invigorated.

. . ." That is obviously Longfellow all over again—the same distaste for the normal tenor of commercial life, the same refusal to fight it, the same surrender to it by "withdrawing" the conscience and then sending it back "invigorated"—to start the ugly business once more. Yet beside this passage is one which could only have come from a noble (however limited) soul. He cherishes poetry as an "incitement to vigorous toils endured for the welfare of communities." "It delights to enfold not only the whole human race, but all the creatures of God, in the wide circle of its sympathies." Grant the enfeebling strain of gentility, grant the coldness, the timidity, but grant also an innate gentleness and humanity. The influence of the young Wordsworth was a beneficent one, not because it introduced him to new ideas or sentiments—those sentiments were natural to Bryant—but because it gave him an example of style and authority. Both are evident in his democratic and pastoral lecture "On Poetry in Its Relation to Our Age and Country." The youthful sage speaks there with the voice of one who knows that he can be derided only by lesser men. It is, incidentally, a good illustration of the *poet* in relation to his age and country, for it was a model expression of the spirit of Bryant's generation. Its climax was an attack on the classical reliance upon mythology for poetic material.

"For my part I cannot but think that human beings," he said, "are infinitely a better subject for poetry than any imaginary race of creatures whatever. Let the fountain tell me of the flocks that have drank at it; of the village girl that has gathered spring flowers on its margin; the traveller that has slaked his thirst there in the hot noon, and blessed its waters; the schoolboy that has pulled the nuts from the hazels that hang over it as it leaps and sparkles in its cool basin; let it speak of youth and health and purity and gladness. . . . If it must have a religious association, let it murmur of the invisible goodness that fills and feeds its reservoirs in the darkness of the earth. The admirers of poetry, then, may give up the ancient mythology without a sigh. Its departure has left us what is better than all it has taken away: it has left us men and women, it has left us the creatures and things of God's universe."

That was the apogee of Bryant's poetic criticism. In an essay written some fifty years later, he did nothing more than echo it, adding only a bow to "a luminous style." A long life changed him little; he matured early and grew no further. There is not much more one can say about him. In his prose, as well as in his verse, he followed his own adjuration and was neither a "subtle thinker" nor a "dealer in abstruse speculations"; his critical writings therefore reveal clearly the cultural sources from which he necessarily drew his essential principles. One has but to read them to understand him. To sum up, one finds that as a mind he was not distinctive against the background of his environment and yet was not submerged by it. One perceives in his writing some of the most pleasant of genteel sentiments: he wrote as he lived—serenely, honestly, and with dignity. He could be erudite without being dreary. He could be naïve and a trifle sugary, but never cheap. His countrymen in the 1820's and '30's had few spokesmen so attractive.

The writers discussed above were all New Englanders, and yet gentility is not peculiarly a New England product. It flourished in old England as well; and it was actually as indigenous to North Carolina, Ohio, and New Jersey as to Connecticut and Massachusetts. That, moreover, does not mean that the "New England spirit" conquered, but only that the middle classes everywhere derived their philosophies from a common source, and there were no forces making for ideological divisions. The people of Cincinnati, for example, had pretty much the same problems to solve and the same goals to achieve as the people of Boston; and the "moral" equality of all regions was affirmed when the dominant social groups elsewhere in America attained the economic and cultural level first attained by New England. Gentility is a geographical or theological phenomenon merely in so far as topographical and sectarian forms are socially conditioning circumstances. When we have finished measuring all the potential influence upon a literary convention of such factors as Puritanism's strict insistence upon godly behavior, the Unitarian's modulated commendation of goodness, or the Anglican's elaborate sophistication; when we have agreed that a mountain people may not have exactly the same "mindset" as a valley people, or that merchants in a seaport may have social customs which are unlike those of plantation-owners, we have gone far toward explaining variations in kind and divergences in time, but we have not invalidated the contention that gentility is the product of a certain class at a certain stage in its history.

One reason why the first—and the majority—of our genteel critics appeared in New England is simply that it was the birthplace and home of America's native literary culture. In comparison, the South was arid, Philadelphia already become somnolent, and New York busy with "worldly" affairs. The differences in intellectual quality, or at least in the intensity of intellectual preoccupations, which distinguished the original colonies were still visible. Not only did Boston shelter the *North American Review*, but also the *Christian Examiner* and the *United States Literary Gazette*, either of which could boast a critical section infinitely weightier than the best in any other city at this time.

Some critical writing did, nevertheless, come out of Manhattan Island. What is particularly significant about much of it is that it reflected the personal philosophy of the city's aristocracy. It would be futile to disregard the contrast in character between the New York and the New England minds.[1] The former was the more urbane and cosmopolitan of the two, more disposed to seek the cheerful life and less the good life.

---

[1] There is no thoroughly satisfactory explanation of what caused this difference in outlook between the two cities. Parrington's chapter, "The Mind of the Middle East" (op. cit., Vol. II), is at least as good as any.

So we are not surprised to find that the reviewers of the *Knickerbocker*, the *New York Review*, and the *Mirror* were not exclusively concerned with philosophical and ethical problems. Not only were they not averse to recommending a writer solely for his ability to entertain, but sometimes permitted themselves to be quite flippant, and even when serious tended to show a somewhat worldlier spirit than the critics of Boston. It was a New York writer (in the *Literary Gazette*) who was infuriated to the point of writing a long rebuttal by the *North American Review*'s incessant attacks upon the character of Byron.[1] It was a rather discursive article, but the gist of it is: "Byron is in his grave, and there the spirit of persecution and misrepresentation should let him rest."

All this does not mean that gentility had no place in New York, for it had. The very men who lightened the local magazines by their interest in the esthetic and narrative aspects of literature were as orthodox as any when they did touch upon moral and social questions. Furthermore, though Bryant was born and educated in New England, he lived most of his life in New York, wrote reviews of various kinds for the *Evening Post* while serving as editor, and delivered his lectures on poetry before the New York Atheneum. Indeed, there was a group of academicians in the city who were altogether comparable with their Harvard colleagues. Gulian C. Verplanck, for example, was descended from a wealthy Dutch family, and yet he would have suffered no maladjustments if he had been transported to Cambridge and condemned to teaching and writing there, among the descendants of the Puritan fathers, forever afterwards.

Verplanck, besides being a lawyer and legislator, enjoyed the title of "Professor of the Evidences of Revealed Religion and Moral Science in its Relations to Theology at the General Theological Seminary of the Episcopal Church." He was a well-

---

[1] Even a fairly liberal and enlightened critic such as E. P. Whipple was not exempt from this passion for judging the man together with his work.

informed gentleman, with good but ordinary tastes, liberal in religion, democratic, and nationalistic. His feet were very much on the ground, but his practicality, the solidity of his temperament, did not detract from his personal kindliness. Even the Diedrich Knickerbocker *History*, which outraged both his sense of decorum and his tribal loyalty, moved him to an expression of sorrow and regret rather than anger. He was a good man and a good bourgeois, and when he wrote that literature should be "directed to the best ends of truth and virtue," he meant just that. There is no mistaking his ideas: they were cut from the general pattern. He said all he could have said when he said of literature that "in directing the mind to whatever is wise, just, pure, or lovely, it exalts and unsensualizes the thoughts. It emancipates the soul from the bondage of the world, lifting it above the desires, the cares, the meanness, and the follies of the present."

There were others like Verplanck in New York; and again we see not only that gentility is not peculiar to New England, but also that it is not an element of Puritanism. We remind ourselves of the Puritan thinker's masculinity, his delight in polemics, his insistence upon realism (his own kind of realism, but realism none the less), and once more it is clear that the always unruffled and optimistic souls whom we have been discussing—souls who had neither a devastating conviction nor an ounce of passion—were of a different breed from the founders of the Massachusetts theocracy. What we concluded before about moralistic criticism in general, applies equally to genteel criticism. Those elements in Puritanism which were middle-class, and thus common to all sects of the Protestant bourgeoisie, were surely fertile soil for the genteel tradition; those characteristics which made Puritanism a distinct theology, a distinct conception of the godliest way to organize society, had nothing at all to do with genteel or any other kind of criticism. What would Jonathan Edwards have had to do with Queen Victoria?

We may pause to consider the wider consequences of the

romantic gentility of Longfellow, Bryant, and their compatriots. Their exaltation of saintliness, of quietude and a sweet passivity —an American hunt for Nirvana by way of immersion in a socially "pure" and morally "uncorrupted" art—was responsible for the intellectual cowardice and anemia of taste of which traces can still be seen in American reading habits and popular literary opinion. What is not so clear, perhaps, is how it arose. The most suggestive explanation is Van Wyck Brooks's. He believes that the common impulse among the writers of this generation was to polish the American scene, to decorate its rawness and make it livable. They were "like prudent women who, having moved into a new house, energetically set to work laying down carpets, papering the walls, cutting and hanging the most appropriate window-curtains, and pruning the garden —making it, in short, a place of reasonable charm and content-ment." We can readily imagine these poets, having seen either with their own eyes or with those of the authors they read a smoother and handsomer life than this country afforded, return-ing home to look wistfully for consoling beauties. This was their land, this their people. They belonged here; they under-stood its spirit and felt at ease with it in spite of any momentary doubts they might have had. Hence they did the natural thing and succeeded in making themselves comfortable.

And yet the ripe end of gentility's attitude toward belles-lettres, of which we have seen the rise and formulation in this period between 1815 and 1840, is the late Victorian spirit. It would first reach the heights in Lowell, and thereafter it would degenerate and thin out in Aldrich, Mabie, and Van Dyke. It would first mature and be truly suave and mellow and cul-tured and, if hardly vigorous, at least not mentally inert; and then, quickly, it would become an aged female. Then softness would manifest itself as squeamishness, optimism as an inca-pacity for facing the truth, and orthodoxy as a querulous com-plaint against "the younger generation." It would then be dis-gusting.

4

The democratization of culture was one of the more notable features of the period 1825-50. There had already been, toward the end of the eighteenth century, a certain diffusion of control over scholarship, an increasing desire to enjoy and contribute to cultural pursuits—from the aristocracy and the clergy out into other sections of the middle classes. Now, however, the movement was extended and deepened, and finally consciously hastened.

A sign of the times was the sudden appearance of numerous anthologies and compendia of American and foreign literature, as well as lectures aimed at neither professionals nor gentlemen dilettantes, but at ordinary laymen. Samuel L. Knapp wrote, for instance, in the preface to his *Lectures on American Literature*, that he was struck most forcibly by the thought that "a single volume of common size, in a cheap edition, might find its way into some of our schools." In the same year, 1829, Samuel Kettell published his three-volume *Specimens of American Poetry* (a ridiculous performance, containing a word of praise for every native scribbler who had ever composed a jingle or a hymn). Longfellow, George Ripley, and others undertook to introduce Continental letters to the populace at about this time. In the 1840's Griswold published his major anthologies—*The Poets and Poetry of America*, *The Prose Writers of America*, and *The Female Poets of America*—and in 1855 the Duyckincks published their two-volume *Cyclopedia of American Literature*.

Griswold's were the best of these compendia, and in them we can find one of the prime motives for spreading knowledge of American letters—namely, nationalism. Our people now had enough leisure to be conscious of America's deficiencies in comparison with the civilizations of Europe. There was balm in glorifying the creations of American talents.

Griswold conceived definite limits to the process of democratizing literature. He was an orthodox Baptist clergyman who found the pulpit an inadequate outlet for his abundant energies, and he went over to journalism and book-reviewing. He became editor of *Graham's Magazine*, and there, as well as in his anthologies, he dedicated himself to what E. P. Whipple gently called "literary patriotism." He was a conservative without any reservations. Once an abolitionist, even his fine emotion for freedom cooled under the spell of his admiration for Henry Clay. Ambitious, aggressive, facile, often unscrupulous, he achieved prominence and authority—proved by the lengthy survival of his calumnies against Poe. Now, Griswold certainly had no interest in the lower classes, no desire to better their lot, no passion to awaken them to the "better things of life." His motive for carrying the banner of literary culture to the non-academic, non-professional public was, as I have said, nationalistic. What kind of "public," then, was he concerned with? We can deduce that from the fact that in one essay he affirmed the inevitability and wisdom of class divisions and made a profound obeisance to "our wise and liberal merchants, manufacturers, farmers and professional men."

The movement for popularizing culture did not, however, end there. It penetrated much lower, reaching the mechanics and poorer farmers. The extension of this process downward in the social scale may be traced to two causes: first, the demands of aroused workers; and, secondly, the interest and sympathy of certain middle-class intellectuals. The pressure exerted by the working classes was aimed specifically at instituting laws for tax-supported general education, but its effect was cultural as well. The instrument of force was the labor union, which had come into being in this period. As an organized labor movement it scarcely resembled modern trade federations, but it was none the less a genuine indication of working-class discontent with industrial conditions and a valid expression of working-class solidarity. The movement collapsed in the Panic of 1837, not because conditions improved to render unnecessary its perpetuation, but, on the contrary, because they became so bad that the labor market suffered complete demoralization.

These early labor societies demanded not simply material betterment, but also the educational opportunities which had previously been available only for the wealthy. "The spirit of the times was expressed in a report of working-men in Philadelphia in 1830. They unanimously resolved 'that there can be no real liberty without a wide diffusion of real intelligence; that the members of a republic, should all be alike instructed in the nature and character of their equal rights and duties, as human beings, and as citizens. . . .' " [1] The struggle for a free public-school system was neither short nor pleasant. It was victorious, however, partly because workingmen could now register their will politically as well as by strikes (which were violently suppressed) and partly because the upper classes suddenly realized that at least some mental training was essential to factory and shop workers, for machine-manufacturing required an adaptive capacity that was missing in the heavy-handed and sluggish toiler of pre-industrial days.[2]

Paralleling the campaign for schooling the children of the lower classes was a movement for educating their parents—not merely in the rudiments of traditional scholastic subjects, but equally in the different branches of liberal thought. This was the lyceum movement, a very important yet underrated factor in the creation of the American mind. The original plan is generally attributed to Josiah Holbrook, supposedly the author of the outlined "Association of Adults for Mutual Education," published in the *American Journal of Education* in 1826, and the guiding spirit of the society corresponding to this project which was founded in Millbury, Massachusetts, the same year.

[1] Carl Russell Fish: *The Rise of the Common Man* (New York, 1927), p. 212.

[2] For an excellent study of this struggle, see Frank Tracy Carlton: *Economic Influences upon Educational Progress in the United States: 1820-1850*, Bulletin of the University of Wisconsin No. 221, Economics and Political Science Series, Vol. 4, No. 1 (1908).

Some commentators have also given credit to Timothy Claxton of Methuen, Massachusetts, who sponsored "The Society for Mutual Improvement" in 1824. The purpose of the lyceum was to establish lecture courses for mature persons who had not attended the higher institutions of learning—the petty bourgeois, the tradesman, the mechanic. By 1830 the system had spread throughout the country, and within a few years a number of state organizations had been formed.[1]

The organizations immediately enlisted wide support and co-operation, sending forth "some of the ablest and some of the most specious men of the times, from New England to the far stretches of the frontier. Similar work was undertaken by mechanics' institutes and other bodies." [2] Webster, Lowell, Emerson, Holmes, Thoreau, Parker, and Phillips were only a few of the great names who gave weight to these various systems. Edward Everett was one of the first to participate. Emerson wrote of him that "by a series of lectures largely and fashionably attended for two winters in Boston he made a beginning of popular literary and miscellaneous lecturing, which in that region at least had important results. It is acquiring greater importance every day, and becoming a national institution." William Ellery Channing was another of the prominent men attracted by the incipient Chautauqua.

All these celebrities were apparently pleased with the opportunity to share their learning with the populace. Regarding many of them, the explanation for this crusading spirit, Fish informs us, is simply that "the fees received for such lectures were an important element in the support of intellectual workers in the United States, who were thus enabled and, indeed,

---

[1] Katherine H. Porter: *The Development of the American Lyceum, with Special Reference to the Mission of the Local Associations in New England* (a dissertation submitted to the University of Chicago in 1914); and H. B. Adams: "Educational Extension in the United States," in the *Report of the Commissioner of Education for 1899-1900*, U. S. Bureau of Education, Vol. I, pp. 284-303.

[2] Fish, op. cit., p. 225.

almost forced to carry their intellectual life to the people in a manner never before equalled." The leaders, however, were undoubtedly actuated by an earnest desire to enlighten and educate the lower classes—in brief, to democratize culture. Theirs was at once an emotional impulse and a philosophical conviction, both being characteristic of a period of romance of which one of the identifying traits was a democratic-humanitarian ideology.

Lectures on literature were common enough to justify the assumption that they were in demand. For a time they were the chief source of intelligence and opinion open to the general public in regard to this and related subjects. And even when magazines with mass distribution, like *Godey's Lady's Book*, did succeed in making the belletristic article a staple, the lyceum still retained its importance, for it reached some sections of the lower classes who were just as unaffected by the popular as by the scholarly periodicals.

As to the quality of the lectures and the points of view expressed in them, we have practically no ponderable testimony. To be sure, many of the lectures of such men as Everett, Emerson, and Lowell have been preserved, but this is only to say that the cream remains, while the bulk has been lost and forgotten. And yet from this fact alone we can make certain plausible deductions. The able, eminent, and reputable men formed a small minority among lyceum lecturers. The majority were patently trivial, incompetent, and untrustworthy—which means that the untrained, uninformed audiences were usually given critical pap of the worst kind. They were fed, we may be sure, the insipidly sentimental and vapid moralism to which gentility always reduces itself when it passes from the drawing-room or the academic hall to address the "people." Thus we conclude that while the aim of this early movement to democratize culture was definitely to inspire and to educate, part of its achievement was the spread of genteel tastes and ideals among the lower classes.

Newspapers and periodicals were also instrumental in accomplishing this purpose. *Godey's Lady's Book* (with a circulation of 150,000) and its imitators and successors helped give the average American woman a notion of elegance that needs no description; we have only to look about us now to see how well they did their job. They bred a literary taste that prized the sterile, the sentimental, and the cowardly, and sometimes we cannot help wondering if the sensational fiction that has prospered in recent years is not, after all, in some ways preferable to the kind of novel that was popular in grandmother's time.

But it is likely that the influence of every one of these vehicles of popular literary intelligence—the lyceum, the mechanics' institute, the newspaper, the magazine of mass circulation—was insignificant compared with the influence of the McGuffey *Readers*. The effect these schoolbooks had upon the minds of the American youth during the nineteenth century has been attested to often, and the results were long apparent in the literary prejudices of the American people.

The McGuffey *Readers* were volumes of prose and verse selected from the works of contemporary and classical authors. They contained, also, instruction in reading and rhetoric. The first and second *Readers* were published in 1836, the third and fourth in 1837, and a fifth (called *The Rhetorical Guide*) in 1841. They were revised and reissued numerous times and sold, in all, by millions of copies, particularly in the Middle West and South. It is safe to say that they were the most widely used books of their kind and that, on the whole, they achieved their purpose, which was threefold: to teach the pupil how to read aloud, to inculcate a love for literature, and to spread "sound principles" of morality.

The last of these aims is the important one for our consideration, for it is the one in which McGuffey functioned as a critic. That is to say, it is the one in which he conditioned the esthetic taste of the students who used his books. Fortunately, there is no need for a subtle analysis of that phase of his general purpose. He never disguised it, and it was stated unequivocally by one of his later publishers: "The reader should cover the whole field of morals and manners and in language that will impress their teaching indelibly on the mind of every pupil. . . . The school readers are the proper and indispensable texts for teaching true patriotism, integrity, honesty, industry, temperance, courage, politeness and all other moral and intellectual virtues. In these books every lesson should have a distinct purpose in view, and the final aim should be to establish in the pupils high moral principles which are at the foundation of character." [1]

The *Readers* were arranged according to the age of the student, the first of them being extremely simple, the fourth and fifth quite advanced. In *The First Reader* "nearly every lesson has a moral clearly stated in formal didactic words at its close." In the later editions, however, open didacticism was eliminated. Now "the moral teaching was less direct but more effective." But at all times, in every volume, and in all editions, McGuffey kept in mind the moral ends of his selections; and his fantastic success warranted the claim that "the author and the publishers were fully justified in their firm belief that the American people are a moral people and that they have a strong desire that their children be taught to become brave, patriotic, honest, self-reliant, temperate, and virtuous citizens." [2]

We recognize here the early code of middle-class morality, not only in respect of sex, but of the social good as well. Virtue, self-reliance, temperance, industry—these are almost Cobbett's terms. They are the desiderata of a pioneering population. As such they were outgrowths of historical necessity, for they were not merely the social heritage of a group that had to place the highest ethical value on its own conduct in order to offset the contempt of others; they were also excellent disciplinary meas-

---

[1] Henry H. Vail: *A History of the McGuffey Readers* (Cleveland, 1911), p. 2.
[2] Ibid., p. 66.

ures in a group that had to create wealth out of a wilderness. Indeed, as abstractions some of the points in that code seem permanently desirable—if considered out of their pecuniary context. But appraised neither as ethical ideals nor as useful rules for behavior, but simply in regard to literature and literary taste, there is no doubt that the code they composed had an unfortunate effect. For the actual interpretation of the code was mean and narrow, and it brought forth not ruggedness, frankness, and simplicity, but sentimentalism and evasion of realities. The rules were being taught long after the passing of the psychological needs they had answered, and so it was the form, not the spirit, that mattered. "Virtue" was translated into niceness.

There was no resistance to the teaching of gentility. The lower classes were brought up to believe in it because there were no alternative ideals, because they were themselves eager to capture and enjoy the prerogatives of the dominant class, and because their education lay in the hands of that class, which taught them what it honestly believed to be good for them. The McGuffey *Readers* are, of course, perfect illustrations of the process and the result. In *The Fourth Reader*, for example, excerpts from the Bible, Johnson, Byron, and Shakespeare stand beside prose and verse by such pious nonentities as Lydia Sigourney, Felicia Hemans, and William Wirt. Here, in other words, was a long period in which the popular tool of literary pedagogy placed its emphasis not on literature but on morality, and the morality in question was largely false. Its immediate effect was to associate moral instruction with literature, so that the average American believed for decades (and some still do) that the purpose of a novel or a poem is to teach the reader to behave in a certain definite way. Its ultimate effect was to make our people resist works of art which did not set out to impart a lesson or which sympathetically depicted behavior contrary to the genteel code.

Finally—and from a strictly esthetic point of view this is its gravest effect—the *Reader* seriously debased the student's taste, for there was no critical discrimination in the book and no standard of inclusion but the moral end. The implication was that Mrs. Sigourney and Mrs. Hemans and Byron and Shakespeare were all good writers and worthy of appreciation, for all of them had something to teach the student. Since the emphasis was on morality, no talk about superior rhythms and richer imagery could be as impressive as the fact that Mrs. Hemans was often clearer and more direct in purpose than Shakespeare.

It would be absurd wholly to divorce motives from accomplishments. We must suppose, then, that many of those who were active in democratizing culture were more or less consciously seeking to influence the masses to think and act in accordance with the accepted proprieties. Judging from today's evidence, we should say that this would apply particularly to the editors of periodicals and schoolbooks. But whatever the terms in which the process was carried on, the fact remains that the idea of democratizing culture grew out of the coming of romanticism. An awareness of the existence, needs, hopes, and potential power of the "plain" people impelled the poets, the sincere and generous intellectuals, to reflect and even take part in the movement. That awareness accompanied the rise to power of the modern bourgeoisie, and it formed one of the significant strands in the complex fabric of romantic literature.

# CHAPTER III

# THE CRITICISM OF ROMANCE

THE literature to which one ordinarily refers when one speaks of "classicism" is distinguished by its spirit no less than its form. There is an emotional as well as stylistic formalism. The art of the English eighteenth century is, of course, the most familiar example of it, although it enjoyed a comparable reign elsewhere in Europe, including even Russia. This classical literature grew out of a society that may also, but with a special meaning, be called "classical." That is to say, it was a literature created for the contemplation and pleasure of an aristocracy presiding over a social order in which the class divisions were precise and the illusion of changelessness obtained. It was a squirearchic and mercantile society, and just as the faith by which it lived was systematic and orderly, so was its art.

Classicism was "un-American" in this country in the sense that it was not a native growth, but its dominance in our eighteenth-century literature had the logic of necessity, because it was part of a larger borrowed culture. It did not, moreover, exist in alien circumstances, for the colonial society that cherished it was profoundly sympathetic to the English way of life of which it was the poetic expression.

Democracy had not exactly flourished here. The merchant princes of the North and the great planters of the South had formed patrician communities that were adorned with London's robes. It was a pleasant, secure, half-feudal life. Joseph Hergesheimer described it rather well, and lovingly, in the first book of *The Three Black Pennys*. Living thus, they could not help becoming, in philosophy and the arts, intellectually corpulent. Easily, naturally, they subscribed to the belief that the world is a divine pattern that is subject at most to the minor mutations of refinement and that progress is not change but merely the patient improvement of incidental details. Nothing could happen without the will and hand of God, they were convinced, and this not only justified in their eyes the structure of their society, but guaranteed its permanence and attached the stigma of blasphemy and insolence to radical demands. Here certainly was an ideal condition for the transplanting of the classical spirit.

Its life here, nevertheless, was brief. It lost its ideological source at the close of the century, when the tide of romance swept over England. Since it was not the fruit of a native culture, had not grown out of an immediate tradition, it was then left defenseless against the criticism that it was noxious and impertinent in a young and hopeful land. But this loss and this criticism were not the primary causes of the supplanting of the classical by the romantic spirit; they were themselves effects of a revolution in the nation's ideals. The change was indeed a philosophical one—when it came, almost a generation later than in Europe—but it hinged, as we have already noted, upon a momentous transformation in economics, politics, and the social *mores*.

The coming of the machine age was the material spark that ignited the spiritual flame we call romanticism. It affected the agricultural regions almost as much as the urban seaports, for it created new needs and vast new markets for the products of the soil. Hope, ambition, visions of conquest, of "progress," of the perfection of human society, flared high in some—those, for instance, who were clustered about the Southern planter, who was now becoming a cotton imperialist, inordinately greedy for slaves and land; and also, and especially, those who were gathered around the merchant of the North, who was becoming a manufacturer, builder, or financier when technological advances made domestic investment more profitable than shipping. Anger and disgust—a withdrawal from the greed and cruelty of a grossly expanding society, coupled with the universal dream of utopia—seeped into the souls of others: those who were disinherited by the industrial revolution, those whose social position was lost through it, those who were not touched by it and were shunted aside and left lonely (and clear-eyed) by a feverish community. Disappointment and anticipation—they are the two faces of romanticism. Both imply a desire for change, a desire for other forms and substances in human life. And that is the heart of romance—either a looking backward or a looking forward to something different, perhaps better, than is now. Thus was lost the immutable universe in which all things, happily, had been constant and classified. Life became fluid.

Romance came late to America. But then, it did not appear in all lands at the same time, for the social changes that formed its "natural" environment did not occur simultaneously in all lands. There was nothing occult or even accidental about its relatively late appearance here. Professor Frederic L. Paxson may well have had just this problem in mind when he wrote, in his *History of the American Frontier*, that "the open frontier and the abundance of land made it hard to drive Americans into factories; and the scarcity of American capital made the rise of manufacturers doubly slow. By 1850, America was at least fifty years behind Europe, with reference to the industrial revolution, and many of the differences between American and European civilization, noticeable to all, were consequences of this." And when one adds such a factor as this country's distance from Europe—which, until the advent of modern communications, made slow the rate of our cultural borrowing—one wonders why anyone has ever found our literary lag inexplicable.

But the lag was really not long, for if we were fifty years behind Europe economically, we were not politically, and in relation to the wealth of the country the changes in the fourth and fifth decades of the nineteenth century were remarkable enough. In any event, when romanticism finally arrived, it came

as a complete school. Its deficiencies were serious and significant, because they were of the spirit, but at least in *form* it
seemed whole. Professor Norman Foerster's comparison of Europe's romantic age with ours could be less sweeping and more
critical and still it would reveal the often unappreciated breadth
of our movement and the multiplicity of its diverse elements:
"We too had our precursors in the eighteenth century, of whom
Freneau is the most distinguished; we had our sentimental prep-
aration, our Werther fever, our Gothic enthusiasms, our fresh
interest in nature, and we had a democratic Revolution before
the French. . . . We had our lovers of beauty; we were fascinated by the Middle Ages; we wrote ballads; we had disciples
of nature; we turned to the national past, to the Indians, the
Puritans, and the Revolution; we cultivated the sense of wonder, the supernatural, the grotesque, the ego, the genius; we
were ardent in social reform, and carried out pantisocratic notions at Brook Farm and Fruitlands; we worked out new theories of poetry and art in revolt against pseudo-classicism; we
were reverently appreciative of Shakespeare, traveled much in
the realms of Elizabethan gold, discovered or rediscovered
Homer, Plato, Dante, Calderón, Rousseau, Goethe, Kant and
the Germans generally. And at length we had our decadence
in Bayard Taylor, Stoddard, Stedman, Aldrich, Lanier, etc." [1]

Professor Foerster confessed, in effect, that his analogy was
too fulsome and generous when he went on to paraphrase Cabot
and define our nineteenth-century literature as romanticism "on
Puritan and pioneer soil"—thereby calling attention to its amazing respectability and its limited ideals. Howard Mumford Jones
has quite justly pointed out that "we have no American Shelley,
no Godwin, no Gautier, no Heine, and no Schopenhauer
to deny conventional values. . . . The American 'Romantic
Movement' is a very correct romantic movement, one that has
no *Lucinde*, no *Mademoiselle de Maupin*, in short, no passion-

[1] In *The Reinterpretation of American Literature* (New York, 1928), pp.
32-3.

ate apology for the senses, just as it has no *Préface de Cromwell* and no first night of *Hernani*, but merely a riot over opera prices. How could it have been otherwise? American educational institutions, dominated by the American church, had no place for esthetics in their scheme of things, and no belief in art, and for that matter, they have little today." He might have gone on to explain that when the church's control over our schools was eliminated, the crudest of secular controls was substituted, and that a rising, energetic, and ambitious people, absorbed in exploiting huge new sources of wealth, is intuitively hostile to art.

The tameness of our romance should not, however, obscure its inclusiveness. When we agree that no Heine and no Shelley arose to confute the masters of our morals and our property, we admit chiefly that among our rebels there were few giants, but not that there were no rebels. As in Europe, so here the greatest moments in the movement were those of protest and non-conformist idealism. They were seldom great moments, but only a prejudiced or myopic observer could overlook them. This is so elementary and obvious a fact that it may seem ridiculous even to mention it, and yet the impression left by many popular essays on the period is a sickeningly pretty one of a whole population greeting a bright tomorrow. Few have dwelt fittingly upon its sorrows and tragedies. The classes on whose toil depended the roseate dawn, and the various classes who were ruined or deprived of eminence by the industrial revolution, have somehow been ignored. How this was done by writers who were engaged in explaining the works of the dissident is an achievement no literary Houdini would despise.

For it is surely clear that the great majority of the poets and essayists of the time were not the voices of State Street and Wall Street. They spoke for other constituencies—some directly opposed to the new greedily acquisitive bourgeoisie, some uneasily aloof, and some only unconsciously and naïvely approbatory. They spoke sometimes too softly, often haltingly, and about some of the crucial questions they spoke practically not at all. They were not, however, always complacently silent. It is suggestive, and ironical, that so much of the literature of romance is not flattering to the class that was benefited most by the very changes of which that literature was the precipitate. The point is that economic and cultural transformations are not confined to a single level of society, but are undergone at many levels. Those who first seized the "means of production" were too busy getting rich to worry about literature and philosophy, which in any event were distracting and "enervating" influences; while, on the contrary, the intellectuals who had not shared in the goods of the new society and to whom equality and democracy were requisites, had every reason to cry aloud on behalf of an idealistic reformation of individual behavior and state conduct. It is worth noting that "the prominent humanitarian and educational leaders of the period, such as Emerson, Thoreau, James G. Carter, George Ripley, J. F. Clarke, William E. Channing, Horace Mann, Henry Barnard, Robert Rantoul, Jr., O. E. Brownson, Theodore Parker, Samuel Lewis and F. H. Hedge, came chiefly from old New England stock; they were sons of ministers, farmers and merchants, and they were nearly all college bred. But they were only remotely connected with the great industrial changes which had been sweeping over New England. These men were representatives of a class in the community which was losing its grip upon social and political authority." [1] It need hardly be said that it is principally these men who make up the subject of this chapter. Most of the uncritical "yea-sayers" (we disposed of many of them in our section on gentility) are in retrospect unimportant. It is the rebels, or at least the dissatisfied, who created the bulk of the literature that survives. There must have been sweet singers of contentment and optimism among the English romanticists, but who remembers them? We remember Blake, Shelley, Godwin, Byron, Keats.

[1] F. T. Carlton, op. cit., p. 39.

There were other literary tendencies in our romantic age besides the humanitarian and educational. They arose, naturally, from other ideological sources. The pursuit of a lavishly poeticized past—the adoration of Elizabethan and feudal scenes—arose largely among the descendants of the mercantile and plantation aristocracies, who found their polite, serene traditions disintegrating in a speculative and expanding world. And among them arose also the romantic delight in the timeless and placeless dreams of the unbound imagination—"pure" poetry, "pure" art, "pure" narrative. The spiritual womb out of which Emerson came was obviously not the same as the one from which Poe came, or Whitman, or even a neighbor like Lowell.

Of course, no analysis which traces the inspiration of particular tendencies in romanticism to specific developments in American life can be followed too rigidly. It is impossible to divide into separate channels, with such precision, the flow of literature in *any* era, for it is a truism that there are never unmingled parallel currents of thought and that men can seldom be placed in a single category. The infiltration of ideas, and frequently of social and economic interests as well, from an originating to a contiguous group is constant.

In a society as fluid as that of the United States before the Civil War, the individual writer was especially susceptible to a medley of not always harmonious sentiments. The cultural streams were at certain points related and were thus disposed to cohere and appear as one, and so he could without any sense of confusion easily assimilate and express the beliefs and moods of several theoretically unsympathetic groups. Today when we look back on the men who were the thinkers and critics of the period, they seem often to be all at odds with each other, often all in agreement, usually both. Such an impression is by no means incorrect. They were the greatest individualists of an individualistic age. They composed no distinct and regular pattern of thought or action. Yet they did belong to their time, they did express (each in his own way and from his own point of interest) something of its spirit, and in the long run it becomes clear that viewed as an assembly they represented the whole of their society. And only by remembering that the "revolution" of which romanticism was a part did not affect the lives of all men similarly, can we explain why the movement embraced such dissimilar men.

The scene was grim and glamorous. For nearly half a century, beginning with Jackson's election, the United States wore a homespun dress. The term "democrat" was then transformed from an epithet into a boast. A commonwealth of "plain people," antagonistic to the tory *Weltanschauung* and contemptuous of aristocratic pretensions, seemed to be the logical destiny, and none but a dwindling number of embittered Whigs would dare decry it. But a democracy, in the highest philosophical sense, it was not. Its determination to prevent the *reigning* capitalists from extending their power was merely part of a systematic policy of encouraging "expectant capitalists," and hence it was essentially as predatory as federalism. It promoted noise, greed, and vulgarity and created the perfect soil for the future growth of Babbittry.

But the important thing is that the democratic *idea* had at last become a genuine and active element in the consciousness and policy of the nation. If it was the boom that acted as a spur to the ambitions of the clamorous democrats, it was the darker side of an emerging industrial capitalism that gave real point to their clamor. This aspect of the period may not have been very noticeable during the quarter-century immediately following the War of 1812, but after the Panic of 1837 the true condition of the masses was apparent to anyone who cared to look.

The boom had been so feverish—in the rise of land values, the expansion of the West, the increase of commodity production—that when the bubble finally burst, the country seemed, for many years afterwards, stagnant. Actually, however, the owning classes recovered quickly and entrenched themselves as solidly as ever. In fact, they grew stronger, while the lower classes suffered bitterly in the depression that ensued from the panic. The gold rush, the railroad speculation, and improvements in agriculture revived Western enterprise. In the East, "by 1843 'big business' was once more in the saddle and making enormous profits," remarked James Truslow Adams. Dr. Adams, in his volume on *New England in the Republic*, admitted that there was "not a little basis for the popular discontent with the corporations and the general attitude of capital." Recovery set in about 1842-3. "It was as natural as it was just that labor should consider itself entitled to some share in the new prosperity. Instead, it found itself losing ground throughout the new decade, whereas capital reaped the entire benefit." A Boston newspaper in 1843 reported that the textile mills were making large profits and that the prices of their stocks were advancing rapidly. They could not help making profits, since wages had been reduced forty per cent since 1840. "By 1845 the Nashua and Jackson corporations were paying twenty-four percent dividends, and most of the mills were distributing large profits, in many cases on watered stock."

As everywhere else in the world, this industrial progress grew out of social brutality. Already a "speed-up" system was piling unbearable burdens on textile workers. Wages were uniformly low. Sanitary conditions in the factories were bad and the hours long. The public asylums and jails were indescribably ugly. Working-class homes were primitive and crowded. Vice and crime were notoriously prevalent. In 1850 the police of New York took a census of the inhabited cellars of the city. Their investigations revealed "that 18,456 persons occupied 8,141 cellars with no other rooms. This meant about one-thirtieth of the population of New York City lived underground." The official report said: "There are cellars devoted entirely to lodging, where straw at two cents, and bare floor at one cent a night can be had. . . . Black and white, men, women and children are mixed in one dirty mass. Scenes of depravity the most horrible are of constant occurrence." Bedrooms in workers' homes were "without air, without light, filled with damp vapour from the mildewed walls, and with vermin." Above the ground, conditions were no better, as an investigation in 1853 showed. The tenement houses were not fit for miserable beasts—and they yielded their landlords "a rent of from 15 to 50 percent on the money invested." [1] (Need we read Engels on the *Condition of the Working Class in England in 1844?*)

These conditions aroused the sympathy and indignation of humane men on the one hand, and on the other proved a fruitful source of discontent and anger on the part of the proletariat. The latter, however, could do very little to change the situation. The labor-union movement, destroyed in its vigorous infancy by the panic, did not take firm root again until the 1850's; and then the crash of 1857 prostrated it once more, and it remained quiescent until the end of the Civil War. But the soil was being thoroughly plowed in these depression years. Professor Perlman put it mildly when he said (in his *History of Trade Unionism*): "As the prospect for immediate amelioration became dimmed by circumstances, an opportunity arrived for theories and philosophies of radical social reform." The German revolutionaries who were then emigrating to the United States—Weydemeyer, Koch, Kriege, and Weitling, for example; old comrades of the youthful Karl Marx—found ready ears at least among the more advanced of the workers. They did not outnumber, however, the native "radicals," such as Beck, Campbell, Andrews, Kellogg, Evans, and Briggs, while the intellectuals Brownson, Greeley, and Brisbane contributed an articulate idealism to which many among the middle classes listened attentively. The period is best known, of course, for the utopian socialist and anarchist schemes imported and nursed by the poets and reformers of Massachusetts and New York. In 1840 Albert Brisbane introduced Americans to the principles

[1] John R. Commons and associates: *History of Labour in the United States* (New York, 1918), Vol. I, pp. 490-1.

of Fourier by publishing *The Social Destiny of Man*. The gospel was spread by the Channings, Dana, Godwin, Ripley, Curtis, Story, and others. Owenism and the principles of Etienne Cabet also became subjects for popular discussion. Josiah Warren's anarchism inspired colonies in Ohio and Long Island. Above all, Brook Farm wrote its name in the history of American idealism. It was founded in 1841 as a community of "kindred spirits" who wished to get out of the business community and live the simple life. Until 1844, when it was reorganized on the basis of the Fourier system, its inhabitants lived pleasantly and peacefully in a libertarian atmosphere engendered by mutual respect and a mild anarchist philosophy. Its residents were transcendentalists and their sympathizers; hence the great names associated with it. Unfortunately, the venture did not prosper for long after 1844.

They all vanished eventually, those Christian philosophies, movements, ideals, utopias. What remained were the inevitable social tendencies accompanying the rise of industrialism. On the one hand an unstable proletariat was developing. Individualism was rampant in its ranks; skilled and unskilled workers were violently antagonistic toward each other; clever politicians fanned the flames of race hatred; and always there beckoned the West. On the other hand a new bourgeoisie was maturing. It was energetic, vulgar, and shrewd; it was speculative and courageous; it was arrogant. Between the two camps, at a distance, stood the intelligentsia, bourgeois by birth, tradition, and culture, but (for causes previously stated) distrustful of capitalist industry, contemptuous of the ostentatious parvenus, and dedicated to the search for a better world.

Lewis Mumford, wistfully looking backward, has called this age of romance the "golden day." Meade Minnigerode, staring wide-eyed at the antics of an adolescent people, has sneered at the "fabulous forties." It happens that both are right. But Mr. Mumford is less so, in a sense, for he has given us to feel that the tiny, scattered battalion of meditative men and women of those electric years represented America—and in doing that, even though he probably does not intend it, he is "literary." No one has pictured well the crime and poverty, but Mr. Minnigerode has sketched, in broad and journalistic strokes, the dazzling vulgarity. "One breathed hope," writes Mr. Mumford, "as one might breathe the heady air of early autumn, pungent with the smell of hickory fires and baking bread, as one walked through the village street." Mr. Minnigerode suspects that village streets are city streets in miniature, and writes: "It achieved the apotheosis of banality in a blaze of wax candles, the sanctification of platitude in a chorus of adjectives." For a few, perhaps, it was the age of Bronson Alcott; for the many, the age of P. T. Barnum.

2

In one of the essays on *Poetry and Religion* George Santayana observed that the transcendentalists wanted "to reject tradition and think as one might have thought if no man had ever existed before." Little need be added to that to describe the spirit of the transcendentalist movement. Elsewhere he referred to the vague, rather complicated theories put forth by Emerson and his friends as "systematic subjectivism"—which is a very neat summary of their philosophy, if by "systematic" he meant thorough or persistent rather than logically constructed, since one of its peculiarities was a total and boasted absence of system.

Emerson's relation to it was that of spokesman in spite of his reluctance to regard himself as such. His differences with the school were not of principle but of execution. Certainly it was he who best defined the ethics, "sociology," and metaphysics of transcendentalism. It is true that he could never feel wholly comfortable in the atmosphere of high moral fervor inhabited by the inner group, nor could he ever do more than sympathize with their political and social radicalism. He was too much the Yankee of legend—cool, reserved, individualistic, cautious—to let himself be drawn deeply into activities which often flouted the conventions and threatened to weaken the stability of the state. But that is only another way of saying that he was a transcendentalist who wouldn't go all the way. With him transcendentalism remained, at most, homiletic, while others tried to convert it into a political reality. Although he cannot, therefore, be listed without reservations among "the pure romantics"—the most selfless and ecstatic of our literary idealists—neither can he be considered separately.

None but a mystic can honestly say that he comprehends transcendentalism in the sense in which Emerson and his colleagues did. Such comprehension assumes a view of the universe and man's relation to it which is wholly irrational and is consummated in a state of emotion more commonly associated with the occult religions than with philosophy. But neither is transcendentalism a mystery to be solved only by initiates. It has philosophical antecedents with which students are thoroughly familiar. In essence an American version of Neo-Platonism, it was derived chiefly from the movement in England which had arisen in the flush of the romantic era. The specific sources were Coleridge's prose writings, Taylor's translations of the Neo-Platonist classics, and, finally, the teachings of Wright and Lane, the English mystics whom Bronson Alcott met during a visit to England.[1]

In his history of transcendentalism Frothingham spoke of it as presupposing "the immanence of divinity in instinct, the transference of supernatural attributes to the natural constitution of mankind." In other words, it reasserted the Neo-Platonist belief in the power of man to go beyond the sensual realm, to perceive what lies above all physical phenomena. The assumption that man is potentially divine, or at least that there is in him a force related to the Godhead, was completed by a belief in the "oneness" of nature. Further, the Concord idealists insisted that a vision of the ultimate "ideas"—in their language,

---

[1] Two studies of the Neo-Platonist strain in transcendentalism have been used here: J. S. Harrison's *The Teachers of Emerson* (New York, 1910) and F. I. Carpenter's *Emerson and Asia* (Cambridge, Mass., 1930).

the Oversoul—is not attainable through reason, nor is it vouch-safed by any church. The aspiring mind, self-purified of grossness and materialism, self-taught that there must be spiritual absolutes, may transcend reason and obtain intuitively (mystically) the desired understanding of the ideal realities. The emphasis, that is to say, is upon man as an individual, as a solitary, independent being, striving for sublime knowledge.

That is the substance of transcendentalism, in so far as it can be reduced to an organized statement. Whatever else it contains is intangible, but it is precisely there—in a kind of soul-drenched poetry, full of affirmations of celestial wisdom—that Neo-Platonism is most evident. The latter was beautifully described by Professor Lowes as "the shimmering mist into which the cloud-capped towers and gorgeous palaces of Plato's luminous fabric had dissolved." He analyzed its origins no less justly when he wrote that "through Plotinus, and Porphyry, and Iamblichus, and Proclus, and their followers, there came about a singular impregnation of Platonic philosophy with the theosophic mysticism of the Orient, and the more esoteric tenets of Judaism and Christianity." [1] The "elusive changeling" born of that union of Athens and Alexandria was adopted outright by the transcendentalists.

They did not adopt it through chance or without cause. For background it should be borne in mind that the men who led the romantic movement in New England were not revolting against Christianity; they were merely attempting to convert an arid Protestantism into something richer, freer, more humane—something that would fit not merely the psychology of nascent industrialism but also the pride and idealism accompanying it. In the foreground there were the peculiarities of Neo-Platonism itself. It was not in opposition to the Christian faith. It had no agnostic or nihilist connotations. Yet it lacked a finite structure and was quite devoid of the tests of error which occur in a theological system and the tests of logic oc-

[1] John Livingston Lowes: *The Road to Xanadu* (Boston, 1927), p. 229.

curring in a philosophical system. It was elusive; it had neither boundaries nor definitions nor method. Of these deficiencies the transcendentalists were fully aware, and they anticipated their critics by defending them as virtues. In the opaque rhetoric of transcendentalism one thing is clear: a passion for individualism and fluidity of thought. Neo-Platonism may be utilized to justify that passion. Therein lay its fatal attraction for the philosophical romanticist who sought a compromise between his Christian heritage and his desire to celebrate the ego and enjoy intellectual liberty.

It is thus suggested that the transcendentalists embraced Neo-Platonism because it was suited to their mood, their aspiration, their interests. In their glorification of "instinct" and their insistence upon man's identity with the universe, the tenets which formed the kernel of their metaphysics, they were but expressing an inspired and rebellious individualism. New England—in fact, the United States—had only yesterday wrenched itself free of a theology and social tradition which explicitly dwarfed and bound the soul of man. Calvinism and the classical society had degraded the individual by minimizing his value, limiting the extent of his movement, and defining his future. These bonds had been loosened by the expanding economy which had followed the Treaty of Ghent. The ideological phase of that revolutionary change in man's social relationships is defined as romanticism, and it is recognized that the vital principle of romanticism is individualism. It is therefore not strange that the transcendentalists, who were individualists above all else, should have appropriated the mystics, for mysticism is the very pinnacle of individualism. One may ask, however, for the specific cause of their mystical tendencies, on the ground that it was possible to be a romantic individualist without also being a mystic. The answer is that the visionary idealists of Concord and Brook Farm were engaged in a struggle against something more than the chains of the past. They were fighting the present too.

This is not a paradox, but a simple reference to the forces which produced a state of emotion that could best find an outlet in mysticism. The situation becomes clear if we glance at the world in which the transcendentalists lived. Industrial capitalism had just been born in the United States. Its history lay in the future. For a hundred years it would grow stronger, penetrating deeper into the daily life of every tiny community with each technological advance. Yet already, in the 1830's and '40's, the transition from mercantilism to industrialism was *psychologically* an accomplished fact. Already it was difficult, almost impossible, for men to think of their world, their wealth, their future, in the static terms of the eighteenth century—the terms of trade and a fixed cosmogony. Already we were psychologically a nation of speculators. And not only in the centers of manufacturing. Every man who marched west, farmer, gold prospector, or real-estate operator, was an entrepreneur risking a small stake in the hope of an immediate profitable turnover. But *intellectually* the nation had changed inadequately. The "cultural lag" was manifest everywhere. The official philosophies (those taught in the universities and preached from the pulpits) and the conventional arts (the poetry and fiction published in the popular magazines and newspapers) were still too close to classicism to represent properly the non-classical psychology of the nation. The current thought did not quite equal the current spirit. The task of the transcendentalists was to render a correct equation.

But this does not mean that the present satisfied them, for it didn't by any means. They did not conceive their task to be merely that of bringing to the philosophy and literature of their times such vital and individualistic tendencies as would match the kind of individualism and vitality that were rampant in the American society of the 1840's. They despised much in that individualism and that vitality. The age, said Emerson (in his essay on "The Transcendentalist"), was "unitarian and commercial." It was an excellent description: the vitality was expending itself in commercial activities, the individualism confining itself to a cool, innocuous theology. James Truslow Adams has explained, in *New England in the Republic*, how this church which had been born of the liberal and romantic movements became now the fashionable religion and was made conservative by the adherence of the wealthy and socially eminent. The men whom we call the transcendentalists were sickened by that smug, materialistic optimism which was apparently the romantic spirit in action. They strove to turn the vitality of the age into creative and humanitarian channels, the individualism into liberty. They sought an equation of spirit and thought predicated upon an uplifting of the spirit to a higher level than was prevalent, which meant that there would have to be an even greater rise in the intensity of romanticism in thought. This implies a degree of belief in the integrity of the individual which can only be termed, as Emerson termed it, an "excess of faith." What species of philosophy other than mysticism could express and justify an emotion which had in it so intense a desire as well as so great a faith?

So much for the impulse which led the transcendentalist to embrace Neo-Platonism. But have we not also pointed to the motives which prompted his interest in those others whom he revered as teachers and leaders? In Wordsworth he saw a democratic simplicity and a love of nature sympathetic to his feelings about the evil consequences of industrialism. In the utopians (particularly Fourier) he found an economic plan the fulfillment of which might satisfy his humanitarian demands. In Carlyle he found, among other things, a glorification of heroism and "great men" which could be so interpreted as to buttress his faith in the creative power of the individual. In the Oriental poets he professed to see a mysticism in accord with his own—but we may wonder if their attraction was not simply their exotic character, for in romance there is always a love for the strange and the unattainable. In the German idealists he found what he thought was a systematic denial of matter as the final reality. And in the greatest metaphysician of modern times, in Immanuel Kant, he found, or thought he did, what he needed most: a logical defense of his basic position. Kant's distinction of the transcendental ideas was eagerly caught up "by young and ardent persons in this country," said Cabot in his *Memoir of Emerson*, "because it fell in with their own assurance of a more direct and intimate mode of access to things unseen and external than was admitted by the prevailing Nominalism. They did not pay much regard to Kant's warning that these ideas, though of the highest value for the regulation of conduct, do not constitute knowledge, since we have no means of testing their correctness. The transcendental consciousness was its own evidence and needed no verification."

The conclusion we arrive at is that much of the snarled erudition of the transcendentalists may be ignored. The origins of the beautiful phrases need not be considered to understand what those phrases meant and what they stood for. The attitude preceded the word: the transcendentalists' inclinations were fairly well formed before they discovered the prophets to echo and the sacred names to swear by. The philosophies they studied and quoted did not influence them so much as make them articulate in the expression of ideals they already possessed. In short, we are dealing with a group of genuine romanticists whose time, place, and circumstance explain them so well that little reference need be made to their cultural borrowings.

The critical writings of the transcendentalists were considerably simpler and more realistic than their metaphysics. Their emotions were definite and keenly felt and when in contact with a specific or familiar subject produced recognizable reactions.

Their chief critical writings appeared in four magaiznes. It is interesting that the first of them was the *Western Messenger*, published in Cincinnati and Louisville from June 1835 to April 1841. Its first editor was Ephraim Peabody, and his successors were J. F. Clarke, James H. Perkins, and W. H. Channing. Obviously, these men were New Englanders, and the *Western Messenger* was nothing but an attempt to transfer the idealism of Concord and Cambridge to the Calvinistic deserts of the West. It has been called "a runaway child of New England." Its editors and sponsors were Unitarian ministers who were propagating their liberal faith among the unregenerated of Ohio, but this task quite naturally involved their non-theological beliefs. They were strongly sympathetic to the transcendentalists, were in constant communication with them, and invited them to contribute to the magazine. The reader will therefore encounter in the files of the *Messenger* the work of such writers as Emerson, Cranch, Dwight, Margaret Fuller, Theodore Parker, Jones Very, and other transcendentalist luminaries.

Was it altogether accidental that the first transcendentalist periodical came out of the West? The movement arose first in Massachusetts; it had many more adherents there than in Ohio; its historical associations were with the New England past. But the West was the perfect environment for an outburst of romanticism—for any kind of romanticism. A boundless optimism, an irrepressible vitality, and a spontaneous democratic spirit were prevalent, together with a generally materialistic outlook and a lack of wide cultural interests; in short, there the ideal conditions, inspiring on the one hand and challenging on the other, existed for an efflorescence of the transcendentalist movement (or its fringe). Moreover, there were no local literary and philosophical traditions to oppress it: it grew up on virgin soil, while in New England the people in the movement were never wholly unconscious of the deep-rooted traditions they were fighting.

At the beginning of its career the editors of the *Messenger* felt a regional obligation as well as a devotion to the cause of transcendentalism. It was not only a matter of principle, according to Professor Mott, for he suggested that the magazine was "also affected by the fever of promotion which is always contagious in a pioneer district." At any rate, in 1835 it announced that "it ought to be one object of a western journal to encourage western literature," which it promptly attempted to do by publishing articles on the religion, culture, and poetry of the West, notices of Western novels and criticism by Mann Butler. But it was not long before its regional interest was dissipated and all eyes were turned toward the East. In 1838 the editors apologized by explaining that "our people, perhaps, have as yet no literature because they have nothing to say. They are busy living, doing, growing. The age of reflection and imaginative reproduction has not yet arrived." These editors were certainly not interested in "doing" and "growing"; they were interested in reflection, and, specifically, transcendental reflection. Their efforts on behalf of Western letters were never so ardent as to interfere with their real interest. The fact is, of course, that the *Western Messenger* was not at all Western, and even in its purely esthetic interests bore little relation to its locale.

The *Messenger's* criticism was written principally by the editors and Margaret Fuller. Special attention was paid to Wordsworth, Coleridge, Shelley, Tennyson, Carlyle, and Keats—the whole gallery of the great English romanticists. It is almost unnecessary to say anything more about the magazine's tendencies. In a period when only a handful of Eastern periodicals were seriously concerned with the romantic immortals, a little journal in Cincinnati was publishing enthusiastic appraisals of them, understanding them, defending them against their enemies, urging that they be read for pleasure and enlightenment! Important also in the career of the *Messenger* were its comments on Oriental literature and the German philosophers and poets. In this regard it did some pioneering work, undoubtedly influencing the *Dial*, the great organ of the transcendentalists which was founded in Massachusetts in 1840. We should note further that the *Messenger* was a passionate champion not only of Emerson but of Orestes Brownson, who was at that time regarded by the conventional laity as a raging heretic in religion, politics, and economics.

The *Dial* lived for four years; its last issue appeared in April 1844. During its first two years Margaret Fuller was editor, during its second Emerson. It was sponsored by the Transcendental Club, an informal association of intellectuals who adhered more or less to the philosophy of transcendentalism. Under Margaret Fuller's editorship the magazine counted as its chief contributors Parker, Cranch, Dwight, Bronson Alcott, W. H. Channing, Thoreau, and George Ripley, in addition to Emerson and the editor herself. Under Emerson's rule Thoreau became more prominent and Charles Lane and W. E. Channing appeared. Wherever we observe the activities of the transcendentalist movement, these are the names that occur and reoccur, together with Clarke, Very, Brownson, Dr. F. H. Hedge, and Elizabeth Peabody, who was the publisher of the *Dial* (and its charwoman). These were not simply the most articulate spokesmen of the movement; they *were* the movement. Its voice was loud and the impression it made on American letters was profound, yet the people of which it was composed were astonishingly few in number. Literary and philosophical movements consist usually of a few intellectual leaders and a host of lay sympathizers; but the transcendentalist movement consisted almost entirely of intellectuals.

The *Dial* was the best and most tenderly edited, as well as the most prominent, of the transcendentalist organs, and better than any other it covered the complete range of interests and personalities. We need therefore go no further to study the criticism of the group as such. And, indeed, in the very first article of the first issue we may read a compact and definitive statement of critical principles. It was written by no less an authority than Emerson. "All criticism," he said, "should be poetic; unpredictable; superseding, as every new thought does, all foregone thoughts, and making a new light on the whole world." We may interpret this request for poetic qualities as an official approval of intuitive, emotional, and spontaneous criticism as against logical and scientific criticism. The desire to supersede preceding thoughts is an expression of pure individualism; the business of "making a new light on the world" points to the transcendentalist conception of art as an instrument for the apprehension of the moral laws which order the universe, the moral laws which are the workings of that principle which is the Godhead itself.

If such a program were carried to its theoretical end, it would produce an entirely personal criticism, a criticism that would have meaning and truth only to the writer and whoever else might happen to have similar private sentiments and idiosyncrasies. Fortunately, the transcendentalists were usually a good deal less extreme, a good deal more reasonable, in practice. Their criticism in the *Dial* boils itself down to a sustained appreciation of their literary idols. Here and there one may encounter a remark, a phrase, which expresses their general spirit or defines their initial premise. Such was J. S. Dwight's query: "Is not God revealed through the senses? Is not every beautiful thing a divine hint thrown out to us?" He there referred to the transcendentalists' conception of a work of art (a "beautiful thing") as a revelation of the Idea of Beauty, which is an aspect of divinity—a conception inherent in the Neo-Platonist metaphysics. Since the transcendentalists, like the Alexandrian philosophers before them, ultimately identified beauty with truth and goodness, we are not surprised to find far more dogmatic statements than Dwight's of the revelatory character of art. Margaret Fuller said that the good critic "perceives the analogies of the universe, and how they are regulated by an absolute, invariable principle. He can see how far the work expresses this principle." Emerson said that the true test of a writer's work is "whether it leads us to nature, or to the person of the writer. The great always introduce us to the facts; small men introduce us always to themselves. The great man, even whilst he relates a private fact personal to him, is really leading us away from

him to an universal experience. . . . The great lead us to nature, and, in our age, to metaphysical nature, to the invisible
awful facts, to moral abstractions, which are not less nature
than is a river or a coal mine; nay, they are far more nature,
but its essence and soul."

But these scattered excursions into philosophy were, as I have
remarked, inconsiderable beside the rhapsodic studies of the
men whom the group admired. The names of these men form a
complete outline of the critical bias of the group, while the
romantic, "intuitive" language in which the studies were written indicate their spirit. German literature and especially the
German philosophical works were conscientiously and thoroughly discussed. Theodore Parker spoke for his friends as well
as for himself when he called it "the fairest, the richest, the
most original, fresh, and religious literature of all modern times."
While Kant was worshiped, Lessing, Herder, Schiller, and
Goethe were regarded as at least minor deities. On Goethe
there were notes by Parker, Emerson, and Margaret Fuller. The
latter reviewed and praised Carlyle's *Heroes and Hero-Worship*.
Thoreau's sentimental lecture on Homer, Ossian, and Chaucer
was reprinted in the last year of the *Dial's* life. W. E. Channing
wrote a poem on the death of Shelley. Emerson's "Thoughts on
Modern Literature" expressed his sympathy with the romantic
poets of England. The doctrines of Fourier were elucidated in
some detail. And Americans, too, were held up for the applause
of the magazine's subscribers. George Ripley saluted Orestes
Brownson; Charles Lane hailed the work of Bronson Alcott;
and Emerson said of Jones Very that he "casts himself into the
state of the high and transcendental obedience to the inward
Spirit"—than which there could be no finer praise in transcendental circles.

In examining the writers of the *Dial* one soon realizes how
thoroughly their critical work was founded on their romantic
idealism. They tried to make their judgment and their style conform to their *Weltanschauung;* they did not often hedge; and

so they created a fairly coherent school of criticism with an identity entirely its own, which is a remarkable achievement in the history of American criticism. Naturally, the *Dial* was criticized by everyone, including its sponsors. Outsiders damned it as "obscure" and "incomprehensible." The reformers, most vigorous of the transcendentalists, said it was a little too "vague" and "aerial." Alcott, and occasionally Emerson and Margaret Fuller, thought it not quite spiritual or metaphysical enough. To us, however, it appears to have functioned perfectly in representing the movement. Each of the criticisms was just, for the *Dial* was certainly too obscure and incomprehensible to reach the world at large, too "aerial" to please those who were concerned with social realities, too practical to please those who sought the "eternal verities" of religion.

The two transcendentalist magazines which succeeded the *Dial* never represented the movement so accurately, precisely because they were somewhat clearer and more definite in their tone and purpose. The *Dial's* immediate successor was the *Harbinger*, organ of Brook Farm in its Fourierist period, and managed chiefly by George Ripley. It was founded in 1845 and lasted until 1849. Among its contributors were not only the orthodox transcendentalists, but also Whittier, Curtis, Henry James, Sr., and the radicals Horace Greeley and Parke Godwin. It was dedicated to spreading the utopian socialism of Fourier and hence stood for the political and social side of the transcendentalist movement. So too did the last of the magazines, the *Massachusetts Quarterly Review*, published from 1847 to 1850 under the editorship of Emerson, James Elliott Cabot, and Theodore Parker. Actually Parker was always its dominant force, and that explains why it earned its reputation as "the *Dial* with a beard." For there was nothing "aerial" about Parker. He was relatively little interested in belles-lettres; he was a militant reformer, and he created a vigorous political magazine. Nevertheless, there was some critical writing in it, notably Parker's own pieces on Prescott, Emerson, and Channing, Henry James's on Swedenborg, and Lowell's on Thoreau. All these magazines had small circulations; the *Dial*, for example, could never boast more than three hundred subscribers. Yet their influence was enormous, although in the main it was exercised, as Professor Mott noted, by the books formed out of the material they published. Their influence was on the whole beneficial. It was favorable to liberalism, tolerance, and democracy. It helped to broaden American taste; to awaken a feeling for beauty in a country where once beauty had been suppressed and where later wit and poise had been held the superior qualities; and to deepen the emotional range of our esthetic appreciation. These were valuable and significant accomplishments, but it must be confessed that they resulted from those tendencies which were common to romanticism everywhere, and not from those which were specific to transcendentalism. The latter, in so far as they directed men's eyes toward heaven, were symptomatic of an idealistic hatred of the drift of American life in the years from 1835 to 1860.[1] Hatred may lead to either of two actions: withdrawal from the object scorned, or an attack upon it. Transcendentalism was neither; it was a philosophical whole, but a sociological compromise, and it could not long serve the social needs of its followers. Eventually the movement disintegrated, some going off along one conclusive road, some along another. Men like Parker, who despised escape, deserted metaphysics and speculative theology in favor of grappling with the real social and political issues of their day. The existence of chattel slavery, the sufferings of the white wage-slaves of the North, and an oppressive sense of what Emerson called "the vulgarity of wealth" made them look earthwards. And because they did not "escape," they retained their strength and sanity. Those who assuaged their disgust by means of a complete withdrawal from the pain of physical fact were in many cases not so fortunate. Escape leads to violence, to negation, to a surrender of reason:

[1] To the Concord prophets, Boston was a place to visit but never to live in.

Alcott ended his life as a mere day-dreamer, Brownson as a Roman Catholic, Jones Very as a psychopath.

### 3

Transcendentalism was not only the theory of a critical movement; it was also a slogan used by several men and women who set down various esthetic precepts which affected much of the literature and criticism that came after them. There were three in particular—Thoreau, Emerson, and Margaret Fuller—whose ideas are permanently fixed in American literary thought.

Thoreau was the least complex, though not the least interesting, of the three. He offers us a direct and immediate insight into the criticism of romance. There were never any qualifications or convenient compromises in Thoreau's career; to believe was to act, in his case. To condemn a government's practice was to refuse to pay its taxes and consequently to see the inside of its jail—a consistency for which he is not honored these days in the schoolrooms of the nation. To despise an urban civilization, its artificial social structure, its conventions, was to retreat from it to the forest. To worship the self-sufficiency of the individual was to test it upon himself by living *alone* in the forest. To profess a belief in the Godliness of nature, to see manifestations of God in brooks and stones and blades of grass, was to seek for himself an actual and constant communion with nature, and not to dream of it while living in the midst of a cultivated metropolis. To ask of men that they look into their own minds, their own souls, for glimpses of that higher Truth which transcendentalism predicates was to him a command that he himself spend his days in contemplation. And so in regard to literature too he was forthright and consistent. When he spoke on poetry there could be no doubt as to his meaning and its relation to his philosophy.

He laid down his fundamental belief when he called poetry "the mysticism of mankind." We must bear in mind what the transcendentalist meant when he used the term "mysticism."

It was not a term of opprobrium. It was not simply a generic term for any and all non-materialist philosophies. Rather it designated, approvingly, a method of apprehending the "ultimate reality," the Oversoul. Thus to call poetry "the mysticism of mankind" is to suggest that it is within the power of the poet, through his unique sensitiveness and intuition, to penetrate the impalpable realm of eternal, final Truth—that a poem is therefore a crystallized vision, as it were, of the immutable God-made laws which order the universe.

What can follow from this except a denial of the value of all writing except poetry? In his *Week on the Concord and Merrimack Rivers* Thoreau wrote: "If men read aright, methinks they would never read anything but poems. No history nor philosophy can supply their place. . . . There is no doubt that the loftiest written wisdom is either rhymed, or in some way musically measured,—is, in form, as well as substance, poetry; and a volume which should contain the condensed wisdom of mankind need not have one rhythmless line." Poetry, to Thoreau, was truly unpredictable, for it was not bound by the limitations of reason. Yet its mystical source did not invalidate its reality. "It is the simplest relation of phenomena, and describes the commonest sensation with more truth than science does, and the latter at a distance slowly mimics its style and methods. The poet sings how the blood flows in his veins."

Elevating poetry above science, the poetic method of describing the physical world above the scientific method, was certainly a conscious and deliberate attack upon materialism. It goes without saying that Thoreau knew nothing about science. It was outside his sphere of interests; it must have represented to him a concern with the trivialities of nature. Science is always materialistic, Thoreau realized, and hence antagonistic to mystical "truths." He was perfectly right, and, as always, completely consistent. And that was his tragedy as a thinker and his weakness as a social force, historically considered. Once he had accepted an untenable metaphysical premise, he *had* to go on (such was his character) to an acceptance of propositions which later proved irrelevant to the problems and struggles that have disturbed his country. Similarly, in his literary criticism he was led by his metaphysical beliefs to attitudes that were sometimes in direct contradiction not only to the common sense of his time but to all those creative impulses which have produced the realistic literature of the twentieth century.

It may be interesting to note that Emerson, who was more often inconsistent than not, more often apt in public to ignore a tradition than to fight it, was seldom guilty of such absurdities as Thoreau's minimizing of science. Emerson greeted the coming of the scientific age, praised the scientists, absorbed the *idea* of science into his own scheme of things. But to acknowledge this is not altogether to honor him. We must remember that Emerson's idea of science was not "scientific." He tried to put a metaphysical or theological brand on the researches of the scientist. In a sense he was a forerunner of such devout misinterpreters of philosophic reality as Eddington, Jeans, Millikan, and Carrel. Further, we may wonder whether Emerson's eager acceptance of science as the equal of poetic and teleological reflection did not indicate simply that he was not as keen in this respect as Thoreau. He did not perceive what Thoreau did: the anti-mystical character of science.

Thoreau's personal austerity, that inability of his to trim his sails, did not consistently lead him to absurdities. His sincere belief in the high station and dignity of art enabled him to detect emptiness and to stigmatize it in a phrase or two. Here, to illustrate, is a remark of his on the genteel verse of his shallow contemporaries: "Much of our poetry has the very best manners, but no character." It is more than a cutting epigram; it is a little essay in esthetics. Or take this plain-worded yet penetrating comment on poetic values: "There are two classes of men called poets. The one cultivates life, the other art,—one seeks food for nutriment, the other for flavor; one satisfies hunger, the other gratifies the palate." But, of course, being what he was and living when he did, Thoreau was not always fortunate in applying his ideas to specific cases. To take only one of many instances, he succumbed to Ossian (as did many of the early romanticists) and praised him as one who speaks "a gigantic and universal language." The truth is that he was usually not a good critic in practice; his perceptions were inferior to his theories. That is to say, he knew what art ought to be, although he was anything but infallible in recognizing its imitations.

Thoreau's was the kind of personality, however, that makes us want to remember him in one of his great moments rather than a weak one. The following passage is not without naïveté, perhaps not even without nonsense. But if we grant him his romantic symbolism, it is also not without profundity: "Men have a respect for scholarship and learning greatly out of proportion to the use they commonly serve. We are amused to read how Ben Jonson engaged that the dull masks with which the royal family and nobility were to be entertained should be 'grounded upon antiquity and solid learning.' Can there be any greater reproach than an idle learning? Learn to split wood, at least. The necessity of labor and conversation with many men and things, to the scholar is rarely well remembered; steady labor with the hands, which engrosses the attention also, is unquestionably the best method of removing palaver and sentimentality out of one's style, both of speaking and writing. . . . He will not idly dance at his work who has wood to cut and cord before nightfall in the short days of winter; but every stroke will be husbanded, and ring soberly through the wood; and so will the strokes of that scholar's pen, which at evening record the story of the day, ring soberly, yet cheerily, on the ear of the reader, long after the echoes of his axe have died away. The scholar may be sure that he writes the tougher truth for the calluses on his palms. They give firmness to the sentence. . . ."

There is more, but that is enough to reveal the uncorrupted

mind, the fine spirit—humane, democratic, independent—from which those lines emanated. So far as Thoreau's effect upon American literature is concerned, that spirit was the really important thing about his criticism, not the errors of judgment or the esthetic blind spots which may be found in it. No better epitaph could be devised for him than this: that he was the first American to urge the union of labor and art—an ideal which has become a catalytic influence in modern letters. It was an ideal to which romanticists everywhere, and surely all transcendentalists, paid homage. It was Thoreau's distinction, however, not merely to make it one of the cornerstones of his critical theory, but also to embody it in himself. Emerson upheld it too, but it was never more than a minor feature of his criticism.

Emerson cannot, in truth, be defined as a critic in terms of two or three impassioned sentiments. It is a platitude that he was complex, many-sided, elusive; that he does not lend himself easily to classification. It has been hinted that his complexity, his poly-faceted character, may be attributed to a "split personality." The term is used here in an ideological rather than the familiar psychoanalytical sense. Philosophically Emerson's was indeed a mind eternally at war with itself. It was the victim of many contradictory strains and stresses, of impulses originating from antagonistic personal and social sources. And it produced, consequently, a body of thought that has been all things to all men. One may find in Emerson's writings at least a partial justification for almost any conceivable doctrine. One recalls, for example, that both the "New Humanists," whose moral and social codes are frankly reactionary, and their most bitter opponents, including some with ultra-radical views, have claimed Emerson as one of their own. Bear in mind also, to take just one other example, that a great variety of rationalists, who demand a sane conception of man's relation to the universe, have leaned upon Emerson as a forerunner and prophet—

but so have the Christian Scientists, who uphold the most irrational of modern theologies.

They have all been right, of course, though not to an equal degree. Emerson was never wholly one thing or another. He knew too much and he was too shrewd to let himself go on behalf of untested, unfamiliar ideas without some reserve or qualification; but at the same time he was too confused to be able to organize into a logical, disciplined system the ideas floating in the intellectual atmosphere of his day.

There are some writers who would regard the latter statement as praise rather than criticism. The word "system" has been the object of sneers in an age of dilettantes and impressionists. The sneers are understandable when they represent a release from the formalism and the static mechanical character of scholastic philosophy. Beyond that, however, they represent only laziness and cowardice—an unwillingness to face facts and assume responsibilities. A "system" need no longer mean a closed cosmogony, a hierarchy of absolutes defining for all time whatever was, is, and will be. It may mean nothing more, or less, than "order": a conformity to a reasonable conception of what life consists of. And to describe as a weakness Emerson's inability to do precisely that is certainly just. We cannot be patient with the contemporary writers who find some peculiar virtue in disorderliness. Emerson's failure to organize his thinking did *not* make him capable of seeing many "truths" hidden from systematic thinkers, nor did it make him a "universal mind," nor anything else—except a disorderly thinker. Flashes of brilliant insight he had without any doubt, and many of them. Excellent perceptions and wise aphorisms were frequent in his essays. But so, also, were hollow epigrams, inconclusive analogies, and rhetorical pronouncements devoid of any real meaning. We must assume that such lapses, even the purely technical, in the case of so conscientious and scrupulous a craftsman as Emerson were caused by something deeper than mere carelessness. Could they have been the physical aspects of philosophical haziness? Inconsistency is a poor soil for stylistic clarity and precision.

Yet we may be grateful for his inconsistency, for it is that which makes him so interesting to study. It is the characteristic that shows him to have been, more than anyone else, the mirror of his age. The divergent tensions within him reflected tensions in the world around him. All the progressive ideological forces of his generation found a response in him. He personified, that is to say, the composite transcendentalist. He was the sum of his fellows, although the parts were modifications of the originals: a reformer, but more ethereal than Theodore Parker; a visionary, but more sophisticated than Bronson Alcott; a rebel, but more practical than Margaret Fuller; a public voice, but more philosophical than Horace Greeley.

The contradictions in his social doctrines are especially revelatory of the man's inner conflicts. A familiar example is his attitude toward the lower classes. It has been pointed out that some of his sayings anticipate Nietzsche: "The mass are animal, in state of pupilage, and nearer the chimpanzee. . . ." "The worst of charity is, that the lives you are asked to preserve are not worth preserving. . . ." "I wish not to concede anything to them [the masses], but to tame, drill, divide, and break them up, and draw individuals out of them." No wonder Herr Spengler admired Emerson above all American writers! Yet the whole story is not thereby told. At other times he could write of the people with sympathy and understanding and a moving faith in their potentialities: "Democracy, Freedom, has its root," he said, "in the sacred truth that every man hath in him the divine Reason, or that, though few men since the creation of the world live according to the dictates of Reason, yet all men are created capable of so doing. . . ." "A man has a right to be employed, to be trusted, to be loved, to be revered. . . ." "We must have a basis for our higher accomplishments, our delicate entertainments of poetry and philosophy, in the work of our hands. . . ." "The people know as much and reason as well as we do." More than once in his life he spoke on behalf of the nameless millions.

But when the problem was lifted out of the realm of theory and translated into a class issue, he wavered once more. On the one hand he thundered against the bankers of State Street, the idle rich, the rapacious mill-owners. No one in his day denounced more bitterly than he the rule of government by property. Parrington's whole chapter on Emerson, in his *Main Currents*, is an impassioned and moving celebration of the man's devotion to social justice and his scorn for the heartless, greedy plutocracy of industrial America. In the heat of emotion Parrington even went so far as to say (with dubious authority) that he "came to attribute a large measure of the cause [of the gap between the real and the ideal] . . . to pernicious social institutions." But we find that Emerson could write such grossly bourgeois sentiments as these: "The consideration the rich possess in all societies is not without meaning or right. It is the approval given by the human understanding to the act of creating value by knowledge and labor. . . ." "In a free and just commonwealth, property rushes from the idle and imbecile, to the industrious, brave, and persevering. . . ." "Success consists in close application to the laws of the world, and, since those laws are intellectual and moral, in intellectual and moral obedience." (This final howler, by the way, moved James Truslow Adams to reflect on the career of Jay Gould. The reader may, if he wish, substitute for Gould any "success" that may come to his mind: Deterding, Kreuger, Morgan, Rockefeller, Mellon, Zaharoff, and other such personifications of intellectual and moral obedience to the laws of the world.) Régis Michaud put it this way: "The considerations on 'Wealth' make one think of Carnegie's *Gospel of Wealth* and Henry Ford's memoirs."

It should now be clear what is meant in calling Emerson "the mirror of his age." His contradictory attitudes toward men and their affairs were equally rooted in the social forces of the mid-nineteenth century. Some men responded to one stream of history, some to another, depending upon their spiritual origins and their circumstances; Emerson responded to all. Why *he* more than others was so sensitive to a variety of antagonistic ideas, why he more than others suffered (without being really aware of it) from "inner conflicts," are questions which have not yet been answered—and which are not directly pertinent to this study, for our interest is not in the individual, but in the limitations of thought confronting that individual to the extent that he was the product of a definite community.

Emerson was the son of a Unitarian clergyman who was well known and admired in the intellectual circles of Boston. His church was an important one, his congregation included some of the first citizens of the town, his writings were respected, his friendships brought him close to the seats of the guardians of culture. His income was modest, yet his social position was high, for New England at the beginning of the nineteenth century still lived in the shadow of the Puritan past, when the clergy (which was then almost a synonym for "the educated") were the rulers and the lawmakers of the state. So long as this self-contained little community remained static, classical, the intellectual was a power and a celebrity. Thus the elder Emerson needed no wealth to gain the satisfactions that men seek in living with other men: recognition, appreciation, influence—the sense of being a significant part of society. His income, however, was not so small that he could not give his son the finest education the United States afforded: Harvard College followed by the Divinity School.

But the son was not so fortunate in his social destiny. By the time Ralph Waldo was graduated, it was 1828 and the nation was already undergoing the birthpains of a new society in which wealth was rapidly becoming the sole measure of power, the main road to position. Without wealth (or its aid) it was becoming difficult to play a role in the affairs of the community capable of supplying that sense of being "significant." The intellectual suddenly found himself disinherited, bereft of his traditional eminence, ultimately declassed.

It would always be possible for an intellectual to occupy a place of prominence in the world of dollar-values if he did nothing to disturb its conventions. A talented clergyman whose talents did not include a dissatisfaction with things as they were could attain a high station. Even he, however, would have to be aware that his station did not include the power to set up the moral and social standards by which his townsmen would live. He could do no more than reflect the prevailing standards and refine them. He was now, in short, the creature instead of the creator of public opinion (except in rural and backward centers). Those to whom that awareness was not too unpleasant lived comfortably. Ralph Waldo Emerson was not one of those who could readily make what are sometimes politely called "adjustments." He resigned from the ministry because of a dogma in which he no longer believed and set out upon a reflective life.

He became the greatest intellectual and moral influence of his time, which is testimony to his fine mind and pure character. It is also a mark of his rightness for the time, his genius for expressing what many others felt vaguely, for he did not bring to his neighbors an idealism of which they knew nothing, but rather crystallized what was already subconsciously stirring them. His teaching has influenced succeeding generations too, which shows how close he was to the hearts of those to whom he spoke: the lower middle classes, whose aspirations have been persistent and basic in our national life. Concretely, his accomplishment was that he formulated maxims (or collections of them in the guise of essays) putting forth a lofty, unvaryingly inspiring philosophy which somehow never conflicted with the pragmatic individualism of a booming society. That meant much to the men and women who listened to him, for their whole lives were now and long afterwards to be spent in efforts to adapt themselves successfully to that ruthless, unrelenting individualism. It is futile to argue that Emerson never intended his words to be put to work for what the Rotary Clubs have since decided to be the good life. We take that for granted. The point is that his words *could* be put to such uses. There was nothing in them that directly violated the philosophy implied in the functioning of the new society; it was only a matter of interpretation. The spirit of Emerson's words—optimism, faith in the ultimate righteousness of whatever existed, unreserved approval of the I—was identical with the general spirit of the age, the spirit of the Western frontier and the frontier of industry. Every schoolboy is familiar with the interminably recurring play on the themes of self-reliance and compensation in Emerson's essays.

Could it have been otherwise? Few men were immune to the rousing temper of the times, and Emerson was infected like most others. It was not only a matter of social energy, arising out of that "fluid individualism" which had swept away the manners and hierarchies of the past. It was also a matter of place. Close to the ebullient East lay a limitless, virgin land in which men were really independent and self-reliant and in which new homes and careers might be built by those who worked hard enough. To an intellectual and poet, the frontier was a moving and inspiring symbol of man's creative greatness. Certainly we know that Emerson was deeply affected by the world beyond the Mississippi.[1] It is to be expected, then, that his belief in the utopian promises of the democratic West, together with his delight in the social and technological achievements of the East, should include an acceptance of the individualistic origins of both promises and achievements.

His difficulties rose, we know, from his dismay on beholding the negative results of the developments he so admired. That

[1] Dr. Ernest Marchand, in a study published in *American Literature* (Vol. III, No. 2), outlined Emerson's emotional responsiveness and intellectual debt to the frontier, and V. F. Calverton elaborated on this essay in his *The Liberation of American Literature* (1932).

life should be dedicated primarily to garnering riches, that men should be avaricious, merciless, and selfish, that starvation, disease, and insanity should be the by-products of progress—these he could not stomach. Alas, he sought to cure the malady by applying the malady: to reform individualism by preaching a purer, finer, yet more ardent individualism. Hence his occasional wavering toward repudiation of the base upon which life was being built in this country. Hence the conflict which manifested itself in so much of his thinking and writing. Hence the idealistic abstractions in his writing which could be interpreted as condoning the things and ideas he seemed simultaneously to be condemning. It explains why today some thinking people regard Emerson coldly. In an extraordinary essay which appeared in the *Atlantic Monthly* in October 1930, James Truslow Adams practically read Emerson out of the company of great writers. Dr. Adams did a masterly job of dissection, and when he was finished there was little left, one might think, of the Concord sage. Shallowness, immaturity, weakness, "lack of understanding of the great currents of thought and action," adherence to a "fatally easy philosophy," a "thin and puerile" cultural equipment—such are the qualities he found in Emerson's essays. And he attributed those qualities correctly to Emerson's acquiescence in and surrender to the Americanism of his age, an Americanism compounded of sentiments the sum of which was equivalent to Mr. Hoover's "rugged individualism." (The sole difference was one of mood, for Emerson joyously beheld the dawn, but Mr. Hoover groped bitterly in the twilight.)

One may applaud Dr. Adams's shrewd and ironical insight without accepting it entirely. There is more that can be profitably salvaged than he believes. In a time when reactionary organizations, financed and directed by a business oligarchy, are poisoning the minds of the American people against humane and libertarian ideals, it is good to remind them that Emerson, like most of the other names they profess to venerate, was no friend of the manufacturers and bankers and their intellectual servants. His faults were not of the heart.

The *Zeitgeist* determined his philosophy of literature. Romanticism, individualism, idealism—they are catchwords, but they are descriptive, and they sum up quite adequately the main tendencies in Emerson's criticism. When he departed from them it was sometimes in response to his private inhibitions, sometimes to the conditioning circumstances of the New England traditions, but rarely because of a genuine, principled opposition to them.

His interest in literature grew out of more than the sheer pleasure he got from the esthetic experience. In literature he found things to cite as illustrations of his doctrines and, like every other transcendentalist, he saw in the great works of art the imperfect yet true reflections or re-creations of the divine ideas. Criticism of the literary arts became, therefore, an integral part of all his writings. That is to say, he was a critic in the larger sense—an expounder of theories—for his book reviews and technical essays were relatively minor and bulked small.

In the theories he put forth, whether privately or publicly, he stayed fairly close to the transcendentalist viewpoint. We have already discussed the critical standards announced by him in the first issue of the *Dial*. It was not a unique example. In *Letters and Social Aims* he said: "Poetry, if perfected, is the only verity; is the speech of man after the real, and not after the apparent. . . . The only teller of news is the poet. When he sings, the world listens with the assurance that now a secret of God is to be spoken." In *Society and Solitude* he said: "The universal soul is the alone creator of the useful and the beautiful; therefore to make anything useful or beautiful, the individual must be submitted to the universal mind. . . . There is but one Reason. The mind that made the world is not one mind, but *the* mind. And every work of art is a more or less pure manifestation of the same. Therefore we arrive at this conclusion, which I offer as a confirmation of the whole view, that the delight which a work of art affords, seems to arise from our recognizing in it the mind that formed Nature, again in active operation." In his essay on "The Poet," in *Essays: Second Series*, he said: "The poet knows that he speaks adequately then only when he speaks somewhat wildly, or 'with the flower of the mind'; not with the intellect used as an organ, but with the intellect released from all service and suffered to take its direction from its celestial life." In the *Natural History of Intellect* he said: "The poet works to an end above his will, and by means, too, which are out of his will. . . . The muse may be defined, *Supervoluntary ends effected by supervoluntary means*."

And so he declaimed, in volume after volume, in one essay after another, variations on the single transcendentalist theme. Just as in the *Dial* he stated what criticism ought to be, elsewhere he laid down the rules for literature. In his essay on "Instinct and Inspiration" he said that "the practical rules of literature" are: "that all writing is by the Grace of God; that none but a writer should write; that he should write affirmatively, not polemically, or should write nothing that will not help somebody . . . that we must affirm and affirm, but neither you nor I know the value of what we say; that we must be openers of doors and not a blind alley; that we must hope and strive, for despair is no muse, and vigor always liberates." Nothing need be added to that to outline the transcendentalist's position in the realm of art.

The whole drift of Emerson's thought was so obviously romantic that an interesting problem is presented by his criticisms of the great romanticists. It is in the *Journals* that we find most of our examples of his "deviations," indicating that he was more apt to speak his mind at home than in public. He did not, however, dissemble when he thought it necessary to speak out, and the fact is that his opinions were often shrewd and just, often nearer the opinions of today than those of his fellows. When he said: "I fear that Time, the serene judge, will not be able to make out so good a verdict for Goethe as did and doth Carlyle. I am afraid that under his faith is no-faith, that under his love is love-of-ease," he anticipated some of our modern iconoclasts. When he exclaimed: "What a notable green-grocer was spoiled to make Macaulay!" he gave us the basis of a portrait. When he alluded to "the parlor and piano music of Byron, and Scott, and Moore," he was unjust to Byron, but put the latter two in their places. So, too, he disposed of Tennyson, whom he called "a man of subtle and progressive mind, a perfect music-box for all manner of delicate tones and rhythms, to whom the language seems plastic, so superior and forceful is this thought.—But is he a poet? We read Burns and said he is a poet. We read Tennyson and do him the indignity of asking the question, Is he poet? I feel in him the misfortune of the time. He is a strict contemporary, not Eternal Man. He does not stand out of our low limitations like a Chimborazo under the line, running up from the torrid base through all the climates of the globe on its high and mottled sides with rings of the herbage of every latitude, but in him as in the authors of Paracelsus [Browning] and Festus [Bailey], I hear through all the varied music the native tones of an ordinary, to make my meaning plainer, nay, of a vulgar man."

But he was not always so fortunate in his judgments. When he said: "What has Lord Byron at the bottom of his poetry, but, *I am Lord Byron, the noble poet, who am very clever, but not popular in London?*" he not only missed the main point in his angry perception of a superficial truth, but also let his moral prejudices run away with him. When he said: "Nathaniel Hawthorne's reputation as a writer is a very pleasing fact, because his writing is not good for anything, and this is a tribute to the man," he was making no sense whatever. When he referred to Shakespeare, in *Representative Men*, with these sorrowful words: "It must even go into the world's history that the best poet led an obscure and profane life, using his genius for the public amusement," a strange Puritan ghost was delivering an arrogant sermon. When he proclaimed: "The poem of all the poetry of the present age for which we predict the longest term is Abou Ben Adhem of Leigh Hunt," he was being so mysteriously foolish that not even his defensible contempt for Disraeli and Bulwer could balance the scales.

Out of all this the boundaries of his moral bias and his taste may be drawn. Clearly, his philosophical and emotional sympathies were with the romanticists. We need not rely entirely upon such an essay as, say, his "Thoughts on Modern Literature" for confirmation. None but a romanticist would have hailed Walt Whitman as he did. He was one of the first distinguished men of letters to welcome the *Leaves of Grass;* he said of Whitman that one must thank him "for service to American Literature in the Appalachian enlargement of his outline and treatment." And none but a romanticist would have said that "Pope and his school wrote poetry fit to put round frosted cake." But we find also that his personal, or idiosyncratic, poetic tastes were not always in harmony with his larger sympathies. In the essay on modern literature mentioned above he criticized Shelley because the latter's "lines are arbitrary, not necessary." In another essay, "Europe and European Books," he extolled Wordsworth for his "just moral perception," but criticized harshly the "slip-shod newspaper style" and lack of "deft poetic touch" in the Wordsworthian line. The mood, the message, the philosophy of romance he worshiped, but the aim and metrical line of Marvell, Herbert, Donne, and Milton were most pleasing to his esthetic palate.

Does that make Emerson a classicist (which Foerster and others of the Neo-Humanist school would have us believe he was)? Hardly. There is no formula for verbal and metrical predilections. He rationalized his in terms of the organic character of poetry—that is, the absolute harmony of word and thought, which denies the possibility of choice, for "there is always a right word, and every other than that is wrong." The inference to be drawn is that seventeenth-century verse, with its compactness, economy of phrase, and crystalline imagery, is more nearly "organic" than the loose, rich verse of the romanticists. Against this it may be argued that what really animated Emerson was his own interest in writing metaphysical poetry. Reaching deeper than that is the suggestion that in romantic poetry there is an acute concern with physical sensation—call it sensuousness—which was distasteful to the ascetic Emerson, who was concerned only with spiritual experience or the perception of divinity. Metaphysical verse, whether Anglican or Puritan, was closer to his notion of what the poet should strive to accomplish, although he remained at one with the romanticists in respect to philosophical values.

It is most sensible, however, to admit that often he preferred classical modes to romantic ones. Our doing so does not surrender him to the embattled Neo-Humanist scholars, for his romanticism was not annulled by his responsiveness to certain forms of classicism. If there was a clash in his critical writing between spirit and form, if there were occasional contradictions representing personal refinements in opposition to intellectual tendencies, they were no more fundamental than the contradictions in his social and political writings. We do not consider him a Bourbon because he justified wealth. In his comments on poetry as in those on social justice, the weight of the evidence is unquestionably in favor of liberalism and romance. The analogy between his esthetic conflicts and his waverings in regard to class issues may, indeed, be carried a step further, and doubtless some will insist that they derive from a common psychological source. His response to the romantic spirit in literature was related to his passion for freedom and democracy in society; his response to the imagery, symbols, and forms of the seventeenth century parallels the strain of aristocratic Puritanism which no one has ever failed to see in him.

An incontrovertible statement of his romantic view of criticism is to be found in his *Journal*. "Criticism," he wrote, "must be transcendental, that is, must consider literature ephemeral, and easily entertain the supposition of its entire disappearance. In our ordinary states of mind, we deem not only letters in general, but most famous books part of a pre-established harmony, fatal, unalterable, and do not go behind Dante and Shakespeare, much less behind Moses, Ezekiel, and St. John. But man is critic of all these also, and should treat the entire extant product of the human intellect as only one age, revisable, corrigible, reversible by him." [1] The words "transcendental" and "literature" have specific meanings here. Concerning the first, Emerson meant simply that the critic must see beyond the given poem to the verities, divine ideas, which the poet has attempted to express or represent. Concerning the second, he referred not to literature as such, not to literary endeavor, but to the actual works produced by the writers of the past and present. His statement is, then, a repudiation of binding traditions, of models and idols, of the theory that finality and perfection were ever attained. It is a denial of absolutes in literature, an affirmation of the right to revalue and reinterpret. It is a statement of critical freedom, which is to say it embodies the chief critical weapon of romanticism. God, it hints, will always be seen with new eyes.[2]

We may now estimate Professor Foerster's triumphant conclusion that Emerson "was even more responsive to the spirit and doctrine of Christianity and of Greek humanism" than to romanticism—a statement made to deliver Emerson from the clutches of the radical critics into the arms of conservatives. We have already suggested that Emerson's responsiveness to "Greek humanism" was insignificant. What he responded to

[1] *Journals, 1838-1841*, pp. 398-9.

[2] This interpretation is distinctly at variance with that of Professor Foerster, who quotes only the first sentence of the above excerpt from the *Journal* and uses it to prove his assertion that Emerson was a Platonist to whom man-made poetry was negligible and perhaps dispensable when contrasted with the immortal *idea* of poetry. That first sentence, standing by itself, erases almost everything else Emerson wrote about poetry. The rest of the quoted passage, particularly the last sentence, gives it its meaning.

was the romantic and somewhat "decadent" Alexandrians. His responsiveness to Christian doctrines, on the other hand, cannot be questioned—and it explains much that was previously puzzling. It should never be forgotten that Emerson, son of a minister and raised in a ministerial atmosphere which suited his temperament, was himself trained for the ministry. Surely it is that, rather than a fancied adherence to some Platonist doctrine, which explains his adverse comments on the great poets and artists. It was the New England minister, not the critic, that denounced Byron. It was the minister that called *Faust* "disagreeable" and "Parisian." It was the minister, in the essay on Milton, that was as much impressed by the poet's chastity, virtue, and goodness as by his verse. It was the minister that complained of a lack of imagination in Shelley, because Shelley presumably lacked a "religious" imagination. It was the minister, strengthening in Emerson as the years went on, that finally turned away from Whitman and came to value Tennyson. All his life he wavered between an anarchist disposition and a ministerial heritage, and if Professor Foerster and his friends really want the minister part of Emerson, few of us will deny it to them.

Most of us will prefer another part of him—the part that was responsible for the sentiments of generosity and tolerance, coupled with an exalted conception of an artist's duties, that are scattered through almost everything he wrote. That spirit breaks not only through the notations of the schoolmen, but also through the restrictions of his own theories and interests. God, the Oversoul, moral "virtue," the divinity of the individual ego—these and all his other grandiose concepts failed to answer his needs. He had to turn toward human beings as he saw them living and struggling from day to day, without reference to the vagaries of metaphysics. And it was then, when he troubled himself with the world just outside his windows, that he spoke best and most movingly. He would dress his speech in the customary terms of a "spiritualist" philosophy, but the sense of a noble passion was there none the less. Innumerable examples come to mind. In the essay on the "Celebration of Intellect" he was marvelously eloquent in defending immediate realities as poetic themes. In a lecture on Michelangelo he said with perfect justice: "In proportion as man rises above the servitude to wealth and a pursuit of mean pleasures, he perceives that what is most real is most beautiful, and that, by the contemplation of such objects, he is taught and exalted." In "Art and Criticism" he approved the growing democracy of literature even in lauguage. "Ought not the scholar to convey his meaning," he asked," in terms as short and strong as the smith and the drover use to convey theirs?" He disliked "superfineness," costume novels, and stories of fashion. He scorned the writer who bows to property. He demanded that American poets forget the ancient and medieval trappings of European romance. He apostrophized the humble homes, the farms, the shops, the fields and forests about us, as subjects just as sublime to the true poet as palaces and cathedrals.

Stuart Sherman once said (in *Americans*) that Emerson, in his more sanguine moments, "goes beyond our most radical leaders in his passion for reconciling art with nature and restoring it to 'all the people.' . . ." When he said that, Sherman was exaggerating a bit (as well as smiling), but he was not too far from the truth. Emerson was unquestionably an important force for the democratization of culture.

One aspect of Emerson's faith in the culture of a democracy was his nationalism. To one who felt as he did about the immediate present, the common people, the frontier, and the novel institutions arising in this young nation, it seemed imperative that the artist turn his eyes forever from the traditions and refinements of older civilizations, including even the burgher civilization of the cities along the Atlantic seaboard, and turn them upon the fascinating spectacle presented by the ebullient life of the new era. He demanded that poets "convert the vivid energies acting at this hour in New York and Chicago and San

Francisco, into universal symbols. . . . American life storms about us daily, and is slow to find a tongue." More than once he reached a degree of emotional intensity on this subject that was remarkable in a temperament that was usually cool in public, when not in contact with questions of religion. It suggests something. . . .

Although certainly it was a legitimate and desirable function of the critic to guide men toward the poetic riches of their own experience, we feel often that Emerson was not thinking wholly of an American art for its own sake. In the back of his mind, becoming sometimes explicit, was the thought that the people of this country ought to be made to realize that God is here and now as well as in the past and in distant lands—that the simplest and most commonplace of physical phenomena and the ordinary experiences of ordinary people contain an abundance of divine hints and signs, from which moral truths may be deduced to point the way to virtue and goodness. That is hardly one of the motives of nationalism as it is commonly understood. It is another of the many traces of an ulterior interest in literature which make us wonder occasionally how we can truly estimate Emerson as a critic. We pause not over the fact that he had ulterior interest, but over the character of the interest. In every age men have tried to find in art some value other than a capacity for affording pleasure, and the differences in their quest have marked the differences in their culture. To obtain power over nature, to propitiate the gods, to instill fortitude in the face of destiny, to arouse the spectator to heroic deeds, to instruct him in chivalrous conduct, to persuade him to accept certain theological dogmas, to uphold bourgeois morality, to inspire revolt against one thing or another—these are but a few of the acts that men have wanted the arts to perform. One can judge the desire for such acts only in the light of one's own desires. For us to judge Emerson's ulterior interest accordingly, we must separate the social thinker from the mystic, although our doing so would have seemed to him absurd.

It is evident that when Emerson hoped for a literature that would help bind men together in mutual sympathy and tolerance, inspire them to fight against the spirit of vulgar materialism engendered by modern business, and enlarge their awareness of the realities of their environment, he was anticipating, even molding, the future. It is also evident that when he wanted a literature that would arouse religious emotions and spread the gospel of transcendentalism, he was traveling along a road that led to nowhere—for the metaphysics he took so seriously has become a mere footnote in the history of philosophy, while with each succeeding generation of critics religion has become a smaller factor in esthetic thought, until today it plays a negligible part (except among certain small reactionary groups). We feel, then, that his "ulterior interest" was beneficial to his critical writing in that it stimulated his perception of the relation between literature and life and led him to appreciate the potential role of the artist as society's conscience. But it was detrimental in that it entangled his wise perceptions with obscure and immaterial notions and impaired his sense of esthetic values.

The effect upon his esthetic faculties was often really serious. It can be felt not only in the moralistically motivated criticisms of Goethe and Shelley (he also wrote other, sounder objections to their work), but also in his habit of putting together names which had nothing in common but their celebrity. There is a downright tastelessness in the way Emerson united the names of the great writers and prophets. Here are a few examples: "Chaucer and Chapman"—"Moses and Confucius, Montaigne and Leibnitz"—"Plato and Paul and Plutarch, Saint Augustine, Spinoza, Chapman, Beaumont and Fletcher, Donne and Sir Thomas Browne"—"Aesop, Aristotle, Alfred, Luther, Shakespeare, Cervantes, Franklin, Napoleon." One is appalled by these indiscriminate unions, until one realizes that, in the heat of his philosophical passion, Emerson was using the names simply as symbols of great men—of individuals, that is, who utilized their inherent power to achieve notable things. He was concerned, in such moments, with the *fact* of achievement instead of the nature of achievement. His "ulterior interest" had thus betrayed him into forgetting his esthetic sense of proportion. Indeed, so deeply ingrained in his thinking were his moral and philosophical prejudices that sometimes he surrendered to them to the extent of repudiating literary values entirely, as when he said: "Literature is an amusement; virtue is the business of the universe."

But his philosophical preoccupations, intense though they were, do not wholly explain his conjunction of Spinoza, Beaumont and Fletcher, and Sir Thomas Browne. We cannot help remembering that more than one critic has complained of a certain "thinness" in Emerson's cultural equipment. Recalling it, we wonder whether he was quite as familiar as he should have been with the works and deeds of the illustrious names he mentioned so casually. It is perhaps impertinent to question Emerson's knowledge of the preachers and poets to whom he referred again and again, but that it should even occur to us to do so is not without significance. It is another of the things that give us pause when we attempt to measure his stature as a critic. That he was, in some ways, not far below the first category cannot be doubted. The more successful of his ventures into the philosophy of literature, as well as his correct appraisals of the pretentious and glittering idols of his time, are achievements which entitle any critic to immortality. Further, he is the author of some of the sharpest and profoundest sentences on poetry and art ever written by an American. His free, undisciplined, roving intelligence, seizing upon some of the more difficult aspects of esthetics, more than once showed remarkable understanding and sensitiveness. One such moment was his summary of art as expression—which endeared him to Ludwig Lewisohn.[1] A second was his anticipation of the modern psychoanalytical critique: "The finest poems of the world have been

[1] *Expression in America,* pp. 128-9.

expedients to keep the writer from the madhouse and amuse him and his fellow men with the illusion that he knew; but the greatest passages they have written, the infinite conclusions to which they owe their fame, are only confessions." [1] A third was his fresh insight into the effect upon literature of historical or social developments, particularly science and democracy. [2]

There are too many important reservations, however, in our summary of Emerson's superior qualities to justify us in ranking him among the immortals of criticism. Too much of his spasmodic brilliance was epigrammatic—a brilliance displaying itself, as many have observed, in "sentences" instead of sustained and cogent discussions. He could not keep his mind on a work of literature or a problem of art long enough to create a complete, perfected essay on the subject. The difficulty was not only stylistic; it was equally that the moralist, the divine, or the metaphysician in him distracted his attention. When we take this into consideration with the deficiencies and faults already remarked, we must doubt seriously that as a *critic* he was great for his own time and place, let alone for a century that produced a Hazlitt, a Coleridge, a Sainte-Beuve, and a Taine. The truth is that transcendentalism produced no great critic, and that within that movement there was another who had a claim to pre-eminence. That other was Margaret Fuller.

But for her style, Margaret Fuller would be recognized as one of the best critics of her generation; but for her character, she would probably be remembered as a critic in spite of her style. She wrote so gracelessly and effusively, and sometimes with such lack of simple clarity, that reading her was anything but a pleasure even to her friends and neighbors. She was, moreover, almost entirely without the gift that Emerson possessed above all else: the ability to write memorable phrases. One recalls a badly expressed thought with difficulty, and for memory's

---

[1] *Journals, 1833-1835*, p. 309.
[2] Ibid., *1836-1838*, pp. 90-5.

sake only the pungent sentence, or the passage composed of
few strokes, but all of them incisive and unerring, can substitute
for the clear, cool, distilled prose of the perfected analytical
essay. Since she could write in neither vein, it was easier to
think of the woman than her words, and so it has remained.
Her "eccentricities," her feminism, her spectacular and tragic
life have been fixed in the pages of our history, but her intelligence and honesty as a commentator on literature have been
forgotten. A revaluation of her work is long overdue.

It is a commonplace of American literary history that she
was a true disciple of Emerson, worshiping the man, sharing
his outlook on life, accepting his philosophical views. But those
historians who have been just to her have emphasized her independence. She was not merely following in the footsteps of the
master; she was a transcendentalist to the bone. So her literary
philosophy varies in no important respect from Emerson's. She
differs from him principally in her greater interest in literature
as such. If she did not actually value it more than he, at least
she was better able to concentrate upon it as a subject for
thought. She could write on books and their authors with relatively few digressions; and she could relate art to life in her
*practice* as a critic and not only in theory. Of particular significance is the fact that she was far more tolerant than Emerson of an artist's conduct, and hence less apt than he to introduce a poet's personal morality into a discussion of his poetry.

No critic is infallible, but her blunders were few. On the
other hand, her specific achievements were too numerous not
to be indicative of sound judgment and good taste. "In her
general view of American literature she follows Emerson rather
closely, finding it in the main derivative and second-hand. Thus
she is unsparing in her condemnation of Longfellow, of whom
she accurately says that 'the ethical part of his writing has a
hollow, second-hand sound.' She speaks sharply of Cooper's
faults, though she is sure that he has virtues that will cause him
to survive, dismisses Willis as trivial, and has no use at all for

Lowell's poetry, which she characterizes as 'a copious stream of pleasant sound.' . . . With considerable acumen, she picks out Poe and Hawthorne as the best American writers of the day. In this judgment she rises far superior to Emerson." [1] Further, she contrived to discuss—"with commendable detachment"— "Byron, Shelley, Moore, all *bêtes noires* of contemporary moralists," and she admired Coleridge, Southey, and Wordsworth (especially the last) for the correct reasons. She knew the meaning of provincialism, recognized nationalism when she saw it, and perceived the dangerous superficialities of the lyceum. Surely these were the "bull's-eyes" of a superior mind! And if anyone is still unconvinced, he should read her remarkable study of Goethe. In a time when Goethe was a universal subject—everyone had something to say about him then, or thought he did—her essay was outstanding for its just appreciation and its sensitive understanding. Ignore her outmoded rhetoric and translate her critical terms into those of today, and you will see that she was cognizant of the vulgarities, the petty snobbishness, and the innate conservatism of the man, yet alive to the all-embracing intellect and the instinctive poet. In short, she estimated Goethe precisely as we do now.

She was also capable of more abstract analyses. Her "Short Essay on Critics," which appeared in the first issue of the *Dial*, was an extraordinarily sensible study of the fundamental types of criticism. Her terminology is, of course, dated, but her classifications are still sound and her comments on the three primary types remain valid to this day. Thus she labeled the first class "subjective"—which is equivalent to our term "impressionist"— and she observed that the author of such criticism gives us "mere records of impressions. To judge of their value you must know where the man was brought up, under what influences— his nation, his church, his family even. He himself has never attempted to estimate the value of these circumstances, and find a law or raise a standard above all circumstances, permanent

[1] De Mille, op. cit., pp. 130-1.

against all influence. . . . The value of such comments is merely reflex. They characterize the critic. They give an idea of certain influences on a certain act of men in a certain time or place. Their absolute, essential value is nothing." The second class she called the "apprehensive"—which is equivalent to our "expressionist" in so far as the term may be applied to the Croce-Spingarn school. To the critics of this type she accorded greater respect than to the former. "These can go out of themselves," she said, "and enter fully into a foreign existence. They breathe its life; they live in its law; they tell what it meant, and why it so expressed its meaning." The last and highest type she called the "comprehensive." Critics worthy of that badge, like the critics of the second category, "enter into the nature of another being and judge his work by its own law. But having done so, having ascertained his design and the degree of his success in fulfilling it, thus measuring his judgment, his energy, and skill, they do also know how to put that aim in its place, and how to estimate its relations."

Is it not obvious that a hundred years ago Margaret Fuller described the antagonists in the literary controversies of the past forty years? What is more, later in the same essay she defined her own position in words that demand applause. She said: "The critic should be not merely a poet, not merely a philosopher, not merely an observer, but tempered of all three. If he criticize the poem, he must want nothing of what constitutes the poet, except the power of creating forms and speaking music. He must have as good an eye and as fine a sense. . . . He must be inspired by the philosopher's spirit of inquiry and need of generalization, but he must not be constrained by the hard cemented masonry of method to which philosophers are prone. And he must have the organic acuteness of the observer. . . . There are persons who maintain, that there is no legitimate criticism, except the reproductive; that we have only to say what the work is or is to us, never what it is not. But the moment we look for a principle, we feel the need of a criterion, a standard; and then we say what the work is *not*, as well as what it *is*." What she said, in effect, was that the battles of literature must be fought over philosophies, not over styles, and she was therefore directly in the movement of the best and most serious modern criticism. Some of our brightest contemporaries have become eminent by saying little more than this scorned and pitied woman said in 1840.

But it is not simply for her excellent perceptions that we must honor Margaret Fuller. We salute her also, and at least as much, for the spirit that informed and illuminated all her critical writing. One may describe it vaguely as a "humanitarian" spirit, but in reality it was more than that. It was a passion for social justice reducing itself, in her critical writing, to two principles: that art belongs to the people rather than the "classes"; and that it is the duty of an artist to inspire the creation of that social and economic democracy which will make possible the dissemination of learning among the masses. Here, of course, was a "utopian socialism," and invariably expressed in the heavier phrases of romantic transcendentalism—and yet it was by no means undisciplined by an awareness of historical process. She knew, at least, that there was such a thing as social evolution and she had some idea of its direction.

"By signs too numerous to be counted, yet some of them made fruitful by specification, the Spirit of the Age announces that she is slowly, toilsomely, but surely, working that revolution," she declared, "whose mighty deluge rolling back, shall leave a new aspect smiling on earth to greet the 'most ancient heavens.' The wave rolls forward slowly, and may be as long in retreating, but when it has retired into the eternal deep, it will leave behind it a refreshed world, in which there may still be many low and mean men, but *no lower classes;* for it will be understood that it is the glory of a man to labour, and that all kinds of labour have their poetry, and that there is really no more a lower and higher among the world of men with their various spheres, than in the world of stars. . . . The mind of the time has detected the truth that there is nothing, the least, effected in this universe, which does not somehow represent the whole, which it is again the whole scope and effort of human Intelligence to do, no deed, no pursuit can fail, if the mind be 'divinely intended' upon it, to communicate divine knowledge. Thus it is seen that all a man needs for his education is to take whatsoever lies in his way to do, and do it with his might, and think about it with might, too. . . . And, as a mark of this diffusion of the true, the poetic, the philosophic education, we greet the emergence more and more of poets from the working class—men who not only have poet hearts and eyes, but use them to write and print verses."

It need hardly be pointed out that a genuinely revolutionary idea is securely fixed within that transcendentalist verbiage. It is implied also in her statement that "the universe is a scale of infinite gradation, and, below the very highest, every step is explanation down to the lowest. Religion, in the two modulations of poetry and music, descends through an infinity of waves to the lowest abysses of human nature. Nature is the literature and art of the divine mind; human literature and art the criticism on that; and they, too, find their criticism within their own sphere." It is contained, too, in this passage: "Poetry is not a superhuman or supernatural gift. It is, on the contrary, the fullest and therefore most completely natural expression of what is human. It is that of which the rudiments lie in every human breast, but developed to a more complete existence than the obstructions of daily life permit. . . . Our definition of poetry is large enough to include all kinds of excellence. It includes not only the great bards, but the humblest minstrels."

How startling these ideas must have been to some of her readers! Many, no doubt, considered them dangerous, but others found that they afforded a new insight into the nature and values of literature. Better than anyone else in America she "explained" the motivating ideology of romantic poetry. That is not to say, of course, that she did not make mistakes. Her very ardor misled her occasionally, as when an expression of sentiments with which she sympathized blinded her to an author's literary weaknesses. De Mille calls attention, for instance, to her overestimation of Eugène Sue. Similarly, she overpraised William Godwin and Brockden Brown: "Born Hegelians, without the pretensions of science, they sought God in their own consciousness, and found him. . . . With the highest idea of dignity, power, and beauty of which human nature is capable, they had courage to see by what an oblique course it proceeds, yet never lose faith that it would reach its destined aim. Thus their darkest disclosures are not hobgoblin shows, but precious revelations."

That was nonsense, unquestionably, but it was not mean or piddling nonsense. It came out of that "excess of faith" which made the transcendentalists seem noble and generous even when they were most absurd. So when Margaret Fuller, at other and fortunately more numerous times, united her fine sentiments to sense, the result was literary criticism that was more nearly in the direction of modern thought than the "sane," uninspired, unadventurous essays of the respectable pedants and journalists of her day. The best, the most vital, the bravest of the romantics were the transcendentalists. In spite of all their faults and weaknesses, they were able to put forth ideas that survived as desirable influences in American letters. And Margaret Fuller was not the least of them. In her writings, no less than in Emerson's, the literary philosophy of transcendentalism was permanently embodied, and it is a tribute both to her and to the philosophy, that so much of what she wrote can still be discussed seriously. Those who have fought on the side of humanity are never wholly forgotten.

### 4

The failure of the South to produce even a small body of significant criticism, in an age when the North was fertile, throws some light on the essential character of romanticism. To the claim that for at least a generation after the Civil War nothing could possibly have come out of the devastated Confederacy it is difficult to reply; but that so little should have come out of the richest, proudest years its states ever enjoyed cannot be explained except in terms of its civilization—a civilization in which the more vital and intense expressions of romance were inconceivable.

To begin with, there were comparatively few literary magazines in the South, despite its boasted culture; and though some were well edited, they were all blighted by the public's indifference. Only three critics of any distinction appeared in them: William Gilmore Simms, Hugh Swinton Legaré, and Poe. In Poe the South possessed, of course, a critic whose historical importance is undeniably great. Indeed, irrespective of his historical position, he was outstanding even in his own time, for most of the magazine reviewers of Boston and New York were competent at best, and often they were merely trivial. But just as Bryant's place in a study of New England culture may be questioned, in view of his long residence and activity in New York, so Poe's place in a study of the South is questionable, for much of his work was done in the alien North. Moreover, Poe was not representative of any class or tendency in the South: he contributed little to its life and expressed little of its thought, except its limitations. It has become evident, in other words, that he was deeply influenced by his early environment, but almost entirely in a negative respect—in his intellectual inadequacies rather than his preoccupations. (That can certainly not be said of Bryant in relation to New England.) The point of view Poe established and the principles he developed were unique, transcending his regional values, and they must be considered in a wholly different line of inquiry. We are left, then, chiefly with the works of Simms and Legaré as specimens of Southern literary thinking.

It is what he stood for, not the quality of his writing, that entitles Legaré to be noticed in this survey. Charleston aristocrat, lawyer, diplomat, man of affairs, he was exceptional among men who professed a love for literature but did little to encourage its growth in their own region; writing was not one of the fashionable avocations of the South's upper classes. Legaré was not exceptional, however, in his opinions. The tastes and standards of his class were his personal criteria; and all his essays reflected, therefore, the mind of a society as well as an individual. These essays, which first appeared in the *Southern Review*, dealt with such subjects as William Crafts, Byron, Cicero, Sidney, "Roman Literature," and "Classical Learning." They were intelligent, but they were also verbose and dull; and in social outlook they were rigidly upper-class, in moral bias conventionally virtuous. To include them in the literature of romanticism we should have to stretch our definitions of the term to cover works with a mildly "forward-looking" tendency and a superficial awareness of contemporary writing. The only other reason one might suggest for classifying Legaré as a romanticist is that his literary and social viewpoints grew out of a fictitious (though ardently cultivated) conception of Southern life.

His optimism consisted in nothing more than a generous faith in "progress," that resounding shibboleth of the nineteenth century, which could be resolved, in Legaré's case, as in most others, into the assumptions that America would continue to grow richer and stronger and its people nobler and wiser. His modest appreciation of contemporary writing was instanced in the essay on Byron, where he recognized the poetic value of imagination, passion, and luxurious imagery. But his optimism was tempered by a doubt that the particular aristocratic society he cherished would long survive; and his appreciation of romantic poetry was almost completely canceled by his zealous love for the ancient classics. In the latter respect he was a true Southern aristocrat, for a devotion to antiquity was one of the literary conventions of his class. He could hardly have disturbed his Charleston readers by his notorious advocacy of classical studies in preference to the sciences. Furthermore, he was parochial, in a peculiar sense; he had no real interest in the cultural possibilities of a society or a region to which he himself did not belong. Parrington points out that his general philosophy represented the Charleston merchants rather than the agrarians of the traditional South; and a recent biographer remarks that he was indifferent to Cooper's novels because he was not interested in the frontier (in spite of his oratorical salutes to the fruitful West). If, finally, we take into consideration his contempt for democracy, we must agree that those overtones of romance that one encounters in Legaré should be attributed not to an acceptance of the true principles of romanticism, or a sharing of its primary emotions, but to the "idealistic" and "romantic" way of life which he and his friends fostered.

It was "romantic" in a purely conventional sense—in the sense that it was an inspired or devised way of life, not a realistic or rational one. Classical it was certainly not: it was not part of an unchallenged cultural order in a rich, closely knit, and apparently stable society, universally esteemed as a final phase in the evolution of mankind. On the contrary, it was at bottom nothing more than a violently emotional response to a need for self-justification and self-assurance. There was not a literate man in the South who was unaware of the world's attitude toward slavery, and there were probably few intelligent ones who had never felt uneasy, if only subconsciously, about that attitude and the bitter criticism it implied. They reacted by subscribing to political and moral ideals which assumed the rectitude and wisdom of the South's social structure. An *apologia* for aristocracy closely related to the rationale of feudalism and a theory of class and racial hierarchies based upon the ancient Greek state were the results.

The manners, ethics, and behavior of the Southern upper classes formed a way of life that was by no means unattractive. As a sentimentalized version of feudal lordliness—with all its accompaniments of *noblesse oblige*, generosity, paternalism, personal bravery—it was, no doubt, psychologically intoxicating. As a way of thinking, however, it was definitely discouraging to independence and experimentation, which were precisely the characteristics of the great art of the romantic age. Any deviation from the intellectual norm might expose the false pretensions of a community built on a vicious system and was therefore frowned upon. Here, then, was a literary mind that was incapable of producing reason, wit, and satire (the fruits of classicism) and equally incapable of producing sensation, iconoclasm, and revolt (the fruits of romance). The literary thought of the South thus had to take the direction of its political and social thought: toward the distant, legendary past. In doing so it was, to be sure, romantic, for when men look away from the life of their own times for their esthetic and philosophical satisfactions, we may call them romanticists. But this was a kind of romance that was anything but creative. In the disposition to dwell in a tinted past there is only sterility. It is the spirit that matters: in every age poets have used old forms and symbols to convey their own ideas and emotions. That is not equivalent, however, to embellishing the present with the heroic garments of antiquity.

The pressure of public opinion, in conjunction with the frustrating qualities of the broader psychological environment, explains plausibly enough, perhaps, why Southern literature was so anemic during the electric years of the pre-Secession era. But it is certain that there was a cause which underlay those phenomena. This was, simply, the absence of a middle class fighting for recognition, power, and wealth. It is an elusive factor, difficult to isolate and measure, but it was unquestionably crucial. For we need only repeat the now familiar observation that the emergence of the modern bourgeoisie is the generative force in the rise of romanticism, to understand why Southern romance was deficient in individualism, boldness, passion, utopian ideals, etc.

Once there had been at least the basis of a genuine middle class—thousands of independent farmers working small enclosures alongside the large plantations. But in the age of cotton imperialism, with yawning markets in Europe and profitable slave labor at home, the planters reached out to buy, steal, and conquer more and more land, and this yeomanry was evacuated, forced beyond the piedmont to the bare and broken soil of the hills. Those who stayed became the "poor whites" of *Tobacco Road;* the others went West. The South was thereby transformed into a community made up of little barons and their black retainers. The myth of "aristocracy" was created and notions of "superior blood" rationalized, and what were said to be the manners and pleasures of the Cavaliers and the eighteenth-century English squires were aped to the point of caricature. The Virginia gentry of the Tidewater region, chiefly tobacco-planters, who formed the nearest thing to a true aristocracy the South has ever known, were contemptuous, but too few in number to balance the scale. The merchants of the cities, whatever their inclinations, were economically tied up with the great cotton-producers. There was no one else to challenge the latter's ideological dominance. No capital was available for manufacturing, while cotton futures boomed, so no industrial bourgeoisie appeared.

In that society the petty bourgeois—the clerk, the professional man—could attain honor and position only by attaching himself to the "aristocracy." He had no alternative but to accept its standards, no ambition but to enter its ranks. It doubtless never occurred to him to revolt; if it did, envy, pride, and fear were in the end sufficient to keep him enchained in the service of what was after all only an arrogant ruling caste. William Gilmore Simms is the classic example, and the story of his personal tragedy as an artist and critic tells us much about the impotence of romanticism in the supposedly romantic South.

Son of an impoverished wanderer, barely schooled, first a drug clerk, then a lawyer with no social connections, Simms had it in him to become the great romantic writer of his region. He was talented, imaginative, enterprising, acquainted with the life of the rural lower classes, fond of the colorful and picaresque characters of the frontier. Most important, his natural impulses were evidently democratic. To this one might add the fact that he had some understanding of the relation of literature to society and at the same time a considerable interest in esthetic values. He began his career as a writer by producing a constant and vigorous flow of novels, essays, sketches, and reviews, while editing several magazines and lecturing on the obligation of the South to support belles-lettres in general and its own writers in particular.

Unfortunately, this rather engaging person had to make a living and gain recognition in a community which allowed little latitude to men of talent. To occupy a position of social importance and be accepted in Charleston's most prominent and powerful circles, one had to be either a planter or a collaborator of the planter in commerce, law, or politics. Simms found it convenient to surrender to the *mores*. Possessed by an ignoble, though not abnormal, passion to associate with the aristocracy —more, to be one of them—he embraced the entire preposterous and reactionary ideology of South Carolina. It was irksome at first. There is proof that he was resentful of caste distinctions, bitter at being accounted a nobody by men and women who had not a tenth of his gifts: he uttered many caustic remarks about blue-bloods and snobs. But after his marriage to the daughter of a prosperous slave-owner and his entry into the ranks of the "gentlemen," the adjustment was easy. He became an advocate of the system he had criticized, an apologist of the class which had ignored him. He grew increasingly interested in politics (as a militant Secessionist) and increasingly snobbish in his own social attitude. And his literary energies thinned and finally dried up. Thus had the petty bourgeois, by playing the game in an arena where there was only one game to play, climbed to eminence, comfort, and intellectual sterility.

Seldom venturing outside the areas approved by the "élite," his critical work was nevertheless proof of at least the potentialities of his gifts. His equipment was meager, for his education and the extent of his private reading were limited, but one could perceive in most of his writing an energetic and inquisitive mind. Of course, he rarely held up for serious discussion the fundamentals: the moral and social issues. He accepted, for example, the orthodox literary morality, insisting that literature incorporate "just principles, generous tendencies and clear, correct standards of taste and duty" and demanding narrative that "elevates our aims." So, too, he conformed to the region's social prejudices, as when he upheld the "sturdy and simple agricultural people" who were far removed, he thought, from "the vices and excesses in city life." He wrote in this connection: "We protest, again and again, against the false asumption, that the city of New York is to be taken as a fair sample of the characteristics of the United States. . . . Sure are we that there is nothing of the same local and moral influences predominating in Charleston and Savannah." [1]

His moral orthodoxy did not, however, encase him in a didactic strait-jacket. He modified it in accordance with his romantic and nationalistic biases. "That sort of poetry," he said, "which is of a didactic or merely moral character, never can possess individuality—will be as characteristic of one country as another, and will fail, therefore, to excite a very strong enthusiasm in any. . . . The contemplative writer [Simms referred here to Wordsworth] is usually a phlegmatic in temperament, who kindles no eyes, stirs no souls, touches none of the more vital strings of the passions and the heart." [2] Each of these quoted statements is patently untrue, but each reveals a current in Simms's thinking. Nationalism, he believed, had a *scenic* base, and romanticism implied physical adventure (derring-do!).

It was therefore logical of him to be an admirer of Scott and Cooper. Regarding the former we must note that Simms's in-

[1] William Gilmore Simms: *Views and Reviews in American Literature, History and Fiction*, First Series (New York, 1845), p. 233.
[2] Ibid., p. 37.

tense admiration was shared by Southerners generally, at a time when New England was discussing Goethe and Carlyle. Regarding Cooper, it should be recorded that Simms understood him as well as imitated him in his novels. He was quite expert in his observations on the structual faults of Cooper's works and quite right in remarking that Cooper awakened his countrymen to the fictional possibilities of the American scene. His analysis of Cooper leads us to another aspect of Simms's criticism. He had a decided interest in the mechanics of composition—plot, invention—a greater interest by far than the famous critics of New England. In this respect he was kin to Poe. It seems, indeed, that most of the critics who came out of the South, since they were indifferent to social and moral questions (taking the status quo for granted), were able to devote some attention to problems of craftsmanship.

Most interesting in Simms is the fact that he was sensitive to the effect of cultural and social forces on literature. There was nothing unique in this by any means, but it was certainly not common among Southern critics. He was especially alive to the frontier: "The temptations of our vast interior," he wrote, "keep our society in a constant state of transition. The social disruptions occasioned by the wandering habits of the citizen, result invariably in moral loss to the whole. Standards of judgment fluctuate, sensibilities become blunted, principles impaired, with increasing insecurity at each additional remove; and this obstacle in the way of our literary progress must continue, until the great interior shall re-act, because of its own overflow, upon the Atlantic cities." [1] This was very clever, and while it suggested subtly the point of view of the urban upper classes, a group to which Simms did not belong by birth, it was actually liberal in recognizing the social phenomenon without condemning or sneering at its human instruments. Elsewhere he predicted that a genuine and original American literature would eventually come out of the West, and he described it in

[1] Ibid., p. 4.

terms partly applicable to Whitman, partly to Mark Twain. This was an achievement that could only have come from a man who was naturally sympathetic to the democratic and individualistic movements of the North and West. We find further evidence of these instinctive sympathies in the fact that in one early review he made a great deal of political equality and *laissez faire* (rivalry, freedom) as factors in our culture that were favorable to the rise of a vigorous and impressive literature. It goes without saying that this was before he succumbed completely to the hollow aristocracy of Charleston and turned his energies to defending snobs and slavery.

The nature of Simms's romanticism is further illuminated by a remark he made to the effect that "it is the artist only who is the true historian." [1] That sounds like transcendentalism, but the meaning is somewhat different. Simms had in mind not the artist's mystical perception of Truth, but the preciousness of his presumed ability to capture in a novel or poem the movement and color of a historical period. History as a science meant nothing to him; he said that "the chief value of history consists in its proper employment for the purposes of art." (No doubt that explains his astonishingly high opinion of the good Parson Weems.) Clearly, these ideas were offshoots of his muscular conception of romanticism. Adventure, brave deeds, violence— these constituted romance. Here Simms spoke for his neighbors, for while Northerners also admired novels containing those pleasant intoxicants, only in the South was Scott revered as a deity. The relation of this esthetic desire to the half-feudal character of Southern life is too obvious to need comment. Simms's positive contribution to this theory, aside from his own novels, was a series of essays on American history as a source of material for the creative writer. His critical employment of it was apparent in his reactions to other kinds of writing. We have already noted his adverse attitude toward contemplative poetry (Wordsworth). For the same reason he was indifferent

[1] Ibid., p. 25.

to works dealing with domestic situations. In such works, he said, "the imagination can have little play. The exercise of the creative faculty is almost entirely denied. The field of speculation is limited; and the analysis of minute shades of character, is all the privilege which taste and philosophy possess, for lifting the narrative above the province of mere lively dialogue, and sweet and fanciful sentiment. The ordinary events of the household, or of the snug family circle, suggest the only materials. . . ." [1]

In that passage one may detect the voice of Southern romance in all its charm and superficiality. How much Simms was intellectually damned by his environment is now evident, for he was defeated not merely by his craving to fraternize with the aristocracy but also by the influence of Southern culture on his general esthetic outlook. He lived in a world made up largely of domestic units which were widely separated and self-sufficient. That intricate and pervasive interdependence of families and businesses which is the foundation of modern society was wholly absent. The few cities of the South were simply the motive-centers of a vast shapeless organism, serving a primitive economy as points through which its raw products were exported and its necessary finished goods imported. The warm, private, common-sense life of the urban bourgeois, so beautifully described by Thomas Mann in *Buddenbrooks*, could not exist there. There, on the contrary, men functioned in public. Life was lived on a stage; and the stage is an art-form which demands action. But it is surely inevitable that the more men's creative and emotional powers are absorbed by the forum and the field, the more they will tend to idealize the home and its sheltered women. The excessive masculinity of public life is compensated for by worshiping an excessive effeminacy in domestic life. Fireside romance became a staple of the North—of England too —but nowhere did it become so popular, nowhere did it find such ardent lip-service, as it did ultimately in the South. "Sweet

[1] Ibid., p. 211.

and fanciful sentiment" on the one hand and knightly adventure on the other: in a later day the perfect symbol for the Southern romance was found to be the pure maiden bestowing a chaste kiss on a bold warrior.

In Simms's day, when the cotton kings were still "on the make" and an untapped wilderness lay just beyond the doorstep, the patterns of Southern culture were just crystallizing. The Scottian temperament prevailed. Perhaps, though, it would be even more appropriate to call it the Byronic temperament, if one abstracts from Byron the bravura gestures, the unbridled imagination and quick temper, and discards the political, moral, and religious nihilism. Understandable, then, is Southern taste in this period. (A recent investigator reports that Byron rivaled Scott in popularity as well as critical esteem. Afterwards Bulwer was idolized. Thomas Moore, too, was widely read and highly regarded.) It was a taste for the sentimental, the archaic, and the athletic, representing the various facets of Southern life. It was a non-philosophic, non-intellectual taste, yet it was not a taste for the extravagances of emotional freedom. It was, we feel, a taste for rather childish things.

When romanticism is barren its peculiar revolutionary character is revealed no less than when it is fertile. Romanticism *is*, in essence, revolt—in American letters as in English, French, and German—revolt against the traditions and circumstances which bind, limit, or repress the individual. It is an assertion of the right to dream, the right to conceive ideals and satisfactions beyond those afforded by the immediate environment. The conclusion is inescapable that it was because the desire for that right was unawakened that the literary thinking of the South remained stagnant and reactionary throughout the romantic age.

Men seek to realize their dreams, and the struggle to realize them in actuality is accompanied by their realization in art. The enthronement of the ego accomplished by romantic literature was never possible in life; and the more difficult it became to win for the ego that respect or consideration which is the theoretical basis of modern thought, the more frequently artists and philosophers were driven to the extremes of romance—and beyond. There have been two distinguishable movements in romanticism. Those who were most concerned with the validity of private experience turned inwards to explore the range of their personal sensibilities. Those who were concerned with the integrity of the individual in a world that was presumably oppressive created that stream of idealism (sometimes mystical, sometimes revolutionary) by which men may still be stirred. They were not mutually exclusive movements; on the contrary, they tended to merge. One readily perceives subtle similarities as well as vast differences in Coleridge, Keats, Vigny, Heine, Hugo, Shelley, Blake. And it would seem that as the century passed, the two fundamental channels of emotion grew increasingly complex. From the enjoyment of the senses came the lushness of Swinburne, the refinement of Arnold, the decadence of Wilde. Yet Wilde could think himself a socialist, Arnold enthusiastically smote the bourgeois, and the Pre-Raphaelites were decidedly interested in social problems. The road from Stendhal's young men is neither short nor straight, but it leads to that huge school of modern novels in which the drama arises solely out of the conflict of a sensitive youth with a coarse and hostile world. Shelley's Prometheus is not unrelated to Nietzsche's Superman. The desire for the nervous stimulants of fantasy and aberration, as evidenced in the Gothic tale, the poetry of Coleridge and Poe, the visions of De Quincey, is afterwards complemented by an interest in the sensory excitation of reality for its own sake, as in the prose of Stephen Crane.

But under the stress of frustration and strife romanticism was finally and irrevocably distilled into its original components, each developing a distinct and unyielding movement. It is the nature of man to compare his apprehension of reality with his dreams. The disparity between the real and the ideal impelled some men to reject violently the bonds of fact in favor of the infinitely satisfying realm of vision and the endless adventure of introspection. It was a choice that led directly to symbolism and its contemporary and more neurotic outgrowths.[1] Others, however, were content to remain on earth, absorbed in the reality that would not conform to the dream. They discovered that studying reality may also be arousing and even gratifying to the ego; and in criticizing reality they found a greater outlet for their idealism. They suggested, then, that the individual expresses himself more truly when confronting the world as it is than when fleeing from it. They saw, in a word, that there is romance in reality.

Realism is an esthetic movement in its own right, unique, definable, but the scholars have not been wrong in describing it as a development from romanticism. For, like romance, it deals with individuals, with suffering and struggling human beings, and not with symbols, manners, or mythology.

[1] The best study of the subject is Edmund Wilson's *Axel's Castle* (New York, 1931).

# CHAPTER IV

# DEMOCRACY AND REALISM

THE meaning of "realism" should not be a subject for debate. It stands for something quite definite—something far more specific than, say, "classicism," which must be redefined and arbitrarily limited by everyone who refers to it. Yet the term "realism" has been widely misunderstood and misused. The average reader of fiction, for instance, may employ it to stigmatize a novelist who seems excessively grim, depressing, and generally unpleasant. Often it is applied to a writer who is thought to be uninspiring, contented with things as they are; often as an antonym to imagination and even to idealism. Perhaps those are merely "vulgar" errors, but unfortunately they occur in more erudite circles too, for occasionally the academic (that is, the reactionary and genteel) critics hang the label on writers whom they regard as rather coarse fellows, or at least as affinities of Sancho.

It would seem that such falsifications derive from a familiar error in logic: applying to a whole group or school the characteristics of one or another of its members. That would suggest that they are caused by simple-mindedness and are therefore of little interest to the student of literature. But the fact that by so falsifying the usage of "realism" it becomes a term of reproach, if not condemnation, points to a situation that is very interesting indeed. It points to the survival of a prejudice which first arose from a failure to comprehend the nature of the movement and then was encouraged by critics who were opposed to its purpose. Nowadays, to be sure, it is a prejudice against a word only, for realism has won its battles. Our "average reader" usually seeks it in his fiction whether he knows it or not. Where the prejudice still exists against the fact as well as the word, it is likely to be among people who are insulated from the problems of modern life, or who desire such insulation —which is as it should be, for it was by them that the coming of realism was fought.[1]

The realists are not related by a common motive: they have included idealists and cynics, revolutionaries and conservatives. Nor are they allied by a single method: some have stood for lavishness in reproducing physical detail, others for the pruning of descriptive matter to the barest essentials. What unites them is their aim. They have all sought to re-create the experiences of men living in a known or observable scene; and he is not a realist whose readers doubt that what he is depicting is consistent with their knowledge of the world they live in. Truth as an abstraction loses its meaning here. Artists have always searched for "truth," for *a* truth. But the realist is concerned with materialistic truth, with fact, with phenomena of which the validity may be empirically determined. Of course, this refers as much to the interior as to the external life of the subject—thought and emotion as well as action and perception. But truth in the religious or spiritual sense, symbolic truth, is rejected.

It is obvious that realism arose with the novel, and if the literature of the past century has been, on the whole, a realistic literature, it is because the novel has been the main art-form of the century. The attempts at realism in poetry have been sporadic and seldom successful; poetry has remained a method for apprehending and expressing the kind of truth that realism ignores. If we were to draw up a list of the great realistic novels, we should find that the emotion and drama they possess flow from their scrutiny of the relation of an individual to other individuals, or of man to his fellow men, or of men to society. These, precisely, are the themes that are best treated by realism. Poetry remains the supreme instrument for a statement of the

---

[1] This is discussed at greater length in subsequent chapters.

relation of man to an abstract concept such as fate, destiny, and God, or to an impersonal force such as nature, death, and time. Certainly there are novels—and several of them are sublime—that treat of those wholly impalpable relations, but no one thinks of calling them realistic (and how many of them have been called "poetic" novels!). In sum, literature becomes realistic when artists and critics begin to study social problems.

Why does the artist turn to authentic, reproducible experience for the material of his fiction? It is, no doubt, a matter of "temperament" to begin with; some men still prefer, as I have remarked, unique emotions and fancied events. If we assume, however, that the writer possesses the required "temperament," we must yet determine the conditions that enable him to make the particular choice. The "temperament" has always existed, but realism, in the sense in which we use the word, has not. The world must have changed, or literature would not have changed. And the first change had to be an awareness of change on the part of the artist; for if life is thought to be static, there is no reason to go on exploring life. That awareness, which arose when feudalism declined and was spread by the climactic struggles against dying feudal orders, was the psychological soil from which, eventually, romance came. Subsequently the realization that human institutions are mutable was associated with another significant development in man's thinking: a belief in the importance of experience and the value of facts. That belief did not exist when men were taught that the earth and its appurtenances are illusory. Then men's emotions were directed toward heaven, and to be serious in art was possible only when dealing with heavenly things and with those beings who were nearest to Godliness—that is, kings and princes. The incidents of common life, the observations of ordinary people, were subjects for comedy and sport. A secular psychology was thus a prerequisite of realism in art.

By the middle of the nineteenth century the psychological revolution effected by the rise of the bourgeoisie was finally completed.[1] Industrialism confirmed the absolute dominance of the new class in Western society. It was now no longer a matter of asserting the rights of man and natural law; political democracy was firmly established and the life of the commoner was everywhere of vital interest. And it was now no longer a matter of destroying the ancient powers of the church; authoritative religion as such was being questioned and materialism was penetrating philosophy. Men began now to look into science for their understanding of the universe, for the rapidity with which living scientists were making epochal discoveries justified the belief that only by re-examining the evidence of the senses could truth, in almost any sphere, be determined. At this time modern physics and chemistry were being founded by an incomparably brilliant group of men working, naturally enough, in England, birthplace of industrialism. A little earlier Smith and Lyell had made their great contributions to geology. Then in 1859 Darwin published the *Origin of Species,* with his theory of organic evolution—and it has frequently been pointed out that this was also the year in which Marx published the *Critique of Political Economy,* which contains the classic formulation of his materialistic law of *social* evolution. In 1857 and 1861 Buckle published the two completed volumes of the *History of Civilization in England* and in 1864-5 Taine published his *History of English Literature,* both written along materialistic lines. The primacy of matter was henceforth taken for granted, in the sense that all philosophical systems now had to square with fact if men were to accept their discipline. Mysticism (a harsh word for idealism in metaphysics) survived, but only in an ever narrowing realm that began at the point at which demonstrable experience left off.

Since artists were also citizens responding to events, literature necessarily reflected the community's new mood and out-

[1] First in England, then in France, a little later in the United States. The point does not *directly* apply to Russia, where other social and cultural factors operated to produce the same end in art.

look. It was at last a defined community, a society whose basic form had clearly been laid down by economic circumstance. The transitionary period, the years of vague but beautiful dreams, of vast aspirations emerging from purely idealistic emotions, was over. The introspective writers, the mystic, the sensualist, the exotic, could ignore their habitual environment, but not so the writers who were perplexed by the problem of setting men free that they might enjoy the good in nature and society. The writer who would not turn his back on the problem had first of all to examine the situation in which men now found themselves. In a revolutionary world—in a time when the passage from one stage of culture to another was at a feverish climax— it was enough to reject the clinging past and set out upon novel and independent paths. But in a time of consolidation, definition, alignment of forces—in a world in which unrestrained hope collided with fact—it was necessary above all *to understand*. And in the mid-nineteenth century, when science was in the public consciousness, to try to understand the behavior of men in relation to other men was to adopt an approach resembling the scientific attitude. Scientists had learned to interpret nature by studying physical phenomena as objectively as possible; why shouldn't artists learn how to guide men to greener pastures by objectively appraising man in society?

In the United States the conditions appropriate to realism and stimulating to its growth were not ripe until after the Civil War. The war succeeded in creating above Mason and Dixon's line the defined community of which I have spoken: the community of industrial capitalism. That was the most important social effect of the four bitter years of conflict. The simple, small-scale, semi-craft factory system of the 1830's and '40's was doomed as surely as agrarianism and mercantilism had already been. From now on, the main line of economic development was toward greater concentration of wealth, increased use of machinery and scientific processes, and a wider gap between producers and owners. The urbanization of American life begun earlier in the century continued relentlessly: we have noted that in 1840 about 8.5 per cent of the population lived in cities (of eight thousand inhabitants or over); in 1860 the percentage was over 16, and in 1880 almost 23. The advance of technology was accelerated: there had been 544 patents recorded in 1830, but there were over 71,000 recorded during the ten years 1860-70, and the average annual number grew to 20,000 in the last decade of the century. Thus, so suddenly that men could hardly adjust themselves, the problems created by the city and the machine were at hand.

Along with technological progress went progress in the pure sciences and scientific thinking generally. English research was widely reported here. Lyell lectured in the United States twice during the 1840's. In 1846 the Smithsonian Institution was founded, and 1848 saw the establishment of the American Association for the Advancement of Science. Darwin's work was immediately caught up by American biologists and passionately debated in public forums as well as in professional quarters. After the Civil War educators began in earnest to fight for the liberalization of collegiate curricula to introduce the teaching of science by laboratory methods. In 1874 Draper published his *History of the Conflict between Science and Religion* as a contribution to the war on dogma, thereby dealing a blow to churchly idealism and encouraging the objective investigation of all phenomena. Science (and in the long run the attitude toward the universe derived from it) strongly influenced even the academic philosophers, notably Fiske, Peirce, and William James.

The state of mind of many critics and artists living in this age when "idealist systems filled themselves with a materialistic content," in an environment where the chief issues pertained less to what the future promised than to what was then being fulfilled, can only be described as the realistic mind. Life in America in the thirty years after Appomattox was certainly bewildering and provocative enough to arouse in the realistic mind its characteristic desire to comprehend and evaluate experience. Here was a nation of unlimited resources which might, in theory, have realized the poets' visions of a free and intelligent commonwealth dedicated to the building of a great culture. Instead it was afflicted by much of the strife, injustice, ignorance, and philistinism of the Old World. The things which had called forth contempt and anger from the transcendentalists and Fourierists had not only survived but grown, hardened, and conquered. The rising class of capitalist entrepreneurs was now socially and politically entrenched, grossly opulent, predatory, at once pious and cynical, creating that era which has been labeled for eternity as "the gilded age." Below them stood a large genteel middle class which even its apologists admit was intellectually narrow and stifled by hoary conventions. At the bottom was a huge yet ever increasing proletariat struggling desperately, sometimes violently, against exploitation and brutality; for this was the period in which the pre-war seeds of trade-unionism grew into a powerful labor movement—the period which brought forth the National Labor Union, the Knights of Labor, the Molly Maguires, and the American Federation of Labor and which witnessed militant strikes in the coal, iron, textile, lumber, and railroad industries, leading to such bloody episodes as the Haymarket affair, the Homestead strike, and the Pullman riots.

The West, too, was changing; and it is likely that the nature of the change had an even greater effect on American intellectuals than the situation in the industrial and commercial cities of the East. The natural man, the man of the fields and forests, unspoiled by decadent civilization, free, simple, and self-sufficient, had been the great dream of romanticism. It never came to life. In its place was the working farmer, caught in the economic orbit of capitalism, producing for distant and unstable markets, dependent on machinery for his daily bread, mulcted by railroads and manufacturers, debt-ridden, soon to become land-hungry. Suddenly it was seen that the typical farmer of the Middle West was far removed not only from the frontiersman and the pioneer but from the idealized yeoman as well. He was simply a toiler fighting an uneven battle to feed, clothe, and educate a family. If he was uncontaminated by the corruption of the city, he was also unblessed by its advantages. Out of his discontent came most of the "radical" movements, all of the rebellious political parties, of the last quarter of the nineteenth century. And even in the Far West, on the last frontier, the romantic ideal failed to materialize. That was a frontier of minerals and timber in which appeared, on the one hand, the grim mining town, and, on the other, the landless, propertyless migratory worker.

However, there were also things in the American scene that were not depressing. There were, as always, admirable men and women in all classes and regions composing a community in which thought was not despised and a healthy, simple attitude toward useful work prevailed. There were the creative tendencies inherent in a rising industrial system, manifesting themselves in the entrepreneurs who were interested in manufacturing and building as well as in the surveyors, inventors, mechanics, engineers, and other technicians who actually developed the machine age. There were farmers who were financing the establishment of state universities and eager to populate them with their own children. There were men in the professions who respected their crafts beyond their potentialities for profits. Thus it was possible for art and education to grow and for their creators to win support and respect in those years of blatant strife and greed. The positive cultural forces were somewhat obscured, but they existed and were fruitful, as Lewis Mumford has so eloquently told us in *The Brown Decades*.

No aspect of this scene was ignored by the alert artists and social commentators of the period. Aside from the political and economic issues, those of manners, taste, and conduct were subjected to critical attention. The behavior of men and women, the urban rich and the rural poor as much as the middle classes, were of great concern as expressions of the problems already arising in respect to marriage, religion, the values of culture, and concepts of justice and righteousness. For in this victorious post-war society, which was so swiftly crystallizing beneath the surface turbulence, it was clear to every observant man that people were thinking and feeling differently from the way their parents or grandparents had thought and felt. The good and the bad were equally examined by writers with diverse ethical and social biases. But whatever the bias, the successful approach was that of realism, for the romanticists and idealists were unable to grapple with such matters.

Realism came out of the West and the expanding industrial centers of the East because they alone offered the favorable stimuli. The social conditions which had diluted the romantic impulse in the South served to prevent the development of realism entirely. The war did not immediately alter the economic structure of the defeated Confederacy; it remained a plantation economy, although on a smaller scale and with new methods of obtaining labor. Industry, technology, science did not enter the South until the early 1900's. And so far as democracy was concerned, there was probably less of it after than before Secession. Now more than ever educated and well-to-do white men had to stick together to retain their position and prestige; and they did this by throttling every democratic lower-class movement, violating the ambitions of the poor whites hardly less than those of the Negroes. In thought and art this resulted in the perpetuation of all the feudal artifices, all the pseudo-romantic attitudes that had made Southern letters seem backward to the point of childishness during New England's "golden age." For now more than ever Southerners had to discourage the depiction of realities, both because of a social need to deny the truth and a psychological need to sustain and glorify their bleeding egos. A realist in the South would have suffered not merely ostracism for having wounded the self-esteem of his neighbors, but violence for attempting to destroy the community. Force was unnecessary, however, for the racial pressures were apparently felt universally, molding the literate and upper-class whites into a fairly homogeneous group with a common outlook. Not until the war generation had died out and new economic and social conditions prevailed did realism begin to appear in Southern literature.[1]

2

When the first edition of *Leaves of Grass* was published, in 1855, Emerson wrote: "I find it the most extraordinary piece of wit and wisdom that America has yet contributed. . . . It meets the demand I am always making of what seems the sterile and stingy Nature. . . . I have great joy in it." Most critics ignored the book, the little men snarled, but Emerson saw that its author incarnated the loftiest qualities he had ever postulated for an American poet. They were romantic qualities, and it was the romanticists who recognized them—not only Emerson, but also (with some reservations) Thoreau and Bryant in the early days, and later (unreservedly) John Burroughs and Horace Traubel.

But Whitman was larger than that frame. He predicted the future while he consummated the past. Giving voice to all the spiritual aspirations of romanticism while insisting that concrete facts, the immediate present, the common people, and the teachings of science are alone worthy of attention by American artists, he marked the transition from "the purest romance" to realism. The views on literature contained in his prose writings square perfectly with the views on man and life expressed by his poetry.

The first elaborate statement of his literary philosophy was

[1] This may be compared with the situation in Russia in the second half of the nineteenth century. There, in a society that was far more feudal than the American South, no racial pressures existed to keep writers attached to the ideological fictions of the nobility and the church. Under the influence of European democratic and scientific ideas, they did not hesitate to picture the realities and speak the truth about their land and their people.

the Preface to the 1855 edition of the *Leaves*. The affirmations of romanticism were never uttered more joyously, more freely. One grasps the whole of this essay by conceiving an Emerson turned warm and passionate, Emerson strong, vigorous, and earthy, Emerson without doubts. It begins with a salute to America as the greatest of poetical subjects: "the United States themselves are essentially the greatest poem" and their people "have probably the fullest poetical nature." "America is the race of poets." The political and social freedom of this vast, seething nation, its democratic and egalitarian ideals, its faith in the individual, its abundance, beauty, optimism, simplicity, and creative energy, its belief in progress and its ceaseless striving, form "unrhymed poetry" which "awaits the gigantic and generous treatment worthy of it." Subjects, themes for song, are not to be selected; the *whole* of this land and its men and women demand treatment: "the American bard shall delineate no class of persons nor one or two out of the strata of interests nor love most nor truth most nor the soul most nor the body most." The instrument is at hand, for English as a poetic tongue "is brawny enough and limber and full enough." And the liberty to use that instrument to compose a work of art appropriate to the unprecedented, incomparable theme, America, may be taken by him who has the strength and courage to take it, for no tradition limits the true creator: "a heroic person walks at his ease through and out of that custom or precedent or authority that suits him not. Of the traits of the brotherhood of writers, savans, musicians, inventors, and artists nothing is finer than silent defiance advancing from new free forms."

Whitman spoke for himself in the Preface, in praise of his own desires, aims, and methods, but that is not its significance. Its intense emotions were not personal; they were the emotions of American romance, and especially of transcendentalism, for Whitman was not merely the flower of the romantic movement, but was influenced specifically by the Concord writers. Aside from his direct admonitions to the poet, which resemble some of Emerson's, the spirit or mood of the Preface springs from transcendentalism. A mystical strain is there, implicit rather than doctrinal, somewhat more pagan than Emerson or even Thoreau was capable of, yet definitely similar to the mysticism of the transcendentalists. This strain in him became increasingly evident as the years passed; in prose pieces written after the Civil War he was more explicit about his metaphysical beliefs.

Yet in that first Preface there were numerous ideas and attitudes which pointed toward realism—and these too, and to a far greater degree than the religious sentiments, became clearer, harder, and more insistent in later years. One which may be thought minor but is certainly indicative was his cry for plain speech: "The art of art, the glory of expression and the sunshine of the light of letters is simplicity. Nothing is better than simplicity—nothing can make up for excess or for the lack of definiteness." Now, this was always a plank in the romantic platform; it derives from Wordsworth and was repeated by Thoreau. Whitman, however, made it emphatic by defining simplicity as definiteness, for the fact is that romance, despite its love for the simple, is usually vague and indefinite. Afterwards he reiterated and amplified the principle into an essential of modern writing. Thus the romantic poet plowed the ground for the realistic novelist.[1]

The second tendency which may be designated an approach to realism was his dogmatic contemporaneity. Here again we must remember that it was a tendency in the thinking of many romanticists, especially the Americans, who had no rich and glamorous past and few of whom had the temperament for fan-

[1] The principle was not invalidated by his own habitual vagueness, just as his nationalism and his praise of English as a poetic tongue were not canceled by his frequent use of foreign phrases and images. The practice of the poet is less reasoned than the theory of the critic. To this we must add that often, in various connections, Whitman explicitly contradicted his plea for definiteness, upholding the "half-tints," the diffuse and undefined. The romanticist forever peeped out of the self-labeled realist.

tasy and grotesquerie. But were any of Whitman's countrymen as determined and uncompromising as he on this question?
In describing the American scene he was obviously requesting
artists to deal with existing things. He then made it a forthright charge: "The direct trial of him who would be the greatest poet is today"; he must "flood himself with the immediate
age as with vast oceanic tides."

Next is the will to deal with facts, to acknowledge all things
exactly as they are, and this takes us to the borderline of realism. It does not take us beyond, because he confronts reality
with the ecstatic expectancy of discovering beauty, nay, *God*,
in every phenomenon, which is an emotion alien to the truly
realistic (non-mystical, non-theistic) spirit. For example, he
writes that the artist must "attract his own land body and soul
to himself and hang on its neck with incomparable love and
plunge his semitic muscle into its merits and demerits." Another:
"Great is the faith of the flush of knowledge and of the investigation of the depths of qualities and things." At the same
time, however, he left no doubt as to his infatuation with truth.
When he said that "men and women and the earth and all upon
it are simply to be taken as they are, and the investigation of
their past and present and future shall be unintermitted and
shall be done with perfect candor," he was moved by the romance of reality, but it was reality none the less, and its literary
result would be realism. The word "investigation" is a hint of
what influenced him. It is a scientist's word. Whitman's thinking was admittedly conditioned by the scientific renaissance of
the nineteenth century. The reports of progress in the physical
and biological sciences—above all, the work of Darwin (in later
years)—impressed him deeply.[1] He rejoiced in the advancing
illumination of natural law and made it part of his esthetic philosophy, utilizing its authority to persuade writers to look at

[1] For evidence see Alice L. Cooke's paper on "Whitman's Indebtedness to
the Scientific Thought of His Day," in *Studies in English,* No. 14, University
of Texas Bulletin No. 3426 (July 8, 1934).

what actually exists if they would determine Truth. He perceived nothing in science inimical to art. "Exact science and its practical movements," he declared, "are no checks on the greatest poet but always his encouragement and support." And he was confident that Americans were truth-seekers and preferred facts to inventions. He wrote: "Great genius and the people of these states must never be demeaned to romances. As soon as histories are properly told there is no more need of romances."

Finally, and obviously of the utmost importance as a prerequisite to realism, the Preface was suffused with a passionate love for the masses which surpassed anything written in that vein by the democratic romanticists who preceded him. The mass was not an abstraction to him, not a poetic concept about which he might sing but from which he remained aloof. He meant what he said; he had worked with the people and lived with them, and then during the war he tended them as a nurse and found them honest and decent and unspoiled. His passion was thus for the masses as living, sweating beings instead of idealized wraiths. In commanding poets to treat of their character and depict their conduct and struggles he was therefore instigating the portrayal of reality—that is, the life of ordinary or recognizable men and women rather than unique or precious individuals. It is not that he was the first to do so; it is that he was the most emphatic. His emphasis justified the realists who followed him.

The peculiar power and originality of Whitman as a critic derived from those four quasi-realistic tendencies. As one traces them through his subsequent writing, with an eye to their increasing force and decreasing sentimentality, one loses any doubts one may have had that he was the link between the idealism of the past and the realism of the present. He changed somewhat during the half-century in which he published his major work, but the changes were only adaptations of color or tone, for his point of view remained substantially the same. Part of the 1855 Preface was converted into a poem, opening *Songs Before Parting* in the 1867 edition of the *Leaves*. In the Inscription which appears in that edition we note that he identified his contemporaneity with his democracy: *"I speak the word of the modern, the word* EN-MASSE.*"* This was the core of his thought, determining his attitude toward the literary heritage. How intense this emotion was in him is evident in his giving it poetic utterance as well as prose statement:

*Dead poets, philosophs, priests,*
*Martyrs, artists, inventors, governments long since,*
*Language-shapers, on other shores,*
*Nations once powerful, now reduced, withdrawn, or desolate,*
*I dare not proceed till I respectfully credit what you have left,*
    *wafted hither:*
*I have perused it—own it is admirable, (moving awhile among*
    *it;)*
*Think nothing can ever be greater—nothing can ever deserve*
    *more than it deserves;*
*Regarding it all intently a long while, then dismissing it,*
*I stand in my place, with my own day, here.*

So, too, his feeling that there could be no American literature which did not take into account the uniqueness of the national character, its incomparable vigor and ruggedness, found its way into his poetry. In *Songs Before Parting* he cried out:

*I say that works made here in the spirit of other lands, are so*
    *much poison to these States.*
*How dare these insects assume to write poems for America?*
*For our armies, and the offspring following the armies.*

*Piety and conformity to them that like!*
*Peace, obesity, allegiance to them that like!*
*I am he who tauntingly compels men, women, nations,*
*Crying, Leap from your seats, and contend for your lives!*

He warned his countrymen to take pride in their "vulgar" strength and simplicity, repudiating the Arnoldian refinements which belong to decadent European cultures:

*Fear grace—Fear delicatesse,*
*Fear the mellow sweet, the sucking of honey-juice;*
*Beware the advancing mortal ripening of nature,*
*Beware what precedes the decay of the ruggedness of states and*
*    men.*

To those who remark that in this long poem there are emotions—anger, fear that the American poem might be corrupted, even a touch of bitterness—which are not present in the Preface of 1855, it need only be pointed out that time and a civil war had passed. Something was happening to his beloved democracy, and he was beginning to see it:

*Democracy—the destined conqueror—yet treacherous lip-smiles*
*    everywhere,*
*And Death and infidelity at every step.*

His anger and fear were fully stated in his most important prose work, *Democratic Vistas*, first published in 1871. In this commentary on American civilization he asserted that the nation had so far achieved notable things only in the material or economic realm and that it was intellectually and spiritually backward and in danger of becoming irremediably crude and mean. He awaited the coming of a class of great native, democratic poets who would act as leaders guiding the people away from grossness and cupidity toward spiritual grace and wholesomeness.[1] It goes without saying that the knowledge of nature and humanity by means of which the nobler way of life would be illuminated would be acquired by the poets having reflected upon, absorbed themselves in, "the average, the bodily, the concrete, the democratic, the popular, on which all the superstructures of the future are to permanently rest."

[1] Fifty years afterwards this prayer was echoed in Van Wyck Brooks's essay on *Letters and Leadership*.

In this sequence of five adjectives Whitman summed up his credo. He predicted therein the literature of the future, but was wrong in two vital respects: it was consummated in the novel and short story, not in poetry; and it was done in critical and pessimistic moods, not in affirmative and optimistic ones. However, as a work of criticism *Democratic Vistas* is more interesting for the way it applied his special values to the art of the past than for its insistence upon those values. He said: "What finally and only is to make of our western world a nationality superior to any hither known, and outtopping the past, must be vigorous, yet unsuspected Literatures, perfect personalities and sociologies, original, transcendental, and expressing (what, in highest sense, are not yet expressed at all,) democracy and the modern. . . . For feudalism, caste, the ecclesiastical traditions, though palpably retreating from political institutions, still hold essentially, by their spirit, even in this country, entire possession of the more important fields, indeed the very subsoil, of education, and of social standards and literature." The existence of medievalism in our thinking and writing was attributable, he believed, to the influence of the poetry, balladry, and songs which grew out of "European chivalry, the feudal, ecclesiastical, dynastic world." (Whitman described quite penetratingly, by the way, the kind of art that was created by the caste societies of the past.) To develop an American (a synonym for democratic and modern) literature we must therefore ignore all previous achievements, for "the great poems, Shakespeare included, are poisonous to the idea of the pride and dignity of the common people, the life-blood of democracy. The models of our literature, as we get it from other lands, ultra-marine, have had their births in courts, and bask'd and grown in castle sunshine; all smells of princes' favors."

It is easy to see that the premise from which he argued was romantic, but that the effect of the argument was favorable to realism. The romantic premise is the belief that the idea precedes the fact—in other words, that art determines ideology, which in turn determines the way people act. Hence Whitman's notion that the medieval community was created by the sentiments and attitudes of medieval poetry, and that the rise of a really democratic community awaited poets who would arouse democratic passions in their readers. (The same conception of the relation of art to human behavior, to reality generally, persists to the very end of romanticism.) But the stimulus to realism implicit in Whitman's thesis was not lessened by his romantic misinterpretation of history. His advocacy of "the average, the bodily, the concrete," etc., and of immediacy, could be detached from his motive.

*Democratic Vistas* is particularly important because of the change it revealed in Whitman as an interpreter of the American scene. It showed that he was becoming more critical, more sensitive, and at the same time more confused. The untroubled faith of his youth was here contradicted by a painful recognition of democracy's blemishes. His joyous oratory was now crossed by uneasiness and foreboding. Thus the extraordinary emotional consistency of his earlier writing was lost. And since he was incapable of analyzing the impersonal factors causing the divergence between the initial ideals and the current practices of his nation, it was impossible for him to resolve the conflict between his hopes and his observations. All he could do in the end, besides calling for poetic leadership, was to reaffirm his optimism.

No matter what one's political bias may be, one cannot deny that to a person of his sympathies socialism alone offered a synthesis of idealism and experience through which he could again be emotionally whole and intellectually clear. But Whitman never understood socialism and never accepted it in any practical sense, in spite of what seems to be a vague approval of collective economy. His recurring doubts about his country altered his outlook in but one respect: in later years he departed from his original nationalism and came to be almost an internationalist. Then he began to use the term "America" as a

symbol for the democratic masses who were everywhere struggling against privilege and hierarchy.

His most serious critical writings, after *Democratic Vistas*,
are those which appeared in *Specimen Days*, 1882-3, and "A
Backward Glance O'er Travel'd Roads" in *November Boughs*,
1888.[1] In them he set down some of his sharpest comments on
European letters and the desirability of withstanding their influence. In the former volume he asked: "Will the day ever
come—no matter how long deferr'd—when those models and
lay-figures from the British islands—and even the precious traditions of the classics—will be reminiscences, studies only?"
And in "A Backward Glance": "Of the great poems received
from abroad and penetrating America, is there one that is consistent with these United States, or essentially applicable to
them as they are and are to be? Is there one whose underlying
basis is not a denial and insult to democracy?" Apparently he
saw with alarm that traditional forms, fashions, and snobbisms
were surviving here, and his way of getting rid of them was to
throw out tradition entirely, which indicates, of course, a grave
deficiency in him both as a critic and as a historian. Even
Shakespeare, he repeated, belongs "to the buried past," and
though he "holds the proud distinction for certain important
phases of that past, of being the loftiest of the singers life has
yet given voice to," the things he wrote "relate to and rest upon
conditions, standards, politics, sociologies, ranges of belief, that
have been quite eliminated from the Eastern hemisphere, and
never existed at all in the Western."

We are not upset by Whitman's announcement that the
plays of Shakespeare are constructed upon the philosophical
and social viewpoints of Elizabeth's England—viewpoints irrelevant to the nineteenth century. On the contrary, we must
credit him with an independent understanding of what has

[1] None of the several prefaces he wrote to new editions of the *Leaves of
Grass* contained anything unique.

since become merely sound scholarship. What is upsetting is his failure to acknowledge the possibility that readers might hold the poet dear, yet be aware of the archaic values in his work and know how to judge them. It would seem that in his role as proselytizer Whitman was impervious to the emotional riches in imaginative experience. But the truth is that he knew better; Shakespeare and Homer were his own favorite reading throughout his life.[1] The importance of what he was fighting for and the difficulty of obtaining it justified his *public* indifference to the classics. Academicians, aristocrats, and idolaters of the dead were plentiful; their opponents still few enough to be excessively ardent. What Whitman said directly after his comment on Shakespeare *had* to be said at that time: "The Old World has had the poems of myths, fictions, feudalism, conquest, caste, dynastic wars, and splendid exceptional characters and affairs, which have been great; but the New World needs the poems of realities and science and of the democratic average and basic equality, which shall be greater."

His faith in the destiny of American literature did not wholly blind him to its actual quality, any more than his faith in democracy blinded him to its present failings. Toward the close of his life, in an essay printed in the *North American Review* (1891), he remarked on the effete and morbid strains in our literature and confessed that it had not yet fulfilled its high promise. Yet he never ceased to believe that if writers would turn from "romances" and "sickly abstractions" to "real things" —"to give ultimate vivification to facts"—greatness would be achieved. He had less confidence, at the end, in the appearance of inspired leaders, but was just as sanguine about the "average."

[1] C. J. Furness, on examining a large collection of unpublished Whitman material, said that it "reveals habits so studious that Whitman himself wished to conceal them from the public, who were already too dependent, he thought, upon bookish literature. . . . Most of his conceptions were the logical outgrowth of sustained and detailed study." In the *American Mercury*, Vol. XVI, No. 64 (April 1929).

In *Specimen Days* he wrote: "Other lands have their vitality in a few, a class, but we have it in the bulk of our people. . . . Sometimes I think in all departments, literature and art included, that will be the way our superiority will exhibit itself. We will not have great individuals or great leaders, but a great average bulk, unprecedentedly great. . . ." Let it be said that though his prediction was overweighted with superlatives, nothing has happened in the last fifty years to make it seem foolish.

We need but glance at Whitman's opinions of modern writers to see in them something besides a yardstick for measuring his judicial intelligence. They provide also a qualitative test of his contributions to literary ideology. Only his mature writing need be considered, although an exception might be made for one, the piece on Dickens, of the many reviews and articles he wrote before the *Leaves*. His appreciation of Dickens, written in 1842, is interesting because it is one of the first instances in which he took his characteristic stand: he applauded Dickens as a true democrat, sympathizing with the masses and portraying their life realistically. The one contemporary whom Whitman loved unwaveringly, placing him at all times in the highest rank, was Emerson. Next to him, and surely above every other English thinker, was Carlyle. The American poets he most admired were Longfellow and Bryant. The British poets he liked were Burns and Wordsworth (the latter despite his betrayal of the democratic cause). He was enthusiastic about Scott, though cognizant of the feudal sentiment in his writings. Cooper, too, he enjoyed. He was intensely responsive to the technical perfection and "sweetness" of spirit in Tennyson's verse, but was equally alive to its weaknesses, descrying in it the "last honey of decay (I dare not call it rottenness)." Poe he did not care for until late in life and even then only moderately, being repelled by everything morbid and abnormal. He never really appreciated Keats, never came to understand Shelley. Matthew

Arnold he disliked as being too elegant, aloof from reality. Of Ossian "he was probably the last important devotee." [1]

It will be remarked that Whitman was in no way distinguished from the leading critics of his time; he was neither a good nor a poor judge of esthetic achievement. If anything he was inferior to his predecessors Emerson and Margaret Fuller. He overpraised Bryant and Longfellow and his evaluation of Scott was fantastically high. That he enjoyed Keats does not obscure the fact that he did not get all that could be got out of him, while his indifference to Shelley is bewildering. Many have felt strongly about Emerson, but Whitman could have done justice to him with a little less idolatry. His antagonism to Arnold was understandable, but showed a lack of understanding, and the same could perhaps be said of his reverence for Carlyle. On the other hand, he was quite just to Wordsworth and superb on Burns. And about Tennyson and Poe he was at least intelligent. [2]

Definitely, Whitman's importance as a critic was not that of a guide to good reading, nor that of an interpreter of the values and meanings of other men's accomplishments. It was entirely, as we have seen, that of a prophet. In his prophetic role he undoubtedly had some influence (most of it on following generations). Therefore the most interesting thing about his estimates of individuals is what they reveal about his social and philosophical ideas. They prove, beyond dispute, that he was a romantic pure and simple. Where his reactions to the eminent romanticists differed in kind and degree from those of other critics, they did not do so because of any vital differences in principle, but because of temperamental differences which were social in origin. He was an American, his background working-class, brought up in a non-theological atmosphere, with little

[1] Foerster: *American Criticism* (Boston, 1928), p. 165. A summary of Whitman's reading is contained in pp. 161-9. For a study of Whitman's esteem for Ossian, see F. I. Carpenter: "The Vogue of Ossian in America," in *American Literature*, Vol. II, No. 4 (January 1931), pp. 413-17.

[2] His tribute to Burns appeared in *November Boughs*.

formal schooling, trained for a craft, spending part of his youth in the country and part in a metropolitan center, and blessed with health and vitality. Compared with his contemporaries, the man's experience was unique in almost every respect. It should explain whatever was individual about his liking for simplicity, nature, physical action, and the common people, his respect for the scholars and philosophers who combined their learning with democratic sympathies, his uneasiness in the presence of emotional complexity, morbidity, and bookishness.

But aside from any peculiarities he may have manifested in those likes and dislikes, every idea and sentiment he put forth allied him with the romantic movement. Thus if a reader were to take Whitman's manifestoes on reality, science, facts, immediacy, and the masses at their *present-day* face value, his plaudits for Bryant, Longfellow, Scott, and Tennyson would make no sense. Hence those manifestoes must be given only their romantic meaning if they are to represent Whitman's own outlook. He never realized what they implied for the future, and he was not enchanted by what he managed to see of the beginnings of modern realism. Pessimism and an absence of spirituality were not to his taste.

A moment ago, however, I suggested that what he said could be detached from his motive for saying it. What follows is that his meaning could be substracted from what he said. We are therefore not surprised that his teachings have been most influential and most widely accepted among men who reject certain aspects of his faith—among men, that is, who are materialists, rationalists, and opposed to a political democracy based on free trade and property. Whitman does not suffer thereby. It is that which has given him his prophetic significance and has made him so monumental a figure. Once the special values of romanticism have been removed, his words take on values transcending the period and the movement which produced him. Many have pointed out that "Whitman thought he was a rooster crowing at dawn, but actually he was singing the swan-song of the once triumphant ante-bellum democracy." [1] If it turns out that in some ways he did enact the role he wanted, it is largely because new meanings were read into his song.

Some may denounce the interpretation of Whitman that has prevailed during the past thirty or forty years and insist upon restoring to his words their original, unsullied spirit. Much would nevertheless be unaffected. There are no two ways of interpreting his love of the people, the masses who are "ungrammatical, untidy" and whose sins are "gaunt and ill-bred," but in whom there are magnificent potentialities, for "everything comes out of dirt—everything: everything comes out of the people." That is the central emotion in the literature arising in our day. Nor is there any way to minimize his contribution to the treatment of sex in art. His influence came chiefly, of course, from his practice in poetry, but he made sexual frankness and naturalness a principle of criticism as well. In "A Backward Glance," apropos of his own literary aims, he said: "Difficult as it will be, it has become, in my opinion, imperative to achieve a shifted attitude from superior men and women towards the thought and fact of sexuality, as an element in character, personality, the emotions, and a theme in literature." Gentility was thereafter on the defensive. And, finally, there can be no disagreement about his liberalizing influence on esthetic form. In that respect, too, his own practice was paramount, but he upheld his practice in his theory, arguing that when there are new facts and messages, "new expressions are inevitable."

Allegiance with the masses, plain speaking about sex, and experimentation with form eventually developed, like realism, beyond his expectations and into channels he could hardly have anticipated. It may well be that he would not have approved. That does not depose him from his place as a forerunner and herald.

[1] The remark in this instance is Professor T. K. Whipple's, from an essay on the literature of 1911-29 which is well worth reading—in the *New Republic*, Vol. LXXXX, No. 1168 (April 21, 1937).

### 3

In the criticism of William Dean Howells we find the two things that were missing in Whitman: an interest in the novel instead of poetry, and a conception of realism devoid of metaphysical connotations. When Howells pleaded for a literature that would contain a realistic treatment of American life, he was talking about prose rather than verse and thinking about conditions rather than ideals. When he upheld the realistic novelists of Europe he was defending the social and esthetic value of an accurate portrayal of character and scene. He was thus a realist in the modern sense, and he was one of the first that America produced.

That is a platitude among professional students of literary history, but is elsewhere not adequately appreciated. The fault lies in Howells himself. He united gentility to his realism, which contradicted his arguments and weakened his own creative writing. During the years 1880-1900, the years in which he was most influential, it was his realism that aroused the passions of other critics; afterwards, it was his gentility. In the twentieth century, when the realists were stripping the novel of all its genteel vestiges, he came to be regarded as a symbol of squeamishness and inhibition by both his enemies and his friends. The former, principally Mencken and his circle, attacked him as one who had helped to make American taste effeminate and helped to exclude from the American novel huge areas of behavior and emotion which demanded treatment by serious artists.[1] They were right, and they advanced the cause of literary honesty and freedom by disabusing the general mind of the notion that he represented the last word in fidelity to nature and in esthetic purpose. Their only error was that they went too far. They portrayed that side of him, the genteel side, as the whole man, minimizing some of his other and equally im-

---

[1] See the reference to Howells in Sinclair Lewis's speech in Stockholm on accepting the Nobel Prize for Literature in 1930.

portant sides and overlooking completely what was most significant in him—the fact that he related realism to the struggle against social injustice. They were guilty of this because they themselves were uncritical of, often content with, the economic drift of society; and they were therefore unable to understand him, unable to understand even the nature of his gentility.

His friends and admirers in this later period did less than nothing to save his reputation. They should have admitted what was obvious, blamed the environment by which he was conditioned while growing to intellectual maturity, and pointed to his great pioneering efforts on behalf of the modern novel. Indeed, they could have kept his memory green simply by recalling that he tried to educate his countrymen to an appreciation of the contemporary Europeans long before Huneker did. Instead, they defended the indefensible. They praised his gentility and sneered at Mencken, Dreiser, Floyd Dell, Sherwood Anderson, and Dos Passos as vulgarians, cynics, apostles of the dreary and the sordid, forgetting that those epithets were applied to Howells himself in the 1880's.[1] They sought to perpetuate his moral viewpoint as the ideal *par excellence* of the novelist and they shuddered at the works of his critics and successors. That was not stupidity, but merely the natural reaction of men who were really Howells's worst traducers. They were the conventional pedagogues and ministers who had in the first place secured his prestige and eminence solely on the fact of his gentility and had deprecated or kept silent about the very things in his writing that made him *live*. Respectable, middle-class, they too were well satisfied with the social order and had no interest in Howells's criticism of it, no sympathy for his desire to see it truthfully described. Thus did his friends collaborate with his enemies to bury him.

How much his reputation declined after his death is indicated

[1] Herbert Edwards: "Howells and the Controversy over Realism in American Fiction," in *American Literature*, Vol. III, No. 3 (November 1931), pp. 237 ff.

by two recent books dealing with our major critics. Professor Foerster's *American Criticism*, containing chapters only on Poe, Emerson, Lowell, and Whitman, offers just a passing mention of Howells. De Mille's *Literary Criticism in America* devotes sixteen pages to Howells as against twenty-three to Stedman, thirty-six to Huneker, and thirty to Stuart Sherman. Fortunately, other historians have been more appreciative of his position and significance. The academic journal *American Literature* has published several intelligent pieces of research on the development of his critical ideas. Lewisohn's chapter on him in *Expression in America* is stimulating and intelligent. Parrington's third volume and Hicks's *The Great Tradition* (1933) sympathetically appraise his aims while commenting sharply on his timidity and naïveté. In the *New Republic* for June 30, 1937, Newton Arvin published a fine essay on "the usableness of Howells" which is perhaps the most cordial re-evaluation of his work that has appeared since his death. There have been still others, but the latter three are of special interest because, being radicals, their authors are not the sort of men we have been taught to associate with the "dean." Such studies, although emphasizing his novels, have re-established Howells as a figure of some importance. But a study of his criticism alone is even more conducive to a proper estimate of his thought, for it reveals him at both his shallowest, most trivial moments and his best. And his best, we must conclude, was a very desirable influence upon his age, however malignant we may think his worst was.

He was born in 1837 in Ohio, a pioneer settlement that was not the savage, lawless, unmoral place that Lewis Mumford once pictured as the typical frontier.[1] It was a piece of New England, sober, industrious, morally strict, without the worldliness of Boston's wealthy classes to serve as a contrast to piety. Add to this the influence of his home, permeated with the mood of

---

[1] In *The Golden Day*.

mystical "Swedenborgian fleshlessness," and Howells's lifelong prudery becomes wholly understandable. He was a fit subject for literary Boston.

As a youth in his early twenties who had already proved himself talented, he went to Boston and Cambridge to meet and pay homage to the great names in American letters. He encountered but did not recognize a senescent culture, a civilization about to begin rotting with refinement. He only knew that it was still the nation's intellectual capital and was therefore an oasis of taste and delicacy which it behooved an aspiring artist to honor and obey. He yielded himself with ecstasy, and the result must have been flattering to his idols, for in 1866 he was invited to return to join the editorial staff of the *Atlantic Monthly*, which was now superseding the *North American Review* as the organ of Brahminism and gentility. During the four years of the Civil War he had lived in Venice as American consul, then for a year he had served under Godkin on the staff of the *Nation*. In the meantime New England's passions had run dry, its idealism sated by the war and its rebels dead or grown old. He arrived to stay in a community that had nothing left but grace. He stayed fifteen years, the last nine as editor of the *Atlantic*, during which time he reveled (worshipfully, of course) in the prejudices and attitudes of the aristocratic natives. The latter had accepted him as one of their own, and he was grateful. After all, he was not altogether a foreigner. Massachusetts was the spiritual home of Ohio and superior to it only in its self-assurance, its polish, and its ritualized manners.

If that were all one could say about his life, he would not be remembered as a critic. The reviews and essays he contributed to the *Nation* and the *Atlantic Monthly* were in no way distinguished from the ordinary run of genteel criticism. His writing was passionless and polite, its scholarship puerile, without force or direction. But in 1881 he resigned from his editorship to devote himself to creative work and in 1885 he began to conduct the "Editor's Study" in *Harper's*. It was then that he first put forth his major critical ideas, and he continued on this new tack until the early 1900's.

The man's mind did not change. He remained a "nice" person, neurotically fastidious, acquiescent to the power wielded by the middle-class Victorian woman in determining moral and cultural standards. He became, indeed, the chief spokesman for the "genteel female," aiding and abetting her efforts to keep this country's literature emasculated and cheerful. Simultaneously, however, he was now preaching the doctrine of realism—against "the foolish old superstition that literature and art are anything but the expression of life and are to be judged by any other test than that of fidelity to it"; and in favor of the assumption "that no author is an authority except in those moments when he held his ear close to Nature's lips and caught her very accent." [1]

There is no mystery in his being a realist. One must bear in mind that by this time the romantic impulse was almost spent, while the social forces productive of realism were beginning to affect even the cloistered souls. Howells was particularly susceptible, firstly because he was a Westerner, in memory at least. Something of his childhood had remained through all the pleasant years of his affiliation to Boston, that something being a consciousness of a world in which there was neither leisure nor refinement. He could recall such things as work and poverty; he could remember farmers toiling endlessly for a bare subsistence. He knew that the people at large and the literary circle surrounding him were no more related than two races of men living in different centuries. That awareness struck something else remembered from his youth; political idealism —for his father was not merely a Swedenborgian, but a militant libertarian and democrat. Hence he could not bury himself, as others did, in pure learning or the enjoyment of art and elegant conversation. The lives of the vast majority of his fellow men attracted his attention beyond the walls of his study.

[1] *Criticism and Fiction* (New York, 1891), pp. 8, 14.

He wanted to know them, understand their problems, evaluate their ways. To this end he himself undertook to portray the *arriviste* aristocracy which had appeared while he had been genuflecting to the old; and he wanted those capable of doing so to portray the rural and urban lower classes.

He was susceptible to the new ideas also because he was sympathetic to economic reform. This was not the romantic idealism of Emerson and Whitman, with its intense emotions about the human worth of the toiler and the superior integrity of the husbandman over the parasite. Simple-minded and utopian as Howells's idealism unquestionably was, it was not simple. It was based on some comprehension of social conflicts and some knowledge (second-hand) of how the masses were living and struggling, and even on some notion of how society should be ordered to ensure justice. He followed the course of the great strikes that were then ripping open the screen of prosperity and class peace—the Haymarket affair in 1886 (in which he courageously demanded a fair trial for the condemned anarchists), the strike of the railroad engineers in Chicago in 1888, the Homestead strike in 1892.[1] The cause of his interest in these events and in the tendencies they represented may, again, be traced back to his social origins. His Boston friends and his associates in New York, insulated from birth against contacts with privation, labor, and the sweat of common people, could be unresponsive to events occurring outside their own little nests. But Howells responded; he had not been insulated, and he was sensitive and honest. That kind of idealism, that kind of sympathy for economic reform, is allied to the desire to learn the *facts* about people and their circumstances and sentiments.

Perhaps the above is only psychological background. But it explains his receptiveness to the writers who were animated by the most vital movements of the time, and those writers brought more of the great world into his study than he was ever ca-

[1] W. F. Taylor: "On the Origin of Howells' Interest in Economic Reform," in *American Literature*, Vol. II, No. 1 (March 1930), pp. 3-14.

pable of experiencing for himself. They confirmed his beliefs, strengthened his resolve. Chief among them was Tolstoy, whom he first read in 1886 and whose champion he remained until the end. Reading Tolstoy had little effect on Howells's novels, but it had an enormous influence on his humanitarian ideals and certainly on his conception of what literature ought to be. He was impressed by Bellamy's *Looking Backward* when it appeared in 1888. He read with keen appreciation the work of the Middle Western realist Hamlin Garland, whose *Main-Traveled Roads* (1891) he defended against the attacks of genteel reviewers; and through his friendship with Garland, who was a single-taxer, he was led to read and eventually meet Henry George. He read Zola, Ruskin, William Morris. He read Laurence Gronlund—"the foremost American Marxist writer of fifty years ago"—and from him he obtained some concrete ideas about a collective society.[1] The result was a mélange of theories and emotions which he was pleased to call socialism. It was not socialism, but it cannot be denied that it was anti-capitalism. At the very least it was an unconcealed hatred for the shocking consequences of industrial progress, to which he reacted by accepting the doctrine of economic equality. The literary expression of this point of view was, of course, his cordiality toward the utopian writers and his enthusiasm for the realists.

Finally, in analyzing his critical philosophy, we must take into consideration his professional interest. He was a novelist. Moreover, he was a novelist who was concerned with reality. That of itself made him a student of the realists who were creating and perfecting the novel in Europe. He was a friend and admirer of Henry James, who encouraged him to study the esthetic principles of the French and Russian writers. He tried to apply to his own craft, within the limits of his narrow personal vision, what he had learned and felt, and in doing so he had to think out, expound, and at last vindicate his adherence

---

[1] *Science and Society*, Vol. II, No. 4 (Fall 1938), pp. 514 ff., and Vol. III, No. 2 (Spring 1939), pp. 245 ff.

to realism. It was not then a popular doctrine in America; he was criticized, derided, maligned. Much of his best critical work, *Criticism and Fiction* (composed of the pieces he had written for *Harper's*), was a direct reply to his opponents. As the years passed he was driven more and more to a positive statement of his theories. The results may be found in the later essays contributed to the *North American Review*—essays on Zola, Tolstoy, James, Ibsen, and Brieux, in which he elaborately, vigorously justified realism. Not only the men abroad, but the Americans too, were of interest to him. His stand for Garland was followed by his appreciative recognition of Stephen Crane and Frank Norris. He was a devoted and generous friend to Mark Twain. He was an early admirer of Ernest Poole, of Edith Wharton, of Booth Tarkington. Quite just is the claim that the first major critic to go before the American public to agitate for modern realism was Howells, the despised symbol of gentility.

The question naturally arises: how did Howells reconcile his gentility with his realism? The answer lies in a passage which has often been quoted. It appears in *Criticism and Fiction* as follows: "It is one of the reflections suggested by Dostoievsky's novel, The Crime and the Punishment, that whoever struck a note so profoundly tragic in American fiction would do a false and mistaken thing—as false and as mistaken in its way as dealing in American fiction with certain nudities which the Latin peoples seem to find edifying. Whatever their deserts, very few American novelists have been led out to be shot, or finally exiled to the rigors of a winter at Duluth; and in a land where journeymen carpenters and plumbers strike for four dollars a day the sum of hunger and cold is comparatively small, and the wrong from class to class has been almost inappreciable, though all this is changing for the worse. Our novelists, therefore, concern themselves with the more smiling aspects of life, which are the more American, and seek the universal in the individual rather than the social interests. It is worth while, even at the risk of being called commonplace, to be true to our well-to-do actualities. . . . Sin and suffering and shame there must always be in the world, I suppose, but I believe that in this new world of ours it is still mainly from one to another one, and oftener still from one to one's self."

Not even this amazing piece of nonsense satisfied him. It was not enough to be superior to the *Continent* in the purity of our mind and to have an advantage in the sweetness of our life; things here were better than in England too. "The American who chooses to enjoy his birthright to the full," he said, "lives in a world wholly different from the Englishman's and speaks (too often through his nose) another language: he breathes a rarefied and nimble air full of shining possibilities and radiant promises which the fog-and-soot-clogged lungs of those less-favored islanders struggle in vain to fill themselves with. . . ." In short, Howells made gentility an ingredient of his realism. It sounds incredible, but it seems he actually believed that in a true picture of the American scene optimism was commendable and sex had no place at all.

He was explicit about his conviction that to be realistic one had to accept the Victorian sexual taboos. In speaking of the novel of gentility he asserted that "it was all the more faithfully representative of the tone of modern life in dealing with love that was chaste, and with passion so honest that it could be openly spoken of before the tenderest society bud at dinner." That he was satisfied with those taboos and apparently confident that they were generally observed, was only in part a reflection of his own squeamish and conventional morality, the environmental causes of which have already been sketched. There were probably personal neuroses involved as well: an unhealthy situation exists when a man of petty-bourgeois origin married to a genteel blue-blood whom he worships, encourages her to be his guide and censor; nor is it healthy for a man to wonder, as he did, if he were not effeminate for liking literature, first as a youth in a frontier community and then as an adult in a practical business world.[1] But surely part of his joy that the novel "now always addresses a mixed company" was due to his downright ignorance about the sexual conduct and desires of the average human being. He could hardly have learned about such things in his home, or in the *Atlantic Monthly* circle which was his finishing school, nor in the well-bred, polite, and often hypocritical society which he frequented wherever he went.

One may also suspect that he condemned sexual frankness for social reasons. It was easier to be brave about philosophical concepts or even about politics and economic conditions than to challenge the moral code, for to destroy the latter was to strike at the manners, the form of family life, the religion—in other words, the culture—he held dear. So he simply refused to carry over his more adult appraisals of authentic material from Europe to the United States. He would acknowledge the possibility that life in Europe was what it really was; his relatively enlightened reviews of the foreign novelists prove that. But since this country, he liked to think, was different, he wanted no jarring note struck. Otherwise the nation might cease to conform to the Boston ideal. A crusading motive rather than a realistic one is implied in his assertion that if "guilty love" *must* be treated, it should be done in the spirit of *Anna Karenina* and *Madame Bovary*—that is, gravely and with a tragic end, to reveal the wages of sin.

What is most puzzling, however, in his rhapsody on the "smiling aspects of life," is the attitude toward the economic set-up, not the attitude toward sex. He seems therein to be flatly contradicting his interest in strikes, his realization that there are masses of underprivileged and exploited men in this prosperous land, his consequent humanitarianism and "socialism." He is even contradicting one of his most powerful arguments for a realistic literature, one never fully stated but frequently

[1] C. Hartley Grattan: "Howells: Ten Years After," in the *American Mercury*, Vol. XX, No. 77 (May 1930), p. 43.

suggested, which was that a truthful depiction of life gives us a "bad conscience"—adds to our knowledge of men and society, awakens us to the existence of tragedies and conflicts to which we were previously blind. If the "smiling aspects of life" are the characteristic ones in America, the need for realism is not very pressing.

Evidently there was some conflict in his social outlook between idealism and contentment. But it was not as sharp as one might think. To begin with, he was quite right about Dostoievsky. A *Crime and Punishment* would not be a fair expression of the United States in the 1880's and '90's; indeed, it is impossible to conceive of an American ever writing anything like it. What we have come to regard as the frontier psychology—a mood of hopefulness and enterprise—was still prevalent. Where it was already turning to cynicism or pessimism, it produced a Mark Twain. In the East, the intellectual who suffered doubts or despairs was likely to be a Henry Adams. A private melancholy gave us Emily Dickinson. None of these, nor anyone else, could speak of such sufferings as Dostoievsky could, or display a comparable insight into the absolute frustration of humanity in a chained and tortured world. Life in America was truly sunnier, freer, more comfortable than in most of Europe.

The prevailing optimism conditioned even the utopian radical movements. Their optimism was not, after all, founded on a social analysis that might provide some historical justification for confidence, but arose simply from the contagious spirit attending industrial and territorial expansion. Nothing in Howells clashed with this buoyant mood. On the contrary, his own optimism, acquired in youth and sustained by a pleasant and successful career, was in harmony with it. We are indirectly saying that there was a certain naïveté in his idealism, but so was there naïveté in all the movements and philosophies that were then attracting middle-class humanitarians. His assumption, like Emerson's, that rich men and wise men are "practically the same thing," is enough to show how little Americans knew of a scientific (a materialistic) method of interpreting the data of economics, sociology, and history. In this period, moreover, Howells was remote from the proletariat with which he sympathized. His knowledge of conditions, of the class struggle, was so definitely second-hand that his failure to feel it deeply is not surprising. That he felt it at all is perhaps more surprising; that he felt it sufficiently to make it part of his literary ideology is one of the agreeable events in the history of American criticism.

A further clue to the emotions behind his apparent *social* gentility is the statement immediately preceding the sentence about the "smiling aspects"—the remark that "all this is changing for the worse." While this is interesting as an indication that he knew very well that everything wasn't rosy, it is most intriguing as a hint of the ideal to which he clung throughout his life. We know that he disliked industrial capitalism. What did he like? The Boston-Cambridge society in which he had lived in the 1860's, a quiet, cultivated community which seemed to be the natural outgrowth of an independent agriculture and small-scale industry. In *Literary Friends and Acquaintances* (1900) it was completely clear, for there he wrote of Cambridge as he remembered it: "Through the intellectual life there was an entire democracy, and I do not believe that since the Capitalistic era began there was ever a community in which money counted for less. . . . Even the question of family which is of so great concern in New England, was in abeyance. Perhaps it was taken for granted that everyone in Old Cambridge must be of good family, or he could not be there; perhaps his mere residence tacitly ennobled him; certainly his acceptance was an informal patent of gentility. To my mind, the structure of society was almost ideal, and until we have a perfectly socialized condition of things I do not believe we shall ever have a more perfect society."[1]

Now, this suggests two things: that Howells hated industrial

[1] Op. cit., p. 180.

capitalism as much because it was destroying a world he loved as because it was inflicting poverty and wage-slavery on the masses; and that, since the "smiling aspects" of life were the disappearing ones, he wanted novelists to be concerned with them in order to influence people to desire similar noble ways of being and behaving. Here again the crusading motive superseded the realistic one. Let no one doubt that he thought art could teach and inspire men to apprehend truth, beauty, and goodness. In *Criticism and Fiction* he wrote: "The finest effect of the 'beautiful' will be ethical and not aesthetic merely. Morality penetrates all things, it is the soul of all things. Beauty may clothe it on, whether it is false morality and an evil soul, or whether it is true and a good soul. In one case the beauty will corrupt, and in the other it will edify, and in either case it will infallibly and inevitably have an ethical effect."

That is bald and narrow, and it overstates dreadfully a tenable position. But in the same volume Howells set forth a derivation from that position in reasonable terms, and the result was a remarkably acute dissection of an opposing movement. "The art which . . . disdains the office of teacher," he said, "is one of the last refuges of the aristocratic spirit which is disappearing from politics and society, and is now seeking to shelter itself in aesthetics. The pride of caste is becoming the pride of taste; but as before, it is averse to the mass of men. . . . It seeks to withdraw itself, to stand aloof; to be distinguished, and not to be identified. Democracy in literature is the reverse of all this."

Thus were realism, gentility, and idealism woven by Howells into one design. Better, we can think of them as three substances in solution, each modifying the others, each lending the others a quality it would not otherwise possess. Consider, for example, his conception of paradise as embodied in Cambridge. Since its civilization seemed to him the highest and most satisfactory yet attained by mankind, how could he abstract from the whole one of the inherent characteristics? Because he could not and did not want to, the Victorian morality accompanied learning, goodness, peace, neighborliness, and comfort in his memory of an ideal society, and it was carried over into his "socialism." With that in mind we can penetrate better the meaning of such a book as his *Literary Friends and Acquaintances*, which consists mainly of essays in praise of the writers he met during his *Atlantic Monthly* days. As literary criticism most of the volume is rather sugary, but the volume is not so much criticism as a picture of a society he thought adorable, a community of people who were gentle and kind and decent. We today may laugh; we know it was grossly different from what Howells thought it. But he saw it myopically, in its loveliest aspects, and his picture of it certainly makes it a more livable place, for men of his temperament and aspiration, than any other in the country. It was a dream, but it suited him, and he ennobled it by wanting to bring it to life everywhere in America. He wanted, that is, the most vulgar business men and their climbing wives to become what the Cantabridgeans were, and the meanest mill town and dreariest village to be converted into versions of Cambridge. Perhaps that desire redeems somewhat his zealous enforcement of the genteel code.

His dream did not completely delude him. At heart he knew that Old Cambridge had died and that the poets and scholars who were its ornaments could never be recalled. He knew at last that there were class wrongs as well as personal ones. "In what business of this hard world," he asked, "is not prosperity built upon the struggle of toiling men, who still endeavor their poor best, and writhe and writhe under the burden of their brothers above, till they lie still under the lighter load of their mother earth?" [1] So he was left in an ideological purgatory: adjusted to a world that was gone, he found it difficult to accept the world that had come; and in the new world he fluctuated between the bourgeoisie toward which he was inevitably propelled by his habits, tastes, and obligations, and the proletariat

[1] *Literature and Life* (New York, 1902), p. 323.

to which he was sympathetic because of his political philosophy and his recognition of the economic and social position occupied by writers in a class society. In this connection he wrote that "the author is, in the last analysis, merely a working man. . . . I wish that I could make all my fellow-artists realize that economically they are the same as mechanics, farmers, day-laborers." [2] This realization was combined with his egalitarian sentiments in the memorable conclusion to his essay on "The Man of Letters as a Man of Business." There he wrote: "Perhaps he [the artist] will never be at home anywhere in the world as long as there are masses whom he ought to consort with, and classes whom he cannot consort with. . . . Perhaps the artist of the future will see in the flesh the accomplishment of that human equality of which the instinct has been divinely planted in the human soul." There could be no clearer statement of the tragic dilemma by which writers have long been faced. It was real in Howells's case, and he was unable to solve it. Some of the strange contradictions in his critical thinking may be traced thereto.

To criticize him for not solving the dilemma by accepting the logic of his declared idealism—that is, consorting with the masses—is to prove oneself a poor historian and a bad psychologist. Neither the man nor the time was right for such an act. He was distinguished simply in his awareness that the dilemma existed; for if his inability to solve it was responsible for some of the contradictions in his thinking, his awareness of it made him a better critic than he might otherwise have been. His most fruitful period was one of constant endeavor to bring art and the people closer together, an endeavor to bring up the masses to an appreciation of art and to teach the artists that the values by which they would be judged, like the future of society itself, would be determined by the masses. We see the salutary results of his thought on this subject in many of his soundest critical observations. There is, for instance, his

[2] *Literature and Life* (New York, 1902), p. 34.

remark that learning always decays into wretched pedantry "when it withdraws itself and stands apart from experience in an attitude of imagined superiority." [1] There is his command that the novel "speak the dialect, the language that most Americans know—the language of unaffected people everywhere. . . ." [2] There is his insistence that "art is not produced for artists, or even for connoisseurs; it is produced for the general. . . ." [3]

Those were commonplaces, to be sure, but they were sound notwithstanding. Not commonplace at the time and equally inspired by his reaction to social issues were his shrewd comments on several of the New England writers. Curiously, they are to be found in *Literary Friends and Acquaintances*. Of Whittier in post-bellum days he wrote: "In the quiet of his country home at Danvers he apparently read all the magazines, and kept himself fully abreast of the literary movement, but I doubt if he so fully appreciated the importance of the social movement. Like some others of the great anti-slavery men, he seemed to imagine that mankind had won itself a clear field by destroying chattel slavery, and he had no sympathy with those who think that the man who may at any moment be out of work is industrially a slave." Of Holmes he said: "In the things of the world, he had fences, and looked at some people through broken palings and even over the broken bottles on the tops of walls; and I think that he was the loser by this as well as they." Apropos of Thoreau's *Walden* he said: "I do not believe Tolstoy himself has more clearly shown the hollowness, the hopelessness, the unworthiness of the life of the world than Thoreau did in that book. If it were newly written it could not fail of a far vaster acceptance than it had then, when to those who thought and felt seriously it seemed that if slavery could only be controlled, all things else would come right of themselves with us. Slavery has not only been controlled, but

---

[1] *Criticism and Fiction*, p. 10.     [3] *Literature and Life*, p. 286.
[2] Ibid., p. 104.

it has been destroyed, and yet things have not begun to come right with us; but it was in the order of Providence that chattel slavery should cease before industrial slavery, and the infinitely crueler and stupider vanity and luxury bred of it, should be attacked. If there was any prevision of the struggle now at hand, the seers averted their eyes, and strove only to cope with the less evil."

Those are admittedly social rather than esthetic opinions, but they are the grounds upon which we are now basing true judgments of the writers concerned. To evaluate Howells's critical work it is thus necessary to consider the whole man. In such a consideration does his gentility obliterate the rest of him? On the contrary, the more one thinks of him in relation to his class and age, the greater his stature is seen to be. His persistent, usually relevant, and often very sensible remarks on the relation of literature to society developed to a fairly high level the point of view which is being tested and refined by the most advanced critics of our day. His intelligence on that subject is reflected in the impressive list of writers whom he defended and praised—a list, by the way, which forms a claim to immortality far weightier than any of his opponents could offer. (To the names already mentioned one would have to add Gogol, Turgeniev, Maupassant, Björnson, Valdés, Galdós, Hardy, Balzac, and Heine.) Beyond those services to American taste there is the inescapable fact that he thought and wrote seriously about serious problems, which is a good deal more than can be said about everyone save James among his contemporaries. It may be that he wrote about them superficially, but at least he wrote about such things as criticism founded on scientific methods, democracy as an active element in the growth of realism, the relation of realism to romanticism, the causes of decadence, the value of classical or antique works to the modern reader. He did so in terms of human life and human needs, which differentiated him from those others who wrote seriously about literature but did so with their eyes fixed upon religious or metaphysical issues.

Hence our conclusion that despite his influence as an apologist of gentility, his work as a whole contributed much to American literary thought. There were many other genteel critics; there were not many advocates of realism and social criticism. As in the case of Whitman, the direction ultimately taken by the critical realists was somewhat different from the one he suggested, and certainly their radicalism went beyond his expectations, but his pioneering role must be acknowledged. In those days a respectable man, an ex-editor of the *Atlantic Monthly* and contributor to *Harper's*, was really doing something when he came out for people like Zola.

### 4

It has been shown that the marriage of democracy and realism was not the product of a region, but rather of a given period in history in which new social and intellectual problems had arisen. Nevertheless, that remarkably potent union of literary philosophies has often been described as the West's special contribution to American criticism; for it was most ardently celebrated there, and it was there that its leading exponents appeared.

Before the development of realism the West had no distinctive critical outlook. That is not to say that it had no interest in literature. On the contrary, as soon as there were permanent settlements, there were magazines which devoted at least a little space to belles-lettres. Among them were the *Western Review*, Timothy Flint's *Western Monthly Review*, the *Louisville Literary News-Letter*, the *Illinois Monthly Magazine*, the *Western Monthly Magazine*, and the *Western Messenger*. A classical bias was apparent in the first expressions of literary opinion that occurred in the West, the eighteenth-century mind having been transplanted to the frontier by men who had been schooled in the Eastern cities. One could find, for example, in what critical writing existed, a considerable admiration for Pope. A more unnatural taste cannot be imagined, and it vanished immediately upon the coming of romanticism.

It may therefore be stated that Western literary opinion was formed in the romantic movement. Romance was obviously in keeping with the scene and the prevailing way of life. It was a particular kind of romance. In the early days Burns and Southey were recognized; later there was some appreciation of Wordsworth and Coleridge; while Keats and Shelley were ignored by every journal but the *Western Messenger*. But invariably during the romantic decades the West was enthusiastic about Byron and Scott. Indeed, the Western critics were among Byron's most vehement American defenders. In this enthusiasm Western and Southern tastes were similar. It was a taste for muscular romance, for action, which expressed the outdoor life and simple individualism of the democratic West as well as the corresponding characteristics of the aristocratic South.

Its suitability to Western life is, however, irrelevant to the fact that romanticism was in no respect original to the West. Like the short-lived classical taste, it was borrowed and nothing was added to it. Western opinion may have differed from other opinions of Scott and Byron on the question of rank, but there were no significant differences in understanding or interpretation. That was also true when romanticism degenerated into genteel sentimentality, when the Victorian novel and poem became popular, for all that the West did was to take over the manners, tastes, and cultural ideals of the East. In part the West was prompted by a natural aspiration to approximate Eastern standards of thought. The primary reason was that Westerners were simply immigrant Easterners. They were neither primitives nor philosophers; they were average men and women who had carried with them their traditional religion and morality when they had struck out for freer and richer economic opportunities.

The influence of the West on American literature was previously described as having been chiefly ideological. Aside from that indirect influence, the West made little or no impression on Eastern writing. "The whole force of a tradition centuries old bore in one direction. Notwithstanding occasional protestations of sectional loyalty, Western writers kept their faces turned toward the East and toward England."[1] Just as once the critics of Boston and New York had praised American writers for their English characteristics, so now the critics of Illinois and Ohio praised their neighbors for the characteristics which made them resemble the great men of the East. In other words, even in regard to American literature Western and Eastern criticism had pretty much the same point of view.

Realism changed this one-sided relationship. The West was ripe for realism. With the disappearance of the frontier in the 1880's, when it was seen that to most settlers the riches of the West were illusory, that farmers were farmers everywhere, a need to sweep away the fancy notions, myths, and romances about the "virgin territory" was inevitably felt by sensitive men. But the West gave to realism an emphasis and a sentiment which long distinguished it from realism as it was commonly understood in the East. That sentiment was the egalitarianism of the old frontier; and the emphasis was the deliberate employment of realism in its democratic garb not merely to tell the truth about life but to alter certain conditions of life. At this time the West's democratic tradition was most evident in the universality and intensity with which the farmers participated in political and economic struggles, which became articulate and purposive in the various "reform" movements; and literature was involved in, became part of, these struggles. Indeed, the Western critics were sometimes more argumentative about the need for a democratic spirit in literature than about the value of the realistic principles. Such an attitude toward realism is clearly quite different from Henry James's or Stephen Crane's.

We saw how democracy and realism were united, and where

[1] Ralph L. Rusk: *Literature of the Middle Western Frontier* (New York, 1925), Vol. II, p. 1.

the emphasis was put, in the later work of Howells, who remained a Westerner after long residence among the Brahmins. The point was made that the Western democratic heritage was the cornerstone of his mature system. His writings were evidence that the West now had something of its own to say and that criticism in America could no longer be based entirely upon the sensibilities and experience of the East, where the profession of letters was usually an upper-class privilege. This shifting of regional forces was confirmed by the work of two younger men writing in the West, Frank Norris and Hamlin Garland, who were among the first of our modern realists in their theory as well as their fiction. They were followers of Howells, and their critical ideas were closely related to his, but they were even more definitely Western and less tolerant of aristocracy and romanticism than he.

Garland's philosophy of art is contained in a volume entitled *Crumbling Idols,* consisting of twelve essays which prove him to have been the most zealous of Howells's allies. The book is one long plea for realism in method and localism in content. He was not satisfied with verisimilitude in general; he wanted writers to confine themselves to their own regions or localities. His logic was simple: that a writer is best equipped to tell the exact truth about the scene he knows best. The interesting thing about that highly debatable proposition is that it repudiates the cultural leadership of the East and implies that the West ought to create a literature of its own, to voice its own emotions and set forth its own problems.

Such, in fact, was Garland's intention. He condemned every dependency upon or borrowing from the cities of the East, whose civilization he considered to be European and effete. He was interested in the indigenous phenomena and the native characters, which he believed could be found only in the West; and while he himself was absorbed in the life of Iowa, Minnesota, and Dakota, he saw the greatest potentialities in California. This was not simply a species of super-patriotism, nor a rationalization of his provincial feelings. And it was not a manifestation of a fear or discomfort felt in the presence of foreign minds. He read the Europeans, learned much from them, and applied what he learned to the things he was concerned with. It is precisely what he was concerned with that explains why he put forward his theory of localism so urgently and emphatically. He was concerned with the embittering efforts of the Western farmer to scratch a living out of the soil, to resist the exploitation of banks and railroads, and to earn some peace and ease through a troublesome and arduous occupation. The literary sum of all this was Garland's conviction that if the American writer, which is to say the Western writer, pictures his immediate neighbors and their circumstances conscientiously, he will communicate a sense of the sufferings and heroisms of the West and will thereby aid the West's social and economic struggles.

Democracy, individualism, and the inevitability of progress were the ideas which animated Garland's critical writing. They were the prevailing sentiments of the Western community in which he grew up. He was thoroughly imbued with them when he came upon the writers who "educated" him: Spencer, Darwin, and Taine, William Morris, Whitman, and Henry George, through whose works he refined and organized his philosophy and justified his radical humanitarianism. His faith in realism as a literary method was confirmed not only by Howells, but by the French novelists—from whom he acquired a slogan, for he substituted for "realism" the French term "veritism."

The ideology of the nineteenth century, optimistic, materialist in its approach to history, unashamed of its generous populism, is on view in Garland's essays on literature. "If the past was bond, the future will be free," he exclaimed. "If the past was feudalistic, the future will be democratic. . . . If the past was the history of a few titled personalities riding high on obscure waves of nameless, suffering humanity, the future will be the day of high average personality, the abolition of all privilege, the peaceful walking together of brethren, equals before nature and before the law. And fiction will celebrate this life." [1] To Garland that was anything but wishful thinking, for he was confident that there were scientific, let alone empirical, grounds for his prediction. He was an obedient Spencerian: "Until men came to see system and progression, and endless but definite succession in art and literature as in geologic change; until the law of progress was enunciated, no conception of the future and no reasonable history of the past could be formulated. Once prove literature and art subject to social conditions, to environment and social conformation, and the dominance of the epic in one age, and of the drama in another, became as easy to understand and infer, as any other fact of a people's history." [2]

The emotions underlying Garland's criticism were little different from Whitman's. He followed Whitman not only in his excessive nationalism, his faith in the future, his devotion to the common people and the doctrine of equality, and even in his partiality to the use of dialect and the vulgar tongue, but also in his interpretation of realism, which was inherently romantic. Garland wanted the drabness and poverty of rural life described, but he did not believe that to do so was the final goal of literature. Beyond the dark scene there were greener vistas; if literature could inspire men to fight against present evils, it could also arouse them to fight for the establishment of a just and beautiful order. He certainly did not believe that America was done for. The fact that it was the duty of a Western novelist to give a truthful picture of his region in order to destroy the East's illusions about it did not mean that the West was without dreams or hopes for the future. In sum, there was no contradiction between Garland's optimism and his insistence that novelists be honest with their subjects and their readers and speak out about the most distressing realities. It was an optimism founded on the admission of unpleasant facts. Garland was a

[1] *Crumbling Idols* (Chicago, 1894), pp. 45-6.
[2] Ibid., p. 43.

materialist where Whitman was a transcendentalist—he depended on the "new science" where Whitman made statements
of faith—and in that respect his conception of realism was
sounder, more nearly contemporary than Whitman's. But they
are nevertheless obviously related, and the similarity of their
diversely expressed optimisms confirms this.

The romantic attitude toward realism was likewise characteristic of Frank Norris. He wrote "A Plea for Romantic Fiction,"
in *The Responsibilities of the Novelist*, in which he defined
realism as the observation of the normal or the known and
romance as the observation of the abnormal or the secret. In
terms of this definition he considered himself a romantic. But
this need not be taken too seriously, for the treatment of abnormal or exceptional subjects is not incompatible with realism. In regard to such matters as the setting of the theme, the
manner in which it is treated, and the consistency of its development with fact and reason, Norris was undoubtedly a realist,
and an enlightened one at that. He was more successful in defining his position in his essay on "The Literature of the West,"
which appeared in the *Boston Evening Transcript* for January
8, 1902.[1] A romantic overtone is easily perceptible in that piece,
but his argument is entirely in keeping with the practice of
modern realism: "In the fictitious presentation of an epoch of a
people, the writer must search for the idiosyncrasy, the characteristic, that thing, that feature, element or person that distinguishes the times or place treated of from all other times
and all other places. He must address himself to the task of
picturing the peculiarity, the specialized product of conditions
that obtain in that locality and nowhere else. . . . One must
observe the typical. It is all very well . . . to urge that the
peaceable citizens, the city-bred men of the Denver office
blocks, are in overwhelming majority to the cowboys, the
miners, and frontiersmen. They are not typical of the West; the
West did not produce them. They are in no way different from

[1] Reprinted in *American Literature*, Vol. VIII, No. 2 (May 1936).

the peace-loving, law-abiding citizens of New York or Chicago. . . . New York produced the financier, Maine the trader, the South the planter, Boston the litterateur, Chicago the business man, but the product of the West from the very first and up to this very hour of writing has always been, through every varying condition, occupation, or calling, the adventurer. You cannot get away from him."

The scene was glamorous enough, Norris thought, so that inventions were unnecessary, and to do justice to it one had to be responsive to its color, its richness, its epic qualities. To *celebrate* the American fact, not merely to describe it, was Norris's purpose. "The difficult thing," he said, "is to get at the life immediately around you—the very life in which you move. No romance in it? No romance in *you*, you poor fool. As much romance on Michigan Avenue as there is realism in King Arthur's court." [1] He did not mean that the novelist should keep an eye out for the charming and delightful aspects of the scene, for he declared that "if there is much pain in life, all the more reason that it should appear in a class of literature which, in its highest form, is a sincere transcription of life." [2] He meant rather that there are more interesting and exciting and surely more significant things in reality than in any imaginary world, which is the first article of any realist's credo.

Norris went farther. The concept of aloofness, of mere observation, was repugnant to him. He urged the novelist to be concerned with all the mundane problems which concerned other men. "The function of the novelist of this present day," he wrote, "is to comment upon life as he sees it. He cannot get away from this; this is his excuse for existence, the only claim he has upon attention. How necessary then for him—of all men —to be in the midst of life! He cannot plunge too deeply into it. Politics will help him, and Religious Controversies, Explora-

[1] Frank Norris: *The Responsibilities of the Novelist* (New York, 1903), p. 19.
[2] Ibid., pp. 31-2.

tions, Science, the newest theory of Socialism, the latest developments of Biology. He should find an interest in Continental diplomacy and should have opinions on the chances of a Russo-Japanese war over the Corean question. He should be able to tell why it is of such unusual importance for Queen Wilhelmina of Holland to give birth to an heir, and should know who ought to be nominated for Governor of his native State at the next convention." [1] There Norris showed that he conceived of the novelist as a guide and interpreter of the moment and as one who necessarily influences social and political affairs. He believed unreservedly in "the novel with a purpose" and asserted that little is left if one takes from the novel "the power and opportunity to prove that injustice, crime and inequality do exist. . . ." [2]

It follows that Norris, like Garland, was a populist. He entwined realism with the democratic idea: "The People have a right to the Truth as they have a right to life, liberty and the pursuit of happiness." [3] The people—"The Plain People who Read"—was the audience at which he aimed and which he predicated for the future. On behalf of that audience, and its problems and strivings, he attacked the "ivory tower" novelists: "They would make the art of the novelist an aristocracy, a thing exclusive, to be guarded from contact with the vulgar, humdrum, bread-and-butter business of life, to be kept unspotted from the world, considering it the result of inspirations, of exaltations, of subtleties and—above all things—of refinement, a sort of velvet jacket affair, a studio hocus-pocus, a thing loved of women and of esthetes. What a folly! . . . She is a Child of the People, this muse of our fiction of the future. . . ." [4] The conclusion is that the novelist is responsible to the electorate: to the farmers and the shopkeepers—in Norris's word, to the "Burgesses." (Populism is not a proletarian movement.)

[1] Ibid., pp. 282-3.　　　　[3] Ibid., p. 11.
[2] Ibid., p. 32.　　　　　　[4] Ibid., pp. 208-9.

And his obligation is to tell the truth about their life, to expose existing evils, to spread the democratic gospel.

The militant realism of the democratic West ended with Norris. There was nothing further to be said; no other idea, no new sentiment was added to the movement after his death. It ended with him in another sense too: as the lingering democracy of the frontier rapidly disappeared, the critics who followed him possessed very little of his faith in the traditional democratic ideal and still less of his optimism about the immediate future of their land. The sort of energy and hopefulness which were displayed by a critic of Western origin like Floyd Dell arose from quite different intellectual sources. The West became sophisticated and produced critics like George Jean Nathan (of Missouri) and Carl Van Vechten (of Iowa). Its disillusioned and oppressed segments produced commentators who were completely pessimistic, especially in the novel and in verse, Dreiser and Masters being the familiar examples.

The one great writer of the West who answered most of the demands of the Howells-Norris school was Mark Twain. He had the simplicity, the folk point of view, the love for the common language, the truthfulness, the critical attitude toward Western life which they regarded as indispensable qualities in a regional artist. But Mark Twain's cynicism is a byword; and while his marvelous pictures of the West are robust and masculine, they are also full of nostalgia. Cynicism and nostalgia had no place in Garland's scheme, nor in Norris's. Their insights were frequently profound, their emotions always moving, but their theories as to what must happen in American literature were based on a sociological error. Their own works came closest to filling their prescriptions for the ideal novel.

# CHAPTER V

# THE QUEST OF BEAUTY

THERE is a theory in esthetics that a writer may create beauty out of any interpretation of experience. The inference is that criticism should not concern itself with an artist's ideas, which is to say his reactions to the way human beings live with one another, but only with his expression of them. It follows that to appreciate a work of literature the critic need only study the means by which the sensation it produced in the reader was achieved. In practice the critic will tend to confine himself to problems of "form"—structure, language, consistency of mood, quality of portraiture, etc. Many names have been given to this theory—the most familiar being "art for art's sake"—but, under any label, the doctrine is founded on the assumption that beauty is independent of the relative truth or historical value of an artist's thought. This may be baldly stated as a belief that the enjoyment of literature depends less upon what a writer is saying than upon how he is saying it.

American criticism has been little afflicted by this doctrine— at least not until recent times. From the beginning ours has been chiefly a criticism of ideas, a sustained polemic for and against various social and moral philosophies as expressed in art. But we have also had an esthetic tradition, an interest in craft, in form, in the non-ideological aspect of beauty. Most often, of course, these interests—the ideological and the esthetic—have been united in the same man, but just as we have had critics who emphasized the idea, so we have had some who emphasized form. In the latter line the first of importance was Poe, the greatest Henry James.

The works of Poe and James are not examples of the "art for

art's sake" attitude, which is rooted in moral anarchism: the notion that truth is wholly subjective. (There is no appreciable difference between the proposition that one man's view of reality is as valid as another's and the proposition that an artist's truth is *the* truth for the purposes of his art.) To associate Poe with such a philosophy is manifestly absurd. It is, in fact, not so much a philosophy as a state of mind, and it is one of ultra-sophistication, the product of a ripe, we may say a decaying, culture. It is inconceivable in the kind of culture we possessed in the 1840's—even in the aristocratic South. James, on the other hand, came much closer to it, as is not surprising when we consider how much worldlier America was in his day than in Poe's and how worldly, in things of the intellect, he himself was. But James was never really a "pure esthete" either, for he was most decidedly interested in ideas. Poe stipulated the way life should be approached in poetry; James could not conceive of some ways of approaching life. In other words, in their different ways and with varying degrees of certainty, both repudiated certain phases of experience as being unworthy of art. That is an ideological act, lending itself directly to ideological analysis. They were frankly preoccupied with form and ostensibly antagonistic to didacticism, but they did not claim to be above the compulsions, problems, and conflicts of society, unlike many esthetic critics of a later time.

Of James that is quite generally understood, but in Poe's case the legend persists that his mind was some sort of immaculate conception, indebted to no race, nation, or age and throughout his life responding to nothing on earth that concerned other men's minds. This attractively romantic theory was cultivated by critics who were baffled by him, and by decadent poets who hailed him as an illustrious antecedent, but the truth is gradually being established. And the truth is that while Poe was indeed psychopathological, he was not insane. He knew very well what was happening around him, had strong opinions about those events, and injected his opinions into his criticism. Further, his opinions were formed—as are any man's—by the environment in which he grew up, the books he read, and the experiences he suffered.

No one doubts that he was affected by his home and his reading, for the once fashionable notion of a writer being "predisposed" to melancholy, individualism, and romance is dead. The doubts now revolve about his experiences—their nature and the way he transmuted them into thought. The modern heresy is to analyze his work entirely in terms of a wounded ego and a frustrated sexual impulse. That is probably a useful beginning; anyone reasonably open-minded cannot fail to be impressed by Ludwig Lewisohn's chapter on him in *Expression in America* and Joseph Wood Krutch's *Edgar Allan Poe,* in spite of the obiter dicta and the flagrant non sequiturs which seem to be part of the psychoanalytical method. But to grant that he was the victim of psychic traumas does not explain the general form and direction of his criticism. It may help us understand the symbols and images he used, the mood in which he wrote, and the peculiarities of taste responsible for some of his weirder statements, just as it helps us understand those things in his poetry and fiction. To understand more we must look into the broader aspects of his upbringing and his period.

It is a matter of simple logic. I have said that the realistic temperament has always existed, but that it did not produce realism until a definite phase of society had arrived. So we may say that Poe's psychological difficulties were not born with him; surely there were writers long before him who were similarly injured; yet they found other kinds of expression. To produce his ideas, his prejudices, there would have to be some interaction between external circumstances and his particular set of neuroses. In turning our attention upon the former factor we are not denying the existence of the latter.

The circumstance of first importance is the time in which he lived. He entered the University of Virginia in 1826 and died, at forty, in 1849. Those dates mark off the height of the romantic movement in America. It is well known that after his brief schooling Poe added little classical scholarship to his intellectual equipment. He read almost nothing besides the books that were popular in his own day. That means that he grew up on Scott, Brockden Brown, Godwin, Moore, Wordsworth, Coleridge, Byron, Shelley, Keats, Hood, Disraeli, and the Gothic romancers, as well as the Americans, great and small, who were writing then. His literary education was thus wholly in romanticism.

He learned some things from Byron a few from Disraeli, and a great many from Coleridge; and he was obviously moved by the Gothic novel. How directly and how consciously he reacted to them we do not know. He left no journals, no large correspondence, and no records of intimate conversations with men of equal intelligence. If he had, the Poe legend would never have flourished; he has been a mystery because there is no documentary evidence to dispute the mystery. The sources of his thought have been mapped through his reviews and essays, but not all of that writing is trustworthy, for at times he would say things that did not represent his initial obligations to, or secret interest in, those more famous writers. Nor do we know when an influence was affected through a natural response to a kindred spirit and when through deliberate study in the hope of achieving success. Disraeli, for instance, he satirized, yet imitated in some of his stories. This we can say, however: that he never showed the impress of any style, tendency, or manner that was not romantic.

What did he acquire from the romantic writers? Not, of course, his desires and inclinations, but certainly a perception of the channels through which he might express himself. That is, he perceived in them the legitimacy of sensationalism, the value of pure imagination, and the enjoyment of self which satisfied his innermost needs. To that degree at least, the romanticists molded the writer Edgar Allan Poe. Their metaphysics, politics, and ethics he had no use for, but the sensibilities they made public were like those he had in private.

The circumstance of next importance in determining his thought was the place he considered home. " 'I am a Virginian,' he was accustomed to say, and anyone who has ever heard that remark made knows what it means." [1] At the age of two he was taken into the home of a prosperous Richmond merchant who later became one of the city's very wealthy men. The atmosphere in which Poe passed his youth was assertively aristocratic, and perhaps his knowledge that he did not belong to it either by birth or legal adoption led him to cling to the aristocracy all the more. At any rate, there is no doubt that he picked up and forever afterwards swore by the social and moral dogmas of a Southern gentleman.

This environmental circumstance was, as I have said, the cause of his intellectual limitations. He hated industrialism; he sneered at feminists; he was opposed to social reform and attacked the humanitarian philosophies that were then current. He was profoundly antagonistic to democracy. He was pro-slavery. He accepted unquestioningly the Southern myth concerning the character, position, and virtues of ideal (chaste) womanhood.[2] That he was an individualist goes without saying, but it should be noted that his typically romantic exaltation of the "dignity of man" was joined to a typically Virginian arrogance, assuming personal superiority over the mass of men.

What species of romanticism could emerge from so feudal a mind? Given the circumstances, could one have predicted Poe's literary views? In detail, of course not—but in outline, perhaps. One could have foreseen his indifference to moral questions and his contempt for inquiries into the nature of society. One might have anticipated his interest in craftsman-

[1] Joseph Wood Krutch: *Edgar Allan Poe* (New York, 1926), p. 28.
[2] These statements are documented in Ernest Marchand's excellent paper: "Poe as Social Critic," in *American Literature*, Vol. VI, No. 1 (March 1934). An earlier discussion of the sources of Poe's opinions is "The Backgrounds of Poe" in Killis Campbell's *The Mind of Poe and Other Studies* (Cambridge, 1933).

ship, his insistence upon the pursuit of pleasure, his absorption in beauty above everything else. Only Poe the individual, the unique personality with its complex of psychological abnormalities, can explain what the writer Poe conceived to be pleasure and what his concept of beauty was. But if those unique elements in his criticism had not been sheathed in the predictable ones, his criticism would not have had the historical significance it now has—would not, in short, have been so important in the development of romanticism.

Poe's hedonism is clearly stated in the "Letter to B——" which prefaced his *Poems, Second Edition*, in 1831. There he opened an attack on Wordsworth by writing: "Aristotle, with singular assurance, has declared poetry the most philosophical of all writings—but it required a Wordsworth to pronounce it the most metaphysical. He seems to think that the end of poetry is, or should be, instruction; yet it is a truism that the end of our existence is happiness; if so, the end of every separate part of our existence, everything connected with our existence, should be still happiness. Therefore the end of instruction should be happiness; and happiness is another name for pleasure;—therefore the end of instruction should be pleasure; yet we see the above-mentioned opinion implies precisely the reverse. To proceed: *ceteris paribus*, he who pleases is of more importance to his fellow-men than he who instructs, since utility is happiness, and pleasure is the end already obtained while instruction is merely the means of obtaining."

The juvenile quality of Poe's mind is self-confessed in that passage. One immediately remarks that happiness is *not* another name for pleasure. Hence while happiness may be the end of instruction, it is nothing short of absurd to say that pleasure is. Bad thinking is also evident in the way he interpreted Wordsworth. "Apparently Poe misconceived both Aristotle and Wordsworth. His reference to Aristotle is obviously based not on Aristotle himself, but on Wordsworth's free rendering, the ambiguity of which ensnared Poe. The 'Poetics' affirms that pleasure, not truth, is the end or object of poetry, and yet a pleasure limited by the demands of truth; whereas Wordsworth bluntly says, 'Its object is truth,' and then goes on to argue that man has no knowledge save what has been acquired by pleasure and exists in him by pleasure, and so leads up to the memorable assertion that 'Poetry is the breath and finer spirit of all knowledge; it is the impassioned expression which is in the countenance of all science'—an assertion that Poe gives no sign of having understood." [1]

How could he have understood? How could anyone have understood who was oblivious of the moral controversies and philosophical speculation of the French Revolutionary era? There must have been some Southern gentlemen who could realize Wordsworth's meaning, but they would be men of greater education and maturer intelligence than Poe. A year as an undergraduate carousing with the aristocratic hoodlums of Virginia, a year and a half as an enlisted man in the regular army, and less than a year as a cadet at West Point are not the kind of experiences that would make a philosopher out of a youth like Poe. His misfortune was that ten or fifteen years later—years of reading, contacts with cultivated people, and intense personal suffering—he was little wiser. No matter what he went through, he grew no deeper a thinker, and the Virginia view of life remained unaltered. And pleasure remained his idea of the end of existence.

His conception of pleasure was then, perhaps, less painful than it became subsequently, but the definition he provided several times toward the end of his life is the one identified with him and the one that has charmed the poets of the romantic decadence. They occur in his two major essays, "The Philosophy of Composition" and "The Poetic Principle," which contain almost everything he had to say about the purpose and value of literature. The former, published in 1846, is that in

[1] Foerster, op. cit., pp. 18-19.

which he attempted to convince the public that he wrote "The Raven" by a process of mathematical reasoning that would make an Einstein envious. He said there that since he regarded beauty as his province—for "beauty is the sole legitimate province of the poem"—his next question "referred to the tone of its highest manifestation—and all experience has shown that this tone is one of *sadness*. Beauty of whatever kind, in its supreme development, invariably excites the sensitive soul to tears. Melancholy is thus the most legitimate of all the poetical tones." Then, said Poe, he asked himself what was the *most* melancholy of all melancholy topics. "Death was the obvious reply." And it was also "obvious" to him that this most melancholy of all topics was most poetical when it was most closely allied to beauty. Therefore "the death of a beautiful woman is unquestionably the most poetical topic in the world." In the next paragraph he spoke of the bereaved lover so framing his questions that he would receive from the raven's answer "the most delicious because the most intolerable of sorrows."

In "The Poetic Principle," published just a year after he died, Poe made the pain-pleasure association personal. Of a minor work of Bryant which deals with death he said: "The poem has always affected me in a remarkable manner. The intense melancholy which seems to well up, perforce, to the surface of all the poet's cheerful sayings about his grave, we find thrilling us to the soul—while there is the truest poetic elevation in the thrill. The impression left is one of a pleasurable sadness. . . . This certain taint of sadness is inseparably connected with all the higher manifestations of true Beauty."

What needs to be said about this theory that sadness or melancholy is an attribute of beauty and that death is therefore the perfect subject for poetry, has already been said by sensible critics: that it exposes the author's mental sickness, that it rationalizes the subconscious motivation of his own poetical writing, and that it is weak, shallow, and evil as an esthetic doctrine. It is profoundly true that sadness and beauty are connected, wrote Mr. Lewisohn, "because life is tragic and all beauty transitory. But Poe did not mean that at all. He meant the 'taint' —significant word!—of a melancholy devoid of moral energy or human contemplation or resistance or power." One is tempted to turn away from this insipid twilight emotion, with a word of sympathy for Poe's twisted soul and a word of contempt for anyone who can seriously discuss the state of mind which is most common among adolescents; but to do so would be to overlook its curious literary potency.

To appreciate the effect of this emotion (it is hardly worthy of being called a theory), it must be considered in conjunction with what Poe rejected in its favor. He rejected truth. Not satisfied with excommunicating didacticism, actually calling it a "heresy" and erroneously blaming the Lake School for it, he specifically banished from the realm of poetry any concern with thought or knowledge—banished, that is, man's striving to grasp the realities of life—thereby striking out all philosophy, morality, and religion, as well as portraiture and the historical epic. "The demands of Truth are severe. She has no sympathy with the myrtles," he wrote. "All *that* which is so indispensable in Song is precisely all *that* with which *she* has nothing whatever to do. It is but making her a flaunting paradox to wreathe her in gems and flowers. In enforcing a truth we need severity rather than efflorescence of language. [The gaudier side of romanticism is on exhibit there.] We must be simple, precise, terse. We must be cool, calm, unimpassioned. In a word, we must be in that mood which, as nearly as possible, is the exact converse of the poetical. *He* must be blind indeed who does not perceive the radical and chasmal difference between the truthful and the poetical modes of inculcation. He must be theory-mad beyond redemption who, in spite of these differences, shall still persist in attempting to reconcile the obstinate oils and waters of Poetry and Truth."

In attacking didacticism Poe was doing the country a service. His frequent and bitter gibes at Longfellow were useful antidotes for the unhealthy veneration with which the latter was then regarded. The didactic poem was a plague that threatened to consume the poetic taste of the American people. But Poe consistently equated truth with moral preaching and further confused the issue by describing truth as if it were something like a syllogism in logic. Never did he show any sign of apprehending truth in the larger sense, nor any awareness of what is known as "poetic truth." Thus from a combination of muddled thinking and narrowness of vision came his anti-thought principle, which denied esteem to most of the great poetry of the past and which has since found steady employment in esthetic theory.

Now, Poe was merely defending his own flight from reality when he substituted pleasure for truth as the end of poetry and attached to pleasure the feeling of melancholy. His was a subjective esthetics if ever there was one, but one implying a certain social attitude which others made explicit. This was an attitude of scorn, even repulsion, for a world in which truth had become so much a matter of argument as to be the prey of philistines, and morality so much the possession of philistines as to be omnipresent and vulgar. It was a world in which aristocrats and artists were uncomfortable—and Poe was both. A "pure" art, an art created for pleasure, prohibiting both vulgar and problematical things, was, as Frank Norris suggested, a last refuge of the aristocratic spirit. Poe's achievement was that he formulated sanctions for the artists who wished to cut themselves off from the experience of the race and enjoy the solitary and wholly unintellectual sensations. This was not a philosophical individualism, but a philosophy of self-devouring egotism.

In Poe's case there was personal grief to justify escapism, but his chief worshipers, the French symbolists, and the inhabitants of the ivory tower who worshiped *them*, were analytical enough to know what they were doing and would justify their immersion in the senses by glorifying the individual in opposition to society. It never occurred to Baudelaire and Mallarmé that Poe was not as sophisticated, nor as introspective, as they. Hence they gave his critical system more than its face value and built upon it a poetic practice which he would probably have denounced as immoral.

To be sure, he developed his idea to its logical end by apostrophizing art for art's sake as did no American before him and few after him. "We have taken it into our heads," he said, "that to write a poem simply for the poem's sake, and to acknowledge such to have been our design, would be to confess ourselves radically wanting in the true poetic dignity and force:— but the simple fact is that would we but permit ourselves to look into our own souls we should immediately there discover that under the sun there neither exists nor *can* exist any work more thoroughly dignified, more supremely noble, than this very poem, this poem *per se*, this poem which is a poem and nothing more, this poem written solely for the poem's sake." A real exponent of that doctrine, however, makes no compromises with the community, and Poe made so many that he all but destroyed his position. In his famous review of Longfellow's ballads he said that poetry "is not forbidden to depict—but to reason and preach of virtue. As of this latter, conscience recognizes the obligation, so intellect teaches the expediency, while taste contents herself with displaying the beauty; waging war with vice merely on the ground of its inconsistency with fitness, harmony, proportion." This he followed with the remark that "a didactic moral might be happily made the *undercurrent* of a poetical theme . . . but the moral thus conveyed is invariably an ill effect when obtruding beyond the upper-current of the thesis itself." In "The Poetic Principle" he went so far as to say that "the precepts of Duty, or even the lessons of Truth, may . . . be introduced into a poem, and with advantage; for they may subserve incidentally, in various ways, the general purposes of the work: but the true artist will always contrive to tone them down in proper subjection to that *Beauty* which is the atmosphere and the real essence of the poem." Clearly, Poe was not prepared to fight respectable opinion to the finish; nay, he shared that opinion in no small degree. He certainly had no grudge against the conventional notions of virtue and vice. He was even disposed to admit that poetry might have some moral utility. The worst of it is that he expounded a glaringly mechanical, unorganic relationship between truth and beauty, or morality and beauty, which eventually became the last-ditch defense of didactic pedagogues.

The qualities he believed essential to the attainment of beauty were derived from his pursuit of sensation. When he sought to describe what a poem or story should accomplish he spoke of "an effect." His aim in both fields was "totality" or "unity"— of *effect*. The reader should be put into a certain mood, should be led to respond to a single sharp stimulus, should be made to *feel*. Literature, according to this view, is an instrument for excitation. Anything that is not strictly relevant to the chosen excitement, anything that does not add to the mood aimed at, must be eliminated from the work. The indispensable qualities are therefore those which can arouse and captivate a reader *without engaging his mind*. They are originality, novelty, strangeness. He quoted with approval Bacon's observation: "There is no exquisite beauty which has not some strangeness in its proportion." He said that he would keep originality "*always*" in view—for he is false to himself who ventures to dispense with so obvious and so easily attainable a source of interest." He used as synonyms, in his essay on Hawthorne, "invention, creation, imagination, originality." He was pleased with himself for having got "some altogether novel effects" in "The Raven."

Did he understand Bacon? Did Bacon prescribe, as Poe did, mere trickery? Could Bacon's dictum have been the standard of a hundred thousand magazine writers? Poe's has become that —and of some of the cheapest writers we have.

His theory of "effect" was completed in his strictures on the physical limits beyond which works of prose and verse could not be successful. A long poem does not exist, he said. The phrase itself, "a long poem," is a flat contradiction in terms, because "all excitements are, through a psychal necessity, transient. That degree of excitement which would entitle a poem to be so called at all, cannot be sustained throughout a composition of any great length. After the lapse of half an hour, at the very utmost, it flags—fails—a revulsion ensues. . . ." Hence *Paradise Lost* is admirable only as a series of minor poems. Hence epics aren't poems at all. The limit to be imposed is the single sitting. This pertains to the tale as well, except that the excitement of narrative is not as intense and may be sustained a little longer— two hours. The novel is of course an inferior form of art, for it cannot be read in one sitting and therefore lacks the force which comes of "totality."

All of which is the most incredible nonsense ever to come from the pen of a reputable critic. It is the result of ignorance of the real effect of art and of a childish conception of what men really seek in art. Poe sneered at the popular phrase "sustained effort," but, needless to say, the populace was right. Our major works are those which tackle major tasks. They could not have been written in a hundred lines or ten thousand words. But major tasks involve more than "impressions" (Poe's alternate for "effects"); they involve thought and the emotions aroused in the contemplation of truth. They would not interest a connoisseur of moods and atmosphere.

Can we, then, take Poe's talk about beauty seriously? He talked much about it; it resounded through his critical writing like a trumpet call to the blessed; it was the war-cry with which he charged the artistically impure. But his idea of beauty was manifestly trivial. This is confirmed in his choice of themes— the themes he praised as well as those he chose for his own verse and fiction—which were inevitably minor. He advocated indefiniteness, an air of mystery, an avoidance of the commonplace, so it is no wonder that this naïve and uncultivated intel-

lect seized upon "a deserted house which the popular superstition considers haunted" as a veritable jewel of a theme—"one
of the truest in all poetry. *As* a mere thesis it is really difficult
to conceive anything better." When he took the trouble actually to list some of the things he regarded as beautiful—the
things "which induce in the Poet himself the true poetical effect"—the caustic Mr. Poe indulged himself in an orgy of sentimentality which differed from Longfellow's only in the lushness of its language.

In the light of these facts, such monographs as Margaret Alterton's *Origins of Poe's Critical Theory* (University of Iowa,
1925) and Floyd Stovall's "Poe's Debt to Coleridge" (in *Studies in English,* Number 10, University of Texas, 1930) do not
seem very important. Miss Alterton suggested that Poe's emphasis on effect was derived from A. W. Schlegel through the
medium of *Blackwood's Magazine* and later from a reading of
Schlegel's *Lectures on Dramatic Art and Literature.* She also
touched on Poe's interest in Coleridge, especially the *Biographia
Literaria,* in which he learned Coleridge's famous distinction
between fancy and imagination. Professor Stovall argues con-
vincingly that the *Biographia Literaria* was the source of
Schlegel's influence on Poe, for he probably read Coleridge's
great work, which analyzes the German's theories quite thoroughly, long before reading anything by Schlegel himself or
even anything else about him. The various parallels between
Poe's ideas and Coleridge's are neatly recited by Stovall, who
is one of our leading Poe scholars. But these elaborate commentaries are based on the supposition that when Poe's words paral-
leled Coleridge's or Schlegel's, their meanings were necessarily
identical. That is not the case. It is likely that Poe discovered
in Coleridge some useful observations—on unity of interest (or
effect), for example—and that he borrowed outright the comparison between fancy and imagination. Unity of interest, however, is simply the means by which a poet successfully conveys
to his readers an aspect of beauty; it is not beauty itself, and

that is what matters. Is it possible that beauty meant no more to
Coleridge than to Poe? Is one to believe that the metaphysical
thinker Coleridge had the same opinion as Poe of the pleasure
to be obtained from art? As for the business about fancy versus
imagination, one has but to examine his remarks in the essays on
Hood, Moore, and "The Poetic Principle" to see how superficial and disorganized his view of the subject was in contrast
with Coleridge's. One need not agree with the *Biographia* to
see a thoughtful mind at work in it.

Poe once said that "every work of art should contain within
itself all that is requisite for its own comprehension." His critical writing lives up to that ideal. Studies like Miss Alterton's
and Professor Stovall's contribute little to our understanding of
it, for it speaks only too loudly for itself.

We can hardly expect sound criticism to issue from aberrant
theories. Poe's judgments of contemporary writers, being fairly
consistent with his peculiar esthetics, were erratic in the extreme. Even his apologists have been hard put to explain some
of his admirations, resorting to the whimsy that he did the best
he could with the poor material at hand. That explains nothing; the way he looked at life and art explains many things.
Consider his moral and social conservatism, his responsiveness
to pathos and fantasy, his championship of the South against
other regions, his craze for technical excellence, and his hatred
of intellectualism; and then consider the absurdly high rank he
gave to Hood and Moore, the fondness he displayed for
Fouqué's *Undine*, the laurels he bestowed upon Tennyson—"the
noblest poet that ever lived. . . . I am not sure that Tennyson
is not the greatest of poets"—and his malicious attacks upon
Emerson, the transcendentalists, and New England writers generally, while praising effusively such Southern gentry as Edward Coate Pinckney and Beverley Tucker. It was not just
willfulness, nor an inexplicable crotchet, that led him to rate
Charles Brockden Brown, John Neal, and William Gilmore

Simms, as well as Hawthorne, above Cooper; it was indifference to the things Cooper dealt with and his manner of doing so. It was not mere stupidity that led him to place *Paradise Lost* below *Comus* and to say of the former that if it were written today "not even its eminent, although over-estimated merits, would counterbalance, either in the public view, or in the opinion of any critic at once intelligent and honest, the multitudinous incongruities which are part and parcel of its plot." While we cannot account for his calling Christopher Pearse Cranch "one of our finest poets" or his ranking John Neal "first, or at all events second, among our men of indisputable *genius*," no one is perplexed by his attack on Lowell, whom he described as "one of the most rabid of the abolition fanatics; and no Southerner who does not wish to be insulted, and at the same time revolted, by a bigotry the most obstinately blind and deaf, should ever touch a volume by this author." Even the compliments he paid to negligible female poets are not altogether bewildering—to the reader who remembers what Southern chivalry was.

Of course, there were happier moments in his role as critic, too. He was among the first to recognize the merits of Hawthorne; he wrote well on Bryant; he treated Shelley, Keats, Coleridge, and Dickens with due appreciation. But he made no original or particularly interesting comments on any of them. Shelley and Keats he touched on only in passing. Coleridge he wrestled with, so to speak; attracted by his poetry, impressed by his learning, but repelled by his philosophizing, he never fixed upon a definite attitude toward him. His piece on Dickens is almost entirely given over to a detailed consideration of the plot of *Barnaby Rudge*. The piece on Hawthorne is remarkable, aside from its theories on short-story writing, for its neglect of the moral intention, of the very sense of the tales, while concentrating on the author's stylistic and inventive powers. The review of Bryant was the most rounded, the least idiosyncratic, "but he based his praise of Bryant upon poems which did not deserve it." [1] What one sees in all these pieces is an extraordinary sensitiveness, but a sensitiveness to specific moods and emotions which he found equally delightful in unequal poets, so long as they were skillful prosodists. Thus he reacted similarly to the lyrical, sentimental side of Shelley and N. P. Willis.

In sum, his critical writing was narrow, special, and usually perverse. Its value is entirely historical, having no pertinence whatever to contemporary interests. That value lies in its total effect, which was that it called attention to the pleasurable aspects of literature in a period of overemphasis on its intellectual and moral aspects. The men who have applauded him in recent years—among others, J. G. Robertson, Edwin Markham, John Macy, and, lately, H. L. Mencken—have been charmed simply by the fact that he went to literature in quest of beauty, for they have been able to use him in their wars upon didacticism and gentility. That he occupied himself with the *craft* of writing, even to the point of attending to word-usage and punctuation, has enchanted some; and no one denies that the critics before him were anything but meticulous in that respect. The Menckenians have rejoiced in his belligerent, sarcastic manner, which truly was invigorating in an age of excessive politeness. His other contributions to American criticism were his ingenious definition of poetry as "the Rhythmical Creation of Beauty" and, finally, his taste—to which one must credit what W. C. Brownell called "the domestication of the exotic."

In after years subtler men than Poe expressed similar viewpoints more cleverly. But Poe's unfulfilled approaches to the

[1] Yvor Winters: "Edgar Allan Poe: A Crisis in the History of American Obscurantism," in *American Literature*, Vol. VIII, No. 4 (January 1937), p. 398. This very clever essay deals with several aspects of Poe's esthetics not dealt with here—especially "The Rationale of Verse" and the interpretation of poetry as music.

ivory-tower philosophy are significant precisely because their timidity and inconsistency reveal how puerile that philosophy can be.

2

Henry James said that to take Poe with more than a certain degree of seriousness "is to lack seriousness one's self. An enthusiasm for Poe is the mark of a decidedly primitive stage of reflection." In his exceptionally fine study of Hawthorne (1879) there occurs that famous passage in which James alluded ironically to Poe's methods and principles and said: "His collection of critical sketches of the American writers flourishing in what Mr. Taine would call his *milieu* and *moment*, is very curious and interesting reading, and it has one quality which ought to keep it from ever being completely forgotten. It is probably the most complete and exquisite specimen of *provincialism* ever prepared for the edification of men."

It is seldom that a critic succeeds so admirably in characterizing both the subject of his remarks and himself. Annoying as those few lines may be to one who has no liking for sneers, they form, nevertheless, an incisive summary of Poe's failings. The way in which they are put is, of course, the key to James's possession of the qualities his butt wanted. Conspicuously he was not provincial: he knew, as Poe did not, the cultures of other lands, the literatures of other languages, and the manners and credos of other classes than his own. Not less conspicuously he exemplified a very high, at least a very complex, level of reflection. Unlike Poe, he explored the mapless areas of mind; the senses were to him important only as they affected mind and not at all in themselves. Their differences were immense, although everything is said when one says that James's sensibilities were adult.

But careless indeed is the reader who permits those differences to obscure their astonishing similarities as critics. The allusion to Poe is part of James's discussion of allegory, which Hawthorne favored and his sympathetic biographer had no stomach for. It is "one of the lighter exercises of the imagination," wrote James. "I frankly confess that I have as a general thing but little enjoyment of it and that it has never seemed to me to be, as it were, a first-rate literary form. It has produced assuredly some first-rate works; and Hawthorne in his younger years had been a great reader and devotee of Bunyan and Spenser, the great masters of allegory. But it is apt to spoil two good things—a story and a moral, a meaning and a form; and the taste for it is responsible for a large part of the forcible-feeble writing that has been inflicted upon the world."

It happens that Poe held almost exactly that opinion of allegory, so after disparaging him James directed the reader's attention to the nuggets of intelligence in Poe's ordinarily "pretentious, spiteful, vulgar" judgments; "here and there, sometimes at frequent intervals, we find a phrase of happy insight imbedded in a patch of the most fatuous pedantry." The notable insight, in this instance, was Poe's "lively disapproval of the large part allotted to allegory in his [Hawthorne's] tales. . . . Poe has furthermore the courage to remark that the *Pilgrim's Progress* is a 'ludicrously over-rated book.' "

It would appear that Poe and James objected to allegory for quite different reasons. Poe believed that literature exists by virtue of its sensuous appeal, which allegory is presumed not to have; James probed for conquests of form and composition, which in allegory are of a minor order at best. A story is debased, one gathers from James, by "symbols and correspondences." An artist confronts his theme and resolves it in its own terms—not by analogies. Unfortunately, the question is not disposed of so easily. One cannot even grant that the day of allegory is past, in view of the vogue for Kafka and his effect upon several of the younger English novelists. A cultivated public still remains for the allegorical tale or poem. It must have some esthetic value. There is also the by no means small matter of historical significance. To deprecate the writing of allegory as "one of the lighter exercises of the imagination" is to overlook its precious role in the development of fiction. Thus, however austere the concept of art which prompted James's statement, the statement itself is unsatisfactory. We are forced to read between the lines for its pertinence to James's whole philosophy. Especially are we struck by the neat little phrase about spoiling "two good things—a story and a moral, a meaning and a form." Now, this was not Poe's language. James did not think what Poe tried to, that morals and meanings were bad things in art. But James did think, as did Poe, of the story first, of the form above everything. The moral or meaning of a work of art was subordinated, in his esthetics, to form—that is, the victory of the artist over his material. In allegory the meaning is paramount and immediate; to James this made for an inferior kind of literature, while to Poe, who wanted to censor meaning, it seemed like an abdication of literature. The differences in approach—more, in the weight and dignity of their feelings about art—need no underlining, but neither does the resemblance between the two men. By a circuitous and difficult route James came to an intense preoccupation with form. Poe had already arrived there, brusquely and with no baggage. It will be shown that, despite all disparities in intellectual equipment, the meeting of their critical philosophies upon that common ground resulted in a certain identity of effect.

James's sphere of criticism was the art of fiction. He was not only the friend of Howells but his associate in promoting an appreciation of the novel at a time when Americans still considered it to be a rather frivolous pastime compared with poetry. Even graver than his friend's was his estimate of the novelist's vocation, even more reverent his contemplation of the craft.

The affinity of realism for the novel is beautifully illustrated here. James had none of Howells's social purposes. There was no moral or political reason, no evangelical impulse, for his insisting that the novelist's duty is faithfully to represent the way men live and act toward each other. Yet he did so insist, no less than Howells. The art itself legislated realism as a method, as he learned both from his own practice and from listening to Flaubert, Turgeniev, Zola, and the rest of that incomparable circle to which James paid eager audience during his stay in Paris in the year 1875-6. "The air of reality (solidity of specification) is the merit on which all its other merits helplessly and submissively depend," he said. He could be emphatic: "The effort of the novelist is to know . . . the only reason for the existence of a novel is that it does attempt to represent life." In the prefaces to the volumes composing the New York Edition of his works, published over a period of years beginning in 1907, he set down his fully ripened, fully elaborated theory of the novel. Among other things, these prefaces reiterate his conviction that reality is the sole source of the novelist's material and the standard by which he is judged. He planned and judged his own works in that light, as he saw it. He tells us, for example, that in writing *The Princess Casamassima* he recognized the danger of making his characters too conscious of experience for their "remaining 'natural' and typical." Of his first novel, *Roderick Hudson*, he confesses that the time-scheme of the story is unreal: Roderick disintegrates too rapidly, and Christina's function as the agent of his catastrophe "fails to commend itself to our sense of truth and proportion." His synonym for "novelist," frequently used, we find, is "painter of life."

The corollaries of realism are energy and seriousness. The artist achieves most when he penetrates most deeply into reality, when he encompasses the broadest of scenes, or when he attempts to know the nearly unknowable and to solve the nearly insoluble. To have represented the simple, the known, the obvious, is a poor victory. Hence one of the crucial tests of greatness is the scope and depth of the novelist's endeavor and the earnestness of his scrutiny of man's affairs and institutions. Accordingly James praised Turgeniev because he gives "no meagre account of life, and he has done liberal justice to its infinite variety." And Hawthorne's tales commend themselves to us by their philosophical weight. "The charm [of these tales]—the great charm—is that they are glimpses of a great field, of the whole deep mystery of man's soul and conscience. They are moral, and their interest is moral; they deal with something more than the mere accidents and conventionalities, the surface occurrences of life. The fine thing in Hawthorne is that he cared for the deeper psychology, and that, in his way, he tried to become familiar with it."

James did not restrict his large view of the novelist's field, nor subtract from his realistic ideal, by excepting sex. He would never condemn an artist for describing the sexual behavior of his characters; he would not evade the issue, in Howells's fashion, by yielding the European's right but denying the American's to represent sensuality. There his detachment from the American scene, his education abroad and long residence in France and Italy, served him well. Consistently sex is a vital factor in his own novels, though quietly, sometimes subterraneously, and not as an act but as a psychological phenomenon. In the preface to *The Portrait of a Lady* he said that "the one measure of the worth of a given subject, the question about it that, rightly answered, disposes of all the others," is: "is it valid, in a word, is it genuine, is it sincere, the result of some direct impression or perception of life?" That reduces to inanity "the dull dispute over the 'immoral' subject and the moral." He continued: "There is, I think, no more nutritive or suggestive truth in this connexion than that of the perfect dependence of the 'moral' sense of a work of art on the amount of felt life concerned in producing it. The question comes back thus, obviously, to the kind and degree of the artist's prime sensibility, which is the soil out of which his subject springs." If this sounds impersonal, it was not always so. His *What Maisie Knew* made many people shudder, and so his preface to it showed more than a little heat. Nothing is an older story to the artist, he cried, "than the grotesque finality with which such terms as 'painful,' 'unpleasant' and 'disgusting' are often applied to his results." As for the people who would frustrate the artist's effort to get at the whole truth of life, he said bitterly: "The effort really to see and really to represent is no idle business in face of the *constant* force that makes for muddlement." That, for James, was anger indeed.

It was no easy thing, in those days, for an American of respectable origin to arrive at such tolerance. It had not been easy for James, notwithstanding his advantages. Born in a home blessed with wealth and culture, brought up in a worldly, skeptical, unconventional atmosphere, carried to Europe at an early age, he had every opportunity to become the cosmopolite he was supposed to have been. Recent studies have undermined the legend of his non-Americanism, revealing the curious tenacity with which he clung to certain American prejudices and the persistence of many American traits in him through all the years of living in Paris and London.[1] But if his worldliness was not as complete as he hoped it was, at least it was sufficient to liberate him from the worst of gentility.

His essays on the celebrated writers of the period benefited from that worldliness, for it enabled him to appreciate their art with a minimum of apologies. Better, he could discuss the sexual elements in their works without hysteria, prissiness, or simpering. The realist could therefore write civilized essays on the novelists and story-tellers he respected—long, coherent, mature essays on the art and personality of Balzac, Flaubert, Tur-

[1] The mind of Henry James has greatly interested contemporary critics—partly, no doubt, because he was inadequately studied, often misunderstood, by the previous generation of critics, but in large part because it illuminates various esthetic and social problems of today. To that interest we owe these valuable essays: Edmund Wilson's "The Ambiguity of Henry James," in *The Triple Thinkers* (New York, 1938); Stephen Spender's "Henry James," in *The Destructive Element* (Boston, 1936); most of the "Homage to Henry James" number of *Hound and Horn*, Vol. VII, No. 3 (April: June 1934); and Robert Cantwell's "A Warning to Pre-War Novelists," in the *New Republic*, Vol. LXXXXI, No. 1177 (June 23, 1937).

geniev, Zola, Gautier, Maupassant, Merimée, and others. He
wrote four on Balzac, in fact, and three on Flaubert, and none
expressed horror at the freedom with which the masters of his
craft referred to physical passion, "illicit" or otherwise.

That, however, was the limit of his acquiescence, the bound-
ary of his worldliness. He could observe, he could tolerate, he
could, up to a point, understand; he could not swallow, let
alone enjoy, the alien morality. With all his respect for the
Europeans, with all his admiration for the great Frenchmen, in
the end he disapproved of them because they lacked, he felt,
a moral sense, a conscience, such as he found, gratefully, in
George Eliot. Only Turgeniev remained permanently flawless,
save for his unrelenting pessimism, which was a blemish James
had no trouble in condoning. The Russian, James assures us,
had "an apprehension of man's religious impulses, of the *ascetic*
passion," as well as a "susceptibility to the sensuous impressions
of life." As for the rest, the moral sense was wanting in each.
He urged that justice be done to Maupassant, who was the victim of a Comstockian conspiracy, and himself did justice to him,
yet did not fail to lament that Maupassant had ignored "the
whole reflective part of his men and women," which he doubtless considered to be the part productive of refinement and
delicacy. Of Merimée, whom he honored as a stylist, he said:
"The moral element in his tales is such as was to be expected
in works remarkable for their pregnant concision and for a
firmness of contour suggesting hammered metal. In a single
word they are not sympathetic. Sympathy is prolix, sentiment
is diffuse, and our author, by inexorably suppressing emotion,
presents his facts in the most salient relief. These facts are, as
a general thing, extremely disagreeable—murder and adultery
being the most frequent. . . ." The esthetic argument is less
important than James's evident need to take note of the "moral
element." That need teased—at times, I think, tormented—him
so that he could not wholly enjoy the novelists for whom on
other grounds his esteem was just short of worship. Nowhere

do we see it more clearly than in his criticism of Balzac. In the preface to *The Golden Bowl* he gave us the distillation of his several detailed studies: "We owe to the never-extinct operation of his sensibility . . . our greatest exhibition of felt finalities, our richest and hugest inheritance of imaginative prose." But in *French Poets and Novelists* (1878) James mentioned his one significant reservation about Balzac's quality, and there is no cause to believe that he ever forgot it: "He had no natural sense of morality, and this we cannot help thinking a serious fault in a novelist. Be the morality false or true, the writer's deference to it greets us as a kind of essential perfume. We find such a perfume in Shakespeare; we find it, in spite of his so-called cynicism, in Thackeray; we find it, potently, in George Eliot, in George Sand, in Turgénieff. They care for moral questions; they are haunted by a moral ideal. This southern slope of the mind, as we may call it, was very barren in Balzac. . . ." The unmoral philosophy of literary Paris was one of the reasons why, at last, he quit the company of the masters and went to England.

James could justify his distaste for the frankly physical. His objection to Maupassant's omission of the reflective part of men and women was restated quite persuasively in an essay on d'Annunzio in *Notes on Novelists* (1914): "That sexual passion from which he extracts such admirable detached pictures insists on remaining for him *only* the act of a moment, beginning and ending in itself and disowning any representative character. From the moment it depends on itself alone for its beauty it endangers extremely its distinction, so precarious at the best. For what it represents, precisely, is it poetically interesting; it finds its extension and consummation only in the rest of life. . . . What the participants do with their agitation, in short, or even what it does with them, *that* is the stuff of poetry, and it is never really interesting save when something finely contributive in themselves makes it so." How revealing that passage is! It appeals, as does James constantly, to one's intellectual snobbishness. It is convincing, for it is true—but not the sole truth, nor the truth all the time. Is the beauty of passion precarious? Is passion by itself incapable of being beautiful? Is it always poetically uninteresting unless it represents something other than itself? Why—one cannot help protesting—must sex be so carefully intellectualized? What should the participants do with their agitation if not *act*? There is surely some uneasiness here, an embarrassment in the presence of nakedness, which is disguised by the suave references to the garments of the mind. That James found it necessary to make a point of an artist's attitude toward sex indicates that he was writing for genteel people; that he arrived at an attitude which differed from theirs yet could not really shock them indicates that beneath his sophistication there were traces, at least, of gentility.

The final sentence of the passage quoted is the key to James's outlook. Its logic is that the sexual passion of ordinary people—of the great masses of mankind—is of no interest to the artist. What passion itself—that is, what the *act*, without regard to anything "finely contributive" in the actors—means in the life of the average individual or the life of society is not worthy of being represented in art. Snobbishness is the word for it, but it would be unfair to call it crass, wrong to call it vulgar. It is a snobbishness of sensibility and manner—perhaps of intelligence. Unfortunately for James, he made the mistake of thinking that the sensibilities he adored, the fine manners, the subtle feelings, the perceptive intelligence, are the possession of the superior classes. That is not to say that he was prostrate before wealth, nor that he was oblivious of baseness and corruption in the aristocracies. The money game revolted him, and its players he loathed: not a few of his stories are grim or ironic, as the case may be, commentaries on the scarring results of greed and selfishness upon character.[1] In the preface to *The American*,

---

[1] In this connection the reader is referred to Newton Arvin's discerning paper: "James and the Almighty Dollar," in the issue of *Hound and Horn* previously cited.

the novel in which he portrayed a family of venal patricians, he said that "it is the misfortune of all insistence on 'worldly' advantages . . . to produce at times an effect of grossness"— which will seem mild only to those who are not familiar with James's style. His famous letter to Charles Eliot Norton on the English upper class, with whom he allied himself and whose attention flattered him and whose homes he frequented, leaves no doubt that he knew that class too well for his own happiness: "The position of that body," he wrote, "seems to me to be in many ways very much the same rotten and *collapsible* one as that of the French aristocracy before the revolution—minus cleverness and conversation; or perhaps it's more like the heavy, congested and depraved Roman world upon which the barbarians came down."

Nevertheless, that was the "body," for better or for worse, to which he felt himself bound. He was interested in "superior people," in people who were complex and introspective, who had knowledge of the most elaborate rituals of "civilization" and might therefore be expected to have curious, subtle, and endlessly provocative reactions to emotional conflicts. Where were such people to be found if not in the aristocracy? The group as a whole might be degenerate, many of its members vicious, some coarse, but among them there would also be the superior ones. Besides, they were picturesque, with their manners, dress, drawing-rooms, gardens, hotels, watering-places, and large affairs generally, while the middle and lower classes were not—and picturesqueness of scene and character is not to be scorned by a novelist. But, as so often happens, eventually his discriminating deference to aristocracy could scarcely be distinguished from a climber's homage to the élite. From it sprang his feeling that the characters in Mrs. Wharton's *Ethan Frome* were "such simple creatures as hardly to be worth the pains the gifted writer had spent on them"; his stigmatizing Ibsen as "ugly, common, hard, prosaic, bottomlessly bourgeois"; and his selection of Anna Karenina as a better subject than Madame

Bovary because Tolstoy "paints the fierce passions of a luxurious aristocracy" while Flaubert "deals with the petty miseries
of a little *bourgeoise* in a provincial town."

There we see how an esthetic preference is interwoven with
class instinct, for it is clear that James is speaking of human as
well as fictional values. The gentry attracted the man no less
than the artist, and for reasons which are not complimentary
to his wisdom or his sympathies. He was acutely sensitive to
the manners of the lower social orders, but not to their hearts
or minds. The one time he dealt with a proletarian subject, in
*The Princess Casamassima*, he assumed that his hero had to be
exceptional, practically a freak, in imagination and intelligence
if he were to be capable of appreciating the fine appurtenances
of aristocratic life. He could not penetrate the mass and could
only interpret a radical sentiment as jealousy turning itself
into an "aggressive, vindictive, destructive social faith." In the
preface to that novel he spoke of "the 'shady' underworld of
militant socialism" and of his hero's opinions as having been
"poisoned at the source." There spoke the tory, and there was
plenty of it in James. Critical as he was of the ruling classes,
he could comprehend no other way of looking at society, at
life, than their way. Of course, he rationalized his convictions
in accordance with his theory of "picturesqueness." Writing of
Balzac's political and religious opinions, he observed that they
were anchored to the monarchy and the Catholic Church. "Balzac is, in other words, a passionate conservative—a tory of the
deepest dye. How well, as a rich romancer, he knew what he
was about in adopting this profession of faith will be plain to
the most superficial reader. . . . A monarchical society is unquestionably more picturesque, more available for the novelist
than any other. . . . A hierarchy [the Catholic Church] is as
much more picturesque than a 'congregational society' as a
mountain is than a plain."

His remarks are true neither in themselves nor as an analysis
of Balzac's motives. But they do reflect his own inclinations.

Perhaps James was furious with the fashionable rich of his day
not because they fell short of an absolute standard of decency
but because they did not conform to his ideal of feudalism.

A critic tags himself when he compares churches and governments with an eye to their "availability" for the novelist.
One gathers that politics and religion do not trouble him much
and that his interest in literature is essentially esthetic. Everything in James's criticism that touches directly on moral, social,
or philosophical issues adds up to but a fraction of the whole.
The rest, the bulk, is an extended inquiry into form.

James believed that the critic's function is to explain and
evaluate what the artist has made of his subject or idea. His
broadest statement of the matter occurs in the preface to *What
Maisie Knew:* "To criticise is to appreciate, to appropriate, to
take intellectual possession, to establish in fine a relation with
the criticised thing and make it one's own." He asked for that
kind of approach to his own work; referring to the prefaces, in
a letter to William Dean Howells, he wrote: "They are, in general, a sort of plea for Criticism, for Discrimination, for Appreciation, on other than infantile lines—as against the so almost
universal Anglo-Saxon absence of those things. . . ." [1] The
very wording of his definition brings to mind the critical ideals
of Croce and his American advocate, J. E. Spingarn, who were
writing at about the same time. And like Croce and Spingarn,
James was effectively guiding the critic toward a consideration
of form or artistry instead of content or substance.

That is not to say that James recommended "art for art's
sake," for he most emphatically did not. The point is stressed
here because his intention has been excessively misunderstood.
The fact is that James was the author of one of the most caustic
attacks on that super-esthetic slogan ever written by an American critic. It is worth quoting at length in order to combat

[1] Quoted in R. P. Blackmur's Introduction to the collected prefaces, published in a volume entitled *The Art of the Novel* (New York, 1934).

confusion—and also for its sharp intelligence on a question that is still not altogether settled. In his essay on Baudelaire, in *French Poets and Novelists,* he wrote: "To deny the relevancy of subject-matter and the importance of the moral quality of a work of art strikes us as, in two words, very childish. We do not know what the great moralists would say about the matter— they would probably treat it very good-humouredly; but that is not the question. There is very little doubt what the great artists would say. People of that temper feel that the whole thinking man is one, and that to count out the moral element in one's appreciation of an artistic total is exactly as sane as it would be (if the total were a poem) to eliminate all the words in three syllables, or to consider only such portions of it as had been written by candle-light. The crudity of sentiment of the advocates of 'art for art' is often a striking example of the fact that a great deal of what is called culture may fail to dissipate a well-seated provincialism of spirit. They talk of morality as Miss Edgeworth's infantine heroes and heroines talk of 'physic' —they allude to its being put into and kept out of a work of art, put into and kept out of one's appreciation of the same, as if it were a coloured fluid kept in a big-labelled bottle in some mysterious intellectual closet. It is in reality simply a part of the essential richness of inspiration—it has nothing to do with the artistic process and it has everything to do with the artistic effect. The more a work of art feels it at its source, the richer it is; the less it feels it, the poorer it is. People of a large taste prefer rich works to poor ones and they are not inclined to assent to the assumption that the process is the whole work. We are safe in believing that all this is comfortably clear to most of those who have, in any degree, been initiated into art by production. For them the subject is as much a part of their work as their hunger is a part of their dinner." [1]

[1] It is beside the point that the contemporary reader will find the essay on Baudelaire one of the least rewarding James wrote. His critical faculty stumbled over his moral conscience. Moreover, he was without the aid of modern

Because his criticism was largely esthetic and only incidentally ideological, are we to regard his practice as a contradiction of his preaching? Not at all. Rather we must think of James
as having *assumed* "subject-matter" and "moral quality." If the
subject of a work was trivial and its morality detestable, he
would have little to do with it. If its subject had weight and
if its morality could command the respect, or at least the interest, of a cultivated adult, then he would train his critical lens
upon it. He would then examine the composition of the work,
the construction of its drama, the vividness of its characters, its
fidelity to the actual, its atmosphere, tone, and style—in a phrase,
what the author did and how he went about it, which is precisely what James gave us in his critical masterpiece, the series
of prefaces. He would summarize an artist's social or ethical
philosophy, express his pleasure or displeasure with it, but rarely
would he argue for or against it on behalf of his own sociology
or ethics. Even less often would he try to find out what the abstracted philosophy meant to the life of men and women in organized society.

He looked at the world as a show or museum, or, more exactly, as an array of intricate human relationships, from which
an artist might pluck the material for his composition. There
was neither sense nor order in life, no pattern to satisfy one's
craving for perfection—but that was the job of the artist: to
create order by evolving a pattern out of chaos. When he does
so he surpasses reality, for while on the one hand we have
"clumsy Life at her stupid work," on the other there is a
"mind." Literature is art only in so far as it is the product of a
"mind," and it reaches its supreme level only when a "mind"
is contained in it to realize and give form to the drama at the
very moment it occurs. It is the inclusion of a "mind" that so
radically distinguishes the works of a Shakespeare from those
of a Scott. "Edgar of Ravenswood for instance, visited by the

psychopathology, which might have enabled him to understand some of the
*Flowers of Evil.*

tragic tempest of 'The Bride of Lammermoor,' has a black coat and hat and feathers more than he has a mind; just as Hamlet, while equally sabled and draped and plumed, while at least equally romantic, has yet a mind still more than he has a costume." In art, "mind" is composition, and "composition alone is positive beauty." "A picture without composition slights its most precious chance for beauty, and is moreover not composed at all unless the painter knows *how* that principle of health and safety, working as an absolutely premeditated art, has prevailed." In its absence there may be life: *The Newcomes, The Three Musketeers*, and Tolstoy's *War and Peace* have life but not composition, James asserts in the preface to *The Tragic Muse;* and lacking composition, those works are lacking in artistic meaning.

He stated his case better than anyone else ever did when, in the preface to *The Ambassadors*, he said: "Art deals with what we see, it must first contribute full-handed that ingredient; it plucks its material, otherwise expressed, in the garden of life—which material elsewhere grown is stale and uneatable. But it has no sooner done this than it has to take account of a *process* —from which only when it's the basest of the servants of man, incurring ignominious dismissal with no 'character,' does it, and whether under some muddled pretext of morality or on any other, pusillanimously edge away. The process, that of the expression, the literal squeezing out, of value is another affair. . . ." It was James's affair as a critic. He would be doing less than his professional duty if he failed to point out that realism is the indispensable choice of method, not merely a preferred one, because fancied events and esoteric emotions and arbitrarily devised conflicts of personalities are small stuff beside the overwhelming variety of tragic, ironic, and amusing provisions of reality. To go outside of reality for nourishment is a mark of defective vision or of ignorance of what the world has to offer. But having established that, James had fulfilled his duty and could go on to his pleasure, which was the study of process.

He reacted so keenly and deeply to mastery of expression that his applause for a novelist's achievement of it was contingent upon the latter's selection of those large, profound themes which are the first indications of his rank. Thus we are told that "to see deep difficulty braved" makes the true artist wish the danger intensified. Hence "the difficulty most worth tackling can only be for him . . . the greatest the case permits of." It follows that the critic in quest of beauty is the critic seeking instances of difficult composition perfectly executed. Naturally, therefore, James, in his capacity as critic, looked at life primarily as material for art. Was this or that phase of man's conduct suitable for fictional treatment? Was it interesting? Did it present a strong enough stimulus to the feeling and thinking reader to warrant the artist's tackling it? Those were the questions he asked. Love, marriage and divorce, friendship, honor, greed, pride, injustice—everything was appraised purely as theme. Once in his life he seized upon a political subject, in *The Princess Casamassima*, and all he could tell us about his sudden perception of the class struggle is that he recognized "an interesting theme."

He had an honorable predecessor in this concentration of criticism on esthetic values. Hawthorne, James's single enthusiasm among American writers, had written prefaces to his novels which were likewise discussions of formal and thematic problems. No one can doubt that the novelist Hawthorne was anything but an esthete, intent as he was upon moral crises, yet his prefaces to *The Marble Faun* and *The Blithedale Romance* are concerned mainly with the obstacles to writing novels in America. It was Hawthorne who wrote that it is difficult to write "a romance about a country where there is no shadow, no antiquity, no mystery, no picturesque and gloomy wrong, nor anything but a commonplace prosperity, in broad and simple daylight, as is happily the case with my dear native land."

And it was doubtless this observation that inspired James to write his notorious catalogue of the "items of high civilization, as it exists in other countries, which are absent from the texture of American life": no sovereign and no court, no country gentleman and no army, no palaces, castles, parsonages, thatched cottages, abbeys, nor any of the other vestiges of feudalism which make England so "picturesque" (and so depressing to a rational man). James has been cursed and jeered at for this description of what makes a country civilized, but his critics have often neglected to explain his motives. He was voicing a predilection for British upper-class life, to be sure, but he was also defining the "accumulation of history and custom" that a novelist requires as a fund of suggestion. It was his notion "that the flower of art blooms only where the soil is deep, that it takes a great deal of history to produce a little literature, that it needs a complex social machinery to set a writer in motion." This was not an attack on the United States, for, said James, "American civilization has hitherto had other things to do than to produce flowers." It was merely an example of his habit of evaluating everything, even a national culture, with reference to its fictional "availability." So far had James carried Hawthorne's thought—to its ridiculous extreme.

All this was in keeping with his theory of the novel, which we now can reduce to pure representation. Representation to what end? Simply, and deliberately, "to swell the volume of consciousness." There is a rule that "bids us learn to will and seek to understand." Excellent, we say, but surely there is something beyond? Do we not will to understand, do we not seek a heightened awareness of life, because awareness and understanding will make a difference in our lives? On this point James had nothing to say. He had no realization that art might lead to action—that by affecting the way men think, art affects their acts. His was a theory of art for the sake of consciousness, and consciousness for its own sake, which is not quite so antagonistic to the theory of art for art's sake as he thought it was.

Now, too, we can put our finger on the reason why many people have found no real enlightenment in James's critical essays. Because there was nothing he wanted to fight for besides artistry, because he had no purposes or ends, he did not deal with the ultimate things for which men go to literature. In the novels we take seriously we look for much more than "picturesqueness," no matter how complex or elusive, and for much more than the subtleties of upper-class conduct in a milieu that is freighted with conventions, traditions, and antiques. Correspondingly, we expect the critic by whom we wish to be taught to talk about more than those things and the way they may best be represented. We expect to learn meanings. James was not a philosopher, as great critics always are. He was the appreciative observer, the man of taste *par excellence*. It was not enough, for taste is a poor substitute for passion, and observing is not the same as living. And there is no compensation whatever for the absence of philosophy, broadly conceived, from a body of criticism. That is why his essays are not definitive. His pieces on Balzac, for example, are superb analyses of method, character, and quality, but give us no sense of the meaning and historical significance of Balzac. Or the essays on Flaubert: they fail completely to place him, because they do not relate him to the social and political currents of his time.[1] Or his extraordinarily thorough discussion of Zola's *Germinal* and *L'Assommoir* (in *Notes on Novelists*): it is a first-rate expression of taste but shows no grasp of the meaning, function, and social value of those novels (and, of course, reveals a pathetic innocence about the life they depict). Or even the essay on Turgeniev: brilliant in its portraiture and its appreciation of artistry, it is poor in interpreting Turgeniev's relation to his land and people. As for his remarks on Tolstoy, they damn the man of taste.

[1] Compare with Edmund Wilson's essay "Flaubert's Politics" in *The Triple Thinkers* and Joseph Freeman's reply to Wilson in the *New Masses*, Vol. XXVII, No. 3 (April 12, 1938).

Indifference to philosophical meanings and their social references is the weakness of James's criticism—and the effect of that criticism, unplanned perhaps, is detachment from the struggles of life. Was that not also the effect of Poe's criticism? Were not his essays pre-eminently appreciative? Neither Poe nor James cared much about the religious and social movements of their respective periods. That is, they were both, in their separate ways, forlorn aristocrats, and their critical writings were similarly aristocratic in their attitudes toward literature.

Much could be said about the various channels through which men arrive at an aristocratic attitude and the various ways they manifest it, but the important thing here is to note that the attempt to isolate beauty from the feeling about life which a work of literature may contain, is hopeless. It cannot produce a full interpretation of the work, nor show us what its beauty really is. Nevertheless, the attempt is still being made, and to many of those who are still making it, James is God. It will be found that they—specifically, some of the critics at first associated with *Hound and Horn*—are, like James, interested in the sensibilities of superior individuals and convinced that the purpose of literature is to add to consciousness for its own sake. In other words, the aristocratic attitude survives. To most of the literary community, James remains the critic who enriched and expanded our appreciation of form—a critic whose appeal is distinctly precious, in both senses of the word.

### 3

Critics speak less of beauty than they used to. Since the decline of romanticism, perhaps because of its excesses, the word is curiously suspect. The words that are taking its place, like "order," "perfection," and "value," do not indicate radical changes in the esthetic quest, for they are meant to suggest much the same thing that "beauty" once suggested. They do indicate, however, that the *approach* to beauty has been changing. When beauty tended to become associated with pure sensation and the indulgence of emotions, those who could not ignore the functioning of the mind began to employ those terms which have connotations of thought. This is the implied distinction: beauty is an object of feeling; order, perfection, and value are objects of reflection. It has never been deliberately stated, because most critics have realized that it is psychologically false: men do not arrive at concepts of order and value through sheer ratiocination, nor do they make decisions as to what is beautiful and what is not on the basis of untutored sensory reactions. There is, in fact, no real border between beauty and value or between beauty and any other concept that involves discrimination. But the impulse to make the distinction is perceptible in the effort to arrive at beauty through ideas rather than colors, sounds, and rhythms.

It is a symptom of resistance to the way a critic like Poe spoke of beauty, or critics like Stedman and Aldrich in the latter part of the nineteenth century, or the impressionist and dilettante critics of the *fin de siècle*—perhaps the last more than any.

James spoke rarely of beauty, but sought it as ardently as did Poe, who spoke of nothing else. His interest in formally perfect representations of reality was the equivalent of Poe's invitation to sensuousness. But the quest of beauty may be divorced from all programs of technique and all preferences in sensibility. It may be a quest of some admired expression—the incarnation in literature of an idea, ideal, or *Weltanschauung* which is deemed beautiful in itself. The idea may exist in any form and appeal to any sensibility—may, in other words, be found in classicism, romanticism, and realism and have nothing whatever to do with the special claims of those ostensibly conflicting schools. This is the quest of beauty through idealism. As different from James's quest as from Poe's, its language is nevertheless apt to resemble the former's, since the idealist, too, reaches beauty by way of the mind.

One of the purest examples we have of a philosophy which

222 FORCES IN AMERICAN CRITICISM

interprets beauty in art as the harmonious expression of a cherished idea is Henry Adams's. Adams was not a literary critic. During the years he was editor of the *North American Review* he contributed only a few reviews to the magazine, and those few dealt with unimportant books (Howells's *Their Wedding Journey*, Palgrave's *Poems*, Tennyson's *Queen Mary*) and contained nothing of any significance. Even his *Letters*, some of them addressed to writers, all of them to intelligent people, are conspicuously devoid of literary opinions. He was a great reader and met many poets and novelists here and abroad, yet his *Education*, which is full of illuminating remarks on history, politics, diplomacy, science, and philosophy, has no more than two or three pages on literature. But there are four chapters in *Mont-Saint-Michel and Chartres* on the poetry of the eleventh to the thirteenth century; and these chapters, in conjunction with the esthetic doctrines evolved by the rest of the book, compose a quite coherent and systematic philosophy of art which has had a palpable influence on contemporary critics. And the *Education*, representing the confessions of a modern mind in search of a defensible outlook upon culture and society, has likewise strongly affected literary thinking in our time.

*Mont-Saint-Michel and Chartres* was privately printed in 1904, revised in 1911, and published in 1913. *The Education of Henry Adams*, written in 1905 as a sequel to the previous book, was privately printed in 1906 and published in 1918. The fruits of a lifetime's study and experience, they are the classic statements of the intellectual dilemmas that closed the nineteenth century and opened the twentieth. In so far as they have some bearing upon literature, they provide us with what James never cared to provide—a commentary on the philosophical problems of the post-Victorian artist.

The fundamental problem was completely described in both books. In the first, summarizing the entire work in his chapter on St. Thomas Aquinas, Adams said of the Thomist philosophy: "The essence of it—the despotic central idea—was that of or-

ganic unity. . . . From that time, the universe has steadily become more complex and less reducible to a central control. . . .
Unity turned itself into complexity, multiplicity, variety, and
even contradiction. . . ." This painful awareness of the bewildering anarchy that is modern life, contrasted with the order
and unified force of the medieval world, is the motivating principle of the *Education*. At the end it reaches the level of tragic
drama as it tells the story of his effort to solve the riddle of
history and acquire an understanding of life that would sustain
him through all his activities and studies, whether scholarly or
political.

The need he felt was the sense of unity, which signified
knowledge of, or faith in, the purpose and logic of the universe.
From that knowledge or faith came power—the power to govern society justly and direct it to noble ends, the power to
build monumental systems of thought, the power to create pure
and organic works of art. Once or twice he flirted with eclecticism. In England, just after the Civil War, he played the part
of a dilettante, frequenting bohemian studios, auctions, galleries, literary dinner parties. He knew that the effect, so far as an
understanding of art was concerned, was "spotty, fragmentary,
feeble; and the more so because the British mind was constructed in that way—boasted of it, and held it to be true philosophy as well as sound method." What was worse, said Adams,
"no one had a right to denounce the English as wrong. Artistically their mind was scrappy, and everyone knew it, but perhaps thought itself, history, and nature, were scrappy, and
ought to be studied so. Turning from British art to British literature, one met the same dangers. The historical school was a
playground of traps and pitfalls. Fatally one fell into the sink
of history—antiquarianism. For one who nourished a natural
weakness for what was called history, the whole of British literature in the nineteenth century was antiquarianism or anec-
dotage, for no one except Buckle had tried to link it with ideas,
and commonly Buckle was regarded as having failed. Macaulay

was the English historian. Adams had the greatest admiration for Macaulay, but he felt that anyone who should even distantly imitate Macaulay would perish in self-contempt. One might as well imitate Shakespeare. Yet evidently something was wrong here, for the poet and the historian ought to have different methods, and Macaulay's method ought to be imitable if it were sound; yet the method was more doubtful than the style. He was a dramatist; a painter; a poet, like Carlyle. This was the English mind, method, genius, or whatever one might call it; but one never could quite admit that the method which ended in Froude and Kinglake could be sound for America where passion and poetry were eccentricities. Both Froude and Kinglake, when one met them at dinner, were very agreeable, very intelligent; and perhaps the English method was right, and art fragmentary by essence. History, like everything else, might be a field of scraps, like the refuse about a Staffordshire iron-furnace." But this was a point of view he was reluctant to accept, though it might win him "a degree from Oxford and the respect of the Athenaeum Club." He came back to his search for unity. It was the ruling passion of his whole career as a student, teacher, writer, historian, and political journalist. "History had no use for multiplicity; it needed unity," he said. "Everything must be made to move together. . . ."

It was not disinterested wisdom that Adams looked for; not an icy, purposeless understanding of the complexities of history. He wanted something to believe in. He wanted a faith. The idea that would make sense out of the confusion around him and explain the dishonest, selfish, pecuniary society of boom-time capitalism had to be an idea which could inspire him and for which he could fight. It had to be an idea such as consoled his eighteenth-century forebears in their contests with agnosticism and instability and guided them to honorable and eminent positions from which they could successfully wage those wars. Obviously, their idea had been illusory, since it had vanished so quickly and had given birth to such impermanent social and artistic structures. Was there an idea which could bind men together, vanquish self-interest, and open the flood-gates of imaginative expression—for more than a season? In the whole of the Christian era he could discover only one principle which had so acted—the Virgin, symbol not only of a church, but of love, of sex, of reproduction. The Virgin had built Chartres; all the steam in the world could not have done it. As a symbol, the Virgin was "the highest energy ever known to man, the creator of four-fifths of his noblest art." With the Renaissance the symbol had begun to lose its force; the decline had been constant ever since. Now there was nothing, no moral energy, no principle of force to give direction and movement to man's progress. Or was there? Was science—from which men were obtaining remarkable insights into the forces of nature and by means of which they were developing the machine—was science the new principle? Was the dynamo a symbol that could be to modern history what the Virgin had been to medieval history?

Adams tried desperately, but the dynamo failed him. Call it symbol, idea, or generative principle, it could not unravel the snarled history of modern society nor give form to the world he lived in. It was not the key to unity. Indeed, it needed explanation itself, and Adams was never quite able to grasp it. Religion alone seemed to promise unity to a man lost in the contradictions of human existence. "If he were obliged to insist on a Universe," he wrote, "he seemed driven to the church. Modern science guaranteed no unity. The student seemed to feel himself, like all his predecessors, caught, trapped, meshed in this eternal drag-net of religion." But he could not accept it. He was intransigently agnostic. He knew too much, thought too much, was too critical and experimental (and felt too deeply his strength as an individual), to welcome the cushioned solace of logic founded upon mysticism. The one thing he could do was to state the problem and hope that the mere statement of it would provide the clue to the pattern. Hence the writing of *Mont-Saint-Michel and Chartres*, which he described as "a study of thirteenth-century unity," for that was the point of history "when man held the highest idea of himself as a unit in a unified universe"; and *The Education of Henry Adams*, "a study of twentieth-century multiplicity."

As we know, the description of the problem did not solve it: the *Education* did no more than confirm the reality of the dilemma. When Adams died in 1918 he was still without his elusive principle of unity. He knew long before then, however, what the sense of unity—that is, what a belief in the functioning of a super-personal, possibly super-sensual, force—could do for the arts. *Mont-Saint-Michel and Chartres* had testified to his conviction that the unifying idea, in esthetic form, was beauty. It made no difference what form: architecture, stained glass, or poetry; and in poetry it was equally valid in diverse moods, styles, or manners. One chapter deals with *La Chanson de Roland*, composed in the eleventh century. He writes: "The verse is built up. The qualities of the architecture reproduce themselves in the song: the same directness, simplicity, absence of self-consciousness; the same intensity of purpose; even the same material; the prayer is granite. . . ." Another chapter, "The Three Queens," rejoices in the charm, gaiety, and elegance of court verse in the twelfth century. A third, on *Aucassin and Nicolette*, is appreciative of the purity and refinement, the "courtesy," of the thirteenth-century *romans*. The chapter on Abélard is likewise sensitive to the beneficent power of the simple and natural piety of the Middle Ages. All this the Virgin had done, through her "constant presence" in men's lives. Adams quoted prayers to her by Dante and Petrarch to show "the good faith, the depth of feeling, the intensity of conviction, with which society adored its ideal of human perfection."

That was as far as he ever got in his education—and it was pretty far for an upper-class American in an age of economic optimism and moral hypocrisy. There is nothing novel but much that is agitating (to mechanistic and pragmatic thinkers) in Adams's discovery that an idea capable of synthesizing multiplicity into unity must be not only a formula representing lines of force but also "an ideal of human perfection." His conviction that such an idea may be the greatest source of beauty in art was even more disturbing. It was, of course, *our* age that found it disturbing, although he was the product of an earlier time. The year in which a trade edition of his autobiography appeared was fatally appropriate: the war ended a few weeks later and two literary generations found themselves adrift in a world of chaos, disillusioned with all inherited beliefs, distrustful of social plans, antagonistic to moral doctrines, indifferent to philosophy, yet aware that nihilism would not suffice indefinitely—that society cannot exist forever without a systematic interpretation of the universe and man's place in it, an interpretation which would justify the past and assure the future. At the very least, it became evident that mere denial is a poisonous soil for literature.

It is now a critical commonplace that the highest esthetic achievements do not spring from a community which believes in nothing. That was the education that American intellectuals strove for, and in some cases strove against, in the 1920's. They made up their minds, one way or the other, when their community collapsed altogether. Three lines of thought have developed. There are critics who have found no way out of agnosticism and have resigned themselves to living in confusion, proclaiming it truth: for example, Joseph Wood Krutch, who embraces what Adams tried to avoid—multiplicity and chance. There are critics who have allowed themselves to be meshed in the "eternal drag-net of religion": for example, Mortimer Adler, whose *Art and Prudence* (1937) is based on that Thomist metaphysics which Adams admired but declined with thanks. There are, finally, critics who have succeeded in becoming what Adams wanted to be but could not: "by rights," said Adams, "he should have been . . . a Marxist, but some narrow trait of the New England nature seemed to blight socialism." [1]

Adams had much to say to all of these critics. They all had something to learn from him. If nothing else, they learned what they had to face, what they had to struggle with, in twentieth-century America. Opinions of the soundness of what might be called his educational procedure are various, but opinions of the inevitability and rightness of his quest are almost identical. Except for the few who still pay rent for an ivory tower—the few who still regard private sensation as the substance of beauty—there is no contemporary critic whose esthetic quest is not reflected in Adams's last two volumes. He was among the most prophetic of his generation, and was therefore one of the most isolated from its major currents of thought. But those currents of thought have been ignored or fought, while he survives—decidedly in the middle of the stream of present-day thought.

[1] Need it be pointed out that it was a class heritage, not a regional one, that blighted his study of Marx?

# CHAPTER VI

# THE ACADEMY AND THE DRAWING-ROOM

HOWELLS and James were not typical of the literary taste and opinion of their generation, except in so far as they reflected its moral inhibitions. In spite of their great prestige and the acknowledged excellence of their critical writings, their influence was limited in the quarter-century, 1875-1900, in which they were at the peak of their power. As champions of realism they dissented from a majority opinion so popular that it took on the sanctity of law. Howells, as a socialist sympathizer and protagonist of the democratic idea in art, aligned himself with people who were not quite respectable. James, as an experimentalist in the formal problems of fiction, was an eccentric. Surrounding them were antiquarians, delicate romanticists, and connoisseurs of the classics—small fish in a vast sea of gentility.

This was the quarter-century in which taste was governed by ladies and gentlemen. The latter phrase is designed to suggest people of means, decorum, and conservative views, for the last great crusade of the bourgeoisie had ended with the abolition of slavery and now there was no species of idealism permissible to persons of breeding. Not only had Calvinism long ago moved out to backwoods regions, but even Unitarianism was disintegrating—into free thought. Individualism had become an established social philosophy, minus its Emersonian flavor. What Henry Adams felt subjectively was indeed the objective situation: no idea, no cause or movement, remained to rouse artists and critics to battle against the weight of authority and usage, except socialism. But that is little more than a theoretical exception; the world of culture, of education and leisure, was distinctly upper-class, and few who dwelt in it desired or dared to be radically critical of capitalism. For there was now not much point in attacking capitalism from an agrarian viewpoint, as the transcendentalists had done. Attacks upon finance and industry would now give aid and comfort to revolutionary workingmen—to "anarchists," the dreaded word. It would threaten the security of the class that supported the universities and literary magazines; it would lead to the end of trust funds and destroy the cultured, leisured world.

There is nothing strange in the fact that almost all the successful and prominent writers of this period were conformists. Such writers have always been at peace with the well-bred community. What is remarkable is how scarce the non-conformists were, and how impotent, how little heard by the reading public, and how difficult it was for them to influence the direction of criticism. The transcendentalists and Fourierist reformers had been non-conformists too, but they not only had been numerically important among the intellectuals of the time, but had found eager audiences and had wielded some power in the schools and journals.

Now only gentlemen—men who had no reason to shock, infuriate, or exalt the reader—were setting up the standards by which the young would be guided, the past interpreted, and the prevailing taste determined. Even the dissenters and skeptics had many of the characteristics of gentlemen. Howells, James, and Adams pursued their subversive thoughts in the politest, most inoffensive manner imaginable: we know how reluctant they were to face the logical ends of their positions. But Thoreau had not been a gentleman, and Emerson, Ripley, and Parker had fallen at least a little short of that title. And Margaret Fuller had not been a lady. As for Whitman, well, everyone knew what he had been. Of course there were still cranks and wild men among the literati! Weren't there Norris and Garland, and wasn't Whitman still alive to recall a lustier age? And there was always Mark Twain to confound the effete, as well as an earnest bohemia in New York and a boisterous gang of journalists in the West. But in the field of criticism the idealists, bohemians, and radicals were poorly represented. Their magazines had small, in some cases purely local, circulations; they seldom got into the best newspapers; and in the colleges they were not represented at all. The major channels of expression were controlled by the critics, editors, and professors who either came from or allied themselves with the old mercantile and landowning classes which, though now devoid of germinal ideas, still dominated the educated public. It was only when the realists and radicals developed a socially influential audience of their own, in the early 1900's, that the reign of the gentleman critic was seriously challenged.

In the meantime bookish people of "inferior" social origin and those who lived in the provinces accepted the canons of the older universities and the elegant drawing-rooms of Boston and New York. Not even in the eighteenth century had the aristocracy more firmly controlled our literary culture. In that intervening century, however, the function of literature in American society had changed. Literary interests were vital interests to the eighteenth-century aristocrat. To him either literature was a weapon in political and religious controversy, or it was a gratifying expression of a state of mind and a way of life. To the upper classes of the 1880's it was a means of avoiding life, a kind of spiritual refreshment, a compensation for what life lacked. The average man in our first era of big business regarded an interest in letters as a mark of detachment from reality, if not downright frivolity. It was a dainty preoccupation, fit only for professors and women and weaker souls. Robust energies found profitable outlets. Our traditional aristocracy could dally with literature precisely because they were not soiled by reality, being secure in their possession of lands and incomes and a temporary monopoly over such genteel professions as the ministry and higher education. Now more than ever, to this class reality was the source of wealth but essentially vulgar and brutal. Literature offered pleasurably refined and delicate experiences to compensate for life's coarseness. The philosophy of Longfellow and his colleagues had borne fruit.

Women had a special place in this government of taste. In the regions where there were no old, well-to-do families and among the new rich and the common people, literature fell completely into the hands of females. They had the leisure for it and supposedly the sensibilities required for its enjoyment. Men were supposed to be too busy and too hard-headed.[1] The character of those women, and what their taste and outlook on life were, the inquisitive student can learn by reading *The Genteel Female*, an anthology edited by Clifton J. Furness (1931). "Frailty," "Sentiment," "Melancholy," "Piety," "Love of Nature," "Humanitarianism," "Fashions," and "Decorum" are the titles of some of his chapters—and they tell us almost all we need to know.

Genteel females were omnipresent; no town was too small, no city too large, to feel the pressure of their demands and dislikes. As a rule they were the final arbiters of literary success and had no small part in the making or breaking of magazines and newspapers. Among them were women of good sense and fine character, but they were as much the products of the civilization in which they lived as their less admirable sisters. They formed the base of the public reached by magazines like the *Atlantic Monthly*, *Harper's*, *Scribner's*, the *Century*, and *Putnam's*. No newspaper of the "better class" could afford to flout them; no lecturer could be sure of success if he did not take their tastes and prejudices into consideration. Even the "journals of opinion"—Godkin's *Nation* no less than the *Independent* and the *Outlook*—were mindful of their existence. In short, they were responsible for much of the literary criticism we are here

---

[1] These generalizations are subject to the usual corrections. Certainly there were liberal masculine minds in the drawing-rooms of Washington Square and Beacon Hill. A few spoke out, but most of them were unwilling to risk ostracism and unpleasant publicity.

discussing, for what may be called the *official* criticism of the time was created by the aforementioned periodicals and journals. There, by gentlemen who addressed themselves to ladies and gentlemen, the reputations of recent and living writers were fixed. Naturally, the literary atmosphere was oppressive to vigorous new talents. To describe it by continually piling adjectives of derogation upon adjectives of contempt would be too easy. They would be justified, but they would explain nothing. and they would obscure the peculiarly useful contributions to taste and culture made by some of the men who are the subject of this chapter. Besides, the scene has already been painted well enough for our purposes: the chapter on magazines in Thomas Beer's *The Mauve Decade* gives us literary New York in the 1890's as seen by a sophisticated writer in the 1920's; and the chapter called "Cryptorchism" in Bernard De Voto's *Mark Twain's America* gives us a Westerner's view of Boston at about the same time. They are not inspiring pictures.

In the last analysis, the main effort of the gentleman in criticism was to idealize art. He tried to differentiate art from reality in two ways: by emphasizing its charms and graces and by establishing tradition as a test of its quality, whereas the world outside the library was at once uncouth and progressive, disorderly and experimental. He worshiped tradition partly because one of the residues of romanticism was sentimentality about the past as superior to any observable present, but more because tradition was the gentleman's handiwork. Tradition was the accumulation of manners and beliefs which gentlemen had evolved and handed down to their sons and pupils; it was the symbol of order, the promise of social supremacy to those who were its guardians.

To the critics of this school the rude life and vulgar language of the masses seemed unfit for literature. Curiosity about sex was excoriated as an interest in the animal rather than the spiritual, the basest rather than the finest, side of man. Materialist philosophies were damned as incapable of creating beauty because they undermined faith and abolished mystery. The politics of levelers were censured as provocative of strife and ill temper. Accordingly, they preferred old forms to new ones and authority to freedom, the abstract to the factual and the precious to the common. Clothing as an indication of personal decency and a proper regard for the neighbors' feelings was a *sine qua non*. All of these biases were applied in judging esthetic achievement, but the sexual more than any. For a man's sexual conduct was the measure of his fineness and spirituality and, above all, his respect for society.

It follows that the very prince of gentlemanly critics was he who ignored living literature altogether, thus attaining the ultimate in detachment from ignoble realities. He was the classical scholar or dilettante, usually to be found in the universities, but often in non-academic circles too. Indeed, a revealing characteristic of the age was its large number of amateur scholars with private means or unexhausting occupations who became authorities on Shakespeare or Dante or the Greek and Roman dramatists. Much of that scholarship, both amateur and professional, was nothing but antiquarianism—the enjoyment of the past because it is the past. There are obviously occasions when looking backward is a necessary and profitable critical act, but when it is purposeless, undisciplined, uninformed by historical or philosophical aims, it is mere dabbling in the classics. In pedagogy it is useful, since to appreciate is the prelude to understanding and evaluation; but in criticism it produces amiable essays proving the greatness of writers whom everyone knows to be great.[1]

Inevitably, the university became the cradle of aristocratic and traditionalist tendencies. Its isolation from the market-place, its unworldly atmosphere, and its pride in being "above the battle" nurtured escapism and snobbishness as well as disinter-

---

[1] To illustrate with contemporary, familiar examples: Bliss Perry accomplishes something; what does A. Edward Newton accomplish?

ested scholarship. And because of its isolation, the academy could retain its gentlemanly character long after the reign of the gentleman had ended in all other channels of critical expression.

2

James Russell Lowell was the *beau idéal* of gentlemanly critics, for he had all the cherished attributes of the breed. In his youth he was a romanticist and radical and was properly ranked among the most advanced contributors to the *North American Review*. He was then a discerning critic of modern and contemporary literature. But that was not the period of his towering eminence. It was after 1850 that he became the Lowell we remember and after the Civil War that his major essays were written; and it was then that he seemed like a colossus bestriding the narrow world of criticism.

Much has been written about that Lowell, and the sense of all those otherwise dissimilar studies is that his geniality, wit, and erudition were the ornaments of a tory mind.[1] He was a Brahmin, said Parrington. Member of a distinguished and wealthy family, alumnus of Harvard and later its Professor of Modern Languages, Ambassador to the Court of St. James's, editor of the *Atlantic Monthly*, he was placed by his background and career among the elect, and the wonder is not that he shrank from the *sans-culottes*, but that he had ever had anything to do with them.

Lowell had no compunctions about advertising his aristocratic views. They are forthrightly stated in many of the essays and public papers written during his middle and old age. The following, from his essay on Gray, is characteristic; it is part of a discussion of the eighteenth century: "In the first three quarters of it, at least, there was a cheerfulness and contentment with things as they were, which is no unsound philosophy for the

[1] In Brownell's *American Prose Masters*, Macy's *The Spirit of American Literature*, Parrington's *Main Currents in American Thought*, Foerster's *American Criticism*, De Mille's *Literary Criticism in America*, and Brooks's *The Flowering of New England*.

mass of mankind, and which has been impossible since the first French Revolution. For our own War of Independence, though it gave the first impulse to that awful riot of human nature turned loose among first principles, was but the reassertion of established precedents and traditions, and essentially conservative in its aim, however deflected in its course. It is true that, to a certain extent, the theories of the French doctrinaires gave a tinge to the rhetoric of our patriots, but it is equally true that they did not perceptibly affect the conclusions of our Constitution-makers. Nor had those doctrinaires themselves any suspicion of the explosive mixture that can be made by the conjunction of abstract theory with brutal human instinct." Also worth citing, because it refers directly to art and culture, is this from his Introduction to a volume on the progress of the world: "The Social Science Congress rejoices in changes that bring tears to the eyes of the painter and the poet. . . . Are we to confess, then, that the World grows less lovable as it grows more convenient and comfortable? that beauty flees before the step of the Social Reformer as the wild pensioners of Nature before the pioneers? that the lion will lie down with the lamb sooner than picturesqueness with health and prosperity? Morally, no doubt, we are bound to consider the Greatest Good of the Greatest Number, but there is something in us, *vagula, blandula*, that refuses, and rightly refuses, to be Benthamized; that asks itself in a timid whisper, 'Is it so certain, then, that the Greatest Good is also the Highest? and has it been to the Greatest or to the Smallest Number that man has been most indebted?' "

But even if he had not stated his social views so plainly, the aristocrat in Lowell would be evident to any reader of his criticism—evident in his choice of subjects, the style and temper of his treatment, and the decisions he reached as to the values in his subjects. Too much has been made of Lowell's failure to translate his feelings about art and society into a rationalized system. True, he was discursive, unmethodical, and frequently impressionistic; yet there is no mistaking his drift, and perhaps if he had been forced to fight for the survival of his point of view, and not merely to defend it against the antagonism of demos, he would have learned how to put it into order and have applied it rigorously. It was left for Irving Babbitt, who *was* engaged in a life-and-death struggle, to systematize.

Lowell's subjects were the undisputedly great and the universally celebrated. Arranged in chronological order, omitting the essays in his *Early Prose Writings*, they are: Dante, Chaucer, Cervantes, Spenser, Marlowe, Shakespeare, Beaumont and Fletcher, Webster, Chapman, Massinger and Ford, Milton, Dryden, Pope, Rousseau, Fielding, Gray, Lessing, Wordsworth, Coleridge, Keats, Landor, Carlyle, Swinburne, Emerson, Thoreau.[1] Swinburne, of whom Lowell published an opinion in 1866, was the only one in that very select list around whom there had not already arisen a large body of criticism. To some of the more modern figures Lowell was antipathetic, but in every case there were precedents. He was warmest, least restrained, almost passionate in the essays on Shakespeare, Dante. Chaucer, Cervantes, and Spenser. Whereas in his youth he had said what he wanted to say about living Americans (Poe, Longfellow, Margaret Fuller, and the rest), he said little about the generation that grew up when he was a mature and settled critic.[2]

To his studies of the immortals he brought his sympathy for their moral, social and religious standards, as well as his fine ear for poetry and his genuine love for the art. He did not bring a new philosophy or a new way of understanding or interpreting their personalities or their times. He seldom ventured

[1] From Foerster, op. cit., p. 111.

[2] He said nothing about Mark Twain. He expressed an opinion about Walt Whitman only in private correspondence—an unfavorable opinion. Of Howells and Henry James he wrote only brief reviews which he did not consider worthy of being reprinted in his books; they were not salvaged until 1920, when Albert Mordell collected Lowell's minor pieces into a volume called *The Function of the Poet*.

to dispute accepted judgments, unless they pertained to textual matters, in which he was an expert. His studies were thus essays in appreciation. Written with verve and humor, invariably sensitive to mastery of language, and abounding with apt quotations and shrewd insights into character, they successfully communicated their author's enthusiasm and made the obvious seem newly discovered.

When he withdrew from the anti-imperialist and abolitionist movements, he lost most of his intellectual contacts with the world in which the mass of mankind worked and fought; and so his significant essays bear little trace of the ideas men developed and the knowledge they acquired in the nineteenth century. He knew something of Taine, but nothing of Marx and Darwin. That is to say, his awareness of environmental theories was superficial, and of evolutionary theories practically non-existent. In fact, science and sociology were realms of learning he never approached. And since he coupled his animosity toward democratic politics with a cheerful ignorance of the commoner's life, he came as close as any man could to being superior to the immediate scene.

But as death is the only absolute insulation against the breath of life, he could not help reacting to those modern sentiments which pursued him into his study, lined though it was with the well-worn classics of many lands and ages. To the literary effects of radical and materialist doctrines he was not indifferent, for they marked the end of venerable traditions and made difficult the perpetuation of classical virtues. His attitude toward realism, for instance, was revealed in many remarks in essays that were not directly concerned with it, for he detested it and could not suppress his detestation. His sneers at Zola and the other "French so-called realists" are well known, as are his doubts about Fielding, who "has the merit, whatever it may be," said Lowell, "of inventing the realistic novel, as it is called." In general he criticized the realists as being untruthful, on the ground that there is a higher reality than the phenomenal, a truth above the factual. The metaphysics of idealism was, of course, a favorite weapon of all genteel critics, becoming at last one of the surest stigmata of a reactionary esthetic.[1]

His *bête noire* among modern tendencies, however, was not realism but the romantic revolt against formalism and the conventions of an aristocratically governed urban society. He fought hard against its literary manifestations—anarchism, naturism, sentimentalism—when he himself was no longer tainted. His singularly obtuse essay on Thoreau was informed by no other intention. It is consequently a masterpiece of misunderstanding and misrepresentation. First he called Thoreau conceited, indolent, and "wanting in the qualities that make success" to explain why he was an individualist who lived in seclusion and despised money and bourgeois enterprise; then he accused him of perversity and eccentricity, while denying him originality; and finally he threw him a little bouquet for his "noble and useful" aim. No one who had not already read Thoreau could gather from Lowell's essay the slightest conception of the real significance, the historical value and meaning, of *Walden* and the essays on "Civil Disobedience" and "Life without Principle," not to speak of the man himself.

Toward the end of the piece on Thoreau Lowell stated his whole thesis: "I look upon a great deal of the modern sentimentalism about Nature as a mark of disease. It is one more symptom of the general liver-complaint. To a man of wholesome constitution the wilderness is well enough for a mood or a vacation, but not for a habit of life. Those who have most loudly advertised their passion for seclusion and their intimacy with nature, from Petrarch down, have been mostly sentimentalists, unreal men, misanthropes on the spindle side, solacing an easy suspicion of themselves by professing contempt for their kind. They make demands on the world in advance proportioned to their inward measure of their own merit, and are

[1] A law of history may be deduced from the fact that in the rise of romanticism it had served a revolutionary purpose.

angry that the world pays only by the visible measure of performance. It is true of Rousseau, the modern founder of the
sect, true of Saint-Pierre, his intellectual child, and of Chateau-
briand, his grandchild, the inventor, we might say, of the primitive forest. . . ." Two years later (1867) he returned to this
thesis and enlarged it into a long essay, "Rousseau and the
Sentimentalists," in which he added Jefferson and Tom Paine
in politics to Byron and the others in literature to show us how
numerous were the ideological offspring of the vile Genevan.
Babbitt's *Rousseau and Romanticism*, published fifty-two years
later, is the ultimate expansion of this thesis, leaving none of
its implications unexplored.

Let us pass over the fact that so far as Thoreau is concerned,
Lowell's thesis was much too strenuously applied,[1] and that, in
any case, it obscured the other and more important aspects of
his thought. Let us, rather, ponder over the fact that Lowell
did not apply to either Thoreau or Rousseau the historical
method that he applied so intelligently to Pope. He had begun
his critical career, as romanticists always did, by refusing Pope
the title of poet at all, but now he learned to appreciate Pope's
achievement by judging him in relation to the history of English society. Why not the same procedure in estimating the
works of Thoreau and Rousseau? Both are fair game for adverse
criticism. Rousseau especially has plenty of nonsense and not
a little that is philosophically bad in his writings. But if justice
can be done to Pope, why not to Rousseau too? In the light of
historical criticism, the Genevan stands out as a necessary force
in the development of modern literature. But that is exactly
why Lowell could not approach him in the spirit of a dispas-
sionate historian. Pope was obnoxiously artificial, snobbish,
dandified, but he was a gentleman. Rousseau—and the same holds
for Thoreau—was not a gentleman. He was a modern. He
kicked holes in the gentleman's picture of an ideal society.
Lowell had learned how to analyze historically the people he

[1] See Henry Seidel Canby's *Classic Americans* (New York, 1931), p. 187.

wanted to understand, but not the people he wanted to purge.

His militant, argumentative moments were rare, however. Usually he preferred the peace of his study, the cloister in which he could indulge his bookishness and serenely enjoy the classics he loved. There his tranquillity was little disturbed by the rumblings of a changing civilization and hardly affected by the manners of people who evidently knew nothing of gentlemanly conduct. Such of the offensive sounds and sights as did reach him when he was in his customary mood, he could dispose of with a phrase or two, while he reveled in the order and decorum that were imperishable in the classics. "What a sense of security in an old book which Time has criticised for us!" he said in a review of the *Library of Old Authors*. "What a precious feeling of seclusion in having a double wall of centuries between us and the heats and clamors of contemporary literature! How limpid seems the thought, how pure the old wine of scholarship that has been settling for so many generations in those silent crypts and Falernian amphorae of the Past!" And that note of escape was accentuated as he grew older and became the bulwark of gentility. "It may argue pusillanimity," he said in the essay on Gray, "but I cannot help envying the remorseless indifference of such men [the scholarly gentlemen of the late eighteenth century] to the burning questions of the hour, at the first alarm of which we are all expected to run with our buckets, or it may be with our can of kerosene, snatched by mistake in the hurry and confusion."

Literature as holiday, literature as "the world's sweet inn from care and wearisome turmoil," was therefore a notion to which he often reverted—"in my weaker moments . . ." he said, "with a sigh, half deprecation, half relief"—but even then his philosophy was at work. He need not have been so coy, so quick to confess as a weakness his going to literature for recreation. All men read for pleasure; books are for relaxation as well as positive experience. The question is: what gives them pleasure, and why, in the books they have chosen to read? The source and nature of one's pleasures are in great part determined by one's emotional disposition. Lowell's delight in the ageless beauties of Dante, Shakespeare, and Cervantes emanated from his feelings about man and morality and culture. He saw in them the qualities of proportion, repose, and unity which are not regarded by classicists as merely esthetic virtues. Lowell himself drew the necessary inferences, referring more than once to the moral import of classical form. Social history, by means of which one may explain why the admired qualities came into being at one time and could not do so at another, was a closed book to him, as it seems to be to all present-day classicists.

A moralist without being didactic, a classical scholar who could carry his erudition gracefully, and a charming guide to the poetic monuments of the past, Lowell was indeed the exemplar of literary gentlemen. His influence was consequently wide and lasting. It has been said that such strikingly different men as Woodberry and Mabie, Norton and Kittredge, and the Neo-Humanists all owe something to him.[1] Perhaps it is sufficient to say that he anticipated every line of thought and endeavor that has since been taken by traditionalist critics and scholars.

### 3

The genteel critic is at his best in appreciation of the past. Then his conservatism and his fears do not seem disputatious, and only in the most indirect way is his point of view a compulsive force inimical to present growth. It makes itself felt in his evasions and the *tone* of his writing rather than in prescriptive statements. Thus, despite his gentility, Lowell can still be read with some pleasure and profit, whereas critics of similar temperament who dealt with contemporaries and philosophized about the place of literature in modern life are unreadable because of their gentility.

In the chapter tracing the origin and rise of the genteel tradition, I said that it grew out of the principle of moral utility but

[1] See De Mille, op. cit., pp. 81-2. Also Foerster, op. cit., p. 119.

as time went on became increasingly divorced from didacticism. We tend today to overlook the fact that didactic writing was condemned at the very time when gentility was most prevalent. Even the most moral of critics, those who could themselves be justly accused of it, condemned it! Take the case of Maurice Thompson, well-known novelist, poet, and essayist of that period and for many years literary editor of the *Independent*. In 1893 he delivered three lectures at the Hartford Theological Seminary which were later published under the title of *The Ethics of Literary Art*. Several times in this volume the author assures us that he is not arguing for didacticism. Throughout his discourse he tells us that the purpose of art is to give pleasure, although he hedged slightly in remarking that "art is for delectation mainly, for moral teaching incidentally or unawares." But all along we have been reading an attack upon realism and a defense of the Victorian moral code which deserves to be recalled as an illustration of bigotry at bay.

Thompson set down his whole philosophy in the first few pages of the volume. He began by settling accounts with the "art-for-art's sake" critique: "life and literature cannot be separated so as to say that what is vicious in life is harmlessly delectable in literature. We live life to enjoy it; we make and read literature to enjoy it. In either case enjoyment is not necessarily a light matter. It is a serious matter in the long run. . . ." After thus denying the esthete's claim to moral irresponsibility, he described the consequences of such irresponsibility: "too often genius sets its face the wrong way, and then, if we are moved by it, our impulse is toward evil. An attack upon our sensibility is more dangerous than one upon our intellectuality." Thompson argued his point as follows: "It has ever been the function of evil to progress by means of fascination, and this fascination is loosely and mistakenly regarded as pleasure or happiness. The thrill of the unholy is mistaken for the calm and lofty ecstasy of pure joy. Ethics does not recognize the legitimacy of evil delights, come from what source they may. The making of a poem which appeals to base sympathies, no matter how perfect the art, is as vile an act as though it were vulgarly done in prose. . . . Young people, even the purest of them, are curious to know what lies between the lids of a scarlet book. A high ethical conception cannot license art to generate such curiosity and then feed it." This argument moved him to wrath: "If we are libertines in art," he cried, "what are we in the finest tissues of character."

Thompson then applied his dogma to living writers. He said: "It is a long cry from Homer and Aeschylus and Shakespeare and Scott to Zola and Ibsen and Tolstoi and Flaubert; but it is exactly measured by the space between a voice which utters the highest note of its time and civilization, and one that utters the lowest. I say that these modern realists utter the cry of our civilization's lowest and most belated element. . . ." It goes without saying that he explained the moral defects of Homer and Shakespeare as reflections of relatively backward societies. Naturally, our society knows better. "Shall we credit our own civilization with an appetency for the *Kreutzer Sonata, Leaves of Grass,* and *Madame Bovary?* Have we moved no farther than this during these centuries of Christianity?" These realists know what they are doing; they are deliberately vile; they are panderers. For example: "If the author of *Tess of the D'Urbervilles* would say the truth, he would flatly confess that he wrote that brilliantly fascinating, filthy novel, not to make poor young girls cling to virtue, not to prevent rich young men from being villains at heart; but to make a fiction that would appeal to human perversity and delectate human animalism."

In contrast with degenerates like Walt Whitman were such admirable men as Scott, Tennyson, Stevenson, Lowell, Howells, and Hawthorne. Those were the writers who justified Thompson's supreme test of quality, which was that if "a novel is unfit for open reading at the family fireside [it] is positive proof that it is not wholesome reading for any person at any place."

It would be unfair to the golden age of gentility to regard

Thompson as its representative. It produced much more tolerant men than he; at least it produced men who were astutely soft-spoken where he was artless and brutally frank. Nevertheless, his credo included its basic principle: that literature is created for enjoyment, not instruction—but enjoyment of a kind that is consonant with the traditional morality. We are a long distance from the utilitarian philosophy when we encounter a direct repudiation of didacticism, but we are carried a considerable distance back to it when we are not allowed to broaden our experience beyond our grandfathers'. The trouble with Thompson was that he went too far back. The vehemence of his prohibitions indicated a certain reluctance to desert moral utility altogether. He had the wit to perceive that literature may condition character, but could not conceive of other virtues than those he had been brought up to respect in middle-class Indiana and Georgia homes.

Since the gap between gentility and didacticism was narrow in Thompson's case, his denial of a didactic intention is most revealing. It proves that the malignant force in criticism at this time was not an insistence that artists vindicate the existing morality, but simply the morality itself—that is, the view of life, which is the determinant of taste. The didactic principle has not been an issue in American criticism since Poe. When recent critics attacked what they said was didacticism, they were really attacking an obnoxious morality. The same critics applauded James Branch Cabell, who is a didactic writer if ever there was one. But they liked his morality.

The crux of the matter, as I said in the earlier discussion of gentility, is the critic's manners—the degree of his assurance, suavity, grace. Thompson showed little development beyond the level attained by critics of the *North American Review* in the 1830's. He was not of the aristocracy and did not speak for them. The aristocracy's intellectual detachment from the common life had become so absolute that they now had only secondary contacts with reality and were therefore absorbed in the pleasures of art rather than its "incidental" purposes, which were assumed. Hence their dislikes were more often manifested as cool reticences than as heated expostulations. The difference between a Thompson and a critic of the most refined gentility is the difference between his peevish admonition that "our associations in art should not be lower than our associations in life" and Thomas Bailey Aldrich's urbane letter written to a rejected author when he was editor of the *Atlantic Monthly:* "Your sonnet is very carefully built, and the construction afforded me pleasure; but while reading the lines I wondered if we writers of verse did not give the public credit for more interest in our purely personal emotions than really exists. Why should we print in a magazine those intimate revelations which we wouldn't dream of confiding to the bosom of an utter stranger at an evening party? In what respect does the stranger differ from the public which we are so ready to take into our inmost confidence?" [1] Their suppressive effects were identical, but their ways of achieving them were not.

Aldrich may be taken as a fair representative of the regnant literary mind. He was one of a circle that included Bayard Taylor, Richard Henry Stoddard, E. C. Stedman, Grant White, Richard Watson Gilder, and William Winter—names which to that generation stood for the nobility of letters. He was a poet, but he fulfilled a critical function as an editor, in which role he helped disseminate the ideal of "niceness." The drift of his thought is recorded in a letter he wrote to Taylor in 1876: "Though politics have lost what little morality they had, literature has not lowered its standard. I have great hopes of it, and I think that a literary weekly journal, 'written by gentlemen, for gentlemen' and discussing *fairly* all topics—social and political— would find ready support." [2] It is hard to see how that passage can be improved upon as a characterization of the genteel classes.

[1] Quoted by Ferris Greenslet in his *The Life of Thomas Bailey Aldrich* (Boston, 1908), pp. 148-9.
[2] Ibid., p. 132.

Everything is implicitly there—the distaste for the undoubtedly cheap and rough life of the state in that day of booming industry, the satisfaction with literature as a charming, well-kept retreat, the moral bias, the mild snobbishness, the conservatism.

His friend Taylor was a critic as well as a poet, and something of a scholar besides, but there is nothing to indicate that his feelings about art and life were not the same as Aldrich's. His scholarship was in the field of German literature, on which subject he published a volume of studies in 1879. His admiration for Goethe and Schiller was great, but his reading of them apparently failed to broaden him in any vital respect, for his papers on subjects nearer home were passionless and respectable. Those papers were collected from the *Atlantic Monthly*, *International Review*, *Scribner's*, *North American Review*, and *New York Tribune* and published, posthumously, in 1880 in a volume called *Critical Essays and Literary Notes*. They are quiet in manner, cheerful in temper, based on a wide classical reading, but quite pointless and of no interest today.

The depth of a man's learning has little to do, unfortunately, with the depth of his mind, as we see in the case of a far more eminent scholar than Taylor. Richard Grant White was one of the leading Shakespearean scholars of that generation and is still remembered by specialists in the field. But his knowledge of Shakespeare did not make him less genteel or less conservative than his friends. Born of an upper-class New York family, brought up on the classics, trained in music (of which he became a distinguished amateur), all his life surrounded by "culture," and becoming in maturity a traditionalist and Anglophile, he was the literary gentleman incarnate. As a reviewer for the *Galaxy*, the *Atlantic*, and other periodicals, he was of a piece with the rest of the circle to which Aldrich belonged.

The outstanding critic of the group was E. C. Stedman. It is he who exemplifies the genteel mind at its most tolerant and who is therefore the most rewarding to study. Stedman was a stock-broker and historian of the New York Stock Exchange, but his heart was in poetry and he wrote much of and about it—which is in itself something to ponder over. His chief contribution to scholarship was his collaboration with Professor George E. Woodberry of Columbia University in the editing of Poe's complete works. What made him celebrated as a critic, aside from his reviews and periodical essays, were his volumes on the English Victorian and American nineteenth-century poets and a theoretical volume called *The Nature and Elements of Poetry*.

Stedman's criticism was a deliberate extension of the past. While other genteel critics were busy anathematizing the realistic novel and advocating the romance as the esthetic ideal of prose fiction, he devoted himself to poetry, which he realized was the true refuge of romantic beauty. To the perpetuation of such beauty he was wholly dedicated, and his interpretation of it was full of Keatsian, Tennysonian, and Poesque overtones. Sensuousness, passion, and simplicity were the essential qualities, while mind was subsidiary, if not, indeed, dispensable. His taste was eclectic and he made a virtue of it: "The author has no theory of poetry, and no particular school to uphold," he said in *Victorian Poets*. "I favor a generous eclecticism, or universalism, in Art. . . ." Nor did he uphold, it turned out, any particular thought, so that he enjoyed not only every variety of form and every kind of diction, but also every point of view and every emotion that did not grossly violate his moral and social standards.

There have been many critics whose work, like Stedman's, had no ideological nerve-center functioning as a selective force, but not many have had so few personal prejudices. It is doubtful that he actively disliked the verse of any poet of recognized metrical and verbal skill. There were, of course, some things to which he was barely or not at all responsive. He had no liking for intellectuality in poetry; he was suspicious, almost afraid, of metaphysical tendencies; and he disapproved of eighteenth-century classicism, of which he spoke as follows: "The essence of Pope's art was false, because it was the product of a false age; Dryden had been his guide to the stilted heroics of the French school, which so long afterwards, Pope lending them such authority, stalked through English verse." [1] But there was no strength in his negative reactions, and they were not founded on a consistent, developed principle; even the passage just quoted, which is extraordinarily heated for Stedman, is surrounded by more favorable remarks about its subject. His "universalism" was no pose; he could find a good word to say about any poet who cared for the "art of verse," which Stedman defined as "the creation of beauty for its own sake or for that of imaginative expression." As that definition suggests, however, his major enthusiasms among the English poets were the romantic lyricists and idylists—Keats above all, Shelley, Tennyson, Landor, and Swinburne. (He was not communicative about Shelley's revolutionary poetry and he deprecated the youthful Swinburne's sensuality.) He treated Hood, Procter, and Horne with the greatest kindliness, while his severest admonitions were reserved, appropriately, for Matthew Arnold as being too intellectual and for the non-lyrical works of Browning as being too metaphysical.

In his treatment of the American poets his "universalism" was at its worst, for here he evinced no discrimination whatever. Nearly every versifier this country has produced is mentioned respectfully, while the names that are popularly revered are treated with the utmost seriousness. Bryant, Whittier, Emerson, Longfellow, Poe, Holmes, Lowell, Whitman, and Bayard Taylor are each given a chapter and each is studied as though he were an important figure—Holmes equally with Bryant, and Taylor equally with Whitman. But this is not inexplicable: it reflects another side of Stedman's gentility—his unwillingness to offend his neighbors, by minimizing their countrymen, all of whom, with two notable exceptions, were respectable men, good citizens, and moral thinkers. The faults and deficiencies of Ameri-

[1] E. C. Stedman: *Victorian Poets* (Boston, 1875), p. 185.

can poetry were related to the limitations of the American mind, which was the creature of gentility and therefore had to be defended. In *Victorian Poets* he answered Swinburne's criticism of our hallowed poets by charging him with ignorance of our feelings and customs. For example: "if Swinburne thoroughly understood the deep religious sentiment, the patriotism, the tender aspiration, of the best American homes, he would perceive that our revered Whittier had fairly expressed these emotions. . . ."

The exceptions to the stupefying respectability of America's poets were Poe and Whitman. In the case of Poe not much courage was needed to rehabilitate him in the nation's esteem. It was a simple matter to prove that his intentions had been honorable; he had fallen from grace through weakness and misfortune rather than an evil nature, and his verse had not been marred by either sexual or political deviations from the norm. On the other hand, his sentiments about beauty and his ethereal melancholy were not unattractive to literary epicures in this age which was anything but beautiful and provided ample cause for melancholy. But in the case of Whitman it required a great deal of courage merely to discuss him in genteel circles, let alone to say favorable things about him. It is to Stedman's credit that he was able sufficiently to overcome his own timidity and squeamishness so that he could study the *Leaves of Grass* in a fairly rational mood. But how nervously he went about it! He first tackled the subject for an essay which appeared in *Scribner's* in November 1880. The way he approached it tells us so much about his age that a recent account of the episode is worth quoting: "Stedman wrote to Gilder on July 1, 1880, that he was 'skirmishing *in re* Whitman'; and after referring to recent suspected activities in *The Californian* of the 'Junta,' as he called William Douglas O'Connor and the rest of Whitman's too staunch admirers, he ended on the note of apology and resolution: 'Never mind. I cannot leave out of my book a poet who is extolled by O'Connor, Emerson, Conway, Burroughs,

Swinton, Rossetti, Swinburne, Buchanan, Dowden, Linton, Clive—but the line stretches out "to the crack of doom." I shall write *honestly* and appreciatively, but judicially, and take whatever results with a clear conscience.' He wrote to George William Curtis on July 16: 'I am *wrestling* with Whitman. Somehow, reading closely a writer of any parts, and no matter how he has irritated me, I always find an immense amount of good in him.' And he addressed Richard Grant White in a similar vein: 'Now I have to write upon Whitman. . . . Can't ignore him—too widely known here and abroad. Shall write the first *judicial* article, also, *in re* Whitman. Shall castigate him for affectation and humbug in his *life, manners,* style; but fully recognize his lyrical and descriptive genius. You are not aware that he has, in the course of years, become an *artist* in his irregular verse. Just glance at his "Captain! O my Captain!" [*sic*] and at "Out of the Cradle Endlessly Rocking," and you will find something to astonish you. The latter long lyric is a wonderful affair, *me judice.*' A letter to Thomas Bailey Aldrich on November 22, 1880, shows the same desire to conciliate hostile opinion toward Whitman and toward himself as a champion." [1]

The product of all this agitation was an essay which handled Whitman very gingerly, but which definitely acknowledged his genius. There is no need to salute Stedman for this accomplishment, since Whitman had already gathered plenty of champions around him, but it was a valiant and honorable deed for a critic in his position. We need not pay attention to his laudatory comments on Whitman, for they tell us nothing that has not been better said by a hundred more enlightened critics; but some of his adverse comments may be treasured as samples of the genteel philosophy. The following is especially interesting: "In Mr. Whitman's sight, that alone is to be condemned which is against nature, yet," said Stedman, "in his mode of allegiance, he violates her canons. For, if there is nothing in her which is

[1] Portia Baker: "Walt Whitman's Relations with Some New York Magazines," in *American Literature,* Vol. VII, No. 3 (November 1935), pp. 283-4.

mean or base, there is much that is ugly and disagreeable. If not so in itself (and on the question of absolute beauty I accept his own ruling, 'that whatever tastes sweet to the most perfect person, that is finally right'), if not ugly in itself, it seems so to the conscious spirit of our intelligence. Even Mother Earth takes note of this, and resolves, or disguises and beautifies, what is repulsive upon her surface. It is well said that an artist shows inferiority by placing either the true, the beautiful, or the good, above its associates. Nature is strong and rank, but not externally so. She, too, has her sweet and sacred sophistries, and the delight of Art is to heighten her beguilement, and, far from making her ranker than she is, to portray what she might be in ideal combinations. Nature, I say, covers her slime, her muck, her ruins, with garments that to us are beautiful. She conceals the skeleton, the framework, the intestinal thick of life, and makes fair the outside of things. Her servitors swiftly hide or transform the fermenting, the excrementitious, and the higher animals possess her instinct. Whitman fails to perceive that she respects certain decencies, that what we call decency is grounded in her law." [1]

By thus defending sexual reticence on the grounds of good taste instead of morality, Stedman was a model of gentility. The moral motive was always present in genteel criticism, at least subconsciously, but the references were preferably to beauty. Stedman was typical of his class also in his way of looking at nature—his effete romanticism, his inability to face biological facts, his willingness to be satisfied with surfaces. Squeamishness is the word for it. It is not pleasant to behold at any time, but especially when it becomes sentimental, as it did in Stedman's writing, which was effusive and metaphorical anyway. He continued his argument against Whitman's "unnaturalness" by stating that "a poet violates Nature's charm of feeling in robbing love, and even intrigue, of their esoteric quality. No human appetites need be pruriently ignored, but coarsely analyzed they

[1] E. C. Stedman: *Poets of America* (Boston, 1885), p. 368.

fall below humanity. He even takes away the sweetness and pleasantness of stolen waters and secret bread. *Furto cuncta magis bella.* The mock modesty and effeminacy of our falser tendencies in art should be chastised, but he misses the true corrective. Delicacy is not impotence, nor rankness the sure mark of virility. The model workman is both fine and strong. Where Whitman sees nothing but the law of procreation, poetry dwells upon the union of souls, devotion unto death, joys greater for their privacy, things of more worth because whispered between the twilights."

Now, Stedman was neither illiberal nor unintelligent; he was as fair and serious a critic as his generation produced. So it is a reflection upon a whole culture, not merely upon his mind, that he could recommend a morbid silence about certain aspects of reality as sound thinking, fine art, and good manners. The conception of literature that was part of that culture was the rationale of its policy of silence, and Stedman was logical in making it the pivot of his argument, as he did when he said that "the delight of Art is to heighten her [nature's] beguilement, and . . . to portray what she might be in ideal combinations." That watered version of romantic doctrine is, of course, familiar to us as the first proposition of gentility. It was utilized in two quite different, though related, ways: in the interpretation of art as a relief from the "mystery and burden of our daily lives"; and in the advocacy of art as an inspiration to the improvement of life. Stedman emphasized the former sentiment. It runs through all his books, usually as an undercurrent, but frequently becoming explicit. He depended upon it to solve the gravest problem he ever faced as a critic—the effect of science upon the future of literature.

This was a problem which many genteel critics were aware of. The rise of the realistic novel had solved it to the satisfaction of the "radicals" and "modernists," but those who upheld the past—those who were trying, that is, to maintain poetry and the prose romance as the major forms of literary art—were engaged in the fight of their lives, and they knew it. Stedman, more than any other critic of his mind, discussed the question in full. He gave a large section of the first chapter of *Victorian Poets* to it, and also the first chapter of *The Nature and Elements of Poetry* (1892), as well as numerous allusions elsewhere. The fact that he did so was commendable, of course, but the results were not. He was shrewd in pointing to the progress of science, and its attendant iconoclasms, as "the cause of the technical excellence and spiritual barrenness" of recent poetry, but he based his faith "that it will in the end lead to new and fairer manifestations of the immortal Muse" upon the notion that "the pure office of poetry is ever to idealize and prophesy of the unknown."

No other really crucial problem of modern criticism is discussed in Stedman's volumes, and where he does touch briefly or indirectly upon one, the concept of art as idealization is a central factor in his attitude. There is, for instance, his hint at what he believed to be the true nature of beauty, which he postulated as the goal of art: speaking of Tennyson, he said that "throughout his work we find a pure and thoughtful purpose, abhorrent of the mere licentious passion for beauty,

> *such as lurks*
> *In some wild Poet, when he works*
> *Without a conscience or an aim.*"

There is also his response to questions pertaining to democracy and social classes: of Landor's *Pericles and Aspasia* he wrote that in it "we penetrate the love of high-bred men and women: nobles by nature and rank;—surely finer subjects for realistic treatment than the boor and the drudge. Where both are equally natural, I would rather contemplate a horse or a falcon, than the newt and the toad." (Henry James's dogma arrived at poetically!) Further with regard to his social outlook, he wrote of Thomas Hood's poetry that to read it is to be thankful for what sunshine falls upon this mournful earth and "to accept manfully, as he did, each one's condition, however toilsome and suffering, under the changeless law that impels and governs all." From these few citations no one can doubt that Stedman urged poets to idealize their material in accordance with *genteel* ideals, so that an esthetic principle that is dubious at best is further compromised by being defined in terms of a reactionary philosophy.

The curious thing about all this is that Stedman considered himself a progressive, even radical, critic. And perhaps he was one—in his circle. His very eclecticism indicated, in his view, broadness of mind. His *The Nature and Elements of Poetry*, which is largely an elaboration of the opinions he set down in his earlier volumes, is the epitome of esthetic tolerance; its definition of poetry is consciously designed to sanction almost every emotion, thought, and sentiment and to exclude almost no poetic aim—except outright didacticism. It goes without saying that his words were braver than his meaning—that is why Stedman rewards our study, for there are few more convincing examples of the curse of gentility. Here was a man of irreproachable intentions, integrity, and uncommon sensitiveness who might have become a good critic but was sapped and stultified by the *mores* of his class and age.

Not as much can be said for all genteel critics. There were many who suffered no doubts and never spoke of what might lie beyond the horizon of conventional respectability. Stedman's friend Aldrich showed no sign of being intellectually superior to the ladies of Beacon Hill. The drama "expert" of their circle, William Winter, carried on a vendetta against realism in the theatre which bespoke not only his acceptance of the Victorian code, but personal narrowness as well. He goes down in history as having been the chief obstacle to the rise of the modern American theatre. Nor was there any hint of broader vistas in the demure sentimentalism of Donald Grant Mitchell, author of *English Lands, Letters and Kings* (1889) and *American Lands and Letters* (1897-9). And there were not many redeeming features in Oliver Wendell Holmes, whose *Breakfast Table* series and *Over the Teacups* are full of literary comment. A militant Unitarian, forever denouncing Calvinism and defending rationalist doctrines, one would suppose that he would be capable of reading modern novels without squirming. Yet he found Flaubert and Zola altogether repugnant—not, to be sure, on moral grounds, but as a matter of taste. He said that the things they dealt with should be left to scientists. This seems to be a rational plea, but the temper of it was prudish and the result was a thesis quite as irrational as the moralist's.

Something must be said, however, of an aspect of gentility which has been too little remarked by recent critics. The genteel tradition was not built entirely of negative and non-creative elements, and it was not always repressive in action. There were productive forces in it, too. There were critics who worked with a social end in mind that was hardly reprehensible. Consider a man like E. P. Whipple, who during the forty years that he wrote and lectured on literature won the esteem not only of the best writers of the time, but also of the widest public that existed for literary intelligence. He began writing when the transcendentalist movement was at its height and continued, with diminishing productivity, until his death in 1886. He was not drawn into the Emersonian circle, but from the start he was a romantic of a kind. Earnest, moral, conventional, he was nevertheless on the side of the liberals. There was nothing exceptional or distinctive about him, however, and if he had confined his activity to writing there would be no reason to recall him other than as a sane and solid critic in a period which was not over-supplied with such critics. But Whipple's career as a lecturer was a quite different matter. He was a tremendous favorite of lyceum audiences—and justly so, for he came to the platform better equipped and with higher purpose than almost any other critic in the circuit.

We see in that phase of Whipple's work one of the initial

tendencies of genteel criticism: the impulse, which was by no means universal but not rare either, to elevate the taste and improve the literary understanding of the lower classes. This was part of that whole movement to democratize culture which, as we noted before, had genteel as well as romantic motives in it. George W. Curtis was another whose work was motivated by those social considerations, and in his case there was, in addition, a practical interest in political reform. Curtis was affected in his youth by transcendentalism and lived for a while at Brook Farm. While much of his writing was on civic questions, he produced books on Bryant and Burns and essays on Emerson, Hawthorne, Thackeray, Dickens, Longfellow, Holmes, Thoreau, and others. He was a gracious, gentle writer, obviously cultivated, and quite as obviously limited in vision and passion. Like Whipple, he continued his work into the last quarter of the century and served as a link between the early and later phases of gentility.

The thing to note here is the form its social conscience took in that later phase. The democratic impulse was petering out—was almost dead in upper-class circles. If anything, there was fear and abhorrence of democracy now that the West was fighting in impolite ways for control of the nation's wealth and government. In an era of pecuniary materialism—a gaudy era in which gentlemen were oppressed by vulgarity—when the Goths in the shape of the *nouveaux riches* were debasing the level of culture in American society, some of the genteel critics thought of themselves as cultural missionaries and custodians of the literary heritage. They were this country's counterparts of Arnold and Ruskin, and as evangelists of taste they chided the parvenus and sought to illuminate and refine the huge new public which stood ready to patronize the arts but had no training in discrimination.

Curtis was touched by that missionary impulse, and his friend Charles Dudley Warner was full of it. The novel Warner wrote with Mark Twain, *The Gilded Age,* was inspired by little else.

It was a recurring motif of his criticism, and in one of his most important essays, "The Relation of Literature to Life" (1886), it developed into a very salutary bit of dialectics: he attacked the common tendency to divorce art from reality—the practical from the intellectual life—and at the same time denounced the "arrogance of culture," the scholars who "regard the rest of mankind as barbarians and philistines." [1] (It would be a poor missionary who would speak pessimistically of the heathen.) The essay is essentially a defense of art against the sneers and indifference of the cynics in the business community. In other respects Warner's critical writing followed the main path of gentility—upholding art as idealization and disparaging the realistic novel. Much the same can be said of Thomas Wentworth Higginson, one of the last of New England's "giants," perhaps the last critic of any importance who came out of the nineteenth-century Boston-Cambridge culture. Unitarian minister, fiery abolitionist, officer of a Negro regiment in the Civil War, and then editor of the *Atlantic Monthly*, essayist, critic, and lecturer, Higginson was a man of genuine stature who deserves the respect of our own century. There was deep sincerity in his desire to see the fruits of learning and literary appreciation carried into provincial homes. He wrote on American literature for the general public and went west on lecture tours during which he was naïvely pleased to find "an audience all ready and always readers of the *Atlantic*, so glad to see me." He is permanently fixed in American literary history because he sponsored Emily Dickinson and kept alive the name of Thoreau, yet how unsympathetic he could be to manifestations of an anti-genteel philosophy! No one has ever written a narrower, meaner essay on Whitman than the one which appears in his volume *Contemporaries* (1899).

When all accounts have been settled, however, it is clear that critics like Curtis and Higginson—and perhaps even Lowell,

[1] In *The Complete Writings of Charles Dudley Warner* (Hartford, 1904), pp. 63 ff.

who was the best of the lot—were doomed to neglect and eventually to oblivion. They helped to develop a serious audience for serious literature in the United States, but they did not add to esthetic thought, offered no new insight to the reading public, and gave nothing to the artist struggling with unprecedented problems. There were more important things to do than to refine the taste of the bourgeoisie. American literature had to be made free to deal with fundamental human relationships and an audience had to be created for it—which is to say that American society as a whole had to become articulate about realities—and gentility was in the way even when it functioned as a civilizing force. The agencies of progress were the radical Westerners, the new white-collar class rising in the industrialized East, and the groups whose intellectual sympathies, often direct attachments, were European. They had no veneration for the *Atlantic* and *Harper's*, saw in them only impediments to experimentation; and the authority of such magazines was consequently, inevitably, deflated.

4

Histories of American literature are usually written by professors. Until recent years the field was so much their property that when a layman ventured into it—even to study only a single period or a special problem—he would be received in academic quarters coolly, if not condescendingly. A Stedman could be tolerated because his sentiments were like theirs, but John Macy and Van Wyck Brooks saw the professors' teeth.

What did the professors make of their field? What kind of history did they produce? The answer tells us how Americans have been taught their own literature, and thus helps to explain the literary mind of pre-war generations.[1] Moreover, it shows us how bad the professors could really be, for on a sub-

[1] "Pre-war" should be emphasized. When the school finally caught up with life (see Chapter VIII) even the conservatives became men as well as gentlemen.

ject that was right at hand and that affected all of our people, they were at their worst.

The answer has fortunately been provided by the academy itself—fortunately because it is so damning that a layman would hesitate to give it for fear of being accused of professor-baiting, a sport that died with Mencken's disappearance as a critic. It is recorded in a volume called *The Reinterpretation of American Literature*, which was published in 1928 but expressed what had evidently been simmering in the colleges for ten or fifteen years. The volume was edited by Professor Norman Foerster, whose conservatism no one questions.

Our first witness is Professor Fred Lewis Pattee, whose contribution to the symposium was "A Call for a Literary Historian" (first published in the *American Mercury* in 1924). He said: "I have nearly a hundred histories of American literature on my shelves, and I am still adding more—a hundred volumes to tell the story of our literary century, and all of them alike, all built upon the same model! I think I could dictate one to a stenographer in three days, with no reference to authorities save for dates: Colonial Period, Revolutionary Period, Knickerbocker Period, New England Period, and so on. Always there is the same list of authors, beginning with Captain John Smith, Anne Bradstreet, and Cotton Mather. A few are treated in chapters by themselves: Franklin, Irving, Bryant, Cooper, Emerson, Hawthorne, Whittier, Longfellow, Holmes, Poe, Lowell, and, of late, Whitman and Mark Twain. The rest are assorted into groups according to chronology, geography, or literary forms.

"But the really stereotyped thing about these histories is their critical method: always the same list of biographical facts with emphasis upon the picturesque, always the repetition of a standard series of well-worn myths. . . . Special purpose and provincial prejudice wave over every one of them like red flags. There is, first, the New England group, headed by the Victorian Charles Francis Richardson, and later by Barrett Wendell, whose bulky *Literary History of America* should have been entitled *A Literary History of Harvard University, with Incidental Glimpses of the Minor Writers of America.* . . . Next comes a group of Southern histories, some of them frankly bearing the title, *Literature of the South.* This region has always been peculiarly sensitive, peculiarly eager to make the most of its scanty literary annals. . . . Between the two extremes lies a belt stretching from Philadelphia and New York westward across the continent. Its textbooks all present close-up treatments of local celebrities. . . ."

Next we have Professor Paul Kaufman, who said: "Only within a year or two has anyone [Foerster in 1925, Parrington in 1927] definitely proposed that in American letters also could be discovered a 'romantic' period. Hitherto we have called our literature between the Revolutionary and the Civil Wars by the noncommittal chronological name Early National, or we have made geographical divisions . . . and if we have hazarded a descriptive epithet at all we have spoken of our 'classic period.' Inner coherence, prevailing tendencies we have not discovered or at least been willing to conceive in terms universally applied to contemporary European literature in the earlier part of the nineteenth century."

And next comes Professor A. M. Schlesinger, historian of American life, who said: "What first impresses the social historian is that his fellow delver in the literary field has been mainly interested in the picturesque, the unusual, and the super-excellent. . . . The historian's scale of values has materially altered as his test of the significance of an historical event has changed from that of the welfare of an aristocracy or ruling class to that of the well-being of the multitude. There have been signs in the last ten years that research in American history is taking a similar turn. . . . The development of literature is constantly affected by the forces which condition the whole course of social growth. American literary history has as yet received little attention from this point of view."

What, in words as few and blunt as possible, have we been told? Firstly, that the professors were imitative and intellectually unenterprising. Secondly, that they were provincial. Thirdly, that they catered to the prejudices of their communities. Fourthly, that they were inclined to snobbishness. Fifthly, that they were loath to grapple with ideas, loath to systematize and generalize. Sixthly, that they abstracted literature from life, ignoring the environmental factors in the development of the art.

The evidence is available in the books on which the teaching and writing of American literary history has been founded. Most respected of all is Moses Coit Tyler's *A History of American Literature during the Colonial Period*, published in four volumes between 1880 and 1897. It is distinguished chiefly by its documentation, representing an extraordinary amount of original research. It is cursed by the author's patriotism and by his philosophy, which was frankly idealist. He said that his book aimed to be "a presentation of the soul, rather than the body, of the American Revolution," and it succeeded in being just that—a disembodied spirit. There is no hint in the book of how any of the Revolutionary writers came to be what they were. Barrett Wendell's *Literary History of America*, published in 1900, is also written from an idealist bias, besides being incredibly insular and, of course, aristocratic. The extreme case of criticism written without any historical sense is Richardson's *American Literature, 1607-1885*, published in 1892. The author's purpose, in his own words, was that "of estimating the rank and analyzing the achievements of American authors"—that is to say, grading them as though they were schoolboys. Professor Harry Hayden Clark wrote in Foerster's symposium: "His work illustrates today the peculiar futility of aesthetic rankings and the neglect of the modern fool-proof historical inquiry and explanation."

Somewhat better in method than the above volumes were George Woodberry's *America in Literature*, and W. P. Trent's

*A History of American Literature, 1607-1865*, both of which were published in 1903. Because they are better, their limitations are instructive. For Woodberry and Trent were superior men, yet with all their intelligence and learning they did not dare break the mold or else could not quite figure out how to do so. Professor Clark said of Woodberry that he "perceived—as behooved a professor of comparative literature—the relations between European and American romanticism, but in such a vague and general way as to indicate slight significance." That could be said of everything Woodberry wrote. He was a sensitive man who caught glimpses of the new currents in esthetic thought—but only glimpses. Always he was vague and general, although even so he was a liberalizing force in the academic world. Trent, too, knew better than most of his colleagues, for there are suggestions of real historical criticism in his work. In retrospect, however, his volume seems just about as cautious and conservative as the others, improving on them mainly in its sense of proportion.

Those are the prototypical histories. Is it any wonder that the other ninety or ninety-five volumes on Professor Pattee's shelves are unreadable? But not all of their characteristics have been described as yet. The one important thing that the *Reinterpretation* group did not touch upon is their gentility. Pattee spoke of Richardson as a Victorian. Did he use the term as an epithet? Certainly Richardson exhibited the unpleasant features of the Victorian spirit. So did they all. They were all timid about opening proscribed subjects. The treatment accorded Walt Whitman by professorial critics, before 1915, is one of the major scandals in the history of American criticism. Wendell solved the problem by writing about him without once mentioning "Children of Adam," as though such poetry were beneath contempt. Richardson was cleverer. He presented the leading arguments in defense of the sex poems, then observed that "the generative faculty, like the sudorific glands elsewhere

gloated over by the same author, is not *per se* a poetic theme,
and . . . Whitman's treatment of it is destitute of the artistic
form which alone makes literature of the corresponding parts
of the 'Arabian Nights' or the 'Decameron.' " For twenty or
thirty years afterwards words to that effect were written in
practically every textbook published in the United States.

A few lines must also be devoted to their esthetic standards.
How seriously they took Irving, Longfellow, Holmes, and
Lowell! In contrast was their treatment of Mark Twain, Melville, and Emily Dickinson, not to speak of Whitman. It was
admitted that Whitman had gifts of a sort, but his form and
style were severely criticized, his mannerisms held up for sar-
casm, and his philosophy of poetry dismissed as an eccentricity
or an aberration. "One can see why the decadent taste of Europe has welcomed him"—said Wendell—"so much more ardently than he has ever been welcomed at home; in temper and
in style he was an exotic member of that sterile brotherhood
which eagerly greeted him abroad." Richardson wrote: "In absolute ability he is about equal to Taylor, Stoddard, Stedman,
or Aldrich." That was a howler, but not a very much greater
one than Woodberry committed when he condescended to say:
"he wrote a few fine lyrics"—which was then the common judgment of professors. Mark Twain was looked upon as a funny
man and a writer of delightfully sentimental stories of boyhood.
Melville was given little space and less understanding, but he
got more of both than Emily Dickinson did. In later textbooks,
when at least Clemens and Whitman began to get their due, the
same kind of superficiality, cowardice, or stupidity, as the case
may be, was betrayed in their handling of Henry James, Stephen
Crane, Frank Norris, and Upton Sinclair.

What the academy feared, in brief, was realism. Broadly defined, the term summarizes all the abominated subjects, emotions, and styles. Americans were not supposed to be disillusioned about the human body and human society. The existing

economic order had to be maintained, the church supported, the gentlemanly ideal vindicated. The professors kept in mind their obligation to train the nation's youth in "right" thinking and living, but one must not imagine that they did not express their own feelings at the same time.

# CHAPTER VII

# THE TWENTIETH CENTURY

GENTILITY and provincialism were dying at the very moment of their supremacy. Their social base had long been weakened, and it was not to be expected that they would forever survive the continuing industrialization of our economy and urbanization of our people. Nor could they withstand the constant infusion of European ideas. As transatlantic communications were bettered, as the racial character of our immigration changed from Anglo-Saxon and Celtic to Slavic, Italian, Magyar, and Jewish, and as the number of American tourists to the Continent increased, the old prejudices were submerged by new and alien tastes, interests, and sympathies, and comparative standards grew where once there had been absolutes. When at the end of the nineteenth century the United States expropriated Spain's Western colonies and made known its desire to participate in the exploitation of China, the parochial aristocracy could no longer hope to impose its dogmas on the arts, for the traditions of a mercantile community are incompatible with empire.

The class which had risen to power and was now acquiring social prestige had its economic roots in industry and international trade. What that means is that the group that was obtaining control of our society, and which was therefore the group that was respected, imitated and served, was made up of people who lived far from the physical source of their income and had little personal contact with it. Their businesses were not family affairs, but corporations. Their interest was in finance, not in the processes of production. They did not regard their economic enterprises as fixed and stable, to be built up,

preserved, and bequeathed, but merely as fluctuating and trans-
ferable investments. They had no knowledge of the men who
actually created their wealth and felt no civic obligations. In
sum, the Buddenbrookses and the Forsytes were being supplanted by financiers.

The social "mind" changed as the nature of our economy
changed. The rising class consisted not only of financiers, corporation lawyers, brokers, and industrial managers, but also of
the men in small businesses who depended upon the dominant
group and of the professional men who served its needs. Among
the last were technicians of various kinds, accountants, advertising men, and journalists. All of them were "free" in a peculiar sense: property in the form of money is fluid; technical
training and administrative ability are for sale anywhere. They
could move about more easily and quickly than men of affairs
had once been able to. Therefore they were experimentalists.
They had fewer community responsibilities. Therefore they
tended toward epicurean attitudes. They had less need of strict
moral codes. Therefore they believed in them less and made
fashionable a certain mild disillusionment. They were, moreover, susceptible to the mood of nineteenth-century science, to
which they were indebted for their material possessions and social rank. Therefore they were pragmatists.

These attitudes and points of view are the elements of what
has often been called the "modern spirit." The class from which
it developed was a city class. It was composed of several racial
strains and was consequently inclined to be cosmopolitan. Acquisitive, conscious of its strength, eager to enjoy the fruits of
its wealth and with sufficient leisure to do so, it had no hesita-
tion about borrowing interesting ideas and appropriate manners
from "foreigners." Thus were the old ways of life destroyed,
for since it was evident to everyone that the social position of
this class was unthreatened, its cultural influence soon proved
decisive.

One could find the shoots of the "modern spirit" timidly

sprouting on the campus of Columbia, the only American university in contact with metropolitan life. Woodberry was a harbinger of the spring to come. Hjalmar H. Boyesen, Norwegian-born professor of German, was another in the '80's and early '90's. His essays on Scandinavian and German literature encouraged realism and introduced new foreign names (and a foreign flavor) into American letters. A third was Brander Matthews, professor of literature, who practiced dramatic criticism and essay-writing. Matthews has been a symbol of gentility for twenty years, and so perhaps it is difficult to think of him as one who advanced the cause of realism. Genteel he was, assuredly, and a very British gentleman at that, whether he knew it or not. Nevertheless he was receptive to Continental literature and helped to break down the notion that to be French was to be immoral. One must compare his dramatic reviews with William Winter's to see how much he stood for progress. But the best of the Columbia group was still another— Harry Thurston Peck, professor of Greek and Latin—and in him we see the conflict between the past and the future.

Peck's mission was to liberalize and broaden academic critical methods and to make contemporary European letters known to American scholars. At times he wrote of foreigners, and even of living Americans, with few lingering traces of the genteel heritage; at other times he seemed no different from Matthews; and when he wrote of a national idol like Longfellow he reverted to type and was just a respectable professor. But he did shock the pedants into looking around at what was actually going on in the world and he did introduce into official criticism a pinch of moral tolerance. Furthermore, as editor of the *Bookman*, he made a great many people conscious of the playful side of literature, of its café-and-studio life, where moral earnestness withered. It was, so to speak, the direction of his work that counted; intrinsically it had little worth. A few historians will remember him gratefully and nobody will read him. He was a stimulating but minor figure even in those days, and nothing he wrote was inspiring for more than a moment only. His audience was continually outstripping him while he oscillated between gentility and worldliness—and that was his misfortune. His qualms and reversions made him an inadequate spokesman for the one class that could have given him a permanent symbolic significance. It was James Huneker, the journalist, who succeeded.

The journalists were naturally less inhibited, less attached to tradition, than the academic critics. Because they raced with the stream of current events and wrote for immediate consumption, they reflected instantly what was happening and were responsive to the moods of the most forward-looking of their audience. Impressionism—the recording of personal sensation as soon after the moment of stimulus as possible—was the very nature of their craft; adventure, exploration, novelty, excitement were the things for which they lived. On the other hand, they were weak in, distrustful of, historical analysis and philosophical judgment. Everything about them, strength and weakness both, qualified them to conduct the innocents into a spicier way of thought than had hitherto been available in this land of noble ideals and ignoble apprehensions. They did well what needed to be done. No literary historian can neglect them; but they weren't critics in the real sense of the word and today they remind us of yesterday's headlines.

Percival Pollard is less than a name to the post-war generation. Is there any way to resuscitate him? He was one of that brilliant group which centered about William Mann's magazines, *Town Topics* and the *Smart Set*, and which included Huneker, Charles Hanson Towne, Willard Huntington Wright, and at last H. L. Mencken and George Jean Nathan. "Pollard showed the first American awareness of the great movements that were transforming continental literature," wrote Ludwig Lewisohn in *Expression in America*—an exaggerated claim, but indicative of his importance to the beginning of the twentieth century. He was a robust figure in a decade dominated by fas-

tidious gentlemen; he was "liberated," vigorous, boldly appreciative of "exotic" ideas. But what remains of all his gusto?
Who reads now his *Masks and Minstrels of New Germany*
(1911) and *Their Day in Court* (1909)? The former, especially,
was for its time an exuberant, amusing, and rather provocative
work. Fatally, both were indecisive and impressionistic, and
neither had anything in it more lasting than the esthetic fashions of his day.

Making quite a noise in that day was also Vance Thompson,
who thought that criticism should be practiced by men-about-
town. In 1895 he founded, with Huneker, a magazine called
*M'lle New York*, on the style of the Paris boulevard papers.
Thompson wrote that "*M'lle New York* is not concerned with
the public. Her only ambition is to disintegrate some small portion of the public into its original component parts—the aristocracies of birth, wit, learning, and art, and the joyously vulgar
mob." Brash, vain, crudely snobbish though it was, that announcement deserves to be recalled as the fertile seed of a pose
that was afterwards immensely fashionable. Time bestowed a
measure of urbanity on the recently emerged middle classes,
but failed to cure their egotism. *M'lle New York* is well forgotten. It was adolescent and postured, its pranks were sophomoric, its bohemianism fake. Yet it was not the least of the
numerous signs that pointed toward the eventual liberation of
American criticism from its moral strait-jacket. Its esthetic
catholicity, its hostility toward the "Puritan," and its interest
in Nietzsche and Stirner were healthy, as were its scoffing at
commercial piety and its determination to describe women as
less than saints. But all of this smacked of naughtiness rather
than considered intelligence; there was too great a consciousness of unconventionality in the tasting of strange and sinful
fruit. Likewise over-ecstatic was Thompson's magnum opus,
*French Portraits* (1913), a volume of superficial appreciations
of the younger French and Belgian writers. In manner and
taste it was wholly indigenous to the *fin de siècle*—the work of

a dazzled American cosmopolite, graduated proudly from the impressionist school.

It was exactly that degree of literary development that Huneker represented and of which he became the master. He did not go beyond it; he merely improved it. He made it—by virtue of his own brilliance—synonymous with the standpoint of the so-called "civilized minority." It would be difficult to find anything in his eighteen books that would not fit the pages of Thompson's magazine, but it would be equally difficult to find anything that is not expressed more plausibly, with greater wit, with neater phrase, than it might have been by any of his friends.

It is a simple matter to describe his performance. The cleverest, best-informed, most entertaining of esthetic guides, he brought into our parlors a host of European writers, painters, and musicians, and made the commonplaces of European intellectual life familiar to our neophyte illuminati. He did so without attempting to draw morals or to prove anything or even to pass judgment. He had no historical sense and little interest in ultimate values. He was content to be an expositor, an appreciator—to re-create the atmosphere of a work of art as he felt it, to reveal its complexion as mirrored in his eyes, to communicate the emotions it aroused in *him*. He was extremely personal —made subjectivism a virtue—but at the same time he was a gifted reporter of other men's sentiments, and the sentiments he reported were as often morbid, perverse, and libidinous as not. He merely reported them, did not explain them. The unusual, the "queer," fascinated him; the speculative was his delight. The man was a hedonist—the first and foremost in our history. He was a man of the city, of music halls, cafés, restaurants, theatres, art galleries, boulevards. Out of his own temperament sprang his will to accomplish what is undoubtedly his chief distinction: his victorious fight against provincialism and the Victorian morality and for an elementary sophistication and tolerance. His epitaph may justly be the label that Mencken applied to him—"anti-Philistine."

Nothing more is required to prove his audacity as a scout than the tables of contents of his books. In *Iconoclasts*, published in 1905, he wrote on Ibsen, Strindberg, Hauptmann, Gorky, Shaw, Hervieu, Becque, Sudermann, d'Annunzio, and Villiers de l'Isle Adam; in *Egoists* (1909), on Baudelaire, Anatole France, Huysmans, Barrès, Nietzsche, and Stirner; in *The Pathos of Distance* (1913), on George Moore, Synge, Verlaine, and again on Maeterlinck and Nietzsche; in *Ivory Apes and Peacocks* (1915), on Joseph Conrad, Jules Laforgue, Wedekind, de Maupassant, Schnitzler, Andreiev, and Artzibashev; in *Unicorns* (1917), on Remy de Gourmont, James Joyce, Claude Bragdon, again on Huysmans and Artzibashev, and in one essay mentioned every French writer then living, including Jules Romains and André Gide. In painting he was equally prescient. *Promenades of an Impressionist*, published in 1910, contains pieces on Cézanne, Degas, Monet, Renoir, Gauguin, and Toulouse-Lautrec; *The Pathos of Distance* pieces on Matisse and Picasso; *Ivory Apes and Peacocks* pieces on Max Liebermann, Van Gogh, and the Italian futurists. In music he was among the first American critics to write favorably of Schönberg, Debussy, Moussorgsky, and Richard Strauss, and passionately of Wagner. The dates given above tell us only when his pieces appeared in definitive form, for they were published in newspapers and magazines months and years—in some cases ten years—before they were collected into books.

In the opening years of the century he was considered daring. It was intoxicating to read him. But re-reading him now is a depressing exercise in fortitude. The time has long passed when the "foreign devils" in the arts were hated and feared, and the war against gentility and censorship seems remote. The truth is that the thrills which he supplied are beyond recall; his job was well enough done to leave him, in the form of his books, nothing else to do. There was no substance in him, no depth, no wisdom. He could write as gravely of Laforgue as of Dostoievsky, as seriously of Barrès as of Tolstoy, as warmly of Artzibashev as of Gorky. One doubts that Whitman meant more to him than de l'Isle Adam or that he was more interested in Joyce than in Carl Van Vechten. And no matter who or what his subject was, he never dealt with esthetic principles or theories of criticism and never showed any understanding of the relationship between art and society. In short, he was not an "intellect." To observe him when he left the narrow realm of esthetic sensation was to witness a shower of smart platitudes. His papers on themes other than the purely esthetic, with rare exceptions, were empty; they were in the glib journalese of a man who had read a great many books on those various subjects, but too many of them second-rate.

Individualism was the only philosophical principle evident in his long list of books—and it appeared in all of them. This was not the idealistic individualism of the transcendentalists, with its humanitarian implications. It was an arrogant individualism: the assertion of personal superiority over the mass of men, the rationalization of class distinctions, the justification of freedom defined as social irresponsibility. In a word, it was Nietzsche's individualism. It was the philosophy, if such it may be called, of the advanced section of the bourgeoisie in the act of liberating itself from all archaic restrictions upon egotism: the feudal traditions of chivalry and service, the Christian traditions of poverty and equality. It was an ideological weapon in the battle against outworn theologies, but also against humanitarian and collectivist doctrines—against anything that limited or threatened the self-directed power of a ruling class that thrived on economic anarchy and wanted to do as it pleased. There were reasons why at this stage of American life Nietzsche became fashionable; and the fact that they created the vogue denotes the social function of men like Peck, Thompson, Huneker, and Mencken.

But it was Mencken, not Huneker, who made the philosophy

an integral part of a critical system. In Huneker's writing it was incidental—certainly not the point of departure. His surviving friends tells us that more than anything else he was a personality: sparkling, keen, colorful. He may be summed up in two words: "sympathy" and "enthusiasm." It was, of course, the first trait that made him receptive to new ideas and forms, but it was also responsible for his preposterous discovery of gold in innumerable ores of the basest metal: he was one of those who brought over here the puny poets and philosophers, as well as the giants, of a decadent European society, and he helped encourage their American imitators. "Sympathy" as a principle of criticism was rejected when the revolt against the tyranny of the Protestant ethic was accomplished. For when everyone had experimented with novel sensations, no one could boast of his ability to find entertainment in the esoteric and exotic. As for Huneker's "enthusiasm," the books themselves bear witness to the ephemeral attractiveness of so personal a quality. The piquant bubbles are gone and the drink is stale. It is the privilege of a child to be, simply, enthusiastic, but the subject of his enthusiasm is the test of an adult.

As long ago as 1917 Mencken was hard put to it to name a really sound and permanent book among the many that his friend Huneker had already published, finally taking refuge in the damning statement that "one no longer reads them for their matter, but for their manner." That is no tribute to a critic as critic. But who today does not realize that the impressionist—the critic who, in Huneker's own words, attempts no more than "to spill his own soul" and "humbly to follow and register his emotions aroused by a masterpiece"—is no critic at all? He is, demonstrably, only a painter of self-portraits. Huneker was just that. The portrait was charming and likable, even if it exposed a certain shallowness in its subject. It was not, however, the portrait of a "universal" man.

But there are men of letters who are elected to historical eminence irrespective of the actual worth of their compositions.

It is likely that when Samuel Johnson's works are on longer read, he will be talked and written about and will represent something concrete and meaningful. He was a type, a perfect symbol of an age. So, too, was James Huneker. In both the man and the writer—in his cosmopolitanism, his contempt for small-town righteousness, his sensuality, and his grim, inflexible individualism—the "smart set" and their zealous apes could find a delightful reflection of their profoundest impulses. Remaining always several steps ahead of the community he spoke to, he was seldom in advance of, or above, its aspirations. It was this class that came to dominate American life after the World War. Those were the years of its plenty. It set the whole tone of the decade in the arts and professions, in manners and politics. And James Huneker was the dream of that class embodied, and indeed it was his friends, his disciples and pupils, who ruled the roost throughout the 1920's. One thinks promptly of George Jean Nathan, Ernest Boyd, and, not quite so promptly, H. L. Mencken, but one should think rather of the way his receptiveness, enthusiasm, and point of view—and, to a degree, his style—were profitably used by the newspaper columnists and reviewers who fashioned the taste of that period. He must have known that his followers would soon acquire authority, for he himself was writing, quite early in his career, for magazines like the *Atlantic Monthly* and *North American Review*—so sweeping was the revolution which the impressionists initiated. As their master, Huneker may be said to have influenced American taste more than any critic of this century.

2

Impressionism was destructive to genteel and classical traditions because it argued the subjectivity of taste. For if taste is subjective, so is thought; and therefore neither standards, precedents, nor social values are relevant to esthetic judgment, the only test of achievement being the degree and quality of the reader's pleasure. But, theoretically, every reader is unique, and if the individual alone is the measure of truth and beauty, no one may say that another's opinion is accurate or false, good or bad. Moral, historical, and psychological criteria are alike beside the point, which is simply whether a work of literature pleases someone.

We can understand why this doctrine was popular, becoming the most effective means of combating repressive authority: it was flattering to those who subscribed to it. It could not, however, satisfy everyone, for there were many who saw that while it banished taboos from the world of criticism, it also banished philosophy and scholarship as objective instruments of valuation. As for its service to art, while it opened the door to the whole of life, it also let in anarchy, for instead of merely freeing the artist and liberalizing the taste of his audience, impressionism condoned irresponsibility and relaxed discrimination. Surely there was some other critical method which could as well demoralize the pedants, the gentlemen, and the classicists and yet be grounded on something more tangible, more reliable than the personality of the reader—a method which did not depend for conviction upon the charm or cleverness of the critic.

Lewis E. Gates, professor of English at Harvard, offered one way out. In an essay on "Impressionism and Appreciation," first published in the *Atlantic Monthly* and then, in 1900, reprinted in a volume called *Studies and Appreciations*, he tried to subject the impressionist method to certain disciplines. He began the essay by writing a fine exposition of impressionism. "Little by little, during the last two centuries," he said, "the human spirit has gained a finer and closer sense of the worth and meaning of every individual moment of pleasure in the presence alike of nature and of art. The record of this increase of sensitiveness toward nature is to be found in poetry, and toward art in criticism. . . . The history of literary criticism from Addison's day to our own is, if viewed in one way, the history of the ever-increasing refinement of the critic's sensorium; it is the history of the critic's increasing sensitiveness to delicate shades of spiritual existence in his reaction to literature; and finally, it is the history of a growing tendency on the part of the critic to value, above all else, his own intimate personal relation to this or that piece of literature. . . ." Then—with some reluctance, for he was sympathetic to that tendency— Gates admitted that the effort to "define a personal impression vividly and imaginatively" was not true criticism. He said that the critic must possess not only sensitiveness but also knowledge of psychology and cultural history; he must be conscious not only of his own feelings but also of "esthetic law." And yet, wrote Gates, "in regarding the work of art under all these aspects, his aim is primarily not to explain and not to judge or dogmatize, but to enjoy; to realize the manifold charm the work of art has gathered into itself from all sources, and to interpret this charm imaginatively to the men of his own day and generation."

Gates called his method "appreciation." Actually, it was merely an enlightened impressionism—that is to say, the impressionism of a man of culture. It was superior to Huneker's method in that it avoided pyrotechnics and acknowledged the need for scholarship. But it confused the critic as an articulate reader with the critic *as a critic*. It would convert criticism into a kind of reportage. That can be enthusiastically recommended to school-teachers who are trying to awaken their students to an appreciation of literature. Criticism is something more than that. It is explanation and judgment. Even dogmatism, which no one cares to defend but everyone practices, has some virtues; at least it is philosophical in intention.

J. E. Spingarn, professor of comparative literature at Columbia University, found the way out of Gates's difficulties: the teachings of the Italian philosopher, Benedetto Croce. Spingarn's famous lecture on "The New Criticism," delivered in 1910 and published the following year, is the best exposition of the Crocean esthetic that has ever been made by an American; and because it was made by an academician who opposed academicians, at the moment when the academy began its enforced retreat from a position of critical authority, it has a historic interest possessed by no other system of similar or comparable intent. Ironically, it owes not a little of its fame to the fact that critics like Paul Elmer More and Norman Foerster—the kind of critics it sought to demolish—have attacked it as a species of impressionism, although it is nothing of the sort.

The climax of Spingarn's lecture was his definition of criticism as an attempt to answer these questions: "What has the writer proposed to himself to do? and how far has he succeeded in carrying out his plan?" According to Spingarn, those were Goethe's words, but Foerster correctly pointed out [1] that Goethe had asked an additional question, to wit: Is what the writer proposes reasonable and comprehensible? Spingarn included the latter question when he translated Goethe's essay; he omitted it from his own essay because he was not a pupil of Goethe but of Croce, and while the first two questions are in harmony with the Italian's philosophy, the third is not. To discuss reasonableness is to introduce ideological problems where only formal ones are desired. For the central purpose of Spingarn's theory was to reduce criticism to purely esthetic appreciation—that is, to eliminate moral, social, and psychological inquiries and confine it to an apprehension of the artist's vision and a study of his expression. In Spingarn's words: "What has the poet tried to do, and how has he fulfilled his intention?" To determine the poet's aim the critic must share the poet's experience—become one with him; to explain the method of achieving the aim and to decide whether he did in fact achieve it, the critic must re-enact the poetic process. Thus, genius (art) and taste (criticism) are fundamentally identical, though obviously not in all respects.

By discarding the problem of value, criticism is limited to formal analysis, however moving or vivacious its transcription of the artist's spirit may be. We cannot ask whether the artist's

[1] In *American Criticism*, p. 119.

view of life is true or significant, nor whether his work may convey to man a meaning which can be justified in terms of man's needs. This critical system is already familiar to us as the logical end of Poe's and James's theory of the critic's function, but they fell short of it by accepting the prohibitions imposed upon the artist by society. Spingarn, in his theory if not his practice, recognized no such restrictions. "We have done with all the old Rules," he said. "The very conception of 'rules' harks back to an age of magic. . . . We have done with the *genres,* or literary kinds. Their history is inseparably bound up with that of the classical rules. . . . We have done with the comic, the tragic, the sublime, and an army of vague abstractions of their kind. . . . We have done with the theory of style, with metaphor, simile, and all the paraphernalia of Graeco-Roman rhetoric. These owe their existence to the assumption that style is separate from expression, that it is something which may be added or subtracted at will from the work of art, a flourish of the pen, an external embellishment, instead of the poet's individual vision of reality, the music of his whole manner of being. . . . We have done with all moral judgment of art as art . . . [for] it is not the inherent function of poetry to further any moral or social cause, any more than it is the function of bridge-building to further the cause of Esperanto . . . [and] the poet's only moral duty, as a poet, is to be true to his art, and to express his vision of reality as well as he can. . . . We have done with technique as separate from art. . . . We have done with the history and criticism of poetic themes. . . . We have done with the race, the time, the environment of a poet's work as an element in Criticism. To study these phases of a work of art is to treat it as an historic or social document, and the result is a contribution to the history of culture or civilization, with only a subsidiary interest for the history of art. . . ."

What, then, did he save that impressionism had lost? Not philosophy: he agreed with the disciples of Anatole France in denying the relevance of ideological inquiry to literary criticism. But learning he did unquestionably save. That was not generally recognized at the time, and the failure to recognize it was the source of error of those who dubbed him an impressionist. The confusion was caused by his sneers at pedantry—the nonsensical adoration of formal rules and the passion for taxonomy which is the refuge of those who fear the unfamiliar and cannot understand the unlabeled. But "learning" is not synonymous with academic scholarship. Scholarship is only part of the critic's "learning"; the greater part is knowledge of the spirit of art and experience in discerning the aims of the immortal poets. In the lecture we are now examining Spingarn touched upon this aspect of his critical theory only once: when he said that the opponents of the impressionists "could combat the notion that taste is a substitute for learning, or learning a substitute for taste, since both are vital for criticism; and they could maintain that the relativity of taste does not in any sense affect its authority." But if taste is relative, what *is* its authority? It could only be its equipment, ripeness, and experience—and this is assumed throughout Spingarn's discussion of the relationship of taste and genius. It is, moreover, the implication of his thesis that enjoyment can be developed into criticism.

In later essays Spingarn clarified his position on this point: he had to, if he were not permanently to be lumped with the impressionists—or, as Irving Babbitt claimed, with the primitivists —for his rather ambiguous affirmations of the kinship of taste and genius had encouraged the moralists and pedants to misrepresent him. His definitive restatement of his theory was his essay on "Criticism in the United States," first published in the Stearns symposium, *Civilization in the United States*, in 1922, and then revised for his own symposium, *Criticism in America: Its Function and Status*, published in 1924. Here he said: "When I wrote the essays which a few years later were collected in a volume bearing the subtitle of 'Essays on the Unity of Genius and Taste,' the pedants and the professors were in the ascendant, and it seemed necessary to emphasize the side of criticism which was then in danger, the side that is closest to the art of the creator. How unimportant it seemed then to weigh and define all the phases of a critic's duty, when one of the highest moments of the life of the spirit, the moment of artistic creation, appeared, at least in America, to be so completely misunderstood. But now the professors have been temporarily routed by the dilettanti, the amateurs, and the journalists, who treat a work of imagination as if they were describing fireworks or a bull-fight (to use a phrase of Zola's about Gautier); and so it is necessary now to insist on the discipline and illumination of knowledge and thought,—in other words, to write an 'Essay on the Divergence of Criticism and Creation.'" Spingarn proceeded to write it, elaborating upon the proposition that "while the critic must approach a work of literature without preconceived notion of what that individual work should attempt, he cannot criticize it without some understanding of what all literature attempts."

The burden of his message was: "Criticism is essentially an expression of taste, or that faculty of imaginative sympathy by which the reader or spectator is able to re-live the vision created by the artist . . . but it attains its end and becomes criticism in the highest sense only when taste is guided by knowledge and rises to the level of thought, for then, and only then, does the critic give us something that the artist as artist cannot give." America had no "criticism in the highest sense" because it lacked three things: "education in esthetic thinking"; "scholarship—that discipline of knowledge which will give us at one and the same time a wider international outlook and a deeper national insight"; and, above all, "a deeper sensibility, a more complete submission to the imaginative will of the artist." Spingarn's final rejoinder to his obdurate misinterpreters was a pamphlet called *A Spingarn Enchiridion*, published in 1929 in reply to Paul Elmer More's assertion, in *The Demon of the Absolute*, that he was teaching the public that "criticism [is] only impression."

Here he rounded up all the statements to the contrary that appear in the essays discussed above and in other papers and published letters.

It is clear that in Spingarn's view the ideal critic is one who, acknowledging the validity of every instance of artistic expression, ascertains whether the expression is really art by means of a taste which has been disciplined by knowledge and refined by contact with numberless works of beauty. This conception of criticism is related to the impressionist's merely by its moral and philosophical tolerance. Otherwise it is vitally different. The impressionist, in effect, rejects all standards; Spingarn erects as his single standard the reactions of men who are extremely sensitive, superlatively well trained, and practically omniscient —men who have little in common with the rest of humanity and whose reactions are essentially incommunicable. If Huneker's principle is anarchistic, Spingarn's is aristocratic. Ostensibly embracing artists, he is actually selecting critics—and those he selects, since they cannot prove their conclusions to readers whose sensibilities are not the same as theirs, are in the enviable position of having their own perfected intuitions as their only authority. Hence Spingarn's critic may be as fine, as discriminating, even as snobbish, as More and Babbitt, but we don't know why he should be so, for while they use explicable points of reference, his critic need never condescend to argue his case.

That is not just a minor weakness of Spingarn's theory: it reflects the fundamental error that makes itself felt wherever the theory is tested. Any system of criticism which is not founded on defined values, and which rejects discussions of value, cannot help being vague. The analyst of esthetics deals with impalpable and often mysterious things; he gives them substance by relating them to human psychology, which, far from being ethereal, is the observable interaction of man's biological heritage with his social and cultural experience. His instincts, conditioning, and thoughts regarding life and his fellow men are deeply involved. In other words, the ideological issues

—moral, political, social, and the rest—which Spingarn so carefully threw out of the window are the *sine qua non* of literary criticism. Devoid of them, criticism is likely to be a game of words—of abstractions which can have no meaning to men and women who laugh or weep at a play because their feelings as human beings are touched. No doubt the kind of critical taste that Spingarn postulates is as trustworthy as anything else in discriminating between that which is human and that which is not. But what is that taste? If it is not something we can scrutinize, then it is something too mystical to talk about.

And mystical is precisely what Spingarn's whole system, esthetic and critical, really is. It depends upon, and is supposed to be justified by, Croce's metaphysics, which is mysticism unashamed. There is no other way of describing a philosophy which, insisting that nothing exists outside the mind, exalts spiritual "intuition" above natural experience and demands of the critic that his "intuition" be identical with the artist's if he is to judge the work of art. We must be Shakespeare when we write of Shakespeare, Baudelaire when we write of Baudelaire, and Ezra Pound when we write of *him*. Of course, there were never such critics, but the intention, again we see, is to confine the field to the elect.

It would seem that it did not occur to Spingarn that while critics are curious about an artist's aim, they are interested primarily in the *effect* of his work.[1] An aim is a private matter, an effect a public one. How a work of literature impresses its reader, what it does to him, what it means to society at large— such is the stuff of criticism. Effects are facts, aims are guesses. It is because most of us take that for granted that we think it exceedingly important to determine that what an artist has expressed is worth expressing in the first place; and also because we take that for granted, we do not have the same respect for all levels of expression: we do not, for example, assess a child's

[1] Not Poe's sense of the word "effect."

story as we do an adult's. It is, moreover, the effect of a poem or novel that people want to learn about in literary criticism. They don't want to find out merely that the poet or novelist has successfully carried out his plan—that he has expressed himself. That is a fine thing for the poet, but it means little to the reader, who, quite rightly, wants to be told how the fulfilled expression may affect *him*.

Because that didn't occur to Spingarn, his theory attracted few adherents, founded no school, and is today forgotten. His ideal critic would have pleased the modern writer far more than did the unimaginative and reactionary professors of the early 1900's, for he would not have been genteel, would not have been antagonistic to radical sentiments, would probably have been hospitable to experimental writing, and would certainly have been able to distinguish between pedagogy and criticism. In those respects he would have fulfilled the needs of that time, but he would not have written criticism that any but a few precious souls would have cared to read. Hence, stimulating and refreshing as Spingarn's lectures were to the pre-war academy, they did not produce the critics who accomplished the great tasks. That was done by critics who were quite as receptive and generous as Spingarn wanted them to be, but for other reasons.

It is likely, however, that one phase of the Crocean theory did influence a number of critics, chiefly because it publicized, as it were, the method which Poe said he believed in and which James partly practiced: the method which narrows criticism to a consideration of esthetic phenomena. At any rate, a simplification—a corruption, if you will—of Spingarn's system is the most thorough defense of criticism as analysis of form ("how the poet has fulfilled his intention") that we have. "The New Criticism," with its confessedly excessive emphasis on the critic's obligation to accept any poetic expression as self-sufficient and valuable, was encouraging to the esthete who ignored the mystical meaning Spingarn gave to "taste" and construed it simply as sensitiveness to form and language. Such a critic assumes the artist's irresponsibility as readily as the impressionists do and differs from them only in devoting his attention to the formal and verbal aspects of a work instead of its general tone and character. On the whole, the impressionist is preferable, for he at least can entertain his readers and can make them want to read the books that inspire him to write so warmly and freshly.

Its preciousness, its subtly aristocratic slant, is the peculiarity of Spingarn's theory to which we must return. It is strange how little it has been noticed. The critic who glorifies taste suggests a way of life, not merely an attitude toward art. Is there a way of life in our times which pretends to be governed by taste rather than ideas and loyalties and emotional wants? There is: taste is the final standard of the most cultivated, most disenchanted of the rootless, cosmopolitan upper class which welcomes experience—"thrill" is a word Spingarn once used—of any kind, provided it be very fine, perfect, of its kind. To be deduced from that attitude is the proposition: all perfections are equivalent. As a proposition in literary criticism, it violates the healthiest instincts of the great mass of readers.

### 3

Huneker and Spingarn represented the twentieth century in conflict with the past from the standpoint of a new bourgeoisie displacing an old. The issues between the two men were trivial compared with their common hostility to the prevailing traditions of the century before. We may assume that there were personal and vocational factors in the evolution of their critical disagreements, but the disagreements themselves, objectively considered, were merely cultural variations within the same social class.

Even the differences between that new bourgeoisie and the classes that had previously dominated American thought—in morality, religion, and politics as well as literature—were small, however, compared with the differences they would both have with a class that would repudiate all inherited values—bourgeois, Attic, and feudal values alike. The revolutionary class would project a way of thinking that implied the end of civilization as we have known it, and, as a result, communication between that class and its opponents would become astonishingly difficult. At that moment Huneker would discover how much he sympathized with Thomas Bailey Aldrich and Spingarn would find that he shared many of the prejudices of Barrett Wendell. Nothing like that has happened in America, but the possibility of its happening began to be perceptible at the beginning of this century.[1]

The existence of an urban, industrial owning class was predicated upon the existence of an urban, industrial proletariat. From the latter class there developed a social "mind" that was wholly different from the "mind" that dominated that period. In no great community has there ever been complete harmony. Society is not static precisely because it is not pacific. The source of its energy are the clashes of thought and ambition that occur in it. An economically and culturally inferior class generates attitudes and points of view that are in essence opposed to those of the superior groups. Because of its inferiority its outlook is likely to be submerged, but it does not disappear and it has a potential energy that may be released under favorable circumstances.

The outlook upon life of the lower classes in America found a new expression during the years when finance capitalism was booming. They shared the democratic and egalitarian sentiments born of the struggles and dreams of lower classes in all societies, all economic orders, in the past, but now, in addition, they had a philosophy, a theory of political economy, and a morality which was unprecedented. Marxism is the name by which this system of thought is known today, but it was not nearly so

[1] As a practical matter, nothing like that could ever happen anywhere, for no class could repudiate all human experience. As a hypothesis, however, the event is a useful instrument in dialectics. I shall touch on its misuse in a later chapter.

widely used thirty or forty years ago. Indeed, the socialist movement of that time was almost as closely related to the utopian and humanitarian movements of the romantic era as to the communist movement of the present. It owed almost as much to Tolstoy, William Morris, and Whitman—and to the leveler tradition in Christianity—as to Marx. But traces of Marxism were there, and they had great significance for literary criticism. Not many people realized it at first, since the Christian sentiments and genteel manners with which every literate man was familiar were quite as evident as the unfamiliar elements in early socialist criticism. Then, in the period 1910-20, the socialists emphasized internationalism, realism, and contempt for gentility, and hence seemed to be cousins of a sort to the realists and cosmopolites and other enemies of provincialism. (The truth is they did have common sympathies and dislikes.) All through those years, nevertheless, a point of view essentially foreign to every other critical ideal and method was being developed. It is that Marxist strain that separates the socialist criticism of the twentieth century from the criticism of Whitman, who had tried to express what he believed to be the reactions to literature and the cultural aspirations of the inarticulate common people, and of Howells, who had tried to further the cause of a literary school that would reveal the need for a classless society.[1]

The Marxist thesis may be briefly stated as follows: a work of literature reflects its author's adjustment to society. To determine the character and value of the work we must therefore, among other things, understand and have an opinion about the social forces that produced the ideology it expresses as an atti-

[1] To speak of the proletariat being Marxist in philosophy and politics is, of course, to refer to its class-conscious, literate segment; and with regard to literature and criticism, it is to speak mainly of the middle-class intellectuals who are allied with that segment in the effort to awaken the masses to an understanding of their economic role in a capitalist state and of their historic destiny as outlined by Marx and his associates and successors. Marxists are aware of the fact that most American workers are bourgeois in outlook and ambition, and that they care little about literature and are content with the shoddy they have been taught to read.

tude toward life. Marxism enables us to understand those forces by explaining the dialectical relationship of a culture to an economy and of that culture to the classes which exist in that economy. At the same time, by revealing the creative role of the proletariat in establishing a communist society, which alone can realize universal peace and well-being, Marxism offers a *scale* of value. Moral as well as political judgments follow from that thesis—and they include a condemnation of the bourgeois sexual code, of woman's traditional place in the community, and of the accepted relative prestige of labor and unproductive leisure. Of immediate significance to the critic is the conception of reality from which the thesis is evolved and which the thesis defines.

In the beginning, socialist criticism was unaware of the potentialities of its own philosophy. It sought primarily to praise the writers who sympathized with the exploited lower classes and secondarily to attract writers to the life of the masses as a theme of incalculable richness which had hardly been tapped. This was a purely propagandistic approach. The socialist critics who were analytical employed the economic interpretation of history as their method—which, in many ways, was a great advance over the methods of critics steeped in idealist metaphysics, but was not Marxism. While it could throw light on the nature of whole periods and movements, it could rarely illuminate the distinctive quality of a single work. Moreover, it tended to confuse motives with effects. In several respects, despite his errors and limitations, Taine would have been a corrective to the mechanical linking of literary ideas to economic phenomena. The more dogmatic socialists overlooked the by now familiar remark of Marx that "certain periods of highest development of art stand in no direct connection with the general development of society, nor with the material basis and the skeleton structure of its organization." They forgot that a writer's adjustment to society complements his adjustment as a human being to the mere fact that he is alive. The two adjustments are related—are, indeed, synthesized in his behavior into one—but far more subtly, more delicately than simple-minded socialists would once have had us believe. The dogmatic tendency has persisted in socialist (or communist) criticism; and so has the purely propagandistic approach, which is not put forward as an objective method of evaluating a work of art, but is defended on moral and political grounds which repel or please us according to our social views. As the socialist movement has grown, however, and as familiarity with Marxism as a philosophical discipline has spread, a body of literary criticism, especially theory, has come into being which is neither mechanical nor of obvious utility to agitators, and which represents something new and formidable in the history of esthetic thought.

Socialist criticism in America may conveniently be dated from the founding of the *Comrade*—"An Illustrated Socialist Monthly"—in 1901. It was first published under the editorship of a board consisting of Leonard D. Abbott, George D. Herron, John Spargo, William Mailly, Morris Winchevsky, Algernon Lee, and Peter E. Burrowes. Later John Spargo became the sole editor. Its first issue contained a book-review department, which appeared regularly until the magazine's demise in 1905. The first review established the principle that ran through most of the literary notices and critical essays that followed. It dealt with three books: a volume of essays on literature by Clarence Darrow, a volume of poems by Ernest Crosby, and a theological work. All three were praised because their authors "are men of the true democratic spirit, and all find their inspiration in the coming of a new society that shall redeem the life of the world."

The critics of the *Comrade* looked for an articulation of socialist beliefs, but were responsive to any expression of humane, libertarian, or democratic ideals. That is the long and the short of the magazine's contribution as a pioneer venture in substituting radical social values for strictly ethical ones. There is nothing more to be said of it, for it was simple and unassuming. The magazine consistently published pieces on literature: Ernest Crosby on John Burroughs, Leonard Abbott on Zola and Edwin Markham ("the laureate of labor"), and Spargo on Freiligrath, d'Annunzio, who was then a socialist, and Heine ("he was one of us in the sense that he ever strove against tyranny for the cause of freedom"). References to William Morris, Whitman, Edward Carpenter, and the English Fabians were frequent. The young Swinburne, who was a rebel, was praised; the old Swinburne, who was a jingo during the Boar War, was despised. Needless to say, the magazine had only scorn for the laureate of imperialism, Kipling. The net result was anything but great criticism, but it fulfilled its function of encouraging American writers of radical sympathies and creating an audience for them.

The *Comrade* appeared at the beginning of the muckrake era. It was superior to the muckrakers in the clarity of its vision as to the basic cause of social evils and the way to cure them; but it was in no small degree a reflex of the very thing that gave birth to muckraking—the revolt of certain sections of the middle classes against governments corrupted by big business and against an economy which permitted the injustices and brutalities openly practiced by the trusts against farmers, workers, and small business men. The popularity of socialism among intellectuals at that time may be described as a left-wing manifestation of what was really a reformist movement. All shades of radical opinion tended to come together under the legal and moral pressures exerted by respectable institutions. Hence ideological confusions were rampant. For instance, it was sometimes difficult to decide at what point anarchism and socialism were divided. One of the editors of the *Comrade*, Leonard Abbott, was soon afterwards widely known as a leader in anarchist circles. One of the men it praised and who wrote for it, Ernest Crosby, was a Tolstoyan. Many of its contributors were merely sentimental humanitarians impelled into contact with the socialist movement because it was the focal point of social protest.

As a consequence there was a feeling of kinship between socialist and other radical critics, even when the latter's writings were unmistakably opposed to Marxism. For example, there is no resemblance between Tolstoyan and Marxist historical methods; yet Tolstoy's feelings about the culture of past ages (as exemplified by his *What Is Art?*) have always attracted over-emotional socialists. An instance of this was the cordiality with which socialists discussed Crosby's pamphlet: *Shakespeare's Attitude toward the Working Classes* (1903). This was an examination of Shakespeare's plays to prove that his attitude toward commoners was typically feudal: that he ridiculed them and had no sense of their worth as human beings. It was Crosby's contention that there were English poets before and during Shakespeare's time who had a nobler, more progressive outlook, and that Shakespeare was therefore a reactionary who had swallowed whole the philosophy of the court. There are several things to be said about all this: it is, to say the least, debatable; it shows no awareness of the real character of the epoch in which Shakespeare lived; it overlooks completely the values in Shakespeare that are permanent for all classes; its approach to a problem in literary history, far from being materialistic, is distinctly ethical. Yet socialists did read and applaud the pamphlet —among them being John Spargo, then considered one of the American authorities on Marxism.

But that was doubtless an exceptional case. The usual situation was that radicals wrote similarly about literature no matter what their political theories were. Consider the essays and lectures on the contemporary theatre by the anarchist Emma Goldman: they did not conflict with socialist criticism and were, in fact, very useful in spreading an appreciation of the stage as a social influence and in arousing writers to a realization of their power to move men in the direction of free thought and rational behavior. Those were among the aims of socialist critics, too. They were propagandistic aims, and it was inevitable that they should be paramount in a time when American critical systems were divided between art for art's sake, art for morality's sake, and various compromises between those two exhausted theories of esthetic purpose.[1] Miss Goldman made no bones about her intentions. Her essay on "The Modern Drama" in *Anarchism and Other Essays* (1911) was frankly a salute to its subject as an instrument for the dissemination of radical thought. In it she discussed Sudermann, Hauptmann, Wedekind, Ibsen, Shaw, Galsworthy, and others, expressing complete sympathy with their ideas and methods, which, said Miss Goldman, would help break down the social injustice and sexual hypocrisies that were oppressing humanity. The essay concluded: "The modern drama, operating through the double channel of dramatist and interpreter, affecting as it does both mind and heart, is the strongest force in developing social discontent, swelling the powerful tide of unrest that sweeps onward and over the dam of ignorance, prejudice, and superstition."

This essay was the germ of her major critical work, *The Social Significance of the Modern Drama*, published in 1914. Here she wrote detailed analyses of the plays of the writers listed above and also plays by Strindberg, Maeterlinck, Rostand, Brieux, Yeats, Tolstoy, Tchekov, Gorky, Andreiev, and others less well known. To Miss Goldman, all of these dramatists were bringing closer the day when there would be no gentility, no superstition, and no exploitation of the poor by the rich. They were the vanguard of a free and intelligent race of men. Miss Goldman was not judging their works for all time, not attempting to discover the classics among current productions, and dealing only superficially with esthetic questions. She was intent upon their social significance for the moment, and so it would

[1] "Propaganda" is not used here as an invidious term. It is used to describe works consciously written to have an immediate and direct effect upon their readers' opinions and actions, as distinguished from works that are not consciously written for that purpose or which are written to have a remote and indirect effect. It is possible that conventional critics have learned by now that to call a literary work "propaganda" is to say nothing about its quality as literature. By now enough critics have pointed out that some of the world's classics were originally "propaganda" for something.

not bother her that she overrated many of the plays she wrote about—found profundities where there were platitudes, inspiration where there was rhetoric, realism where there was sentimentality. But she did emphatically dig out of them their social value, their moral implications, *for that moment.*

She worked from premises which had emotional vitality and were in keeping with the spirit of a period much larger than her own day. No one who is "on the side of life" can be pained or bored by her credo: "The modern artist is, in the words of August Strindberg, 'a lay preacher popularizing the pressing questions of his time.' Not necessarily because his aim is to proselyte, but because he can best express himself by being true to life. . . . Both radical and conservative have to learn that any mode of creative work, which with true perception portrays social wrongs earnestly and boldly, may be a greater menace to our social fabric and a more powerful inspiration than the wildest harangues of the soapbox orator. . . . The Modern Drama, as all modern literature, mirrors the complex struggle of life,—the struggle which, whatever its individual or topical expression, ever has its roots in the depth of human nature and social environment, and hence is, to that extent, universal. Such literature, such drama, is at once the reflex and the inspiration of mankind in its eternal seeking for things higher and better. . . . The Modern Drama . . . mirrors every phase of life and embraces every strata of society . . . showing each and all caught in the throes of the tremendous changes going on, and forced either to become part of the process or be left behind. Ibsen, Strindberg, Hauptmann, Tolstoy, Shaw, Galsworthy, and the other dramatists contained in this volume represent the social iconoclasts of our time. They know that society has gone beyond the stage of patching up, and that man must throw off the dead weight of the past, with all its ghosts and spooks, if he is to go foot free to meet the future."

Miss Goldman exaggerated. Many of her beloved dramatists were merely concerned with manners and ethics, seeking reforms within the framework of the old society. It was she who read into their works the need for a new society. Her naïve political predictions need no comment. Nevertheless, it is instructive to compare her dated and rather ingenuous essays with those of Huneker on the same subjects. There were some truths which he, with his sophistication and esthetic sensitiveness, easily perceived, while she missed them entirely. But there were basic truths about meanings and morals to which he was blind and which she glimpsed. It is likely that her essays will be the more fruitful to future historians of those subjects.

It must not be assumed that there were no "scientific" socialist journals in the pre-war period. There were several which tried to be definitely Marxist. Perhaps the most substantial of them was the *International Socialist Review*, published in Chicago from 1901 to 1918 by Charles H. Kerr. Like the rest, unfortunately, it contained little criticism of literature, but that little was animated by doctrines presumed to have been derived from Marx. Typical was John Spargo's review of Marcus Hitch's *Goethe's Faust*, which gave him much "pleasure and satisfaction," wrote Spargo, because "what Comrade Hitch sets out to demonstrate is that, just as the popular psychology is determined by economic conditions, so is the psychology of the masters of literature; that in a word, the ethical standards of such great writers as Goethe reflect the economic conditions of their time. . . ." [1] Hitch's monograph illustrates the inadequacies of an economic interpretation of literary history, and Spargo's remarks about it show how superficially Marx was then understood in the United States, but both were symptomatic of the battle against esthetic mysticism—a battle in which the socialists were philosophically in advance of the others who were trying to bring art down to earth. In general, however, the fragmentary criticism of the *International Socialist Review* indicated that the main interest of socialist critics, like most Amer-

[1] *The International Socialist Review*, Vol. VIII, No. 11 (May 1908), p. 711.

ican critics in the first decades of the twentieth century, was to encourage realism.

The socialist's affinity with realism was stated very forcefully in the leading editorial of the *Masses* in February 1911—the second issue of a magazine (then edited by Thomas Seltzer) which was a successor, on a more mature and "politicalized" level, to the *Comrade*. It said: "It is natural that Socialists should favor the novel with a purpose, more especially, the novel that points a Socialist moral. As a reaction against the great bulk of vapid, meaningless, too-clever American fiction, with its artificial plots and characters remote from actual life, such an attitude is a healthy sign. But it is doubtful whether if the best Socialist novelists were to follow the popular demand, the result would not be harmful to imaginative literature. The writer of fiction, even if Socialistic, may not be restrained by a theory. He must be free from all preconceived notions, even though they may be scientifically true. He must devote himself merely to the reproduction of life as an impartial observer sees it. The less hampered he is by theories, the more likely he is to see and depict life as it actually is. And this is the most important function of the novelist. . . . Socialism has more to gain from a free, artistic literature reflecting life as it actually is, than from an attempt to make facts fit the Socialist theory. Socialism has nothing to fear from a true reproduction of life, because life is never opposed to Socialism."

That represented the best socialist thought of the time. It has been repeated, in various forms, ever since in order to restrain doctrinaire enthusiasts from imposing didactic formulas upon critics and writers. But its psychological insight was childish. One did not have to be a Marxist to learn that no writer comes to a theme without preconceived notions, that no one is an impartial observer of anything, and that progress in thought is impossible without theories. The Marxist would add to that that the disposition of one's partiality—the nature of one's theories—is the question, and it can be answered only in terms of non-esthetic criteria. In a few years the *Masses* would begin, under the literary editorship of Floyd Dell, to speculate about such problems—to examine the real connections between ideas and society and creative genius. For it was Floyd Dell who raised socialist criticism to a plane that would entitle him to be called the true precursor of Marxist critical writing in America.

Dell did not immediately occupy himself with those problems. He had made a reputation in Chicago as a critic whose mind was unfettered by genteel and classical dogmas—a young man of fresh and liberal views, responsive to every experimental and unconventional movement. When he joined the staff of the *Masses*, his further development as a socialist did not, at first, materially alter his literary outlook, which was stimulating to socially-minded artists and readers anyway. The *Masses* had no rigorously defined philosophy, aside from being, as it proclaimed on its masthead, devoted to the working classes. It was as much an organ of bohemia as of socialism; it was a rallying center for all who were enemies of bourgeois respectability, whether in politics or in art. Socialism was, as it happens, a plank in the bohemian platform, partly because it was an extreme form of opposition to the smug burghers, and partly because bohemians, living on the disreputable edges of the capitalist world, were keenly aware of the indecencies and cruelties of a profit economy. But bohemianism has no actual relationship with socialism, and the mixture of the two in the *Masses* resulted in the overshadowing of the latter by the former—probably because American literature in those years really needed the bohemian more than the socialist. At any rate, the critics in the *Masses* were as anxious to free men from bourgeois and academic standards—in life no less than in art—as to create a socialist culture.[1]

[1] It is indicative of the character of the *Masses*, of Dell, and of the era that while its editorials by Max Eastman and its cartoons by Art Young were intensely political, its book-review section was filled with discussions of psychoanalysis, sex, love, and marriage. There was a definite split between politics and everything else in life. No one illustrates that better than Eastman him-

We see that tendency particularly in the *Masses'* criticism of poetry—written chiefly by Louis Untermeyer: it was much the same as that in *Poetry: A Magazine of Verse*, founded in 1911 by Harriet Monroe to champion what we now know as "the poetic renascence." It was decidedly to the good that Lindsay, Masters, Frost, Edna Millay, the imagists, and so on, should be appreciated, but there was no special understanding of what the new poets stood for and no grasp of the significant causes of their sudden and approximately simultaneous appearance. Those are the insights one expects from socialist critics, whose ability to explain cultural phenomena is what first impresses even hostile readers. A decade afterwards—in his remarkable little volume *Intellectual Vagabondage* (1926)—Dell proved that he knew, or had learned, what it was all about, but he did not prove it in 1915 or 1916. Certainly Louis Untermeyer had no such insights. When, in a review of Braithwaite's *Anthology of Magazine Verse for 1915*, he hailed the young modern poets because they had "discarded the faded and moth-eaten loveliness of tradition," he was speaking the truth, but not the whole of it and not explaining it. That can also be said of many of Dell's reviews of contemporary prose works—the novels of Wells and Chesterton, Shaw's *Androcles and the Lion*, Rupert Brooke's *Letters from America*, and others: they were fine, they were alert, their spirit was lively and adventurous; they were not, however, extraordinary. They might have been written by any liberal critic. (It must be confessed that liberal critics were not so plentiful then.) He was a good critic for that time principally because he favored realism, as he made plain on numerous occasions. That is the sole basis, for example, of his keen admiration for *Windy McPherson's Son* by the newcomer Sherwood

self, who was a socialist but whose criticism of poetry contained not the slightest hint of it. Dell, who wrote long pieces on Freud and Jung, made psychoanalysis a literary vogue. Of his generation and his era he wrote, in *Intellectual Vagabondage*, that "we might for a time cease to trouble ourselves about the State; but we could not for long remain untroubled concerning Woman."

Anderson, whose talent Dell was among the first to recognize.

But there was another side to his criticism—a side inspired wholly by his revolutionary principles. Although it was usually only implied, his preference for realism in the novel was, we know, an expression of the socialist's belief that to portray reality is to reveal the need for social change. Sometimes the revolutionary impulse was explicit, uttering statements which could only have come from one who was prepared to break with the old order. In a review of *The Genius* he analyzed Dreiser's mind and past achievements brilliantly—said what had to be said about *Sister Carrie* and *Jennie Gerhardt* and about their author's bewilderment and awe in the face of life's strangeness, cruelty, and beauty—and then, addressing himself directly to Dreiser, he pointed out that the greatest tragic themes are those of rebellion, which Dreiser had never touched. "Life at its best and most heroic is rebellion," wrote Dell. "All artists, big and little, are in their degree rebels. You yourself are a rebel. . . . Why do you not write the American novel of rebellion?"[1] Again, in a review of George Moore's *The Brook Kerith*, Dell wrote: "Mr. Moore has something lacking in him. He does not understand heroism. It may be true that heroism ends in disillusion, just as life ends in death. But to view the magnificent audacities, the tremendous enterprises of idealism, from the plain of disillusion is to fail to understand what it is all about."[2] Here was an esthetic insight that grew out of an insight into life which belonged, though not exclusively, to socialists. Here was a new principle of criticism taking root in America. Eventually it was so strengthened in Dell that it became a major element in his literary thinking.

The *Masses* was banned when the United States entered the war. It was followed by the *Liberator*, edited and written by the *Masses* group minus those who had become patriots and plus a few younger men who were soon to lead the magazine into the

[1] *The Masses*, Vol. VIII, No. 10 (August 1916), p. 30.
[2] Ibid., Vol. IX, No. 1 (November 1916), p. 16.

communist movement. Dell was still the leading critic of the group. By now he had observed the victorious course of the Soviet Revolution, which he had greeted with joy and continued to support; he had been placed on trial along with the other editors of the *Masses* for seditious activities and had seen America become war-mad; he had come to realize how serious was the revolutionary struggle, how much its victory could transform society, and how much it was needed to make imperialist wars impossible. Yet even now his criticism smacked of pre-war moods. It was still, for the most part, an assault upon "bourgeois pieties," still overly interested in Woman and Love, still a defense of individuality against convention. His contributions to the *Liberator* formed a volume called *Looking at Life* (1924), which was so playful and light-hearted that it seems incredible that a socialist could have written such pieces when the socialist movement was fighting for its very existence. He could go so far as to write: "I am not ashamed to say that to me art is more important than the destinies of nations, and the artist a more exalted figure than the prophet. . . ." [1] This was to explain why he believed that art is one thing and politics another.

It was a difficult position to maintain—for anyone sincerely devoted to the kind of politics which may lead to a revolution in culture as well as economics. If, on the one hand, he could praise verse created out of private, sensuous experience, on the other Dell could hail Whittier as "the poet of rebels and revolutionaries." If he could get indignant about Conrad's romanticizing of women, he could also discuss the Catholic "guild socialism" for which Chesterton was an untiring propagandist and the Americanism of Whitman in an age of greed and exploitation. He knew, always, that genuine criticism "begins where sympathies and hatreds alike leave off; it endeavors to understand the movements and tendencies which arouse these emotions"—which was Dell's slap at impressionism.

[1] *The Liberator*, Vol. I, No. 12 (December 1918), p. 45.

Literary movements and tendencies are replies to society's demands; they refuse or comply with those demands. To study a literary movement is, for a socialist, to study its social origin and meaning. When at last Dell began seriously to examine his literary ideas and their antecedents, he produced a work in which the history of literature is related to the history of social thought—the volume entitled *Intellectual Vagabondage*, which ran serially in the *Liberator* in 1923-4 as "Literature and the Machine Age." And when at last he was confronted with a novel which had come out of a socialist culture—a novel built upon emotions and attitudes that were new to literature—Dell thought more deeply than ever before about the effect of a culture, economically and politically defined, upon art, and the result was a piece of criticism more nearly Marxist than anything else he ever wrote. The occasion was a review, in January 1924, of Libedensky's novel *A Week*, which, said Dell, "belongs to us not only because it is about Russia, in which our revolutionary hopes are centered, but because it deals with that revolutionary movement of which we ourselves, however humbly, are a part." He continued, after shrewdly analyzing Gorky's career up to that time, as follows: "The great stories of the past have been stories of individuals; and because all individual effort meets with final defeat, even if it is only the defeat of old age and death, these stories have been tragedies, seen as such by the story-teller. The greatest art of the past has been tragic art, for this reason, since from the individualist point of view life is a tragedy. But the time has come when life can be viewed otherwise; and in the revolutionary art of the present, which presages the art of the future, it must be seen otherwise. The deaths of these men and women, in this story of Libedensky's, do not constitute a tragedy. . . . For they are part of a cause that goes on, that goes on to triumph and would go on no less even if this moment were one of temporary defeat; they belong to that cause, their deaths no less than their lives, and its triumph is their triumph. Their effort, their hope, their heroism, lives on in that cause. There is much that is sad, but nothing that is tragic, about such deaths. Libedensky's book foretells in this matter new conceptions of art, as of life."

We must not exaggerate Dell's growth toward Marxism in our recognition of his pioneering role. As a critic he barely perceived the class factor in culture. That is to say, while he saw that ideological and social tendencies are interwoven, he did not, in his criticism, make use of his knowledge that society is not a harmonious entity but is composed of conflicting classes. It was left for younger men to investigate, clarify, and apply that principle. Dell himself was too much a product of pre-war conditions to be able to participate vigorously in post-war movements.[1] He knew, in the end, the limitations of his own school. In *Intellectual Vagabondage* he remarked that the younger generation "may well feel called upon to liquidate the liberal-and-radical 'freedom' movement which has so obviously reached the point of bankruptcy." Yet Dell's was no mean part in the sowing of what has become this century's major contribution to criticism. Most of our present-day critical theories and practices had their genesis in America during the nineteenth century. Marxist criticism is of recent birth, and its influence and potentialities for future growth (and improvement) are incontestable, while impressionism and expressionism, which were also developed, if not formulated, since 1900, have been either discredited or greatly modified.

---

[1] Floyd Dell's autobiography, *Homecoming* (1933), is an honest and charming account of his intellectual history. Joseph Freeman's autobiography, *An American Testament* (1936), contains an excellent analysis of the *Masses,* the *Liberator,* and Dell.

# CHAPTER VIII

# THE WAR OF TRADITIONS

ITS militancy is the most obvious characteristic of American criticism since the war. In the whole of the nineteenth century there was only one critic, Poe, who was deliberately and consistently disputatious. No one else made polemics the basis of a critical method. Whitman was a maverick, but he was exclamatory rather than argumentative. Now, however, it is customary for critics to be bellicose, and there are few who have let politeness stand in the way of controversy.

The reason is not hard to find. Criticism in our time has been largely a war of traditions—a struggle between irreconcilable ideologies. On one side stand the defenders of various antiquated faiths, by no means in agreement with each other but all opposed to the principles and methods peculiar to the twentieth century; on the other stand the exponents of modern tendencies, their mutual antagonisms unresolved even in their conflicts with the traditionalists. These critical wars are not just esthetic debates. They have been passionate, they have often been acrimonious, because they involve social, political, moral, and religious philosophies; they are conflicts between ways of life, between classes, and between cultures.

Huneker, Spingarn, and Dell were the founders of our modern schools. Almost all contemporary American criticism, when it is not simply a continuation of the past, may be outlined according to the ideas or sentiments they advocated. But within the outlines there are significant departures from the original patterns: profound reservations, advances along lines previously only suggested, crosses with older ideas and practices, and unions with one or both of the other modern systems. Most striking has been the later development of socialist criticism. In its present form, however, this school of thought was a minor force in the 1920's; it commanded a small public, attracted few critics, and affected scarcely a handful of writers. Mencken and Van Wyck Brooks were the representative critics of those years. Each made use of ideas we have already encountered, but adjusted and reformulated in terms of latter-day needs and issues. They had stature and power because they mastered their material and expressed their points of view clearly and confidently. They were able to do so because they knew whom they were speaking to. They weren't beckoning from a mountain-top to the crowd on the plains; they didn't have to be self-conscious about deviating from convention: their audience was always right at hand. Journalism in an age in which history began to be measured by years instead of generations was having its effect: literary movements spread and receded faster now than formerly; the public kept up with its prophets.

First, as an influence, came Mencken. He captured, trained, and led the audience Huneker had discovered. There were, to be sure, critics who were even more like Huneker than he was: for example, Ernest Boyd, whose volume of *Studies from Ten Literatures* (1925) is studded with phrases like "good Europeans" and "civilized man of cosmopolitan and international culture"—phrases used to indicate how wise, how admirable, what fine thinkers and artists are the subjects to which they refer. He was no less subjective than Huneker, affirming that "personal taste and emotion . . . in the last analysis, is the only basis of literary criticism." And like Huneker he wrote chiefly of European letters, seeking to function as an antidote to provincialism and to educate a rising generation in the achievements of foreigners (in this case mostly Irishmen). Mencken's former associate, George Jean Nathan, was also closer to Huneker in both spirit and style. He was for many years America's most celebrated dramatic critic because he helped do for the theatre what Huneker had started to do for the arts generally; drove out the moralists, the sentimentalists, and the prissy gentlemen, and made it a place where one might enjoy every variety of sensual and intellectual experience (except the social revolutionary). He, too, has written much about Continental artists. He, too, is a subjectivist pure and simple. And his hedonism is a matter of record: he has described it as his total credo in a symposium called *Living Philosophies*, published in 1931. He is the perfect type of the leisure-class cosmopolite —ethically skeptical, physically indulgent, politically cynical. He is to William Winter what Huneker was to Aldrich.

But Mencken had qualities of which none of his colleagues, allies, or imitators could boast. He had style: his prose was distinctive, energetic, packed with explosive phrases. He had humor: he could entertain his readers, make them laugh—not with subtle wit, but with "wisecracks" that seemed very funny, at the time they were written. He had a purpose, which is to say that he was frankly a fighter and could therefore excite people, unlike a man like Nathan, who professed to have no enthusiasms. He had the gift of making his readers believe that they were among the "civilized minority" that was supposed to uphold reason and taste against the onslaughts of the stupid, loutish mob. He had the shrewdness to stay at home, preoccupying himself with the American scene, which is easier to comprehend and more amusing to talk about than the arts and letters of distant and unfamiliar lands. And, most important of all, he had a philosophy: his prejudices were completely rationalized— his theory of criticism becoming part of his interpretation of life, which overlooked no phase of human behavior. In short, his esthetics, his sociology, and his ethics were all one—which is as it should be.

*Nietzsche Americanized* is about as accurate a summary of the intellectual content of Mencken's philosophy as we need. For the rest—he merely brought energy to despair, Waldo Frank once remarked. Here, in brief, was his credo: class distinctions are not economic and conventional, but congenital and genuine. The few at the top of society are naturally aristocrats. Without them there can be no art, no disinterested thought, no fine manners, and none of the blessings of civilized society (good food, good wine, good conversation, and so on). The masses are essentially brutish, evil, and incompetent; they are instinctively hostile to culture, to rational conduct, and to esthetic discrimination. The first problem of politics is to keep them docile; the second is to prevent them from interfering with their betters. There are no such things as truth and progress. The superior man expects nothing but an opportunity to enjoy himself. One of his major pleasures is to laugh at the antics and idiocies of the herd.

The following excerpts from *A Book of Prefaces* (1917) and his several volumes of *Prejudices* (1919-27) show how his social and literary ideas were interwoven, his thoughts in one field illuminating his thoughts in the other: American literature is mediocre because "the United States has not yet produced anything properly describable as an aristocracy, and so there is no impediment to the domination of the inferior orders. . . ." The South is a "Sahara of the Bozart" because it has been "drained of all its best blood. The vast blood-letting of the Civil War half exterminated and wholly paralyzed the old aristocracy, and so left the land to the harsh mercies of the poor white trash, now its masters. . . ." "The primary aim of the novel, at all times and everywhere, is the representation of human beings at their follies and villainies, and no other art form clings to that aim so faithfully. It sets forth, not what might be true, but what actually *is* true . . . [and] if it departs from that representational fidelity ever so slightly, it becomes to that extent a bad novel. . . ." Joseph Conrad "brings into the English fiction of the day, not only an artistry that is vastly more fluent and delicate than the general, but also a highly unusual sophistication, a quite extraordinary detachment from all petty rages and puerile certainties. The winds of doctrine, howling all about him, leave him absolutely unmoved.

He belongs to no party and has nothing to teach, save only a mystery as old as man. . . . He stands apart and almost alone, observing the sardonic comedy of man with an eye that sees every point and significance of it, but vouchsafing none of that sophomoric indignation, that Hyde Park wisdom, that flabby moralizing which freight and swamp the modern English novel."

Let us see how, in one of his most famous essays, he applied those doctrines to a living American novelist: "The general ideas which lie at the bottom of all of Dreiser's work . . . are not unlike the fundamental assumptions of Joseph Conrad. Both novelists see human existence as a seeking without a finding; both reject the prevailing interpretations of its meaning and mechanism; both take refuge in 'I don't know.' . . . The struggle of man as he [Dreiser] sees it, is more than impotent; it is gratuitous and purposeless. . . . Man is not only doomed to defeat, but denied any glimpse or understanding of his antagonist. . . . But this skepticism is often tempered by guesses at a possibly hidden truth, and the confession that this truth may exist reveals the practical unworkableness of the unconditioned system, at least for Dreiser. Conrad is far more resolute, and it is easy to see why. He is, by birth and training, an aristocrat. He has the gift of emotional detachment. The lures of facile doctrine do not move him. In his irony there is a disdain which plays about even the ironist himself. Dreiser is a product of far different forces and traditions, and is capable of no such escapement. . . . One half of the man's brain, so to speak, wars with the other half. He is intelligent, he is thoughtful, he is a sound artist—but there come moments when a dead hand falls upon him, and he is once more the Indiana peasant, snuffling absurdly over imbecile sentimentalities, giving a grave ear to quackeries, snorting and eye-rolling with the best of them. One generation spans too short a time to free the soul of man."

His notion of realism as a means of expressing a fatalistic and cynical philosophy was much broader in practice than in theory. The emphasis was on the philosophy rather than the method. It had to be, for the method was likely to be inspired by motives—and to lead to conclusions—that were contrary to his. Thus he championed men who were not realists at all—men like Cabell and Hergesheimer—but whose view of life was as pleasing to him as Dreiser's. His inclination to agree with those who "take refuge in 'I don't know' " was doubtless the source of his praise for Sherwood Anderson. In Anderson he saw also a confirmation of his feelings about the meanness and cruelty of rural and small-town life. His contempt for moral hypocrisy and his hatred of social and political cant were evident in his loud cheers for Sinclair Lewis. Any writer who laughed at idealism, jeered at the superstitions of the common man, conceived of life as essentially meaningless and therefore unknowable, and portrayed men as creatures of dignity and wisdom only when they held themselves aloof from the mass, refused to rebel against injustice and tyranny, and scrutinized their fellows with a nicely balanced mixture of pity and scorn, was almost sure to win Mencken's esteem. For such an artist he would create an audience—not merely in the sense of collecting potentially sympathetic readers, but in the sense of educating them to a full appreciation of the approved attitude. More, he found the material for his artist: pointed out the manifold aspects of life in America that would lend themselves to such treatment.

If one simply names the writers whom Mencken selected for applause, his perspicacity as a critic seems proved beyond cavil. A critic makes himself immortal when he does for a novelist of magnitude who is neglected or maligned what Mencken did for Dreiser. A critic may justly take pride in knowing that he contributed to the success of a *Main Street* and a *Babbitt*. In the light of such feats, his succumbing to a Hergesheimer seems unimportant. And the fact is that Mencken's service to American literature cannot be measured: by establishing Dreiser as a contemporary classic he smashed whatever barriers to realism still remained; by making *Babbitt* fashionable, he sanctioned critical and satirical studies of American manners. But if one examines the reasoning behind his selections, doubts enter. It occurs to us that it was possible for Floyd Dell and Randolph Bourne to appreciate Dreiser, and for the former to appreciate Anderson, from standpoints quite different from Mencken's. It occurs to us that younger critics have been impressed by Lewis's novels on other grounds than Mencken's— that they have drawn inferences from *Babbitt* and *Main Street* that must enrage Mencken.[1] It occurs to us, then, that we *cannot* ignore his unfortunate enthusiasms, for, being similarly arrived at, they were no less ardent and persuasive than the fortunate ones. Cabell and Hergesheimer were not his only errors: what are we to think of a process of reasoning that convinces a critic that he ought to embrace a trivial comedian like George Ade, whom he called "one of the few genuinely original literary craftsmen now in practice among us . . . a great instinctive artist"? Such a selection makes us recall the curious fact that he had no plaudits for Hemingway and Dos Passos, although he saw the worth of their contemporary, Scott Fitzgerald.[2] Clearly, his reasoning did not encompass the whole of a subject and it was not infallible. It was successful, we know now, when the works it led him to admire had wider significance and other applications than he thought to be the case; and it was unsuccessful when the works it led him to reject had values with which he had no sympathy.

[1] See Robert Cantwell's essay on Lewis in *After the Genteel Tradition: American Writers since 1910*, a collective work edited by Malcolm Cowley (New York, 1937).

[2] His uniformly bad criticism of poetry is a problem in itself. Some have said that he had no ear or feeling for poetry. A more tangible source of error was his conception of the art: he defined poetry as "a comforting piece of fiction set to more or less lascivious music." From such nonsense came, inevitably, his statement that "Lizette Woodworth Reese . . . has written more sound poetry, more genuinely eloquent and beautiful poetry, than all the new poets put together—more than a whole posse of Masterses and Lindsays, more than a hundred Amy Lowells. And there are others [who are superior to the 'new poets'], Neihardt and John McClure among them. . . ." Later he praised Masters extravagantly.

Hence to evaluate his criticism we must appraise his entire philosophy, for we subscribe to his literary opinions only if we agree with his interpretation of life. That is to say, we see in his favorites what he saw in them, we fail to see in them what he failed to see, and we refuse recognition to the writers he disliked, only if our beliefs about the nature of the universe and the history of the race coincide with his. Mencken would assent to that basis of judgment. His criticism was subjective, but it was not restricted to sensory impressions. He often spanked the genteel professors for grounding their criticism upon ethical criteria, arguing for "a purely aesthetic judgment upon an aesthetic question," but his own procedure was never purely esthetic. Indeed, when he took the trouble to write a more or less formal theory of criticism, he chided the esthetes and gave to critics the latitude their profession requires: in his essay "Criticism of Criticism of Criticism" he said: "beauty as we know it in this world is by no means the apparition *in vacuo* that Mr. Spingarn seems to see. It has its social, its political, even its moral implications. The finale of Beethoven's C minor symphony is not only colossal as music; it is also colossal as revolt; it says something against something. Yet more, the springs of beauty are not within itself alone, nor even in genius alone, but often in things without. Brahms wrote his Deutsches Requiem, not only because he was a great artist, but also because he was a good German. . . . To denounce moralizing out of hand is to pronounce a moral judgment. To dispute the categories is to set up a new anti-categorical category." Again, in his essay "Footnote on Criticism," he said: "The feelings that happen to be dominant in him [the critic] at the moment the scribbling frenzy seizes him are feelings inspired, not directly by life itself, but by books, pictures, music, sculpture, architecture, religion, philosophy—in brief, by some other man's feelings about life. They are thus, in a sense, secondhand, and it is no wonder that creative artists so easily fall into the theory that they are also second-rate. Perhaps they usually are. If, indeed, the critic continues on this plane—if he lacks the intellectual agility and enterprise needed to make the leap from the work of art to the vast and mysterious complex of phenomena behind it—then they *always* are, and he remains no more than a fugleman or policeman to his betters. But if a genuine artist is concealed within him—if his feelings are in any sense profound and original, and his capacity for self-expression is above the average of educated men—then he moves inevitably from the work of art to life itself, and begins to take on a dignity that he formerly lacked."

Let us now, therefore, weigh the "vast and mysterious complex of phenomena"—the precepts, biases, insights, theories, knowledge which compose the philosophy—behind Mencken's criticism. Our first observation is that his is consciously and frankly a class philosophy. If you do not belong or do not desire to belong to the class for and to which he spoke, the substance of his philosophy is repellent to you. It is the very opposite of a universal or timeless system of thought. It is a doctrine of inhumanity and quiescence. Our second observation is that it includes a host of notions about genetics, sociology, political economy, and history which are either unproved or disproved. They are notions born of upper-class prejudices and advanced by upper-class apologists, but they are not defensible upon scientific or logical grounds.

If through those observations we can understand where and why his vision was limited or faulty, what do we find to explain his successes? We observe that the general drift of his philosophy was in the direction of agnosticism and determinism. He was against the churches, against mysticism and spiritualism. To that extent he was in the broad movement of modern thought and was close to the hearts and minds of modern novelists. We observe, further, that he despised the provincial petty bourgeois. His motives were aristocratic, but the result placed him, in that respect, on the side of the bohemians and the socialists. Those two factors in his thinking were responsible for his most useful, best executed, and most effective critical writings. They produced, for example, his essay on "Puritanism as a Literary Force" and all the subsequent attacks upon comstockery, philistinism, and gentility. Finally, we observe that because he was untouched by the ideals of refinement that prevailed in genteel and academic circles, he was capable of enjoying the specifically American tendencies in our cultural tradition. This was directly responsible for his greatest work, *The American Language*, and was an element in his appreciation of writers whose "vulgarity" the professors deprecated.

The fate of his philosophy explains the rise and decline of his position as a critic. When his political and moral ideas were popular, his literary influence was great; when they weren't, his influence declined. His career is thus a key to certain aspects of the social history of the past quarter-century.

The first issue of the *American Mercury* appeared in December 1923. Menckenism was at its height in the five years that followed. To whom, in those five fat years, was despair a comfortable and pleasant mood? Who could afford to be tolerant and skeptical, yet argue that attempts to reform or improve this miserable world are futile? Who was it that could calmly, even eagerly, describe man as half wolf and half jackass? The question almost answers itself: the educated among the prosperous middle classes of the large cities, and especially the young ones. The elders functioned in the public world in a truly realistic and cynical manner, but in their private worlds they were often afflicted with vestigial cravings for respectability. Their sons and daughters were too sophisticated to make such arbitrary and artificial distinctions. They were the "emancipated"—a generation which had passed beyond the stage of flirtatiousness and was asserting its desire to enjoy every pleasure provided by a society of which, for very good reasons, it was disdainful.

In Mencken's editorials and essays they found an intellectual pattern for the urban tory. One must study his battle with the orthodox professors to realize what that meant—that his conservatism was a revolutionary force. His sneers at such timid souls as Mabie and Van Dyke, whose gentility was sickly, were doubtless needed, but much more important was his grappling with the New Humanists—Paul Elmer More, Irving Babbitt, W. C. Brownell, et al. This was not a war between tories and liberals, but between two kinds of tories—between the culture of a squirearchic and mercantile community and the culture of a community whose wealth was mobile. The clash was over the question of regulation. Mencken and More agreed that men are knaves and fools, but while More deduced therefrom that they must be ruled with an iron hand, Mencken claimed that their greed and stupidity ensure the permanence of an individualistic society and that to regulate it is to deny the superior man the pleasures to which his superiority entitles him. More was terrified by a literature of unrestricted exploration and expression, while Mencken regarded that literature as the sustenance of the free-thinking and the disillusioned. Let us not have books, More (or Babbitt) would say, that stir up thoughts and emotions which are inimical to a proper veneration of the ancient rules of conduct, or society will collapse. Preposterous, Mencken would reply; you are not keeping the mob in its place, but simply denying the civilized man the privilege of experience.

An aristocratic attitude based on laissez-faire sentiments could hardly fail to be attractive in the fat years—when people were on the make and, to the contented and the short-sighted, it seemed naïve to hope for radical social changes. It became unattractive, to put it mildly, when the lean years arrived. Then its accent on personal freedom became less conspicuous than its fatalism and exclusiveness. As a principle of literary criticism, what had once been a tool to squeeze the desiccated culture of New England out of America's literary life was now useless. Of what interest was it in an age corrupted by poverty, threatened by war, and rotten with a fear of living? How could it possibly interpret the ideological movements that were rising out of the chaos of capitalism's desperate hour? It was no longer a creative principle, but a conservative one.

2

Freedom of expression is the one issue on which the critics of this century have been united. They have all fought against taboos and on behalf of the artist's right to strike out in new directions. In that sense they have all been liberals. But they have also sought to point out the directions that the artist would be wise to choose, and the fact that their preferences have been dissimilar is an indication of the ambiguity of liberalism. As a social philosophy which grew out of the idea of liberty, individualism is always and under any guise its central force. Individualism, may, however, be based on either of two sentiments: respect or contempt for mankind. The former, crystallized into a belief that human beings are potentially good and that they must therefore be protected against those who are in a position to enchain, degrade, or exploit them, is as much in opposition to Nietzsche's adulation of the strong as to classical philosophies. It is that sentiment, of course, that is usually associated with liberalism; and it is not the "rugged individualist" but the idealist that we think of as the typical liberal.

Humane individualism—in its modern form largely a product of the French Revolution—was given its greatest impetus in America by the transcendentalists. After Whitman, however, it took on new characteristics: the mystical gave way to materialist strains; and because of the pressures of a capitalist society which utilized the principle of liberty in unexpected ways, certain compromises were made with collectivist ideas. Who were now the liberals? They were mostly writers of middle-class birth who expressed the sentiments of people who had occupations or professions that were either unconnected with or in some degree despoiled or frustrated by the workings of modern finance and business. The writers themselves were part of that stratum of society. It was an educated and rather proud class, for its members were doctors, teachers, ministers, independent farmers, and small merchants, and allied with them were many technicians and white-collar workers who resented their social status as dependents of corporate enterprises. Their position was anomalous. On the one hand they were hostile to capital because it was corrupting American politics and regimenting the thought and mechanizing the life of the community; on the other hand they were resisting socialism because it denied the sacredness of the individual. They sympathized with the common people, yet were close to the upper classes in education and manners. They participated in political contests that were waged over economic interests, yet they were concerned principally with problems of social and personal morality. Confusion was the consequence: the range of social attitudes for which the title of liberal could be claimed was astonishingly wide. The kind of cultural and literary criticism that was called liberal was accordingly chaotic and contradictory. Nevertheless, generalizations are not impossible: there were main currents.[1]

Consider the group that ran the *Nation* when Carl Van Doren became its literary editor. He served in that capacity from 1919 to 1922, during which time he had as his associates Ludwig Lewisohn, Mark Van Doren, and Joseph Wood Krutch. Van Doren told his readers what he demanded of a book, to wit: "Is it alive?" He said further: "The measure of the creator is

[1] Here the main currents are necessarily merely touched upon. The time is too recent, the number of its critics too large, for justice to be done to either the period or its individuals. The materials available for the future historian include *Farewell to Reform* by John Chamberlain (1932), which is the best study we have of American liberalism in action and is itself an example of liberalism become self-critical; and numerous autobiographies, including Randolph Bourne's *History of a Literary Radical* (1920), Ludwig Lewisohn's *Up Stream* (1923), Sherwood Anderson's *A Story-Teller's Story* (1924), Alfred Kreymborg's *Troubadour* (1925), Harold Stearns's *The Street I Know* (1935), Carl Van Doren's *Three Worlds* (1936), Mabel Dodge Luhan's *Movers and Shakers* (1936), and Burton Rascoe's *Before I Forget* (1937), as well as Floyd Dell's and Joseph Freeman's volumes.

the amount of life he puts into his work. The measure of the critic is the amount of life he finds there." This, in itself, was meaningless. The question is: what does the critic consider to be vital? Van Doren subsequently answered that question. "We were held together," he wrote of his colleagues and himself, "by a shared passion for literature as an art so interwoven with life that neither could be understood without the other. This passion set the tone of criticism in the new Nation and has marked it ever since." The point of departure was, then, a conviction that literature must deal with real emotions, real thoughts, real experience. A work did not have to be realistic in the technical sense, but it did have to express what men and women were actually feeling, thinking, or suffering. The points of arrival were the essential liberal faith in freedom and enlightenment and an eagerness to share in the revolt of the "younger generation" against the *mores* of the village.

That faith and that cordiality toward the younger writers made the *Nation* a healthy and positive influence in the days when a wide public was first beginning to welcome the "new poets" and the non-genteel novelists. And it made Van Doren one of the better historians of American literature, as well as an enthusiastic guide to contemporary writing. But, by his own admission, it did not make him a philosophical critic; he did not concern himself with the nature or the movement of American culture, nor with esthetic theory, nor with the tendencies that indicated the future relationship of the artist and the people. "More and Babbitt, Sherman and Mencken, Lewisohn and Van Wyck Brooks, all demanded that literature take more certain courses toward more certain ends than I felt any need for," he wrote in his autobiography. "They took part in controversies. I never did."

Lewisohn was the *Nation* critic who inquired into the purpose and the psychological sources of literature and criticism. He was easily the most militant of the group and, at that time, its philosopher. He made the doctrine of individual liberty a stick with which to beat the More-Babbitt school, but for ends that had no resemblance to Mencken's. In *The Creative Life* (1924) he said to the prophets of the "inner check": "You speak of us as undisciplined. You do not know what discipline is. To narrow the possible choices of life is to eliminate discipline more and more. Your true conservatives are the animals whose habits know no change in a thousand generations. They practise no discipline because they need none." Lewisohn's own purpose was as remote from the disciplinarian's as could be: "It is the remediable moral suffering in the world that crowds my vision—the remediable moral suffering, remediable by a little hard thinking, a little tolerance, a little more goodness, a little less righteousness. If I write a criticism it is to further that supreme end; if I write a novel it is to further the same end." This he justified by what is now a platitude of criticism, but none the less a truth: "Literature, since it deals with the actions and passions of men, must express both the values which men hold and live by and the author's attitude toward those values which is, in turn, the necessary expression of his own. Hence literature can no more avoid moral and philosophical and even political and economic issues than a man can jump out of his skin."

Two significant traits of the liberal mind are already evident: a disposition to talk about social and cultural phenomena in moral and psychological terms; and hopefulness founded on nothing more substantial than a faith in the social efficacy of appeals to reason. Lewisohn's next step was the logical one—a plea for the "open mind" that was once the liberal's pride and which was really nothing but uncertainty, for an unwillingness to make decisions is a sign of doubt and confusion. "Literature must go upon a voyage of discovery. It must immerse itself in a study of human nature as human nature really is," he wrote. "We have not yet reached the stage of interpretation; we cannot yet build up an intelligible world. We shall not reach that stage for years, perhaps not for generations. Salvation is far off.

But again the analogy of the sciences should help us. In regard to morals we are still in what might be called the alchemistic and astrological stage. We are still in the grip of fiction and superstition. We must have patience and bear with the artists who give us facts and confessions, in order that some day the age of chemistry and astronomy may dawn upon that world of conduct and spiritual values which is the supreme concern of us all."

With all his talk of science, it is plain that Lewisohn's misty and emotional philosophizing reflected a wholly unscientific, a non-materialist, conception of the history of society. It reflected that idealistic individualism (the adjective to be emphasized equally with the noun) that made most liberal thought humane, charming, and unrealistic—the last because it was deficient in understanding of the modern state. Everything Lewisohn wrote was a defense of individuality, of personality interpreted with no reference to its origins in social relationships. An earlier work, *The Spirit of Modern German Literature* (1916), was precisely such a defense, asserting "the eternal separateness and uniqueness of the individual and his struggle for liberation from the weight and uniformity of life." Toward the end of the 1920's he moved away from the traditional liberal position, without, however, revising the emotional individualism that was the root of both his critical method and his social philosophy. But then, when liberalism was in crisis, it was not Lewisohn but the third of the *Nation's* celebrated critics, Joseph Wood Krutch, who came forward to defend the free and skeptical intellectual.

Van Doren was tolerant and inquisitive, Lewisohn was passionate and affirmative, but both were concerned primarily with liberating the artist on the premise that the truths he would learn and the beauty he would find would inspire and enlighten the rest of us. Men might be made finer, more reasonable, by an art born of sincere and uninhibited self-expression. There were liberal critics who did not go that far—who were interested in the art with little regard for its wider moral implications. Such were Francis Hackett and Burton Rascoe, both of whom got their start in Chicago, the former becoming the first literary editor of the *New Republic*, the latter becoming editor of the *New York Herald Tribune "Books"*—a post he lost eventually because he championed the foes of gentility. Their critical writings had no discernible philosophy behind them, no social values to correct and illuminate their subjective tests of esthetic value. They were entirely personal in approach, and their charm was personal. Both encouraged an adventurous and experimental literature; neither touched on first principles. Their affinity (especially Rascoe's) with the Huneker school is obvious.

But there were liberal critics who went much farther than the *Nation* group—critics whose major interests were the truths the artist would learn and the beauty he would find after he was liberated. They refused to believe that they had to wait generations to build an intelligible world. They knew that the materials for reaching the stage of interpretation were right at hand. "Self-expression to what end?" they asked. What constitutes fineness?—reasonableness? Above all, how is the artist to be liberated? Questions of that order led them to fundamental problems. They transcended the ego of the intellectual, realizing that the quality of the individual is determined chiefly by the quality of the community. They saw, in other words, that the problem was greater than the mere destruction of taboos. First they had to evaluate a culture: what were the social pressures that have warped, weakened, or hampered the artist? And what traditions have favored him ("the usable past")? Secondly, they had to decide what aims they would strive to achieve. Thirdly, they had to create standards of judgment out of the experience, the aspirations, and the known potentialities of human beings.

Among those critics were Van Wyck Brooks, Randolph Bourne, Waldo Frank, Harold Stearns, James Oppenheim, and

Lewis Mumford, writing, at various times, for the *Seven Arts*, the *New Republic*, and the *Freeman*. From them came the most challenging, the most fruitful, and probably the most important body of critical writing that this century has yet produced. Their significant accomplishment was their analysis of the history of American culture, which showed us, as we had not before been shown, the sources of America's literature and the idiosyncrasies of the national mind. But they had fatal weaknesses. They stemmed, to a greater degree than some of them knew, from Emerson and Whitman. They were idealists, although it had long ago become apparent that idealism is incapable of assimilating all the facts of history; they were individualists in an age when individualism was becoming a reactionary force. They tended toward romantic attitudes, toward the same adoration of the artist as a seer that was betraying Ludwig Lewisohn. Romantic, too, was their treatment of society as a unit. "Wholeness" was Waldo Frank's fetish, and he merely exaggerated what was in the minds of all of them. Van Wyck Brooks was their leader—the first, the ablest, the most prophetic of them in their liberal stage—and his development reveals where and why they were frustrated, and predicted their dispersion.

It was in 1915 that Brooks's voice, curiously strong despite its gentleness, urbanity, and patience, became significant in the councils of criticism. In that year, in a volume entitled *America's Coming-of-Age*, he made certain observations about our literature and asked certain questions about the future of our culture that were startling to a people habitually determined upon treasuring the former and saluting the latter. We know that he was not the first to trouble the waters. But Brooks was not a "foreigner," not a Catholic, not a Jew, not a Westerner, not a radical, not even simply a New Yorker corrupted by those alien influences. He was a Yankee of Protestant descent who had been graduated from Harvard. That was the crucial thing. He was a native, brought up in the traditional home of our dearest literary heritage. Its past was in his bones, its spirit was his spirit. Yet he turned against it. His turning was not merely a skirmish; he was not satisfied with picking inadequacies and pointing to desirable adventures. He wrestled with the whole of American life, with its literature and philosophy and their relation to the soil from which they had grown, and he did so in the very language of his subject. *His* conclusions, ironical, subtly contemptuous, but ultimately inspiring, could not be repudiated on the ground that he was incapable of understanding the things he dealt with.

He was a brilliant youth, but *America's Coming-of-Age* was not an immaculate conception. He had plowed the ground for it. Seven years before, he had published a little book called *The Wine of the Puritans* in which he examined (although without arriving at a final decision) some of the issues that became his lifelong preoccupation. Then had come his studies of Symonds and Wells and a collection of essays on European writers, three books in which he dwelt upon figures who were products of a richer, older, and presumably freer civilization than ours, yet whose lives illuminated the problems *we* faced. When Brooks turned again to the mind of his own country, he knew exactly what he wanted.

As a practicing critic, he wanted more than anything else a great literature made "out of American life"—a literature that would constitute the soul of his people, at once born of the race's spiritual experiences and upholding those experiences for the race to live by. Only Whitman, of the classics, could be accepted in the light of such an ideal, he said. In all the others—Hawthorne, Irving, Bryant, Longfellow, Emerson, Lowell, Poe—"something has always been wanting . . . a certain density, weight and richness, a certain poignancy, a 'something far more deeply interfused,' is simply not there."

Having said so much, Brooks went deeper—to the civilization which created that literature. (For literary criticism, he said elsewhere, "is always impelled sooner or later to become social criticism . . . because the future of our literature and art depends upon the wholesale reconstruction of a social life all the elements of which are as if united in a sort of conspiracy against the growth and freedom of the spirit.") And about that civilization, that way of thought, he could say little or nothing that might flatter the intellectual jingoes. He wrote: "From the beginning we find two main currents in the American mind—both equally unsocial: on the one hand, the transcendental current, originating in the piety of the Puritans, becoming a philosophy in Jonathan Edwards, passing through Emerson, producing the fastidious refinement and aloofness of the chief American writers, and resulting in the final unreality of most contemporary culture; and on the other hand the current of catchpenny opportunism, originating in the practical shifts of Puritan life, becoming a philosophy in Franklin, passing through the American humorists, and resulting in the atmosphere of our contemporary business life."

It was true in its time, and utterly damning, and it was sufficient to make his book extremely important. But not even then was his thesis complete, for he was courageous enough to confront the end of his reasoning and honest enough to state it. Since it was the American mind, American culture, society, that was the source of our failures and frustrations in literature, it was necessary to put forth a new social ideal—one "that shall work upon us as the sun acts upon a photographic plate, that shall work as a magnet upon all these energies which are on the point of being released"—an ideal that would fuse matter and spirit into an "organic whole." Simply and briefly, self-fulfillment as an ideal had to be substituted for self-assertion. "On the economic plane, this implies socialism; on every other plane it implies something which a majority of Americans in our day certainly do not possess—an object in living."

But this, after all, is an old and rather dull story, you may say. Precisely; and because you have said it you have shown how deeply his theory has penetrated into our literary thinking.

It was not an old story when he first told it. Consider again the points made by Mr. Brooks in the course of his argument: America's esthetic taste, after a hundred and fifty years, was still immature, its belles-lettres still afflicted with pernicious anemia; the reasons for these conditions lay in the Puritan and pioneer traditions, the springs of an excessively utilitarian and commercial environment; the artist could function in that environment only by escaping to an ethereal private world or by conforming to the artifices and duplicities of convention, neither of which was a happy choice; and no other way out existed than the way toward collectivism.

Now, it cannot be said that any of these points was "original" or "revolutionary." We have seen that the utilitarian character of American life was damned for its strangling effect upon our literature many times by many writers in the nineteenth century; indeed, a glance in that direction was made as long ago as 1799 by Charles Brockden Brown. Certainly an interest in the unity of literary and social criticism was not unique: William Dean Howells, to take just one example, had occasionally approximated it. Nor was he alone in his belief in socialism as the prerequisite of a great art in the twentieth century: the socialists had said the same thing before and were saying it better, more persistently, and more vigorously. But who before Brooks, in a study of American literature and culture, had united all those elements so clearly, cogently, and persuasively? And who else, in the years just before and during the World War, had so accurately keyed the pitch of his argument to the *Zeitgeist*?

The time was the Wilsonian era, the period of the "New Freedom," when one could justly say, as Brooks himself said, that "a fresh and more sensitive emotion seems to be running up and down the old Yankee backbone." The scene has already been sketched. It need hardly be demonstrated that Brooks's work was a perfect and glowing expression, in criticism, of the temper of those years.

To say that he fitted his age is in no way to detract from his accomplishment. It is to say only that the age was ready for him, for his sentiments were such as belong to rebels and idealists always. The particular ideas in which his sentiments were embodied could not have exercised so great an influence before then, but they have since become the *minimum* platform of liberal and radical writers, who, it happens, have consistently formed the "younger" generation of critics. In a sense, he had nothing more to say, except to refine, strengthen, and at last systematize his principles. In one respect he had overstated his position: modern American literature was not really so barren as he would have had us believe. Dreiser had already published his masterpieces. In another respect he had understated it: the broad tendencies he described and judged were too generalized and inclusive. The history of American society is not a simple, continuous line, but a complex of conflicts, tensions, and resulting progressions. It was essential that Brooks analyze the charted streams into their obscure but definitely separate currents in order to clarify the points of agreement and disagreement between diverse groups of artists and philosophers in the past as well as the present. Otherwise he might be accused of distorting a reality that was damnable enough without distortions.

If we may be allowed for a moment to project the experience of the 1930's into 1918, we may see at once that his next book, *Letters and Leadership,* was not quite the work anticipated. It was unquestionably a brilliant performance; it is probably the most effective piece of writing he has yet given us. But it marked an advance in style, not thought; in polish, not analysis. It did neither of the two things it should have done: it did not dig into the subsoil of American history, in which might lie the completed explanation of the contradictions in our cultural evolution, nor did it apply Brooks's known point of view to the writings of living men, which might explain the value and destination of contemporary thought. It referred to Dreiser and the *Spoon River Anthology* of Masters only to use them as illustrations of the gracelessness and cruelty of American life—references that tended to overlook the vast creative energy and the rebellious outlook inherent in both men. It castigated More, Babbitt, and Brownell, but failed to place them, failed to interpret them. For the rest, it was an enlarged and bolder treatment of the residual theme of *America's Coming-of-Age*, a study of the hollowness of our literature, the shapelessness of our culture, the grossness of our life. There was but one additional note: a new emphasis on "leadership," on the need for "a race of artists, profound and sincere," who would bring us "face to face with our own experience and set working in that experience the leaven of the highest culture. For it is exalted desires that give their validity to revolutions, and exalted desires take form only in exalted souls."

It was a superlative statement of the liberal idealist's philosophy. Its impassioned call for a "collective spiritual life" was both humane and eloquent, and its eloquence was all the more remarkable in that the author's delicate, lucid prose managed also to be firm and incisive. To be sure, that hint of distortion we found in the previous book was here too, aggravated perhaps by Mr. Brooks's insistence that artists inspire men to find salvation "from within," but there was so much truth in the sermon, so much gravity in the plea, that such objections would have seemed picayune if they had been made.

Ours is hindsight, of course, but the fact remains that they would not have been picayune. To look inward in the search for either origins or solutions of social and cultural phenomena is apparently suicidal. In the public, not the private, world reside the forces whereby the community's cultural pattern may be altered. The will of the individual derives its authority from the needs of the masses, not from a personal vision of the Good and Beautiful. It was Brooks's error that he pondered overmuch on the brute strength of men as compared with the frailties of man. By so doing he came gradually, no doubt unconsciously, to concentrate upon the effort required of the individual to lift himself out of the swamp. This in turn led him to an acutely sorrowful pity for the artist in his tragic dilemma. We are now, surely, discussing an attitude that is downright unhealthy for a social critic.

In an essay on "The Literary Life in America," published in 1921, the reader may find some indications of the change in Brooks. It put forth nothing substantially different from the burden of the two books we have just examined; the difference was solely one of tone. The piece was tinged with despair, its apparently defiant conclusion speaking not for the nation but for the few sensitive intellectuals who retained an urge to independent creative activity. We may grant that there was ample reason for despair if we pause to recall what America was like in the post-war years. The Wilson catastrophe, the horrible vulgarity of Babbitt triumphant and prosperous, the Red hunts and the steel strike—these must have left their mark on him. He could see that liberalism was not merely defeated but almost destroyed as a social force. Justified or not, however, he was yielding to an unfortunate emotion.

We saw it functioning in *The Ordeal of Mark Twain* the year before, and again, and more intensely, in 1925, in *The Pilgrimage of Henry James*. It is unnecessary to elaborate on the themes of these biographical critiques. They are well known, they have been written about frequently. In essence they are applications of his familiar thesis to the study of single writers. It was his notion that both were frustrated by the American environment. Twain stayed at home and compromised with the conventions and tastes of the "gilded age," and hence lost his soul. He suppressed the best in himself, suffered, grew embittered and even impotent. In another environment he would have been one of the great satirists of all time. James, on the other hand, fled to Europe, "and the uprooting withered and wasted his genius." The moral, in brief, is that the artist is inevitably thwarted by American life, directly if he stays here, indirectly (by depriving him of the nourishment to be got from one's own soil) if he departs.

It is difficult nowadays to deny that there was a palpable distortion of reality in these biographies. Bernard De Voto's *Mark Twain's America* has convinced most of us that Twain was exactly what he was meant to be. Whatever else De Voto's book contains, it demonstrates that Huck Finn's creator was *not* frustrated and that what genius he possessed found expression. He wrote numerous bad books because that was the kind of mind and background he had, and his two or three excellent books were also written because of that mind and background. If he had been different he would not have been Mark Twain. In short, Brooks exaggerated his potentialities. As for James, recent treatises have made us thoroughly dissatisfied with Brooks's theory. Grave questions are still unanswered. Was James, after all, untrue to himself? Was he so American in character that he had to wither through absence from America? Was he not cosmopolite from youth? And did he not write what he wanted to write? In short, we suspect that Brooks minimized James's achievements.

Here we see the consequence of introspection upon his esthetic judgments as well as his social interests. His attention was shifting from the latter, his mood warping (no matter how minutely) the former. In the Mark Twain book we read that "an environment as coercive as ours" obliges us "to endow it with the majesty of destiny itself in order to save our own faces!" In the James book we perceive Brooks lamenting over the fate of the first novelist "to present the plight of the highly personalized human being in the primitive community." Introspection is an indispensable critical instrument. The critic can discover the meaning and effect of a work of art only in himself, but he can give his discoveries the weight of universality and the aura of truth only by holding them to the light of historical social values. To slight the second process is to slight the rail of science that parallels the rail of poetry in the line of criticism. It is therefore not surprising that Brooks's prose was no longer "firm and incisive." It was elegiac. Softness is evident on every page of the book on James. Waldo Frank complained once of "a petulant delight in pain."

Pain, sorrow, despair—they are seldom permanent. Sometimes from their distillation comes the impersonal passion by which prophets are seized. More often what comes out of them is the calm, lightly melancholy adjustment that is akin to resignation. There is no other way to describe Brooks's *Life of Emerson* (1932). It was intended to complement the James and Twain studies in so far as it would portray an American writer who neither compromised nor fled, yet was able to live in joy and harmony with his environment. It was not, however, a critical or a psychological or a social study. It was a re-creation of Emerson's life in his own words. How, then, could it give us the truth about Emerson's world and his place in it? It could not, and the reader who puts it down thinking it has enabled him to understand Emerson is mistaken.

From our point of view, the implications of this reverie—for that is what the book is—bear exclusively upon Brooks's relation to the critical movement of which he was the father. He had now no relation to it whatever, except a reminiscent one. That this is a continuing phase is proved by his most recent book, *The Flowering of New England*. It is composed in the same manner and the same temper as the Emerson "biography." The writing is superb, the images it evokes are memorable; in many ways it is the finest portrayal ever made of the artistic and intellectual life of New England's "golden age." But it is wholly lacking in analysis. It explains nothing, neither causes nor consequences, and therefore it truly estimates neither the meaning of the "flowering" nor its lasting influence. It is purely description and narrative, and it indicates that its author has turned to scholarly story-telling. If he finds peace and pleasure in so doing, we must be glad, for no man deserves them more. No man ever wanted less for himself and more for his fellow men.

Nevertheless, we cannot help regretting that he is not still an inspiring leader; and part of our regret is a recognition of the flaws in liberalism which ensure its defeat: its impractical reliance upon the individual and its romantic misunderstanding of history. The retreat from liberalism is typified by Brooks's recent inclination to blame "human nature in general" for the faults he formerly attributed to society.[1]

### 3

There was once a notion abroad that the liberal movements in criticism were created entirely by journalists and periodical writers and that the academy has remained conservative, unenterprising, and genteel. It is true that most of our traditionalists and tories are university teachers; it is true that the liberals are still in a minority in the universities. But that liberal, even radical, professors have been rare is not true, and that they have not influenced modern literary thought is wholly false. The academy has changed, though slowly, with the changing world. It has reacted to, and acted upon, the economic, political, and ideological tendencies of the contemporary scene. Peck and Spingarn were only the first of many. Carl Van Doren was a member of the faculty of Columbia University before and after he was literary editor of the *Nation*. Ludwig Lewisohn had taught at the Ohio State University for many years. At the University of Chicago there was Robert Morss Lovett, socialist, libertarian, friend of the younger writers. At the University of Wisconsin there was William Ellery Leonard. At Yale there was Henry Seidel Canby. At the University of California there was T. K. Whipple, author of *Spokesmen: Modern Writers and American Life* (1928), which is one of the most sensible studies we have of twentieth-century American literature.

The academy was growing up. It was beginning to share the

---

[1] Perhaps this sentence will have to be amended at some future date. See Brooks's "Writers and the Yankee Tradition," in the *New Republic*, Vol. LXXXXVIII, No. 1264 (February 22, 1939).

emotions of serious adults who were trying to adjust themselves to an America become rich and imperialistic. In its own special field, literary history, it was beginning to achieve mature and realistic interpretations. In 1927 it came of age: V. L. Parrington, professor of English at the University of Washington, published the two completed volumes of his *Main Currents in American Thought*. With that work the academy was at last brought face to face with the ideas, sentiments, and historical methods of today. The tories and mossbacks have remained; but the old ones are dying off and the young ones are retreating. In 1936 Professor Arthur Hobson Quinn of the University of Pennsylvania could publish a work—*American Fiction: An Historical and Critical Survey*—from which no one could gather that any advances had been made since the early nineteenth century in psychology, political theory, or sociology; but such works are no longer common and soon they will be freaks. Parrington's volumes marked finis to the sort of literary history we had been getting from the heirs of Tyler, Richardson, and Wendell.

To appreciate fully what Parrington's work represents, it should be approached from the standpoint of method. Historiography in this country had been undergoing a pretty thorough transformation for about twenty years. The study of economic and social forces as determining factors in the politics (and hence the ideology) of any given period, had gradually increased until it was now almost respectable as a method of analysis. By the 1920's the older historians were on the defensive before the "vulgarians" who were not satisfied with an "inspiring" narration of events and refused to treat the affairs of parties and states as reflections of ideas which had sprung absolutely from immortal mind. Moreover, these new historians were usually progressive, in the sense that they were not blindly patriotic and were sympathetic to the struggles of the small business man, the farmer, and, in some cases, the worker. The new history expressed, in brief, the rise of middle-class liberalism. Its fruits were such writers as James Harvey Robinson and Charles A. Beard, whose method, it is fair to assume, was influenced, however remotely, by Marxism, although Beard quite shrewdly gave credit to James Madison.

This academic revolution had barely touched the writing of literary history before Parrington. Our numerous professors of American literature had doubtless read Taine, but they were apparently unimpressed when it came to using a comparable procedure in the study of their own specialty. They had, of course, never read the dialectical materialists. Several praiseworthy short histories had appeared since Wendell's time, but their worth rested upon their scholarship and *esthetic* liberalism rather than any fundamental difference from the older works in either method or political philosophy. The time was overripe for Parrington. A definite expression of the liberal spirit had long been due. A change from the historical bias that Dr. Canby so politely labeled "Federalist"—in other words, Brahmin and right-wing Republican—in his salute to Parrington as a refreshing and valuable novelty, had too long been delayed.

The materialist approach, in the form of economic determinism, was already attracting notice as a way out of what Parrington called the "arid desert" of romantic philosophy on the one hand and the sterility of pure esthetics on the other. For one thing, historians like Beard, Turner, Adams, and Schlesinger, by investigating economic and social problems, were revising previous notions of America's past, and their revisions made the old-fashioned textbook conception of our literary past look a little silly. Furthermore, increasing interest in American literature had stimulated research in the sources; monographs on the circumstances in which the classic Americans had done their writing, doctoral theses on cultural as well as esthetic borrowings, were appearing in the journals and upsetting familiar prejudices. Brooks's studies and the insistence of the radical critics that literature is a social product and that its history cannot otherwise be understood, were having some effect.

Parrington's *Main Currents* arrived to supply the most needed things: an account of our literary history which squared with recent works on the history of our people and a realistic technique for analyzing the relationship of a writer to his time and place—in addition to a militantly progressive spirit. Professorial and literary circles had consciously been waiting for such a work, and if the one that did come forth was far more radical than some people cared for, it simply could not be rejected. The author was a professor too; his scholarship defied scrutiny; and his ideas were couched in terms that were native American, most of them having come over shortly after the *Mayflower*.

One must emphasize Parrington's radicalism because it is probably the most significant aspect of his work. He sharpened, gave point to the economic interpretation of literary movements because of his desire to reveal the motivating interests and real direction of specific works of literature. Thus his method was part of his general intention. It is inconceivable that he would have investigated with such firmness the social ties of individual writers, or been so eager to expose the sectional and class issues underlying the ideological tendency which each writer represented, if his sympathies had not been lower-class. Nowadays "class-angling" is not a sport of kings.

Radical—not merely liberal or progressive—is the correct term. He had none of that amiable tolerance which comes of cynicism, nor was he the kind of optimist whose buoyancy is based upon an Olympian idealism. He was partisan from the start—passionately so. He was optimistic because he believed, after serious economic and political study, that when the illusions of the frontier were completely dispelled and wage-slavery grew openly oppressive, the people would take matters into their own hands and enforce their due rights. The third volume—published uncompleted, because of his death, in 1931—with its chapters on Whitman, Henry George, Wendell Phillips, and Bellamy—all of whom he embraced, yet softly, unobtrusively impugned as lacking in political acumen with regard to an industrialized, corruptly governed state—is proof enough. In the earlier volumes, dealing with figures whose words barely touch upon modern problems, his sentiments were not quite so apparent, although surely they inspired his tributes to Roger Williams, Sam Adams, Paine, Theodore Parker, and others, and his pieces on the tories for whom his scorn shone through his poised and judicious treatment of them.

His radicalism was not altogether obvious. He was certainly not so foolish as to flaunt it; he expressed his point of view as being "liberal rather than conservative, Jeffersonian rather than Federalistic"—a formulation which is not merely traditional to this country, but which has a strong appeal to large numbers of its citizens. His method he would likewise describe with classical references; in commending Beard's *An Economic Interpretation of the Constitution* he remarked: "Underlying this significant work was a philosophy of politics that set it sharply apart from preceding studies—a philosophy that unsympathetic readers were quick to attribute to Karl Marx, but that in reality derived from sources far earlier and for Americans at least far more respectable. . . . It goes back to Aristotle, it underlay the thinking of Harrington and Locke and the seventeenth-century English school, it shaped the conclusions of Madison and Hamilton and John Adams, it ran through all the discussions of the Constitutional Convention, and it reappeared in the arguments of Webster and Calhoun." Professor Eby, who edited the final volume, said that Parrington was inspired first by Taine and then by J. Allen Smith, "who applied to the abstract theorizings of political science the economic realities. . . . Parrington was quick to realize the fruitfulness of economic determinism when applied even to literature."

We cannot know whether Parrington made these "respectable" attributions because he realized that that was the only way to win a fair hearing or because, being himself wholly American in temperament and thought, they were natural to him, came to him more easily than such names as Marx and Engels. Probably both reasons operated. Nevertheless, I can state dogmatically that he had some acquaintance with Marxism, had been influenced by it, and knew that his method was related to it. I have seen a letter by him in which he said as much. Is that influence not written into the book itself? He did not speak merely of "environments" or vaguely of "economic groupings"; he did not describe a given epoch as a whole, possessing characteristics shared by all who lived in it; he spoke clearly of classes and class struggles. Essentially agrarian in mood and outlook, he was yet aware of the problems of the urban masses and, I suspect, convinced of the futility of rural individualism and the potential fruitfulness of a socialist community. This has been overlooked by those metropolitan intellectuals who were charmed by his agrarian leanings. The evidence is strewn throughout the completed parts of the third volume and is confirmed by Professor Eby's statement that Parrington had planned a vindication of Daniel De Leon, Eugene Debs, and Victor Berger.

It would be wrong to infer, however, that he was an outright socialist or a true Marxist. So far as his personal attachments were concerned, he was too much the agrarian ever to absorb himself in a fundamentally urban movement and too much the Western libertarian to stand exclusively for collectivism. He would not repudiate the philosophical "main currents" that formed his own mind. As for the differences between his method and the Marxist's, some of the major shortcomings of his work arose from that earlier and so-called "American" species of materialism—shortcomings caused, that is to say, by the inadequacies of economic determinism, which would not have been caused by a subtler approach. For example, the brief chapter on Longfellow, excellent as a characterization of the man and his writings, made no real attempt to explain his cultural origins and none whatever to show us the ultimate effect of his sentimentality. We must suppose that Parrington failed here simply because economic determinism is too crude and vulgar an instrument for such purposes. Another example was his lamentable chapter on Poe, where he just threw up his hands and said that Poe was "quite outside the main currents of American thought" and had therefore best be left alone. In other words, economic determinism could not contribute anything toward an understanding of Poe. But a sounder materialism—one in which cultural and psychological phenomena are integrated with the social—might have contributed something.

There were compensations, however. If Parrington had been a socialist of unmistakable redness and had adopted an "alien" materialism, he would probably never have won so wide an audience or had so profound an influence. The time was ripe for him, but not for a genuine Marxist. His willingness to shelve his method when confronted by esthetic problems was pleasing to literary scholars who had learned only yesterday of the applications of that method to political controversy. That early American materialism enabled him to insinuate his ideas into quarters ordinarily closed to radical ideas. The thought itself was early American—in language. He spoke always of democracy, one of the noblest words we know, but one subject to various definitions. Parrington referred to economic democracy, which hasn't an explosive sound. His devotion to that kind of democracy, which takes all other kinds for granted, and his persistence in evaluating writers in the light of it, got across. And that was his great achievement.

It was important for a weightier reason than the fact that it ended the monopoly on academic literary history previously enjoyed by conservatism, which is inherently anti-democratic. It restored the original poets, prophets, and preachers whose real characters had been hidden or suppressed by the genteel school. It showed us their true faces—their antagonism to the robber barons, their love of freedom, their faith in the social decencies. Only an impassioned democrat would have brought to light those neglected features of men like Bryant and Howells or have refurbished our rusty pride in rebels like Tom Paine and

Sam Adams. The job was so well done, so undeniably valid, that no one has since tried to undo it. Parrington's portraits of America's libertarians and revolutionaries are permanent, no matter how much his estimates of their minds may be corrected by the future. His esthetic errors of judgment were many, but time is taking care of them. They are being forgotten. No one will be harmed by his fantastic overpraise of Cabell, while many will be benefited by his insight into the American mind.

He was thus one of the critics who have been reinterpreting our heritage while searching for a "usable past." Indeed, he was the product of that self-conscious activity: the critic who did find the usable past. Since his time American radicals have followed his lead and have begun to adjust themselves to the native democratic tradition which he brought back to us and unashamedly glorified. Direct and immediate was his effect upon the writing of literary history: several recent textbooks are noticeably different from any produced ten or twenty years ago, whether because he gave the professors heart or because he taught them. It is safe to say that thanks to him a consciousness of social forces and a progressive political spirit are present in those recent volumes, and to predict that they will be present in a great many more in the future.

4

The "enemy" fought on several fronts: metaphysical, moral, and political; in criticism, education, religion, and social history. Wherever they fought, in whatever spirit, they were the "enemy" because they defended the past and berated the present. The past was civilization before the French Revolution; the present was the world created by science, industrial capitalism, and democracy.

The "enemy" was not a generation, but some of the moderns thought it was. They spoke of the "old men," as though the conflict were simply between youth and age; or they alluded sarcastically to the "Victorians," as though the struggle were simply against a particular set of manners with special reference to sex. Now that freedom of speech about sexual matters is taken for granted, we are apt to forget how pressing an issue it once was. It was important, but it was not the primary issue. It had a symbolic value, but the symbol tended to overshadow the substance. The real struggle remained after sex was liberated, and then it was seen that age was not the point and that manners were significant only as behavior involving social relationships.

Those among the "enemy" who stood merely for "purity"—for sexual reticence and idealizations of domestic virtue—were easily disposed of. They were not the true defenders of the past. They compromised with the present in too many ways: by being sympathetic to the progress of science, or by being politically liberal, or by failing to rebuke agnosticism and atheism. As often as not, they were romantics, as Stedman had been before them. Their inconsistencies betrayed them: the things they accepted or compromised with destroyed the sexual taboos. The real "enemy" understood that to preserve the gentlemanly ideal —with all that that implies in the realm of ethics, in the organization of society, and, consequently, in literature—the whole of the present had to be repudiated. They were aware of the symbolic value of the sexual question far more than some of the moderns were; they used it as a springboard for discussions about individualism and order, freedom and authority, skepticism and the church, science and the supernatural—which were their major interests and which were aspects of the one great issue: should society be governed by a cultured aristocracy according to classical traditions, or by the collective will of the masses in the shape of elected representatives?

Eventually the "enemy" was defined. Time eliminated not only the prudes but also those who were merely "old men"—men who disliked the new ways for no other cause than their newness. Circumstances forced others—notably Stuart Sherman —to qualify their enmity to contemporary movements. Sherman's career was the triumphant retort of the liberals to the tories, of the journalists to the professors. When he was a teacher at the University of Illinois he was probably the most vindictive and belligerent of America's conservative critics. He wrote what Ernest Boyd not unjustly called Ku Klux criticism, for with all his liveliness, scholarship, and wit, he was a jingo, a Red-baiter, a son of Mrs. Grundy. When, in 1924, he became editor of the *New York Herald Tribune "Books"* he grew tolerant, kindly, even progressive. Such, at least, is the legend. Its moral is supposed to be that once a man is delivered from academic convention and small-town bigotry, he becomes susceptible to liberal influences. It is too pretty a legend, too facile a moral. A great city can do wonders, but nothing quite that wonderful. The fact is that the seeds of liberalism had always been in Sherman. New York was the fertilizer. The man had been trained by Babbitt and employed by More; from them he had learned how to defend genteel prejudice and provincial fear of urban and alien manners. But he had never been an artistocrat, nor an authoritarian. Long before his arrival in New York he had written of his admiration for Emerson and Whitman, confirming his own idealism and his own democratic predilections. It was a short step to discovering virtues in Dreiser, startling though it seemed at the time.

Let the Neo-Humanists themselves tell the story (they tell it better than the liberals who believe in miraculous conversions); the following is from Norman Foerster's preface to *Humanism and America:* "The tendency toward humanitarianism, emotional sympathy with divine or undivine average humanity, appeared . . . in the post-war writings of Stuart P. Sherman. A student under Professor Babbitt, a contributor to the *Nation* under Mr. More, Sherman became the author of two books written in a vigorous and accomplished style and permeated with humanistic principles, one on Matthew Arnold conceived as a Victorian humanist, and one *On Contemporary Literature* conceived as a chaos of naturalism. Then, carried away by admiration of Wilsonian idealism and hatred of 'Prussian autocracy,' and by an uncritical devotion to Emerson, he drifted from his humanistic position into an ever vaguer faith in the common man, and at length, as a literary journalist in New York, into a rather indulgent impressionism." In the same volume Gorham B. Munson wrote: "In his growth Sherman was influenced by the books of three conservative critics, Mr. Paul Elmer More, Mr. Irving Babbitt, and the late W. C. Brownell; and here again his conduct was significant of some lack of desperation in him or of some softening influence on the fibres of his mind. For under the pressure of the ideas of Mr. More and Mr. Babbitt he was a little impatient. They were too austere for his taste, whereas he could not admire Brownell sufficiently. But of the three critics Brownell dealt least in the primary ideas of life: he elaborated with a great deal of fine sense secondary ideas about literature and society. He had, it appears to me, a mind more localised in the nineteenth century than the minds of his two colleagues. And nineteenth-century minded, rather than classical minded, was Stuart P. Sherman. . . ." The suggestion that there was something wanting in Sherman—a softness of mind, a lack of critical integrity—to explain why he tired of the venom of More and the fanaticism of Babbitt beclouds the point; it was a tactical move to cover up the Neo-Humanists' embarrassment at Sherman's defection from their ranks. But the suggestion that he was never really a classicist is perfectly sound—and if Munson and Foerster had made it before Sherman's apostasy, we could compliment them on their discernment. The democrat in Sherman emerged when he entered a congenial environment and discarded the classical bias he had picked up at Harvard. The democrat grew tolerant when democracy itself became tolerant.

In the passage by Munson quoted above we see that Brownell, too, fell short of perfection in the eyes of the Neo-Humanists, and, indeed, his final position was distinctly at variance with theirs. Foerster wrote: "In a broad view of the 'movement' the late Mr. Brownell doubtless merits a conspicuous place. Entering criticism, like Mr. More, by way of journalism, Brownell performed valuable service through his acute non-provincial book on *French Traits* as far back as 1888, and through his perennial insistence on high standards in literature and the fine arts. Never a humanist in the strict doctrinal sense, before his death he inclined to respond to the humanitarian optimism of America." Brownell was the flower of that line of genteel critics who were troubled by the crudeness, superficiality, and disorderliness of American life and thought. He was so much the best of that line—the most learned, cultivated, and serious—and so much the best stylist, that he alone is really worthy of being compared with Matthew Arnold, who was disturbed by the same discreditable characteristics in English life and thought. Men like Curtis, Warner, and their circle were pained by crudity—by the vulgar and the tawdry—and hoped that a refined literature would bring refinement into the nation's life. Brownell saw deeper: he saw the thinness, the insubstantiality, of American literature as a whole, and decided that provincialism was the cause; he saw that artists were becoming socially irresponsible, and realized that that was unfortunate for both art and society; he saw the chaos of thought that resided in the anarchy of modern life, and concluded wrongly that the former was the cause of the latter.

His perceptions led him to certain definite prescriptions: as a cure for provincialism, he recommended the study of European culture and himself studied the culture of France, describing its traits with the hope that his callow countrymen would thereby be shamed and stimulated; he observed that artist, critic, and reader were intellectually dependent upon one another and argued for an unflagging sense of social responsibility as an essential of high esthetic achievement and serious esthetic thought; and he insisted that "standards" be recognized and adhered to, as ideals toward which artist and critic should strive and which would serve as measures of value and correctives of perversity. All of this was commendable—in the abstract. But Brownell was talking about an ethical obligation and ethical standards, and the ethics in question added up to gentility; it was the same old story retold more persuasively and in more sophisticated terms. "For forty years he taught his moderate and urbane gospel of discipline, decorum, and intellectual tact. The heresies of 'self-expression,' naturalism, and impressionism he considered aberrations from a desired norm. He insisted so austerely on this norm, this admirable but ultimately abstract principle, that he lost his hold on the very 'substance' he demanded in his prose masters. When he faced the literary productions of the new age around him, or when he attempted to understand tradition as a reality that is valid only by its success in surviving in the present, he proved almost abjectly incompetent." [1]

However, his principles as such were wise, just as Arnold's were when detached from their social context. Like Arnold, Brownell wondered if democracy was not the ultimate cause of disorder and vulgarity; and, less gravely than Arnold, he flirted with aristocratic sentiments. But Arnold at last came to suspect that social inequality and economic injustice made the building of "a perfect civilization" impossible; and Brownell came to respond to "humanitarian optimism," which was America's substitute for the English socialist movement by which Arnold had evidently been affected. In other words, Brownell was a better Arnoldian than the Neo-Humanists who worship Arnold as a gentleman but are silent about his liberalism. Both Brownell and Arnold were nauseated by the rampant philistinism of a bourgeoisie grown prosperous; neither was prepared, in the end, to turn back the clock.

The "enemy" is now almost defined. There is just one other distinction to be made: it used to be thought that a critic who paid little or no attention to contemporary literature, seeking poetic wisdom and experience only in the classics, was necessarily opposed to romanticism and enamored of discipline, de-

[1] Morton Dauwen Zabel: *Literary Opinion in America* (New York, 1937), p. xxiv.

corum, balance, and the other shibboleths of the militant classicists. Thus, for example, in its single reference to the New Humanists, the *Cambridge History of American Literature* placed John Jay Chapman beside More and Babbitt. This was a gross misrepresentation of Chapman's position. He was an Emersonian —a philosophical reformer, a violent individualist, and finally a mystic. His romanticism was essentially aristocratic, *but it was romanticism*, which must automatically align him with the anarchists when Babbitt calls the roll of the angels. Moreover, he was anything but genteel so far as sex is concerned, and not at all decorous in his political conduct, nor disciplined in his personal life. Chapman's adventures among the classics were much like Emerson's: an appreciation of great individuals, of great character rising above convention, of sublime truths glimpsed through divine intuition.

The "enemy" were the critics, led by More and Babbitt, who advocated a return to pre-romantic principles in thought and conduct. Their writings may seem complicated, may seem abstruse and learned, and are certainly confusing to anyone who is intellectually adjusted to the modern world, but actually they are informed by very simple ideas and rather transparent emotions. It is to the credit of these men that they have not disguised their beliefs—that, on the contrary, they have been unambiguous and methodical. Their beliefs need only be stripped of their scholarly accretions to be revealed as a set of arguments in defense of gentility.

These critics had an advantage over their nineteenth-century predecessors, however, in having witnessed the genteel community's collapse and the maturing of a society in which appeals to tradition were futile. They realized, therefore, that the literary problem was really a philosophical one, which, in turn, involved social and political problems. In essence, their realization was that since gentility prevailed only when gentlemen reigned over society and culture, it was their job to find out why the reign of the gentlemen had ended and how a restoration might be effected. They discovered that the source of their literary troubles was romanticism, with its emphasis on individual freedom and its deification of nature in place of the supernatural. They discovered that science was the initial influence in favor of naturalism and experimentation. They discovered that democracy is incompatible with aristocratic privilege and absolute authority of any kind and that it tends, in the long run, to liquidate class rule. In short, they discovered that the energies released by the Reformation, the Enlightenment, and the Industrial Revolution were ultimately subversive to classical forms of morality and art.

They did not lack the courage of their convictions. They understood that to preach restraint, decorum, moderation, and so on, is not enough, although assuredly such preaching was one of their major occupations. They began by attacking monistic philosophies, upholding an unqualified dualism and asserting the primacy of spirit. Then they attempted to find a psychological equivalent for religious dogma, arguing that there is in man an instinct, or intuition, or insight which, if properly encouraged, would bid him honor the ethics of the golden mean. In this connection More invented the notorious phrase "the inner check," which Babbitt exploited mercilessly. At this point some of the reactionary critics were moved to protest, exclaiming that there is no substitute for dogma, no guide so sure and firm as an orthodox church. This has been T. S. Eliot's complaint. The debate is not to be taken too seriously, however, for Babbitt himself said: "I range myself unhesitatingly on the side of the supernaturalists. Though I see no evidence that humanism is necessarily ineffective apart from dogmatic and revealed religion, there is, as it seems to me, evidence that it gains immensely in effectiveness when it has a background of religious insight." [1]

[1] In *Humanism and America*, edited by Norman Foerster (New York, 1930), p. 39.

To proceed: the Neo-Humanists then declared that science is all right in its place, but its place is not where it can deal with moral and philosophical issues. Further, only the presumptuous and the credulous believe that science has established determinism or invalidated a faith in immaterial forces or justified moral relativism. Finally, the Neo-Humanists denounced all egalitarian and libertarian doctrines as contrary to instinct, reason, and experience and productive of evil.

These doctrines compose an attitude toward life which has had some very interesting practical expressions. Naturally, the Neo-Humanists have execrated socialism; but they have also condemned humanitarianism. They have even sneered at humanitarian religions, by which they mean the liberal and democratic Protestant churches; they have been cordial to the Anglican and Roman churches. They have interpreted the Gospels as being in no way inimical to class and hierarchic social orders: Paul Elmer More wrote that Christ "never for a moment contemplated the introduction of a religion which should rebuild society. His kingdom was not of this world, and there is every reason to believe that he looked to see only a few chosen souls follow in his footsteps. . . . He nowhere intimates that the law and custom of the world can be changed; he accepts these things as necessary to the social system. . . . Not a word falls from his lips to indicate that slavery should be abolished, or the hierarchy of government disturbed . . . [and] when tempted by the Pharisees he replies in those ringing words: 'Render to Caesar the things that are Caesar's, and to God the things that are God's.' " [1] They have sneered at feminism and pacifism. They have attacked labor unions, popular education, and universal franchise.[2] They have bewailed the elevation of science above Latin and Greek in collegiate curricula and urged a return to

[1] Paul Elmer More: *Shelburne Essays: First Series* (Boston, 1904), pp. 243-5.
[2] See More's *Aristocracy and Justice* (Boston, 1915), and Babbitt's *Democracy and Leadership* (Boston, 1924).

the ancient concept of education for the benefit of the leisure classes.[1]

The practice characterizes the theory. What the Neo-Humanists want is a squirearchy, which is to say, an urbane and refined feudalism. How to bring it about in a society already industrialized is one of the two things about which they have been silent; the other thing is what form such a state would take in such a society. But present-day events provide us with the answers. Attempts have been made to create industrialized feudal states. The process is called fascism. It is not one of moral persuasion, however, and the states that result from it are not urbane and refined. Murder is the method, and the result is the obliteration of reason, the death of culture, and the canonization of force. There seems to be no other way to abolish humanitarianism, or to restrain science from interfering with ethics, or to curb labor unions and pacifists, or to guarantee the subordination of the masses to an "aristocracy." Are the Neo-Humanists fascists? Of course not! These American professors who sound so bloodthirsty in print, are really very mild men. At least we must acknowledge their sincerity in pleading for decorum and self-control. No, they are not fascists; they must shrink with horror from the fascist state—and with disgust from its literature.[2] The question is introduced here for just one purpose: it shows how childish are their complaints about the modern world, how childish are their remedies, how childish their social ideal. Their ventures into sociology, politics, and the philosophy of science are the ventures of children. But they are children playing with fire. Their urbane and decorous state can never be realized, but

[1] There are also hints of a racial bias in some of the Neo-Humanists' writings. In *The Demon of the Absolute* (Princeton, 1928), More wrote: "New York is . . . a place where millions congregate to do business and to eat and die, where Yiddish or Italian and occasionally a kind of English is spoken. . . ." T. S. Eliot, who is sympathetic to this group, addresses himself almost exclusively nowadays to "Anglo-Saxons."

[2] This does not preclude the possibility that an American fascist government, if ever it happens here, will appeal to the Neo-Humanists as Mussolini appealed to Giovanni Gentile.

their lectures may impress some of their students in unexpected ways. Are the sons of bankers and corporation lawyers—or of small-town merchants, for that matter—likely to be turned into Aristotles by discourses on the lamentable consequences of democracy?

As literary critics the Neo-Humanists have been most successful in their sallies against the impressionist and "art for art's sake" theses. They have pointed out that when a critic refuses to judge a work of art he abdicates his primary function; that there are more important things for him to do than to exhibit his personality; that there are sounder, more reliable standards of taste than his whims; that critical anarchy leads to creative anarchy; and that criticism cannot be divorced from philosophy, nor art from moral and social experience. As theoretical principles these observations are incontrovertible, and in debates over theory the Neo-Humanists have often been remarkably effective. It is significant that these principles correspond to the principles for which Marxist critics have fought. They concur on social responsibility as the touchstone of value in literary criticism. Their disagreements as to the nature of that responsibility and the standards to be referred to are, of course, absolute.

The standards that the Neo-Humanists have depended upon have made them bad critics of modern poetry and fiction, while the critics whose theories were so easily refuted have been, on the whole, much more competent in these fields. Why the former have been uniformly wrong and frequently obtuse is obvious: their preposterous philosophy has made it impossible for them to understand any writer who is sympathetic to modern ideas, and their passion for traditional forms has made them incapable of appreciating esthetic experiment. The absence of such biases has been the source of strength in the criticism of the illogical, unsystematic subjectivists and esthetes, who have, however, erred in other ways. The Neo-Humanists have been quite shrewd at analyzing the drift of contemporary literature—at describing, that is, its temper and character. They have been especially apt at detecting the symptoms of introversion and decadence. But they have denounced those tendencies as violations of laws that have been moribund for centuries, for they have studied living literature without being themselves parties to the anxieties, hatreds, and ideals of living men. Everything that literary criticism ought to have, their criticism has—except one thing. The touch of life is what is missing, and without it scholarship is pointless and an interest in philosophical issues is futile. For without it reality is hopelessly distorted.

Compare the studies of Proust and Joyce in the last volume of More's *Shelburne Essays* (1936) with Edmund Wilson's studies of the same writers in *Axel's Castle* (1931). It is astonishing how they parallel each other in their remarks on the psychological tone and the moral implications of their subjects. It is even more astonishing how divergent are their attitudes toward their subjects' achievements and significance. They divide at the moment when a genuine understanding of our present environment is required. Wilson approached his problems with the alertness and compassion of a man participating in Proust's and Joyce's experiences; More regarded them from the standpoint of the dead past. One had some knowledge of what the Western world was like and what the intelligence of the twentieth century hoped it would be like in the future; the other depended upon an artificial conception of the world and knew only what the intelligence of remote times had tried to make it. Wilson grasped the reality; More distorted it. This was not an accidental or unique failure. How many men have come out of More's and Babbitt's studies subtly twisted out of their natural shapes! Consider the very first of More's *Shelburne Essays*, a piece on Thoreau which portrays him as a sort of primitive Neo-Humanist—a portrait intended to be appreciative, but actually even falser than Lowell's spiteful caricature. Consider also Babbitt's *Rousseau and Romanticism* (1919)—a work of great erudition and sustained thought, the final effect of which is grotesque. The ideas in Rousseau that seem most useful and progressive are lumped with his perversities and posturings. All his ideas, to Babbitt, were evil, and since he was one of the first and least inhibited of the romanticists, Babbitt made him his personal devil and fantastically exaggerated his influence. Again the distortion of reality.

There is no mystery about "the touch of life" that criticism needs. It consists in knowing human beings as they are and sympathizing with their efforts to achieve peace, freedom, and happiness. Part of the history of criticism is a history of the way our knowledge of human beings has changed and of the way our sympathy has been extended to an ever larger section of the human family. The Neo-Humanists know little about humanity and sympathize with only a small section of it. They tell us that confusion exists; we agree. They tell us that it is an unhealthy condition; we agree. But when they offer us an inhuman moral absolutism as a remedy, we smell—as Santayana has said—fustiness and faggots. It is one of the critical jokes of all time that these men should have bestowed upon themselves the title "New Humanists." To quote Santayana once more, the humanists of the Renaissance "believed in the sufficient natural goodness of mankind, a goodness humanised by frank sensuality and a wink at all amiable vices; their truly ardent morality was all negative, and flashed out in their hatred of cruelty and oppression and in their scorn of imposture. This is still the temper of revolutionaries everywhere, and of philosophers of the extreme Left. These, I should say, are more truly heirs to the humanists than the merely academic people who still read, or pretend to read, the classics, and who would like to go on thrashing little boys into writing Latin verses."

## 5

In the meantime the quest of beauty went on to its logical end. It was pursued independently of the wars in which Mencken and Brooks and More were engaged, and developed into a separate tradition, yet it was not oblivious of them. It could not be, for the directions it took were determined by the forces those men represented.

The fact that they were clashing forces was the first determinant, for out of their conflict came that condition of moral sophistication and intellectual instability which permits the belief that the study of beauty is wholly a study of expression. Thus the setting that had been unavailable to Poe and James was the familiar environment of the modern esthetic critic, and the state of mind they could never attain was his normal state. Under those circumstances relativism could easily be converted into nihilism: if the thesis that an artist could create beauty out of any ethical conviction seemed lukewarm to the critic, he could maintain that ethics and art are unrelated. In either case he took part in the revolt against gentility. He was the truest liberal of them all, *if he was consistent*, for he alone had no preferences as to what paths the artist should follow. This pertains not only to ethics; to be consistent the esthetic critic had to reject social as well as moral purposes, or to maintain that social philosophy and art are unrelated.

Actually, so "pure" an esthetics never existed. The only approach to it is an escapist conception of literature, on the basis of which a critic may propose to deal exclusively with sensation and with form as a victory of the creative will. We have learned, however, that that in itself is an ethical and social attitude: it reflects the critic's adjustment to society. It may be symptomatic of some personal weakness in the critic—of a morbid shrinking from reality; if that be so, his contemplation of literature is likely to become the shallowest kind of impressionism. If he is excessively fastidious yet mentally disciplined and analytical, he will perhaps be the kind of critic who conducts a research into the process of creation as a sort of game whose interest is its difficulty and preciousness. But the critic who wants art to compensate for life's failings may be expressing a violent distaste for an objective condition, the properties of which he can describe with perfect clarity and understanding. And that, precisely, has been the "motive" of much of the esthetic criticism written in this country during the past thirty or forty years.

Here the setting to be considered is the one surrounding the little community of intellectuals: the philistine business world—with its fetish of being "practical"—of which Mencken and Brooks and More were alike scornful. But while those critics went to history, politics, and religion to investigate causes and suggest correctives, the esthetic critic became a propagandist for beauty itself. Emerson's maxim, "beauty is its own excuse for being," taken out of the philosophical background which gives it its transcendental meaning, is the idea to which he dedicated himself. Interpreting beauty as form—for art is a refuge from the world that taints the poetic spirit only in so far as it can be enjoyed without regard for meanings—his criticism became an investigation into methods. This had the salutary effect of encouraging esthetic experiment, while teaching the layman something about the artist's technical problems. When the extremes of experimentation had been reached, his criticism became an aggressive apology for an art deprived of its power to communicate anything; and now the layman was taught something about the artist's social problems.

The " 'esthetic opposition' to the norms of business," as Kenneth Burke recently called it, has been most active and articulate in the criticism of poetry. For in poetry, much more than in prose, one derives pleasure from the non-ideological elements of the composition; more easily than in prose, its beauty may be abstracted from its meaning. The emotion expressed in a lyric need not be particularized or traced to the specific objects that arouse it. Hence it may appear to be an expression uncorrupted by purpose. Sensitiveness to colors, sounds, rhythms, and images is accordingly idealized for its own sake; and the life of art is thus directly opposed to the economic life. It could be shown that this was the unconscious background—perhaps, indeed, not altogether unconscious—of the "poetic renascence." The latter was a realization of Stedman's dream in a form and with a character Stedman never dreamed of; and its critical theory was Stedman's stripped of its genteel and sentimental qualities.

Immediately upon its founding, Harriet Monroe's *Poetry: A Magazine of Verse* became an important organ of the "esthetic opposition." Miss Monroe herself was a liberal, probably more sympathetic to Brooks than to Ezra Pound, who was her foreign editor and her most distinguished contributor. But there was little antagonsim, in those days, between the esthetes and the liberal social critics, for they were both too busy attacking the same things. Her magazine bore the imprint of an enthusiasm for Whitman, yet published criticism reminiscent of Poe; simultaneously it criticized our cultural traditions and agitated for the cult of beauty. Pound was the leading esthetic critic of the time. He was then identified with the imagists—John Gould Fletcher, Hilda Doolittle, Amy Lowell, and Conrad Aiken—whose interest in the esthetics of poetry was unconventional and impressively serious. Amy Lowell was the noisiest and best publicized of the group—which is not to say that she did no good. On the contrary, as a popular lecturer she introduced modern poetry to more people than any other critic of that generation. But her criticism was woefully superficial; when it was not mere press-agentry for her friends, it was simply an exaltation of beauty conceived as something apart from moral and social beliefs. She stated her position in her volume on *Tendencies in Modern American Poetry* (1917); no one who compares her remarks on Sandburg and Masters with her remarks on H. D. and Fletcher can mistake it. Aiken was also a practicing critic for a while. In 1919 he published a volume called *Scepticisms*, containing his reviews of current volumes of poetry. It was admittedly a work of unqualified subjectivism. It began with an "Apologia Pro Specie Sua" in which Aiken described all criticism as self-portraiture and concluded with an "Appendix" in which he wrote that "human judgments or tastes reduce themselves under pressure to the terms of the pathetic ego which stands as judge." Pound was shrewder than Aiken and better equipped than Miss Lowell; and his was certainly the best mind of the lot.

He had the advantage, of course, of being personally noticeable. His clothes and his beard advertised his defiance of the commercial spirit. As an expatriate he was one of that long line of artists who had damned the materialistic atmosphere of their homeland by fleeing from it, but his flight was rather more spectacular than James's or Whistler's had been. His stylistic eccentricities, his esoteric erudition, his enthusiasm for novelty— everything about the man and the writer breathed the esthete. But there were occasions of understanding and sensitiveness that made his criticism something more than the amusing intellectual circus that it seemed to be. It was that too, to be sure, for he appointed himself trumpeter to any number of obscure writers and artists, and he blew his horn loudly and weirdly. Many of the obscure ones became famous afterwards; some were nothing but "modernist" poseurs. For Pound was apt to get excited about anything new and original, anything that smacked of experiment, so he was bound to fall for charlatans as well as authentic explorers.

He criticized poetry as music—its sound, cadence, and perhaps especially the excellence of its orchestration. Perfected complexity in the orchestral structure of a poem was his special interest, no matter what movement or school he was flirting with at the moment. A more ecstatic enjoyment of form was never known. It was not mystical, however. It was an exercise of the intellect, to which his senses were presumably subservient, but it was an intellect preoccupied with esthetic abstractions—until recent years. His criticism of the novel was similarly devoid of philosophical content. In *Instigations* (1920) he said that he subscribed to the theory of realism expounded by the Goncourts in their preface to the first edition of *Germinie Lacerteux*. On the surface, at least, it seemed to be the realism of esthetic "scientists"—artists "superior" to temporal issues, intensely conscious of their craft, extremely inquisitive about the phenomena of life *as material for art*. That Pound was among the first of our critics to appreciate Remy de Gourmont, James Joyce, and T. S. Eliot and one of the earliest to study Henry James on the latter's own grounds is thus proof of his critical intelligence, but also an indication of his interests. For those are the writers who would naturally attract a critic immersed in the problems of form. And Pound dealt only with their formal thought and achievements. In that period of his life he had but one philosophical principle— one fitting to an individualist in quest of beauty; in *Pavannes and Divisions* (1918) he wrote: "Bad art is inaccurate art. It is art that makes false reports. . . . If an artist falsifies his report as to the nature of man, as to his own nature, as to the nature of his ideal of the perfect, as to the nature of his ideal of this, that or the other . . . if the artist falsifies his reports on these matters or on any other matter in order that he may conform to the taste of his time, to the proprieties of a sovereign, to the conveniences of a preconceived code of ethics, then that artist lies" —which was splendid rhetoric to affirm a much abused platitude, for Pound's whole point was that every man is different from every other man!

Pound was the foreign editor of another American magazine: the *Little Review*—and to this one he was really suited. Founded in Chicago in 1914 by Margaret Anderson, who later brought it to New York, it was published sporadically until 1929. It was the maddest, bravest, and most stimulating experimental magazine America has ever had. If for no other reason, it will be remembered as the periodical in which Joyce's *Ulysses* first appeared, running serially for three years starting with the issue of March 1918, during which period it was burned four times by the United States Post Office authorities and at last successfully prosecuted by the Society for the Suppression of Vice. Pound was responsible for Joyce's appearance in the *Little Review;* and it was he who sent in T. S. Eliot's and Wyndham Lewis's work. But the editors (there were two now: Jane Heap had joined

Miss Anderson) needed no persuasion from him. They were willing to try anything—including even the Dadaists, whom they introduced to this country. They also tried Ernest Hemingway
when he was just beginning to write, and editorially put themselves on record that he was the best of the new Americans.
Such instances of foresight were rarer than their numerous attempts to secure immortality for exotic nonentities.

Their perspicacity and foolishness alike exhibited their daring. Neither ridicule nor reason restrained their rebellion against
convention. Unfortunately, they never stopped to examine the
conventional in an effort to discriminate between that which is
natural or useful and that which is artificial or repressive. That
would have been a philosophical act productive of social criticism, which they despised as vehemently as the criticism of Phi-
listia. They preferred to discard convention as such in favor of
individuality as such. Freedom so conceived is almost inevitably
expressed as a passion for adventures in form and sensation.
Here there is no need to speculate about motives. Contempt for
the practical, common-sense world was evident in everything
the magazine said and did. To be absolutely individual and to
live as though inspired—which turned out to be a state of emotional intoxication—was the professed aim. Miss Anderson suc-
cinctly described the movement in which she participated, as
well as her own behavior, when she opened her autobiography,
*My Thirty Years' War* (1930), as follows:

> *My greatest enemy is reality.*
> *I have fought it successfully for thirty years.*

It was, in truth, a movement that the *Little Review* anticipated. Its career was not, at any rate, a unique episode in our
literary history. It was imitated or succeeded by half a dozen
magazines, almost all of them published abroad by American
exiles. In the era of Harding and Coolidge, Paris and its suburbs
—among which Italy, Spain, and Austria were counted—became
the Greenwich Village of the new "younger generation." Before

the war a young man who was unhappy in the bourgeois atmosphere of his home, and who wanted to write and act without deferring to tradition, embraced socialism or anarchism. His disgust with a land that worshiped the dollar made him a revolutionary (pro tem), in the sense that he acknowledged the possibility of cleansing the human spirit by destroying the environment which had soiled it. In the Village he felt sufficiently distant from his home to be able to express himself freely. Now, in the post-Versailles reaction, when a defeatist mood pervaded the liberal camp and socialism was impotent, the esthetic life seemed to be the only effective protest against a land that young men with a taste for art believed to be irremediably corrupt. And only in Europe was such a life plausible. In America it was either pretense or perversion. To go to Europe, moreover, was to remove oneself from all the compulsions and dislocations that made America unbearable—in a word, to escape. An act which is at once a personal escape and a social protest—how delightful! There was a great exodus.

The *Little Review* itself had been transported to Paris before it died. *Broom*, founded in 1921—edited by Harold Loeb, Alfred Kreymborg, Malcolm Cowley, Matthew Josephson, and Slater Brown—was published in Rome, Berlin, and finally New York. *Secession*, founded in 1922—edited by Gorham Munson, Kenneth Burke, and Josephson—was published in Vienna, Berlin, the Tyrol, and finally New York. In 1925 Ernest Walsh and Ethel Moorhead founded *This Quarter*—published in Milan and Cannes. In Rapallo Ezra Pound brought out his own little magazine, the *Exile*, in 1927-8. There were several more. They were all alike, and they all died after a year or two. They stood for various interpretations of "art for art's sake" and discussed literature as an experience in sensation. Since the senses are easily satiated, they had constantly to search for more novel sensations, intenser experiences, so that esthetic experiment degenerated into a psychopathological activity. Now the end of the quest of beauty was in sight. It was reached by *transition*, "the last and biggest," the best known and most uncompromising, of the expatriate magazines—founded in Paris by Eugene Jolas in 1927, with Elliot Paul as co-editor, and published until 1930, then revived in 1932 and issued from The Hague until 1936.

Dada had merged into surrealism, which was the ultimate fruit of French symbolist esthetics, ripened in the anarchic moral climate of Europe in the 1920's.[1] The "esthetic opposition" to certain aspects of reality was not an opposition to the whole of reality. The study of form became a study of the dissolution of form, and the enjoyment of sensation became an approach to hysteria. *transition* was in the midst of this turmoil, responding to it and stimulating it. It functioned as a link between the American and European esthetes, contemporary style. "Angry, sophisticated, high-spirited, tired, primitive, expressionist, objective, subjective, incoherent, flat, it included everything that seemed new; rhapsodies to the machine were printed side by side with poems of escape from the machine, while Functionalism, Superrealism and Gertrude Stein all nudged one another. But that was chiefly in the beginning. As the magazine continued, it began to work toward a policy of its own, one that would combine the editor's three principal admirations, for Rimbaud (the hallucination of the senses), for Joyce (the disintegration of the English language) and for the Superrealists (the emphasis on dreams and on the 'autonomous' imagination). . . . The campaign was launched in the June issue [1929], in the form of a 'Proclamation' signed by sixteen writers. It begins: 'Tired of the spectacle of short stories, novels, poems and plays still under the hegemony of the banal word, monotonous syntax, static psychology, descriptive naturalism, and desirous of crystallizing a viewpoint, we hereby declare that'—but the document is worth quoting in full. It is funny; and it sets forth the doctrines that writers were willing seriously to uphold in that year when even the craziest little magazines were saner than the Stock Ex-

[1] See Wilson's *Axel's Castle* and Malcolm Cowley's *Exile's Return* (New York, 1934).

change." [1] This is the document, these the things the sixteen writers declared:

1. The revolution in the English language is an accomplished fact.

2. The imagination in search of a fabulous world is autonomous and unconfined.

3. Pure poetry is a lyrical absolute that seeks an a-priori reality within ourselves alone.

4. Narrative is not mere anecdote, but the projection of a metamorphosis of reality.

5. The expression of these concepts can be achieved only through the rhythmic "hallucination of the word."

6. The literary creator has the right to disintegrate the primal matter of words imposed on him by textbooks and dictionaries.

7. He has the right to use words of his own fashioning and to disregard existing grammatical and syntactical laws.

8. The "litany of words" is admitted as an independent unit.

9. We are not concerned with the propagation of sociological ideas, except to emancipate the creative elements from the present ideology.

10. Time is a tyranny to be abolished.

11. The writer expresses. He does not communicate.

12. The plain reader be damned.

There were esthetic critics who were neither expatriates nor verbal anarchists, critics who were moderate, poised, and cultivated. Some critics kept reality at a distance, so to speak, rather than being implacably at war with it, and some did not fight it at all, but were simply interested by it the way James had been. There were the merely fastidious, the consciously aristocratic, and the classically trained. There were analysts of the psychology of expression. There were connoisseurs of experiment (which is not synonymous with experimentalists). . . . They were all different, yet they were all the same. They were the

[1] Cowley, op. cit., pp. 274-5.

same because they did not criticize the artist's interpretation of the way human beings live with each other, but only the manner in which his interpretation was expressed. The "motive" might be a desire to find relief from the chaos of existing thought by assuming that it was somehow resolved in esthetic form, or it might be an acceptance of chaos as an unavoidable condition and therefore not a subject for debate. Whichever the "motive," the result was criticism designed to further an appreciative and discriminating apprehension of experience.

The result was less admirable than the intention. Inactive, morally purposeless, detached from the social conflicts that are the basis of experience, such criticism tended to become excessively refined and intellectualized. The goal was sterility. The perfect critic of this type is Paul Valéry, his perfect creation "M. Teste." No American critic went so far, but there was a definite tendency in that direction. Simplicity, human warmth, naturalness were blighted by the complicated speculations of the latter-day Jameses. Or perhaps the superbly discriminating esthetic critic turned out to be a superior kind of impressionist—one whose taste and manners made a Huneker look vulgar and incompetent. Yet the philosophical faults of a Huneker were his faults too.

The *Dial*, in its new incarnation as a magazine of the arts—published in New York under the editorship of Scofield Thayer from 1920 to 1925, and by Marianne Moore from 1925 to 1929, when it died—provided a forum for every kind of esthetic critic except the intransigent experimentalists. The latter hated its catholicity and politeness; and *Dial*-baiting became a sport of the *Little Review* and *Broom* groups. What really infuriated them was its ultra-fineness, its rather exquisite air—that air which brings to mind the epithet "Harvard esthete." It was nevertheless the most solid and intelligible of American esthetic magazines, and it was precisely its tolerant and eclectic policies that enabled it to educate a whole generation in the problems of form, feeling, and taste—the things that Mencken and his friends knew or cared nothing about. Everyone, European or American, who had anything to say about art and its appreciation contributed to it. The Americans included Stewart Mitchell, Cuthbert Wright, Gilbert Seldes, Charles K. Trueblood, Paul Rosenfeld, Kenneth Burke, Yvor Winters, Edmund Wilson, Pound, Eliot, Aiken, Fletcher, Cowley—a heterogeneous company bound together by their common interest in the means by which beauty is created in literature. But the impressionists, if not dominant, were the critics most at home in the *Dial:* it was their special haven, while the more intellectual and systematic critics of the poet's practice were identified with such periodicals as the *Criterion,* edited in London by Eliot, and the *Hound and Horn,* edited in Cambridge, Mass., and New York by Lincoln Kirstein, Bernard Bandler, R. P. Blackmur, Allen Tate, Yvor Winters, and Varian Fry. Despite its hospitality toward a wide variety of tastes and methods, the *Dial* seems in retrospect to have been the organ of the Walter Paters and Arthur Symonses of the 1920's, who cultivated a sensitiveness so delicate that grosser mortals were often mystified and sometimes overwhelmed by it. Marianne Moore was probably responsible for imparting that tone to the magazine. Impressionists like Aiken and Wright were slovenly compared with her. Impressionism, in her hands, lost whatever resemblance to a critical method it had ever had. Her essays and reviews were prose poems—the style dazzling, the thought tenuous.

There was one critic who apparently possessed all the virtues —fine taste, poetic sensitiveness, intellectuality, an experimental inclination. His literary scholarship was beyond dispute, his writing deft and memorable. He was, moreover, a poet of the first rank, which gave his criticism of the art an extraordinary authority. He was universally respected: by Pound, by the later expatriates, by the impressionists of the *Dial,* by the *Hound and Horn* group. This critic was T. S. Eliot. His volume of essays, *The Sacred Wood,* published in 1920, is still considered to be one of the truly distinguished works of esthetic criticism produced in this century. . . . The reader will note that he is here described in the past tense. He is no longer an esthetic critic, or is one only secondarily. His works are many now, but *The Sacred Wood* alone is a consideration of esthetic problems. In the rest the emphasis is on the esthetic effects of moral and social beliefs. His development is one of the "consequences" touched upon in the following chapter. At this point, however, it is worth observing that the aristocratic implications of the quest of beauty—that strain of aloofness from the common life, of indifference to the fate of the community, of a sense of superiority to the passions and ideals of the mass of men, which is obvious in esthetic criticism from Poe and James on to the present day —are fully realized in T. S. Eliot.

# CHAPTER IX

# CONSEQUENCES

AS the 1920's drew to a close, it was evident that American critics were becoming obsessed by the need that Henry Adams had felt. The failure of traditional philosophies of history to explain the intolerable chaos of the present and the way to an orderly and reasonable future was certainly more deeply and universally felt than it had ever been before. Men were freer now than they had been in Adams's day, and their freedom emphasized the urgency of the need. For there were still fewer conventions to adhere to, still fewer sacred institutions, still looser social controls. Science had destroyed Adams's religion, industrial capitalism his social ideal, but at least he had had the gentleman's morality. (It was one of the few things he was reluctant to criticize; it was sanctified by his faith in his family.) Now that was gone too, and with it was gone the last remnant of the elaborate ethical system created by the bourgeoisie in the three centuries that followed the Reformation.

Symptomatic of what was happening was the confusion that prevailed in liberal criticism. Whatever sense of unity, of a common purpose and goal, had existed among that not quite definable group, was disappearing with the passing of the decade, until at last one could justly say that the most fruitful movement in the literary thought of this century was done. Van Wyck Brooks's disillusionment with his own youthful idealism was one of the more temperate reactions. There were others who abandoned the liberal faith with rather violent gestures. Take the career of Harold Stearns, who had come down from Harvard insisting that the idealist need not be sentimental, but must, on the contrary, be tough and realistic. That was the motif of his *Liberalism in America* (1919), which showed that he was unawed by glamorous reputations and alert to the weaknesses of his comrades-in-arms. Two years later he brought out *America and the Young Intellectual,* a collection of spirited essays, so hopeful, so confident in the will and the intelligence of the rising generation, that it seemed logical to deduce therefrom that there were liberals who would not succumb to the disillusionment and disgust of the post-Versailles reaction. Commercialism and vulgarity would not, after all, conquer! In 1922 he edited his famous *Civilization in the United States,* a volume suckled by sorrow and pain, and immediately fled to Paris, the Dôme, and silence. He returned early in the 1930's and has since been making his peace with his country, enthusiastically discovering virtues in it that were always there and minimizing the faults that once excited him and which have not vanished.

There are some who have been less resilient, but no more fortunate in retaining the buoyancy and optimism of their past. Look, for evidence, at the transformation in Ludwig Lewisohn (who is at least still fiery). Shortly after publishing *The Creative Life* he removed every trace of liberalism from his thinking. He returned, as he says, to his people and "to the religion of his fathers," which is a nice way of saying that he became a nationalist and a mystic. For a critical method in keeping with his new position he relied upon psychoanalysis, which is not innocent of mystical tendencies and which permitted free play to his interest in the quirks of personality and discouraged whatever interest he had ever had in the impersonal environment in which personality is shaped. His chief critical work in this later period was *Expression in America* (1932), which is full of sharp and memorable insights that are like unexpected dramatic asides, for the book as a whole is ill-begotten. It is an ambitious attempt to write a history of literature from the Freudian viewpoint, and it is a convincing proof of the inadequacy of Freudianism when applied to a problem that is essentially cultural and social. Freud and Judah compose a faith which offers nothing to mankind;

it can lead only to obscurantism. Yet it is Lewisohn's faith today, and it is a thoroughly reactionary one, as can be seen by his rancorous gibes at every expression of collectivism.

Or look at Waldo Frank, who, like Lewisohn and unlike many other liberals, has kept his zeal and passion. In 1919 he published a volume called *Our America*, an interpretation of the history of American life and literature. It showed the influence of Van Wyck Brooks—its general thesis resembled that of *America's Coming-of-Age*—but there was much in it that was fresh and original. It was an attack on materialism, a hymn to the idealistic and poetic spirit. The seeds of dissolution were there—in the diffused and formless prose—but health and sense were there too. An even decade afterwards he published *The Rediscovery of America*, one of the most depressing books of our times. Aside from a few penetrating remarks on our poets and philosophers, it consisted wholly of an emotional fog of terrifying opaqueness. Metaphysical phrases, mysticism largely derived from Gurdjieff, an involved restatement of Brooks's old search for leadership, made up a muddled, morbid volume. Then, a few years later, he turned to communism—not as a Marxist, however, but as a sort of primitive Christian, still full of the moral fervor and the mystical emotions which had found other outlets in other years. His was essentially a religious faith rather than a social philosophy, and it could not survive the bitter experience of the Moscow trials. What can he look forward to, in what can he now believe? To what end can he henceforth direct his zeal?

Several of the liberal critics who have neither worshiped new gods nor resigned themselves to a cynical agnosticism have remained what they were fifteen or twenty years ago, unchanged in a changing world. Those who have never had passion have never suffered disillusionment. All they have suffered is a loss of position. Men like Van Doren and Lovett once stood for that imprecise and ambiguous something known as progress: they were liberators and friends of the unorthodox. But they stood

still, and today they have no special distinction. Their lessons
have been absorbed and forgotten. No one who feels keenly the
need of contemporary criticism looks to them for satisfaction,
for they have rested with the negative victory of liberalism—the
routing of the bigots and the pedants.

What is that need of criticism? It is always the same: a tool
that will enable the critic to measure the extent and value of an
artist's comprehension of reality. But reality in the twentieth
century is complex, uncontrolled, frightening. None of the old
tools will do. Liberalism proved that. It did not, however, succeed in developing substitutes. The vision of a reasonable and
pacific life that was the core of its striving has faded—faded because the means by which its attainment was held to be feasible
have been demonstrated, by history itself, to be utopian; and
also because it has come to seem less lovely, as a way of life in
the world we now know, with the realization of how much of
the past it retains. It cannot too often be repeated that liberalism
is merely an idealistic form of individualism. It has run its course,
the liberals themselves tell us, as the premise of a social scheme—
and hence as the basis of esthetic and philosophical criticism. It
was at its height in Emerson's day; then there was a moment of
renewal in the Wilsonian era; and then it withered. It was at
this time that theories of psychic and moral therapy became
popular: the frustrated idealist decided that it was easier to
manage an individual than a society.

There was a compensating reaction, however. In contrast
with those who came to believe that, as one of them put it, in
order "to have a great society we must have great individuals,"
there were liberal critics who began more realistically to study
the apparently unmalleable environment and its effect upon
thought and art. We can see such progress in the work of Lewis
Mumford and Matthew Josephson. Mumford's *The Golden Day*,
published in 1926, is a study of New England's culture in the
era of Emerson and Thoreau—a Periclean age which he made
to seem even more golden than it was by comparing it with

the newly settled West, where a pragmatic and materialistic civilization was being founded. He was unfair to the West and too generous to New England, but the really unfortunate thing about the book was its nostalgia for the glorious epoch of individualism. For that yearning for a situation and a mood which could never be recaptured could have no effect but the unintended one of weakening creative impulses, since it nurtured a species of idealism which, at bottom, was escapist. His *Herman Melville* (1929) was a further retreat from actual, urgent problems, for in it he did no more than weep beautifully over the fate of an artist in a land of business—a theme already fully exploited by Brooks, and in Mumford's work extremely suggestive of defeat and bitterness. Yet in *The Brown Decades* (1931) Mumford turned his attention to the positive and fertile elements in America's cultural history, and in his succeeding works —*Technics and Civilization* (1934) and *The Culture of Cities* (1938)—there is little nostalgia for the past and no defeatism. In them, despite a large residue of esthetic romanticism, there is a serious attempt to estimate the social and technological factors that make for brutal chaos or rational order in Western culture. If Mumford should again write literary history or biography, he could hardly revert to the personal sentimentality that perverted his earlier books.[1] Matthew Josephson's development is even clearer than Mumford's. His *Portrait of the Artist as American* (1930) was frankly a variation on the familiar theme of Brooks: it was an essay on the tragic destiny of the poet oppressed by a "practical" community. It was an oblique confession, as Mumford's *Melville* had been, of how little assurance the liberals had. They were no longer fighting for the fulfillment of their desires as men, but pleading for privileges as intellectuals. Within a few years, however, Josephson began to write political studies—*The*

---

[1] There is no evidence, however, that Mumford has overcome his habit of discussing the existence or non-existence of cultural "wholeness" or unity without regard for the presence or absence of *social* "wholeness" or unity. This habit, which he may have acquired from Waldo Frank, suggests a by no means insignificant strain of mysticism in his social philosophy.

*Robber Barons* (1934) and *The Politicos* (1938)—which were anything but lachrymose and which indicated a more objective view of society and a less tender-hearted attitude toward its control than had been fashionable in the 1920's.

I have said that notwithstanding their differences the liberal critics had once been sufficiently related so that we could speak of a movement, and that in the 1930's we could no longer do so. But it is not only that there was now no "movement"; it is also that its characteristic hopefulness, its adventurous spirit, its *energy* had disappeared, signifying the decline of liberalism as a creative force in American critical writing. When we find critics today who can provide their audiences with genetic ideas, we find that they stand well to the left or right of what we once knew as the liberal standpoint. The latter has become mere opposition—a source of criticism of those who have positive philosophies or faiths; and liberalism has become a search for evidence to confirm one's doubts rather than a quest of certainty. Such criticism may be exceedingly useful. It may be indispensable as a defense of victories already won. It can never acquire power, however. It cannot, that is to say, inspire conviction or stimulate the creative will. Power comes to those who fight for something, not to the skeptic, however bilious and arrogant may be his defense of skepticism.

The work of Henry Hazlitt, sometime literary editor of the *Nation*, illustrates the temper of much liberal thought in recent years. Hazlitt's *The Anatomy of Criticism* (1933) is an exposition of two types of critical thinking: the academic and the experimental (or the traditionalist and the subjectivist). A synthesis of these methods, which is interwoven with the argument, is presumably a statement of the author's own attitude. Actually it is less a synthesis than a compromise, and it is unfortunately apt to strike us as passionless catholicity rather than reasonableness. It is a wholly negative critique. It is shrewd enough as an exposure of the logical flaws in the methods of his opponents, but it is non-creative; nothing can come out of it that can arouse either the artist or his audience. This is confirmed by the appendix to the volume, which contains two essays on Marxist criticism. They are destructive analyses of the subject. Whether they are correct or not is beside our point, which is that Hazlitt's work is lacking in that generative principle for which Adams searched and which is the quest of most contemporary critics. Those who still think of themselves as liberals have evidently given up the search.

The *reductio ad absurdum* of this tendency is to be found in Joseph Wood Krutch. He has been attacked by other liberal critics, but perhaps if they were as guileless as he and insisted upon developing a thesis to its logical conclusion, they would accept his work as a fair expression of their own sentiments. In *The Modern Temper* (1929) Krutch wrote an elaborate justification of absolute skepticism. The intelligent man could not, nowadays, believe firmly in anything at all, he said—not even in art, which "affords no more than another solvent, another critical instrument by means of which the various sciences of life men used to live by may be proved to be false." Art may, however, "furnish a means by which life may be contemplated," or it may provide us with "a new way of meditating and perhaps even a new way of despairing. . . ." Three years later, in *Experience and Art*, Krutch qualified his gloom sufficiently to declare gravely that if we want to live we have got to have a faith, and since all faiths are false it doesn't matter what our faith is so long as we hold to it—and literature can give us a faith. Needless to say, this suave pessimism made no impression upon the small but intensely alive community in which literature is created and assimilated.

The best of the liberals have not succumbed to such futile intellection, any more than they have resigned themselves to quiescence or gloom. They have moved on to a higher level or inquiry, retaining their democratic faith, their distaste for the *mores* of a commercial society, and their experimental temperament, but with a greater interest in collectivism than they

CONSEQUENCES 367

had before and a more scientific approach to historical and ideological analysis. In effect, they have deserted liberalism. (One wonders if it will soon be regarded as an archaic term, for it is rapidly losing its philosophical connotations and is now used chiefly in American politics, where it is a title to which tories pretend.) The first of the modern liberal critics to repudiate his own liberalism was Randolph Bourne, who, in 1917, paid his respects to the illusions that had previously inspired him: in an essay on "The War and the Intellectuals" he had his bitter say about his idealistic friends who had "willed" the war to make the world safe for democracy; in an essay called "Twilight of Idols" he severed his ties with John Dewey, who had been his teacher and who was then a god of liberal critics, educators, and journalists. It was clear that Bourne was about to take a new line. He was done with short-term ideals; he no longer believed that freedom alone could ensure a rational world; he no longer had any faith in the power (or the stability) of independent intellectuals with humane sentiments. Bourne was now prepared to criticize the social order—and, of course, its culture—from a militantly radical standpoint. He might have become the foremost socialist critic of his generation if he had not died two years later. There were few who emulated him in the 1920's, but the pervading disillusionment bore fruit in the '30's. Then, in the face of an economic crisis which was evidently permanent and in view of the inability of "men of good will" to halt the spread of fascism, it was widely acknowledged that the premises of nineteenth-century idealism were untenable. Liberalism was symbolically buried when the editors of the *New Republic,* in an editorial on the twentieth anniversary of its founding, redefined its policy, producing a credo which could be called many things, but not liberal.[1] Subsequently, they denied that it was a liberal magazine and stated that they preferred to call it "progressive."

[1] *The New Republic,* Vol. LXXXI, No. 1051 (January 23, 1935).

This has been a period of clarification. The war of traditions has been simplified. There are no longer any debates about social or sexual realism, nor about the right of the artist to experiment with form. Freedom, in those respects, is assumed. The debates are now about the purposes for which realism and experimentation are being employed—the ends to which they are being directed. Thus the conflicts are expressly concerned with ways of life—they are frankly between classes and cultures— where once they had been obscured by esthetic and philosophical abstractions.

The degree of simplification must not be exaggerated. It is the war between the classical and radical critics that has been simplified—through reducing their differences to the fundamental issues. There are a great number of critics who are neither classicists nor radicals, but who side with one or the other group on specific points. Within the two defined groups there remain unyielding antagonisms, which are in some cases more intense than that felt for what is supposed to be the major opposition. In short, we have achieved clarity not because there are fewer fights but because we understand what the main fights are all about and because the fights are being conducted in terms that reflect the life around us rather than in the metaphysical jargon of the old schoolmen. In the early 1930's many of us believed that literary critics, like political parties, would soon be divided into a militant left wing and a die-hard right wing. We know better now. The process of division is long and slow. There are loyalties, there are habits of thought, feeling, and conduct, that cut across it. There are problems of expression that touch both wings equally, and problems that neither has solved to its own satisfaction, let alone to the satisfaction of the opposing camp. Nevertheless, the outlines of such a division exist. The process was begun and it has continued. The rise of Marxist criticism was the catalyst.

In the fabulous '20's Marxist criticism was no more than a phrase to the literary world at large—a somewhat mysterious

but not at all intriguing phrase which sounded foreign and un-
esthetic. Its exponents were obscure and not obviously gifted.
In 1922 the editors of the *Liberator* had presented their magazine to the Communist Party, which soon afterwards converted
it into an organ of political propaganda. From then until the
end of 1924, when it ceased publication, the *Liberator* contained
nothing of critical interest except Dell's contributions and a few
pieces by Michael Gold and Joseph Freeman. In 1926 the *New
Masses* was founded, with a board of editors including Gold,
Freeman, and James Rorty, and a contributing board which
included John Dos Passos, Max Eastman, Freda Kirchwey, Louis
Untermeyer, and Edmund Wilson. For two years this magazine
attempted to revive the tender-hearted, bohemian radicalism of
the pre-war *Masses*. It failed. The *Masses* audience had been
decimated by patriotism and prosperity: the Socialist Party had
dwindled, the labor unions had retreated and lost much of their
membership, and Greenwich Village had become fashionable.
The writers themselves were undecided as to what road they
ought to take. Many of them were only superficially interested
in the revolutionary doctrines they were supposed to be sup-
porting; they were really interested in resisting Babbittry, in
asserting their individuality as intellectuals against the conform-
ism of Rotary, just as their expatriate friends in Paris were. In
1928 the *New Masses* was reorganized under Gold's editorship,
and now for the first time an attempt was made to create a
popular literary magazine with an explicitly Marxist policy. For
two or three years it had several thousand readers in labor circles, but reached very few in the literary community and by
those few was naïvely regarded as a sort of politicized *transition*.

During those years the leading interpreters of Marxist criticism were Joseph Freeman and V. F. Calverton, its leading example Michael Gold. Strictly speaking, Gold was not a critic
at all. He lacked the scholarship and the analytical mind that
are among the primary requisites of a critic, and in his own field

he was handicapped by an inadequate knowledge of Marxist theory. But he also had uncommon advantages. A child of the proletariat, for and to which he spoke, unencumbered by the dead weight of academic learning, possessed of a rare feeling for the simple human values in a work of art, profoundly sincere and impassioned, he was able to communicate his point of view as no other radical critic of this generation has been able to. He contributed nothing to what has usually been the preoccupation of Marxist critics: the study of the interplay of class bias, social heritage, esthetic tradition, and individual psychology. He rarely touched upon the problem that has always troubled this critical school: the relation of theme to form. He did, however, exemplify the attitude toward contemporary writers of one who has rejected many of the most dearly cherished, the most universally accepted of contemporary beliefs—and that is an important aspect of Marxist literary thought.

For that system of thought is, as I said in the earlier section on "Socialist Criticism," based upon a new conception of reality: that the nature and intensity of the class struggles in modern society determine society's "mind" and structure; and that justice and the logic of history are both on the side of the common people in their contests with aristocracies. The Marxist then argues that writers cannot truthfully portray any phase of the social "mind" if they have not taken into consideration the factors that molded it; and that the social "mind" is a significant factor in all human relationships. His categorical imperative is that, so far as they are able to do so, writers should take their stand with those who represent progress, which is to say, the mass of humanity striving to obtain justice and to establish a classless, rational, planned society. From this thesis one is led— through steps too numerous and complex to be dealt with here —to an attack on nationalistic and aristocratic sentiments, on attempts to substitute religious or mystical consolations for earthly blessings, and on glorifications of the individual at the expense of the many. And such, precisely, were the attacks that Gold specialized in writing. He did not often improve his readers' understanding of the reasons why, or the means by which, writers came to express the objectionable attitudes, nor did he often succeed in elucidating the effects of those attitudes on esthetic form, but he succeeded very well in estimating their implications with respect to the conflict between socialism and capitalism. In sum, his role was essentially that of an advocate of the literary interests of a radical working class against a conservative bourgeoisie.[1]

Freeman complemented Gold's efforts. He had the equipment and the ability to undertake psychological and esthetic analyses. Yet that represented a minor part of his writing. He spent his energies arguing the case of Marxist criticism—explaining what it is, describing its methods, and proving its validity. This was an unavoidable task in a period when writers generally and critics in particular knew practically nothing about Marxism and its disciplines. Within the communist movement itself there was little knowledge of its pertinence to literature; and the notion inherited from early socialist criticism, that the sole duty of a Marxist critic was to applaud writers who expressed radical sentiments and to chastise those who did not, was prevalent. Hence, as a contributor to liberal and radical journals and as a lecturer to labor audiences, Freeman tried not only to get the Marxist method recognized by the critical fraternity, but also to correct the misconceptions of his own party. Realizing that some of the more controversial issues had already been explored in the Soviet Union, he studied Soviet literature and criticism on the spot and produced a volume called *Voices of October* (1930), in which he sought to describe the development of literary thought in a country where Marxism is the state philosophy. This volume is still the basic work in its field. There is,

---

[1] The best and most easily obtained of Gold's essays happen to be two he wrote at the end of the period here discussed: an essay on Thornton Wilder, in the *New Republic*, Vol. LXIV, No. 829 (October 22, 1930), and one on Archibald MacLeish, ibid., Vol. XXXV, No. 973 (July 26, 1933). They are, however, characteristic of his earlier (and later) critical writings.

indeed, no comparable exposition of the critical principles under discussion.[1]

In 1923 V. F. Calverton founded the *Modern Quarterly*. Soon afterwards he began to publish essays by Marxist scholars on political and esthetic theory and on current problems in the social sciences. Moreover, he encouraged discussion in these fields, organizing debates and symposia to represent diverse viewpoints. This magazine alone offered a forum to the younger radical critics who wanted more space and a more intellectual audience than the *New Masses* was able to provide at that time. Thus, as an editor, he promoted the critical ideas associated with Marxism in a period that was not congenial to such ideas. But he was also a critic. In that capacity he did two things: he wrote long essays defining the advantages of the critical system he espoused; and he applied that system to the study of American literature. Examples of the first endeavor are his book *The Newer Spirit* (1925) and his pamphlet *The New Ground of Criticism* (1930), and of the second endeavor his book *The Liberation of American Literature* and his pamphlet *American Literature at the Crossroads* (1931). In so far as these essays helped make Americans aware that there *is* a Marxist method of criticism, Calverton did a service to the movement with which he was then identified. The mere fact that he was the first critic who tried using that method in writing a full-length history of American letters entitles him to a prominent place in a historical survey such as this.

But Calverton's interpretation of the method was anything but subtle. For a long time he called it "sociological criticism," which, if not the result of confusion on his part, is certainly confusing to the reader. By suggesting that literature is to be criticized from the point of view of sociology, it minimizes the philosophical and ethical criteria implicit in the truly Marxist ap-

[1] Joshua Kunitz and Louis Lozowick collaborated with Freeman to produce the book, which deals with the Soviet theatre, cinema, painting, and music, as well as literature.

proach and it seems to disregard esthetics altogether. In the latter respect he was no different from many others who considered themselves Marxists at the beginning of the '30's. To him, however, is attached the stigma of being one of those who set an unfortunate precedent, especially because he had the ear of the literary world, for a while, more than any other Marxist critic. What he argued for, what he practiced, came to be regarded as the genuine thing. Calverton also misrepresented his school in setting up an indefensible distinction between "ideas" and "craft" (or substance and form), which included a conception of craft that no literary critic, of any school, could possibly accept.[1] On the whole, Calverton's influence was in the direction of a mechanical materialism which proved to be inferior even to Parrington's rather inflexible method. Parrington had compensated for the failings of economic determinism by his own passion and his stylistic gifts, neither of which Calverton possessed.

It is clear that Marxist criticism was a negligible force at the beginning of the '30's. There were few who practiced it, and their total output was astonishingly small. The most prolific writer of the three mentioned above was not a fair representative of what this tiny movement would soon become. The most influential, Gold, was not a judicious and trained critic, although forcefully expressing the significant emotions of the movement. The ablest, Freeman, published less than any of them. This condition was now changing rapidly. With the coming of the economic crisis, it became obvious that our society was not as secure as it had seemed to be. Therefore the pessimism of certain liberals about the usefulness of striving for social justice was unwarranted. Immediately, the century-old struggle of the artist against the business man took on a new meaning. In a collapsing econ-

---

[1] An extremely enlightening discussion of this question, in the form of a debate between Hazlitt and Calverton and a commentary by Granville Hicks, appeared in the *Modern Monthly*, Vol. VI, No. 1 (Winter, 1932) and Vol. VI, No. 2 (Summer, 1932). The jumping-off place was Gold's historic essay on Thornton Wilder.

omy, collectivism ceased to be regarded as a utopian concept. It became, indeed, the only seriously considered alternative to a cruel and irrational situation. I am referring here not only to the material situation, but also to the paroxysms of fear and anxiety which seized American writers and thinkers. Everything but capitalism had come to seem unsubstantial and fleeting; that alone, for this generation at least, was something one could be sure of—something to which one had to adjust oneself, even if one did so unhappily. When capitalism began to crack, no certainties whatever were left. The very form, not to speak of the content, of traditional thought became questionable. One scarcely knew *how* to think. With all his pessimism Adams had never dreamed that a fixed point would become as desperate a need as it did now. The inevitable step was toward Marxism; nothing else offered both a goal and a method of attaining it. To the artist collectivism had a special appeal—an appeal in addition to that which attracted him as a human being: it posited a society in which the "instinct of workmanship" was encouraged and work performed for other than merely pecuniary ends was the norm. In this moment of crisis a considerable number of our intellectuals turned to the radical movements, many of them becoming Communists. The decade of disillusionment and cynicism was finished. Liberals and esthetes began to study Marxist theories, and Marxist criticism suddenly became a widely felt force.

The critics who thus rejected their previous philosophies and methods were, of course, of the younger generation—men who had come to maturity during or soon after the war and had never believed in the existing social scheme and its prevailing thought. Such of them as had been liberals of the school of Van Wyck Brooks—notably Granville Hicks and Newton Arvin— found the adjustment to Marxist ideas relatively easy, for Brooks had always emphasized the social values in literature, had studied literature as part of a broad cultural pattern, and had long been a declared socialist. The degrees of conviction were not identical: Arvin, for instance, has not adopted the systematic and revolutionary Marxism that has characterized Hicks's writing, which, by the way, was at one time influenced by Mencken as well as Brooks. But in the main their sympathies were obviously related.

The acceptance of Marxism by certain critics who had once been considered "pure esthetes" was much more remarkable. Consider such of them as Kenneth Burke and Malcolm Cowley. The former had been associated with the *Dial* and had contributed to the "little" magazines; the latter, despite a perceptible debt to Brooks, had been active among the expatriates and had flirted with the Dadaists. They had never consciously displayed any social awareness—except that hatred for bourgeois society which had led them to experiment with the most individualistic forms of esthetic expression. Obviously, it was that emotion that had made them susceptible to Marxist teachings. The Marxian dialectic enabled them to comprehend the world against which they had so blindly and ineffectually revolted; it enabled them to explain their own position; and it offered a means of achieving a realism unmixed with despair and a purpose devoid of theatricality. The whole story of the rise and fall of the esthetic nihilists and of the conversion of many of them into Marxists is told in Cowley's book *Exile's Return* (1934). It is a personal narrative which happens also to be the history of a significant literary movement.

In this summary of the growth of Marxist criticism I have deliberately named only the most prominent of those who have been identified with it *throughout* the 1930's. Marxist criticism has undergone extraordinary changes within this decade. Its interests, its emphases, its temper, with respect both to contemporary literature and to the perennial problems of esthetics, have not been constant. It has reacted to the increasingly dangerous threat that fascism offers to Western culture. It has responded to self-criticism and to the attacks of its opponents. It has not been unaware of the shifting temper of the American people. And as the substance and method of Marxist criticism have changed, so have personal allegiances. In this school, politics, social philosophy, and literary doctrine are not dissociated. When there is a clash in any of these spheres of thought, there is likely to be a clash in the others. Accordingly, there have been violent controversies among the critics, resulting in divisions so bitter that to use the term Marxist to cover all the critics who have at one time or another applied it to themselves or had it applied to them by undiscriminating observers is to fail to designate the real sense of their dissimilar positions. The term is here applied only to those whose intentions have not been in doubt for some years. That eliminates those who once embraced the Marxist credo and then immediately began to revise it, and those who, hostile to present tendencies in the Soviet Union, are now pointing toward a kind of philosophical anarchism.

These developments are taking place at this very moment. There is no prospect of a resolution of forces in the near future. We lack perspective. Moreover, the full history and meaning of the controversies cannot easily be explained to those who have not been close to them: it would take a volume to do so, even if the time were propitious. I propose, therefore, to do no more than to indicate the main currents in Marxist criticism as a whole.[1]

In the first flush of enthusiasm many of the younger radical critics were apparently prepared to discard the entire literature of the past. Their thesis was approximately the following: until now art has expressed the sentiments and philosophies of feudal

---

[1] To those who want to know something about the controversies, these two essays are recommended: James T. Farrell's *A Note on Literary Criticism* (New York, 1936), and Edmund Wilson's "Marxism and Literature," in his *The Triple Thinkers*. They are the most celebrated attacks on the Marxist critics that have been written from a radical standpoint.

Farrell's book was severely criticized by V. F. Calverton and James Burnham, two critics with whose political affiliations Farrell is sympathetic and who are as contemptuous of the more or less "official" Marxists as Farrell himself is. For Calverton's piece see the *Modern Monthly*, Vol. IX, No. 12

and bourgeois societies; hence those who are striving to create an equalitarian socialist society cannot obtain from such art the essential satisfactions that art is supposed to afford us. The single reservation to be made is that one may profit from studying the art of the past from the viewpoint of craft. To this thesis there is one reply: our culture is a development, not a mutation. It is continuous; its roots are in the past. There is a relationship between what we feel and think now and what men felt and thought one, five, ten, or twenty centuries ago. A work of art cannot mean to us what it meant to men in other and older civilizations, but it means *something* to us—something we cannot and must not hold lightly. And that will be equally true for those who come after us even after the economic and political structure of society has been transformed. As for the notion that craft may be abstracted from the emotions and the sensitiveness to life that have made a work of literature survive, no more need be said than that it is unworthy of adult discussion.

Paralleling the attempt to bury our literary heritage was the thesis that "art is a weapon"—that is to say, a weapon in the class struggle. The argument presented was that since works of literature express class attitudes, the literature of today has value only if it expresses the attitude toward life of the most progressive groups. They are those who recognize the decadent and retrogressive character of the bourgeois community and are prepared to fight for collectivism and the new culture that will arise from it. The highest artistic consciousness is attained with that recognition and the decision to act upon it. The artist then intentionally produces works that will make men aware of their social

(August 1936), pp. 16 ff.; for Burnham's see the *American Socialist Monthly*, Vol. V, No. 7 (October 1936), pp. 62-4.

During the '20's Wilson was distinguished as an esthetic critic who, as he said, "saw the connection between works of art and the environments in which they were produced" and who frequently discussed "the role played in the work of various artists by the factors of period, nation, race, and social status." His *Axel's Castle* was the product of that period. Since then he has made several turns—first toward Marxism, then away from it. His future is unpredictable.

role. Now, it is true that art *may* be a weapon. It has often been one. But it has been other things as well. Furthermore, the artist does not ordinarily create a work with the intention of stimulating a specific act or a specific line of thought. He seeks to present an experience that will heighten his reader's understanding of life. Such understanding is not purposeless; it will influence his conduct—but only in a general direction. To determine the actual point of arrival is the philosopher's problem.

Both of the theses described above exemplify what may be called the political criticism of literature. It is perfectly legitimate, but it is not, by itself, literary criticism. No one can say to what extent literary criticism is related to the social sciences, but it should be obvious that the political criticism of literature belongs to them completely. It may be sanctioned by the importance and urgency of the political conflicts of our times. One may, indeed, argue with great reason that those conflicts are crucial to the future existence of any culture whatever, so that no other kind of criticism matters at this moment. But that, too, is political criticism, and those who uphold it should so realize and be careful to observe its proper place in the larger literary criticism.

Actually, however, the Marxist, far from denying the value of literary criticism, has come to regard it as one of the indispensable instruments of cultural survival—which is quite as dignified and noble a conception of his profession as any other critical school has evolved. The "ultra-leftist" theses were probably inevitable in a young and ardent movement. To a degree they were reactions to attacks upon the movement made expressly from a class angle. To a perhaps greater degree they were produced by a condition within the movement itself. There was a strain of anti-intellectualism in it—a hostility toward those who live by the fruits of thought—which had been bequeathed to it by the I.W.W. Freeman had fought against that tendency; the newly recruited intellectuals fought against it in the early '30's; and then as the movement grew and broadened, it was overcome.

There are not many instances of "ultra-leftism" in the writings of Marxist critics today. The theses we have been examining are dead, while the principle that literary judgments must be founded on determinable social values is permanently established. The reviews that are being written today by the most popular of journalistic critics prove how much the social consciousness of the Marxists has affected contemporary American criticism.

That is not to say that Marxist critics have solved their problems. On the contrary, they are now at last facing them. To begin with, they have consistently slighted esthetic appreciation. They have failed to analyze the interaction of idea and form, of emotion and expression. Secondly, they have not effectively dealt with the problem of communication. The Marxist uses innumerable words differently from the way they have traditionally been used. These words mean things to him that are quite different from what they have heretofore meant. That is a natural consequence of a revolution in social, moral, and psychological values. But he is communicating with people who have carried over the habits of speech acquired in the traditional environment, and he is constantly trying to persuade people outside his movement that his methods and ideals are correct. Hence communication is always difficult, often confused, sometimes frustrated. It is a problem of immense significance, yet there is only one Marxist critic in America, Kenneth Burke, who is energetically and seriously concerned with it.

Clearly, Marxist criticism is still in a formative period. Nevertheless, its contributions to date can be assessed. The least that can be said is the following taken from an article by Malcolm Cowley: "For all their narrowness and, on occasion, their insensitiveness to literary values, they [the Marxists] have contributed something to the discussion—new answers to old questions, new questions that remain to be answered and, most of all, a consistent method of interpretation and evaluation. . . . Critics for at least a century have been trying to judge literature purely in terms of literature. When that line of thinking gets them into trouble, as it is bound to do, they merely stop thinking and write a finely evocative phrase. Or else they make use of some abstraction—Beauty or Ecstasy, or Personality and Character—to gloss over conflicts that couldn't be resolved without hard thinking and tedious research. Rather than being scholarly or scientific or merely informative, critics want to be the high priests of a literary tradition. They go on repeating their own errors and those of their predecessors, which custom has rendered almost sacred. The result is that criticism in our times has advanced scarcely farther than in those of Aristotle; much of it is really pre-Aristotelian. And most of it won't amount to more than a learned game until it consents to let its results be tested by outside disciplines—by philosophy, psychology, sociology, medicine, and by history most of all. That explains the importance of the Marxist critics. The chief service they render is to introduce non-literary standards that change the rules of the game, that make it more of a science, that bring it closer to the rest of life. These standards are often crude and impolite, especially in the beginning, but at least they can be tested and verified and altered at the points where they disagree with information from other sources; in other words, they are capable of improvement." [1]

One must conclude that the Marxists possess what Adams wanted. They have a philosophy of history to explain the present and guide them to a desirable future. They have a faith. They have a unifying idea. And therefore as critics of literature they have principles by which any work may be rationally interpreted and which may inspire and direct the creative impulse. No critic can ask for more; no critic should be satisfied with less. He who cannot accept their principles is obliged to offer alternatives for which as much can be claimed and which are as susceptible to being tested by reason and experience.

[1] *The New Republic*, Vol. LXXXXVIII, No. 1263 (February 15, 1939), pp. 49-50.

One school has risen to meet that challenge. Most conservative critics have either ignored the need or denied it. Typical
is Bernard De Voto's remark that he is "a pluralist, a relativist,
an empiricist," which he elaborates into a truculent defense of a
state of mind inimical to simplifications, generalizations, and abstract logic, to systems, theories, and prophecy—in other words,
to thinking.[1] But there are, as we know, conservatives who are
not averse to thought, and one group of them has undertaken
to complete Adams's quest as vigorously and thoroughly as the
Marxists. They are the classicists. They have formulated a philosophy that is a good deal short of being systematic, but which is
at least a way of life, an interpretation of human conduct, and
a social and esthetic ideal. They have critical principles that
enable them to explain their preferences coherently.

The classicists have frequently been lumped with the Neo-
Humanists, whose brief notoriety in 1930 was a warning to
complacent democrats that the aristocratic mind was still with
us. For thirty years Babbitt and More had cursed the world they
lived in and tried to bludgeon its literature. The world had been
deaf and its literature had grown less and less "classical." They
had trained a few disciples, but their influence upon the public
at large, always small, had decreased constantly, until at last it
had been confined to the academy, where they formed the extreme "right wing" of a traditionally conservative body of men.
Then suddenly they began to reach a somewhat wider audience
than they had enjoyed in almost a decade. In 1928 the *Forum*
formally opened its pages to their onslaughts upon the liberals
and impressionists. Shortly afterwards the *Bookman*, under
Seward Collins's editorship, followed suit. In the issue for January 1930 Collins published a manifesto in which he declared that
naturalism and its concomitant evils were dead and that the new
decade belonged to "Humanism." The journalists, aware of the
restlessness and discontent among the younger writers and sens-

[1] *The Saturday Review of Literature*, Vol. XV, No. 16 (February 13, 1937),
p. 8.

ing that a revolt against the idols of the post-war period was already under way, were quick to seize upon Collins's statement for editorial comment. Subsequent issues of the *Bookman*, containing essays by Babbitt and More and their allies, and Foerster's symposium, *Humanism and America*, were likewise extravagantly publicized.

The journalists were quite right in assuming that they were witnessing a reaction against pessimistic and escapist moods in favor of certain traditional faiths. But they chose the wrong horse. The furore over Neo-Humanism soon died down. The absolute inability of More and Babbitt to appreciate the literature of the twentieth century, plus the fact that unmistakable traces of gentility still clung to them, defeated their campaign to win to their side the young, non-academic critics who were inclined to conservative or traditionalist sentiments. The latter have learned much from Neo-Humanism and they acknowledge their respect for and indebtedness to its leaders, but their true prophet is T. S. Eliot. The present-day classicists were yesterday's esthetes; they remain intensely interested in formal problems and are sympathetic to verbal experiment; and, withal, they are not genteel. Their aristocratic bias is buttressed by their leaning toward the Catholic churches. Manifestly, they have learned much more from Eliot than from Babbitt.

One occasionally hears Eliot being referred to as an American critic. It is absurd not because Eliot has long been an English citizen, but because he has adopted an English philosophy and speaks directly to the English upper classes. It was in the preface to *For Lancelot Andrewes* (1929) that he made his famous remark that his "general point of view may be described as classicist in literature, royalist in politics, and anglo-catholic in religion." Is there anything American about that point of view? To be sure, in *After Strange Gods* (1934) he referred to himself as a Yankee, but that was a pretty conceit devised to flatter his audience at the University of Virginia, where, in 1933, he had delivered the lectures that formed this volume. *For Lancelot*

*Andrewes* was a volume of essays of which three, including the title essay, were devoted to praising the styles and ideas of obscure English divines. It is difficult to believe that they made any sense to American readers. Everything he has written since then, and especially his most recent volume, *Essays Ancient and Modern* (1936), is aimed at members of the Anglican church who swear fealty to the King of England.

Why has he been able to influence so many American critics? It would be too glib to say that his converts in this country are the snobs of criticism, and it would obscure something that is both interesting and important. Eliot had suffered the sense of frustration, had felt the disgust and horror that life in our society inspired in the war and post-war generations. His poem *The Waste Land* was the perfect expression of that loathing and bitterness. But he had eventually found a faith—a faith that gave him hope, that gave him standards in terms of which he could logically criticize modern culture, that explained (to his satisfaction) the causes of decadence and chaos, and that constituted an ideal worth fighting for. In brief, he had found a unifying idea. It was one which did not look forward to a social revolution, but, on the contrary, looked backward to a restoration of privilege and hierarchy.

At first this faith impressed his American admirers only in its strictly literary phase. It was partial to classicism and was the basis of his appreciative essays on Dryden, Donne, Middleton, and the English metaphysical poets, and his depreciative comments on the romantics. Those who were sick of introversion, disorder, and egotism welcomed a return to the orderliness and objectivity of the classicists. Eliot was certainly responsible for the renaissance of classical taste that occurred in American criticism after the war. But in the years of crisis—the psychological crisis that accompanied the economic—the literary side of his traditionalism became less important. It was submerged in his criticism of culture in general. His followers were forced to think their position through, as he had thought his through.

Their taste, their moral beliefs, their conception of the good life, were nakedly revealed as the fruits of an archaic social system which required an established church to guarantee its stability.

One wonders if Eliot's insight and honesty were not sometimes embarrassing to the classical schools. For he raised the war of traditions to a plane of dignity that no one who had read the Neo-Humanists would have thought attainable. Nothing could be more calmly or simply stated than this (from *Essays Ancient and Modern*): "There are two and only two finally tenable hypotheses about life: the Catholic and the materialistic [i.e., the Marxist]. . . . It is quite possible, of course, that the future may bring neither a Christian nor a materialistic civilization. It is quite possible that the future may be nothing but chaos or torpor. In that event, I am not interested in the future; I am only interested in the two alternatives which seem to me worthy of interest." Eliot chose not only the Catholic hypothesis, but also its political corollaries. His literary opinions were thus given a firm philosophical base to rest upon, and from that fact drew the reasonable conclusions. He wrote: "Literary criticism should be completed by criticism from a definite ethical and theological standpoint. In so far as in any age there is common agreement on ethical and theological matters, so far can literary criticism be substantive. In ages like our own, in which there is no such common agreement, it is the more necessary for Christian readers to scrutinize their reading, especially of works of imagination, with explicit ethical and theological standards. The 'greatness' of literature cannot be determined solely by literary standards; though we must remember that whether it is literature or not can be determined only by literary standards."

To this had esthetic criticism at last come—to a realization that non-esthetic criteria are the ultimate tests of value. Whether they be called philosophical, moral, or social criteria, they are still the ideas that men have about the way human beings live together and the way they ought to live. The quest of beauty had become the quest of reality. It had become, in essence, literary

criticism as socially conscious and as polemical as the criticism
of the Marxists. Now, is it not significant that the polemics of
the erstwhile esthetes are on behalf of an aristocratic society?
Critics like Cowley and Burke are exceptional; most of the critics
who once were absorbed in formal analysis and have since acquired a consciousness of the extra-literary forces that go into
the making of literature, are reactionaries. It *is* significant, but,
on reflection, not surprising. Esthetic criticism has always been
an aristocratic exercise. We are haunted by the ghosts of Edgar
Allan Poe and Henry James. Early in our own century Amy
Lowell, propagandist for "pure beauty," delivered an argument
against the propaganda of a socialist poet that was plainly animated by an upper-class bias. She said: "If we admit that the
degraded are degraded, there is not much danger of losing our
perspective; if we hug them to our hearts and turn a cold shoulder
to the sober and successful of the world, then we are running
fast toward chaos, and our mental processes may fairly be considered a trifle askew. If nature had deemed the unfit so important, she would doubtless have heaped her favours upon them
instead of markedly reserving these tokens for the fit." [1] And
today we find Ezra Pound, supreme esthete of the pre-war era,
apologizing for fascism and exalting Mussolini. We can understand why the Marxists have neglected esthetic criticism.

The American traditionalists, the classicists who are the new
defenders of the old faith, have had similar backgrounds. Consider such of them—the best known and probably the most gifted
—as Allen Tate, John Crowe Ransom, and Yvor Winters. They
were esthetic critics; their inclinations were toward individualism and aristocracy; they are now religious and political reactionaries. Winters is the author of two volumes of criticism:
*Primitivism and Decadence* (1937) and *Maule's Curse* (1939).
In them he denounces naturalism and advocates "the discipline
fostered by the Catholic and Anglo-Catholic Churches." Ransom's volumes are *God without Thunder* (1930) and *The*

[1] In a posthumous volume, *Poetry and Poets* (Boston, 1930), p. 152.

*World's Body* (1938). They attempt to prove that literary criticism must be founded on religion—which, admittedly, flourishes in a hierarchical society. Tate's volume is called *Reactionary Essays* (1936), and the title describes it perfectly. If there be any doubts about the political character of this passion for the church, they may be settled by *I'll Take My Stand* (1930), a symposium to which Tate, Ransom, and other Southern critics contributed. It was a plea for an agrarian society such as the South possessed before the Civil War. These critics have apparently not yet confessed, even to themselves, that the old agrarian South could not have existed without slavery.

Eliot spoke of alternatives, not of choices. A choice implies two things of more or less equal value. He believes that one of the alternatives has greater value, is nobler, is in a sense more real, than the other. The question is therefore not simply one of personal taste. It is a question of evidence and reason. But the alternative he favors admits of no evidence and derogates from reason. His philosophy is, in the last analysis, wholly mystical. It is not capable of being tested and verified and improved. The alternative he rejects is, on the other hand, the one that is favored by those who are determined to be as scientific as one can be in a non-physical field. The literary criticism of the neo-classicists is a criticism composed of obiter dicta inspired by intangible emotions. The literary criticism of the materialists stands or falls by the findings of the social scientists, psychologists, and historians. Eliot's alternative involves a revulsion against democracy; the materialists are partisans of democracy. The literary criticism of his school tends to create a literature that will express the sensibilities and experiences of a few fortunate men. The criticism of the opposing school tends to create a literature that will express the ideals and sympathies of those who look forward to the conquest of poverty, ignorance, and inequality—to the material and intellectual elevation of the mass of mankind.

To whom does the future belong? In January 1939 Eliot announced that the *Criterion*, the literary journal he had edited since 1922, would no longer be published. His Europe had crumbled; the culture in which he had put his faith was dying. The *Criterion* had served its purpose. Eliot had arrived at a mood of detachment. There was nothing he could hopefully fight for now. But those who believe in scientific methods, in realism, in social equality and democracy, are hopeful and are fighting.

# INDEX

Abbott, Leonard D., 289, 290
Abélard, 226
Academic criticism, 259-65, 268-9, 328-35
Adams, H. B., 60
Adams, Henry, 168, 222-8, 229, 230, 360, 380, 381
Adams, James Truslow, 74, 82, 98, 102, 330
Adams, John, 24, 332
Adams, Samuel, 332, 335
Addison, John, 8, 9, 10, 12, 276
Ade, George, 308
Adler, Mortimer, 227
Aeschylus, 244
Aesop, 112
*After Strange Gods*, 382
*After the Genteel Tradition*, 308
Aiken, Conrad, 350-1, 358
Akenside, Mark, 9, 15
Alcott, Bronson, 77, 78, 86, 88, 89, 91, 97
Aldrich, Thomas Bailey, 56, 221, 246-7, 251, 255, 264, 286, 304
Alfred, King, 112
Alterton, Margaret, 198, 199
*Ambassadors, The*, 216
*America and the Young Intellectual*, 361
*America in Literature* (Woodberry), 262-3
*American, The*, 210-11
*American Criticism* (Foerster), 155, 160, 190-1, 235, 237, 242, 278
*American Fiction: An Historical and Critical Survey*, 329
*American Journal of Education*, 59
*American Language, The*, 311
*American Literature*, 33, 101, 155, 159, 160, 163, 181, 189, 201, 251
*American Literature at the Cross-roads*, 372

*American Literature, 1607-1885* (Richardson), 262
*American Magazine*, 7
*American Mercury*, 153, 167, 260, 311
*American Prose Masters*, 235
*American Review, and Literary Journal*, 16
*American Socialist Monthly*, 377
*American Testament, An*, 301
*Americans*, 110
*America's Coming-of-Age*, 319, 320, 324, 362
*Anacreon*, 21
*Anarchism and Other Essays*, 292
*Anatomy of Criticism, The*, 365-6
Anderson, Margaret, 352-3
Anderson, Sherwood, 159, 297-8, 307, 314
Andreiev, Leonid, 272, 292
Andrews, Stephen Pearl, 75
*Androcles and the Lion*, 297
*Anna Karenina*, 167, 211-12
Annunzio, Gabriele d', 272, 290
*Anthology of Magazine Verse for 1915*, 297
*Aristocracy and Justice*, 343
Aristotle, 11, 112, 190-1, 332, 345, 380
Arnold, Matthew, 132, 154-5, 249, 257, 337, 339
*Art and Prudence*, 227
*Art of the Novel, The*, 213
Artzibashev, Boris M., 272, 273
Arvin, Newton, 160, 211, 374-5
*Assommoir, L'*, 219
*Atlantic Monthly*, 102, 161, 167, 171, 175, 232, 235, 246, 247, 258, 259, 275, 276
*Aucassin and Nicolette*, 226
Augustine, St., 112
*Axel's Castle*, 133, 346, 355, 377

389